The
Liffey
in
Dublin

The Author

J.W. de Courcy is Associate Professor Emeritus in Civil Engineering at University College Dublin. He has made a lifelong study of the Liffey and is the co-author of *Anna Liffey – the River of Dublin*, an illustrated guide to the river. He has had a career of over half a century in engineering practice, including twenty-four years as a university teacher. In addition to qualifications in engineering, he is an Honorary Member of the Royal Institute of Architects in Ireland and a Fellow of the Royal Society of Antiquaries of Ireland. He has lectured and written extensively in Ireland and abroad on engineering and general topics and has organised and edited the transactions of various Irish and international conferences. He is a past president of SEFI (Societé Européenne pour la Formation des Ingenieurs) and a past chairman of the National Library of Ireland Society.

The Liffey in Dublin

J.W. DE COURCY

Gill & Macmillan

Gill & Macmillan Ltd
Goldenbridge
Dublin 8
with associated companies throughout the world
© J.W. de Courcy 1996
0 7171 2423 1

Copy-editor: Angela Rohan
Index compiled by Helen Litton
Typeset in 10pt Garamond Narrow and 11pt Frutiger Light by Peanntrónaic Teo., Dublin
Printed by ColourBooks Ltd, Dublin

5 4 3 2 1

For Sheila, with love

The author is deeply grateful to his sponsors,
CRH plc
and
the Custom House Docks Development Authority,
for the generous support which has enabled this book to be published.

Contents

Illustrations

Foreword

This book is a treasure. It is a history of a river but a history told with a difference. In a unique way, John de Courcy, formerly a professor of civil engineering at University College, Dublin, vividly unfolds the life story of our grand, and dear, old River Liffey, James Joyce's Anna Livia Plurabelle.

The River Liffey has, for several thousand years, followed substantially the same course, rising as a stream in the Wicklow Mountains between Kippure and Tonduff, swinging in a great curve through the counties of Wicklow and Kildare, then turning back to flow through the now capital city of Ireland and meet the sea at Dublin Bay. The changes that did take place over the years – the influence of the river on the lives of communities along its banks; the development, by the people, of the river to their needs – are depicted by de Courcy in a dialogue between the people and the water.

The introduction to the book is a masterly and lively overview of the historical development along the Liffey of the city of today. Concise and economical in style, it is at the same time visually evocative and, with an apparent effortlessness, stimulates imaginative reconstruction of an earlier age. Behind the pockets of frenetic traffic of our time are clearly seen the 'extensive areas of waiting-space for stock, pack-animals and vehicles on both banks'.

The various sections in the introduction encompass a multifaceted story of the river and provide a promise of the riches to be discovered in the descriptive index entries which form the core and central treasure trove of the book.

These almost 1,400 entries, enhanced by some 200 illustrations, form a landmark book of reference. But it is much more than that. While it may be used as a most valuable and authoritative source for tracking down a particular item of information, it may be dipped into just as profitably with delight at any time. It makes for fascinating reading, and leads compulsively from one enlightening, unusual or amusing signpost to the next.

John de Courcy has an innate sense of history, an infectious enthusiasm for his subject, and for this work has completed a mammoth undertaking in meticulous research. Happily, too, he has the capacity, the great gift, of transmitting the knowledge he has gathered in a clear, attractive and entertaining style. And his extensive bibliography will surely satisfy the specialist scholar, and whet the appetite of the general reader.

Finally I would say with reference to the author's mention of 'inadequacies . . . that arise from the limitations of his study', this work may, in future years, be added to by others, or elaborated on; it will never be surpassed. I feel truly honoured to be associated with it.

F.X. Martin, OSA

Introduction

And in the night-time in the dark, in all the sleeping silence of the earth, the river, the dark rich river, full of strange time, dark time, strange tragic time, is flowing, flowing out to sea.

(Thomas Wolfe, *The Web and the Rock*, 1947)

Ah, but she was the queer old skeowsha anyhow, Anna Livia trinkettoes!

(James Joyce, *Finnegans Wake*, 1939)

O tell me all about Anna Livia! I want to hear all about Anna Livia. Well, you know Anna Livia? Yes, of course, we all know Anna Livia. Tell me all. Tell me now. You'll die when you hear.

(*Finnegans Wake*)

SPACE AND TIME IN THIS BOOK

The River Liffey rises in the Wicklow Mountains between Kippure and Tonduff, 21 km due south of Rory O'More Bridge in the city of Dublin. It flows in a great loop, first west across the counties of Wicklow and Kildare, and then north and east across Kildare and Dublin. It passes through the city and 'disembogues itself into the ocean' (12)* at the mouth of Dublin Bay on a line extending from the Baily lighthouse to the Muglin Rocks.

The river has been tidal up to the weir at Islandbridge since about 1200. Before that date, spring tides probably flowed further upstream towards Chapelizod. The distance from the weir to the mouth of the bay is approximately 16 km. In the late 18th century what is now known as the mouth of the Liffey was formed at the Poolbeg lighthouse, some 9 km below the weir. Before then, the mouth of the river was indeterminate, although one might see it in the vicinity of the Abbey Theatre or indeed even further upstream into the city.

The territory covered by this text lies in the 16 km from the weir at Islandbridge to the mouth of Dublin Bay. So much of the history of the river is related to the bay that to choose the 18th-century mouth would offer an incomplete picture.

The Liffey has flowed east, substantially along its present course, through what is now the city of Dublin for several thousand years, since times unrecorded by history or tradition. From the earliest times, man has lived near its banks. The river and the mouths of its tributaries have been fished since the beginning, and the fords have been crossed. One might, however, suggest, albeit arbitrarily, that no significant change was made to the river by man until the Norse built the first earthen bank under the escarpment of Christ Church Cathedral in about 900; and that date has been chosen to start this book.

The material described, then, will be within a frame having, on a time axis, the period from AD 900 to the present, and, on a space axis, the 16 km from the Islandbridge weir to the mouth of the bay. And as the subject is essentially the interaction between the city and the river, the

---

*Numbers in parentheses refer to the bibliography.

treatment will not stray unnecessarily beyond the medieval high-tide shoreline and the land close by on each bank.

THE CONCEPT OF INTERACTION

What is the interaction implied in the title? It is between a river and the people of a city built on it.

Cities may be distinguished, in the context of this interaction, as those that do not acknowledge any significant river, as for instance Brussels, Milan, Birmingham or Mexico City, those lying upstream on great rivers, for example Paris and Cologne, and those on significant tidal rivers, such as London, Rotterdam and Dublin. In the first category, there is no interaction. In the second, interaction can occur through regular seasonal flooding following spring thaws, and random storm floods. In the third, seasonal and storm inundations also occur, but are imposed upon a regular twice-daily cycle of tidal rise and fall.

In Dublin the tidal range can quite frequently reach an amplitude of 3 m. A ninth-century Celt living on the bank of the Liffey in certain places in the future city might go to sleep one night with a still sheet of water 100 m or more wide lapping at his front door, and wake early next morning with a mud or shingle bank sloping away from his house down to a narrow thread of water perhaps 50 m away and 3 m below his doorstep. To both the Frank at Cologne and the Lombard at Milan this would be an absurdity.

The Celt and Frank would, however, be at one about the effect of unexpected flooding. Each would have accepted such inundation as an act of God, to be guarded against if possible but otherwise to be endured. Many such inundations were caused by the River Liffey in Dublin over the centuries, and this danger was not finally brought under control until the river was harnessed in the mid-20th century by dams at Pollaphuca, Golden Falls and Leixlip. We know that the people who lived on the spit of Ringsend also recognised the possibility of having waves generated by easterly gales at sea flow in through their back doors and out through their front doors, a hazard that was removed only when Ringsend was cut off from the open bay by the South Wall and the land intakes of the 18th and 19th centuries.

The interaction or dialogue in the text is between people and water, between the Liffey and the community living along its banks and shores. The following table shows the elements of this interaction. They arise from the nature of the river and the needs of the people.

Nature of the River Liffey	Input by the people
Estuary	Early settlement
Ford	Internal trade routes
Tides	Ferries
Floods	Bridges
Material forming bed	River containment
Fish and shellfish	Land intake
Location in Ireland	Quays
	Harbour and port
	Flood control

Dublin and the Liffey have developed together as a result of the vast series of interactions, large and small, that has continued during the last 1,100 years. The broad areas in which the interactions have occurred may be listed under the following headings:

population growth
defence
crafts
trade
centres of influence   – religion
                       – government and administration
                       – law
                       – industry
                       – commerce
                       – culture
                       – society and living.

One cannot say that the river has been hostile to the people of the city. A tree is not hostile if one must climb in it to gather fruit and risk falling. The Liffey had many fish and the shores of the estuary in the bay teemed with shellfish. Clothes could be washed in the river, timber could be rafted, animals watered, rubbish thrown out, boats floated, children and others could swim. In all of this, as man began to live along the tidal banks, the people and their river came to terms. But in 1,100 years both have changed. We no longer live in fear of inundation, but we do not eat the shellfish any more. We can now cross dry-shod at many places 24 hours each day, but we may, if unduly sensitive, be offended at low tide by the condition of the strands. We no longer float great rafts with timber or fodder up or down the stream, but we have perhaps demolished an island to make concrete. And we have converted the river-banks into sadly overloaded service ducts for traffic.

The city can never, no more now than before, ignore the river. There always has been, and always will be, a relationship that shows itself in a myriad of ways. The Liffey is always there, in storm and calm, in peace and war, as thoroughfare, defence line, access for attack, escape route, source of water, food and energy, main drain and waste disposal channel, grave for the bodies of men or women killed by themselves or by others, a stream for work and recreation, for spectacle and sport. It is this unceasing interaction between people and Liffey that has prompted the present work.

WHAT IS OFFERED BY THIS BOOK

By definition the text is not in narrative form. Instead, it describes various discrete matters alphabetically, to present the whole subject in what might perhaps be suggested as an exercise in pointillism. The conditions for the inclusion of an item are that the matter must relate directly or indirectly to the city–river interaction, and that, if it is a place or an event, the site must be close to the high-tide river-bank or shore. It will be seen, however, from Figures 1 to 4 that the high-tide shoreline has altered greatly since 850, so that what was properly accepted as close to the bank or shore for perhaps the first 750 years of the period covered may now be believed to be quite remote from any water's edge.

The 1,400 or so items in the text may be grouped broadly under the following headings:
areas outside the city
banks, fords, pools and strands
bathing
battles
boats and shipping
bridges
buildings, old and new
defence, and military establishments
Dublin Bay
fishing
folklore and tradition
formal inscriptions on bridges and monuments
government, civic: assembly, committees, boards, officers, franchises, property
government, national
guilds
historical events
hospitals and infirmaries
illustrations
industry
land intake
literary references in prose and poetry
maps and mapmakers
men and women
mills and other energy sources
natural phenomena and conditions
port and harbour
precincts and quarters
public amenities and amenity areas
quays
refuse disposal
religious institutions
secular institutions
streets, roads and lanes
tides, inundations and water levels
transport on land: vehicles, railways
tributary rivers
water supply
wrecks.

Sources are listed for all the information given, other than that explicitly offered as speculation. However, a bibliographical reference system has been adopted which regretfully lays the onus on the specialised reader personally to consult the listed references for further detail.

THE LIFFEY IN 850

c. 3000 BC	Newgrange tumulus
c. 3000 BC	Kitchen middens at Sutton and Dalkey Island
AD 50–400	Roman port of London (289)
100	The great roads of Ireland 'discovered' (120)
c. 300	Tara capital of Ireland (36)
432	St Patrick returns to Ireland
550	Tara in decline
c. 550	Clonmacnoise founded
841	Norse establish permanent settlement at Dublin (99: Clarke)

There appears little evidence that durable structures were built before 850 on the banks of the Liffey between the future site of the Islandbridge weir and the sea. The monastery Cill Maighneann was possibly the only stone building near the river, if indeed it was built in stone. It had stood from the early seventh century (244) on the high beak of land between the Liffey and the Camac, where the Knights Hospitallers of St John of Jerusalem would later establish their hospital.

The first step in considering the appearance of the Liffey in 850 is to visualise a landscape with, substantially, no buildings. Small, isolated or perhaps, in places, clustered timber dwellings would have made little mark. Secondly, one recognises that the land surfaces above high tide were then as nature had made them, generally coarse river meadows with some bushes and trees. The impact of human deposits would be minimal, and the man-made humps arising 1,000 years later from canal construction would not exist. Thus for example a track along Ballybough Road from Summerhill would have fallen steadily downhill to the Tolka rather than switchback over the Royal Canal, and the hump of Newcomen Bridge would not have interrupted the natural flatness of the North Strand. Thirdly, there are no cartographic or precise textual records of the period, so some measure of speculation must be introduced.

The early location of the high-tide shorelines north and south of the Liffey are proposed in an entry in the text entitled Shoreline, The Medieval, and it is useful to recognise that the high-tide levels in the river were fundamentally the same in 850 as they are today. The river was tidal up towards Chapelizod. It passed through a swan-neck where the Islandbridge weir would be built about 350 years later, and then flowed roughly due east through a quite narrow alluvial plain with river gravel terraces to a point near the Abbey Theatre. There the shores diverged to form the west side of Dublin Bay, in which the only two features breaking the high-tide water surface were Clontarf Island, now under Bond Road, and the spit of Ringsend. The huge Bull sands lay north and south of the channel of the river, but it would be nearly 1,000 years later that man would cause the formation of the Bull Island.

Following the river downstream from the weir, the first notable feature in 850 was Kilmehanoc Ford, just above modern Island Bridge. Next, on the south bank the River Camac appeared

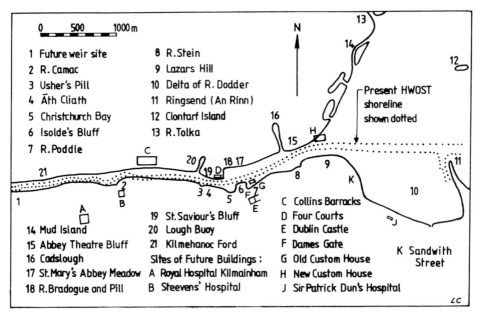

Figure 1: Liffey shoreline in the city, 850

around the end of the Kilmainham beak and flowed into the Liffey, with probably a wide confluence at Heuston railway station. In the downstream angle of the Camac and Liffey lay meadowland that would be converted, almost certainly by man, into an island to be known more than 600 years later as Usher's Island. The inlet of Usher's Pill lay a little to the east, and just here was located Áth Cliath, the most important ford on the river and the first cause for the building of Dublin.

Slighe Midluachra crossed the Liffey at this ford, and linked up near the south bank with other great roads of ancient Ireland. The importance of this crossing at the nearest practicable site to the coast was enormous, although the tidal fluctuation made the ford quite inefficient; and one may envisage, even at that early time, extensive areas of waiting-space for stock, pack-animals and vehicles on both banks. It will be observed that the direction of the river changes near here, to curve around the land on the north bank on which St Saviour's Priory would be built 400 years later. Arguably this land was a 'hard spot' in the river, formed perhaps with boulder clay, and the existence of this quite small 'hard spot' may have influenced the immediate location of Áth Cliath. A mere 250 m downstream on this bank, the confused confluence of the River Bradogue flowed through a strand of alluvial mud, and formed what would become known as 'the Pill beyond the water'. From the Bradogue this strand extended downstream along the north bank until it reached another probable 'hard spot' at the Abbey Theatre. Beyond this place the tideway opened up into the bay.

Opposite the Bradogue a strand on the south bank extending eastward from Áth Cliath widened to form what might be called Christchurch Bay, in which 50 years later the Norse would make the first significant human intervention in the river. The east side of this little bay, roughly from Fishamble Street to Exchange Street, was a rock-based bluff on which Isolde's Tower would be built about 500 years later, and at the east edge of that bluff lay the mouth of the River Poddle with its island.

Some 700 m east of the Poddle confluence, the small River Stein flowed into the Liffey from the south with, to its east, the long west–east ridge of Lazars Hill, now Townsend Street. Beyond that again lay the great bay of the Dodder delta, into which the Swan River also flowed. Once past the spit of Ringsend, the shoreline fell away to the south-east, past the future rabbit warrens behind the murrough that fringed the South Bull sands at Sandymount and Merrion, and on along the rocky shoreline past Blackrock and Dún Laoghaire, with its inlets at Monkstown, Sandycove and Bullock, to Dalkey and its islands.

East of the Abbey Theatre on the north bank, the shoreline turned to the north-east along the North Strand to the mouth of the River Tolka, and it probably, even in 850, formed at high tide the strange isolation of Mud Island near Newcomen Bridge. From the Tolka, the high-tide shoreline ran east and then north-east by Clontarf and St Anne's Park to Sutton Cross, which some thousands of years earlier lay under water with Howth as an island to the east, and from there it ran by south of Howth Head to the Baily lighthouse.

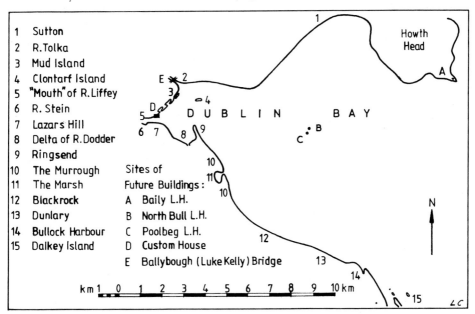

1 Sutton
2 R. Tolka
3 Mud Island
4 Clontarf Island
5 "Mouth" of R. Liffey
6 R. Stein
7 Lazars Hill
8 Delta of R. Dodder
9 Ringsend
10 The Murrough
11 The Marsh
12 Blackrock
13 Dunlary
14 Bullock Harbour
15 Dalkey Island

Sites of Future Buildings:
A Baily L.H.
B North Bull L.H.
C Poolbeg L.H.
D Custom House
E Ballybough (Luke Kelly) Bridge

Figure 2: Liffey shoreline in the estuary, 850

Much of this 39-kilometre-long shoreline from Dalkey to Islandbridge weir to the Baily could support a population, as there was ample seafood and generally some rough pasture available. There may have been some hamlets. One would see the possibility of these at the fords of Kilmehanoc and Áth Cliath, at the fishing-centres of Ringsend, Clontarf and Bullock, and at Ballybough near the mouth of the Tolka. Other sites might be added, but this is clearly an area for speculation, and one unlikely to be resolved.

A VIEW OF THE RIVER IN 1577

900	First earthen bank at Wood Quay
1066	Battle of Hastings
1170	Anglo-Normans capture Dublin
1492	Columbus reaches New World
1494	Poynings' Law
1537	Henry VIII orders dissolution of monasteries

In 1577 Richard Stanihurst, born into an influential Dublin family, and tutored by Edmund Campion in Dublin in 1570 (290), wrote 'a plain and perfect description of Ireland' for *Holinshed's Chronicles*. In it (*CARD*, II) he noted, 'If you be delited with fresh water, the famous river called the Liffie, named of Ptolome Lybnium, runneth fast by. If you will take the view of the sea it is at hand.' In his opinion, 'the onlie fault of this citie is that it is lesse frequented of merchant estrangers, bicause of the bare haven'. He mentions the Woodkeie and the Merchant Keie and records that 'the Bridge street with the greater part of the Keie was burnt in the year 1303'.

How then did the Liffey appear to Stanihurst nearly 700 years after the Norse built the first earthen bank at Wood Quay? How had the interaction proceeded during those 700 years?

One can now recognise that the year 1577 was close to the end of a long period, nowadays largely forgotten, during which the people of Dublin very much took the river as they found it. A new vigorous 200-year era would begin within 25 years, bringing a campaign of development that would completely transform the river down to Ringsend. But in 1577 the walled city lay on the south side of the river, and one might truly say that the Liffey ran by the city of Dublin rather than through it. Two great monasteries, St Mary's Abbey and St Saviour's Priory, arose in the seclusion of the north bank and flourished there for several centuries. By 1577, however, both had succumbed to the personality of Henry VIII, one falling into the hands of the law and the other going to private developers.

The Norse and, later, the Anglo-Normans continued the development of the quays that had started in 900, and they had, perhaps by 1250, completed Wood Quay and Merchants Quay to a river wall line not far from the modern walls of these quays. From the 14th century, if not earlier, the city wall, punctuated by towers, ran close by these quay walls.

At the west end of Merchants Quay the first bridge was built across the Liffey, to supplement Áth Cliath and to give access for commuters to the new north bank suburb of Oxmantown and to the two monasteries and their surrounding settlements. This bridge, now Fr Mathew Bridge, was the only road bridge that the people felt to be necessary at Dublin until 1670, and it had already been destroyed and rebuilt, probably twice, before that date. Upstream there was a narrow footbridge, supplementing the ford at Kilmehanoc, from the earliest times. It is a coincidence that when Stanihurst was writing his account in 1577, Sir Henry Sidney was in that year replacing this footbridge with a stone-arched road bridge close by, on a site that was the second ever to be used for a road bridge across the Liffey between Islandbridge weir and the sea. The weir itself had been built by the community of Kilmainham early in the 13th century. Part of its function was to form a mill-race, and it is the island that was made by the Liffey and the mill-race which gave the name of Islandbridge to the district near Sidney's bridge in the late 16th or the 17th century.

Down by the city no further quayage had been added since the beginning of the 14th century. Such scattered river works as were made would have been associated with the monasteries or with private landholders. A grant of King John in 1192 had declared that 'every citizen may for his own advantage build wherever he wishes on the bank but without damage to the city or citizens'.

Out in the estuary, east of the future site of the new Custom House, the Liffey at low tide flowed through a web of shallow channels, between shoals and occasional deep pools, to cross the sand bar east of the Poolbeg lighthouse and so into the deep water of the bay. It was this dangerous entrance combined with the absence of any protection against storm in the bay which led Stanihurst to describe Dublin Harbour as a 'bare haven', and which forced the city merchants and shipowners into endless protests about the hardships of their trading conditions. Virtually no attempt was made prior to 1600 to improve this position. Again the people appeared to take the river as they found it, and to suffer the problem rather than confront it.

Many historic events on the banks of the Liffey and its estuary would have been known to Stanihurst. In 919 the high king of Ireland, Niall Glundubh, was killed at Kilmehanoc Ford in a battle with the Norsemen. In 1014 Brian Bóruma was killed as he defeated the Norse along the shore of the estuary and the mouth of the Tolka in the battle of Clontarf. Some of the last slaughter on that Good Friday was at the Droichet Dubhgaill beside Áth Cliath (where indeed there had also been many deaths 'in the full tide' during a battle at that ford in 770). In 1171 the final battle between the Anglo-Normans and the displaced Norse of Dublin was fought at Hoggen Green along the south bank of the Liffey between the Poddle and the Stein. And in 1317 the citizens strengthened the river walls along Merchants Quay and Wood Quay and blocked the gates and slips to frustrate Edward Bruce, who had come from Scotland to challenge Edward II for the lordship of Ireland. In 1534 it was in the Chapter House of St Mary's Abbey that Silken Thomas Fitzgerald, the young deputy governor for Ireland, threw down the gauntlet to Henry VIII and mustered a Geraldine army to take Dublin. It would be the stubborn resistance of the people of the city to the assaults of Silken Thomas that would later lead Henry to reward them by making over to the city as a gift the priory of All Hallows, which he had acquired from the Augustinians in 1538. This would in due course become the site of Trinity College. The map or plan made in about 1592 to illustrate proposals for the new college, the Hatfield Plan, would be the first map to show a building in Dublin in its relation to the 'Liffe Fluius'.

A VIEW OF THE RIVER IN 1800

1588	Defeat of the Spanish Armada
1601	Battle of Kinsale
1641	Rising in Ulster
1649–50	Oliver Cromwell in Ireland
1660	Restoration of Charles II
1667–1745	Jonathan Swift

1691   Treaty of Limerick
1782–1800 Grattan's Parliament
1789   French Revolution
1798   Rising of the United Irishmen

In 1600 Dublin entered a period of entrepreneurial turbulence and rapid expansion. The names of Newman, Hawkins, Jervis, Amory, Ellis, the Ushers, Rogerson and Vavasour enter history as individual developers of the river-banks; Dublin Corporation, the Society of the King's Inns and the Crown also played large parts. The population of the city grew sevenfold in the 200 years to 1800, from about 26,000 to 180,000. The aggregate length of the quays, which in great part constitute the actual interface between man and river, increased sixteenfold in the same period, from 450 m to 7.2 km. Five new bridges were built across the Liffey, and indeed some were destroyed and built a second time in the 200 years; this programme included an astonishing output of four new crossings in the 13 years from 1670 to 1683.

The intake of new land along the river-banks began with Jacob Newman in 1606 and extended through to William Vavasour in 1798. It is a matter of personal choice to rank the many projects in order of importance, but, if area alone were the criterion, one would have to mention the Corporation for the work of the Ballast Office in taking in 195 ha on the north bank, in the area known broadly as the North Lotts, and Sir John Rogerson, who, supplemented by Vavasour, took in 115 ha from the delta of the Dodder. As a result of other intake projects further upstream in the city, three of the Liffey tributaries, the Stein, Poddle and Bradogue, disappeared into culverts.

Craig (3) has observed that the Renaissance arrived in Ireland on 27 July 1662, when James Butler, duke of Ormonde, 'stepped out of his pinnace on to the sands of Dublin Bay'. He had returned to Dublin as lord lieutenant of Ireland and was to be influential in the country for a further 23 years. Among many achievements, he made a vital contribution to the interaction of the city and the river by persuading the riverside developers, in particular Sir Humphrey Jervis, to form quays of generous width and to build only on their landward side.

Not surprisingly, this 200-year period was also the first age of Dublin maps. No useful map of the city existed before 1600, but between then and 1800 some 20 major sheets appeared, showing the growing city in detail, with some illustrating also the estuary in the bay. There are in addition countless maps and plans in the records from this period dealing with small areas and individual projects.

It is not a coincidence that the first artist to illustrate the Liffey, Francis Place, began his work at this time, with his drawings of 1698/9. Unlike in other major European cities, there were no earlier topographical illustrations of the Liffey in Dublin. Place was followed during the 18th century by a stream of artists, all reacting, it may be suggested, to the increasing influence of the Liffey on the built environment, and to the increasing interest of the people in their river and port.

It was at the beginning of the 18th century that the city first began to solve the problems of its inadequate port and harbour. The epic 100-year achievement of the young and impecunious Ballast Office in building the South Wall, among the most dramatic marine works of the 18th century, worldwide, was the first step in providing a safe haven for mariners and in eliminating the 900-year-old scourge of the Bar. This work, coupled with the abandonment of the old port in the city in about 1795 and the building of a new Custom House and dock downstream, was an essential step towards the development of the modern port.

The abandonment of the old port at Old Custom House Quay immediately downstream of Grattan Bridge came about only after the most bitter controversy that had ever arisen in the city in the context of the river. The dominant classes in 18th-century Dublin were urbane. A battle had not been fought in the metropolis since 1649, when Colonel Michael Jones routed Ormonde and opened the east coast to Cromwell. Faction-fighting did occur among the dispossessed and as an entertainment for lusty young college students, but the landed, professional and merchant classes rarely resorted to collective violence. Even their fury was civilised. It tended to be expressed in wit and satire, in lampoons and anonymous broadsheets and in angry informal assemblies. The proposed building of Carlisle (now O'Connell) Bridge, which was at the focus of the controversy, was first mooted in the middle of the century, but its opponents, principally the merchants established in the old port precinct and along the older quays, held up its construction for nearly 50 years.

Thus, a long open letter was published in 1752 'from a Freeman to the Citizens of Dublin, occasioned by an extraordinary Kind of subscription, begun by the Aldermen, on a very extraordinary Account'. It commented, 'Ye see what a bustle is made about this new Bridge; in consequence of a Pique between some Persons of Distinction . . . too often is the publick Good sacrifized to private Passion'. A year earlier, in a strong attack on the project, Eugenius, an anonymous writer, had asked, 'Is not Citizen and Inhabitant, Words of like Signification: But if at present the Name of Citizen should be confined to Hucksters and Pedlars etc., and an Odium thrown on all the rest on their account as if they were the Whole, would not that be a very pretty story?' Again in 1752, in a broadsheet entitled 'The State Tryal', another anonymous writer expressed the hope that

> the Great Personages who can Give the Authority for carrying on such an Undertaking and have a clear and distinct perception of the remotest Consequences thereof . . . they who have the true Spirit of Patriotism in them, will never prefer the Private Advantage of any Particular Person however great and powerfull nay that of their own to the general or Publick good.

But, in the end, the power of the few, led by John Beresford, prevailed and the bridge was built, though still under a civic cloud, and opened in 1795. It is quite clear now, one must say, as indeed it was at the time, that building the bridge and moving the port downstream was the right thing to do in so far as the proper use of the river and the development of Dublin were concerned.

Despite Eugenius's claim, the words citizen and inhabitant were by no means always 'of like Signification' in Dublin in these centuries. The citizens' franchise controlled the administration of the city. The inhabitants merely dwelt there. The citizen and his wife were entitled to free oysters one day a year at Clontarf. Mere inhabitants were not. And it was also the citizens, rather than those dismissed by James Gandon as the populace, whose parliamentary suffrage supported the notable planning activities of the Wide Streets Commissioners and the erection of the great riverside buildings of the 18th century, the two Custom Houses and the Four Courts. Mere inhabitants did not at the time have a say in such matters.

Not all anonymous *cris de cœur* were in the public domain. Individuals also addressed one another. In 1726 a spurned lover, xxxx Esq., gently rebuked his fickle 'young lady' in couplets printed for him in London, for sixpence in boards (291). He likens her to Anna Liffey:

> Among th'Iernian nymphs for beauty famed
> There dwelt a beauteous Nais, Livia named.

He traces Livia's lineage:

> Her mother Lamia, Neptune was her sire.

Lamia is identified as Lambay Island. He sees his lady as Anna Liffey, wooed by the great rivers of Ireland, which he names.

> If mortals you reject; caught with those charms
> Know many a God of Rivers seeks thy Arms.

But his lady has left him:

> Still does the quickness of her ancient course
> That once enforced her feet her streams enforce
> Which tumbling from the mountains to the plain
> Thro' thee, beloved Eblana, seek the Main.

He envisages his lady enhancing the splendour of the Phoenix; and he entreats her to beware of his rivals:

> You on those Streams, Pride of those Streams, that dwell
> Yet tread the dangerous paths by which they fell.

He sees her walking on the strand

> to view the conquests you have won
> (Where oft those Eyes supply the absent sun).

In a footnote, he describes the strand as a 'place of parade, chiefly for the winter-season, upon the Liffy lying below Dublin'.

The immediate effect of this 18th-century lament on the young swain's fortunes is not known, but it is intriguing today to see Anna Liffey cast in a mythological role and with this particular imagery in the literature of more than 250 years ago.

A VIEW OF THE RIVER TODAY

1800	Act of Union
1829	Catholic Emancipation
1840	Municipal Corporation Reform (Ireland) Act
1845–9	Great Famine
1914–18	First World War
1916	Easter rising
1921–2	Anglo-Irish treaty
1939–45	Second World War

It is convenient to divide the people–river interaction during the 200 years since 1800 into two parts, one above and one below the East Link Toll Bridge.

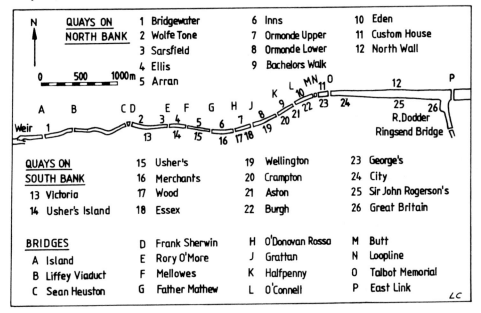

N	QUAYS ON NORTH BANK	1 Bridgewater	6 Inns	10 Eden
		2 Wolfe Tone	7 Ormonde Upper	11 Custom House
		3 Sarsfield	8 Ormonde Lower	12 North Wall
		4 Ellis	9 Bachelors Walk	
0 500 1000m		5 Arran		

QUAYS ON SOUTH BANK	15 Usher's	19 Wellington	23 George's
13 Victoria	16 Merchants	20 Crampton	24 City
14 Usher's Island	17 Wood	21 Aston	25 Sir John Rogerson's
	18 Essex	22 Burgh	26 Great Britain

BRIDGES	D Frank Sherwin	H O'Donovan Rossa	M Butt
A Island	E Rory O'More	J Grattan	N Loopline
B Liffey Viaduct	F Mellowes	K Halfpenny	O Talbot Memorial
C Sean Heuston	G Father Mathew	L O'Connell	P East Link

Figure 3: Liffey shoreline in the city, today

In the first of these, from Ringsend to the weir at Islandbridge, the interaction has mainly been a continuation of the city development of many centuries. Eight new bridges were built, including two to carry railways across the river, and two as private ventures to be paid for by tolls. Several of the older bridges were reconstructed. Among them was the venerable Old Bridge, which was demolished after 400 years of service and replaced in 1818 by what is now Fr Mathew Bridge.

The quays west of O'Connell Bridge, somewhat uneven and irregular in surface and width, were taken in hand by the newly established Ballast Board, and were converted, in a sustained operation over 25 years, into the disciplined form that they have today, with their remarkably uniform parapets and copings. The continuity of the quays from O'Connell Bridge to Sean Heuston Bridge was completed on both banks, and, in the construction of Heuston railway station, the River Camac was confined in a culvert.

Below O'Connell Bridge the quays were completed on both banks down to Ringsend, and it was these quays that, early in the 19th century, had to meet the first demands of the new downriver port. The cross-section of the river had to be levelled and the quay walls deepened in this reach to receive the new steamships, which had arrived at Dublin for the first time in 1815. Large enclosed docks, which in the event would have mixed commercial success, were built on both sides of the river, and the infant gas industry established itself on the south bank. Both banks in this area would become industrialised, and the railway companies would in due course extend their lines down to the north bank waterside at several places.

While general riverside building did continue during the 19th and early 20th centuries between Ringsend and Islandbridge, one must recognise in the late 20th century a particularly vigorous outbreak of redevelopment on both banks of the river. During this surge, still flowing, many public and commercial buildings have been newly erected along the quays, and, in a significant modern interaction, the people of Dublin are being cajoled into making their homes again along the river-banks. There is much to be admired in the new works, but it will be for our descendants 100 years in the future to regard what then remains, and decide on the taste and wit of the 20th century.

For the principal development of the Liffey since 1800, however, one must look to the new estuary of the river, east of East Link Bridge, and to the older and larger estuary in the bay.

In 1800 the Bar was still the treacherous obstacle it had been for 900 years. Ringsend still perched on its narrow spit, and the Pigeonhouse precinct, approached by a narrow causeway along the South Wall, was being strengthened as a military fort. Sailing-vessels were still at the mercy of gales from all quarters as they ran for shelter into the new river-mouth or anchored in the bay to ride out stormy weather. The tragedy of the *Prince of Wales* and the *Rochdale* in 1807, however, showed how little faith could be placed in the open bay as a sanctuary in time of storm, and these wreckings very much encouraged the construction of the great asylum harbour of Dunleary a decade later.

The coming of steam power largely freed mariners from the perils of storm in Dublin Bay, but it did not remove the danger of the Bar to all shipping. This had become the dominant concern of ship owners and masters and of the port authority, at that time the Ballast Board; and it was the Board and its advisers that solved the age-old problem through the construction of the Bull Wall, completed during the 1820s, and the development of a programme of dredging which has continued to the present day. One result, quite unexpected, of the building of the Bull Wall was the formation outside it of Bull Island, which had scarcely existed above high tide in 1800, but which now accommodates two golf-links, extensive sand-dunes and, at all stages of the tide, a sandy strand more than 4 km in length.

Between 1833 and 1837 the southern shoreline of the bay was reorganised by the construction along its edge, from Merrion Gates to Dún Laoghaire, of the trackway for the Dublin and Kingstown railway. Sea walls were built, and new causeways enclosed a bird sanctuary at Booterstown and a tidal pond, later filled in, at the old Dunleary Harbour. A Martello tower was demolished. The railway would later be extended to Dalkey and beyond, but in the area covered by the text, the line would follow an inland route that did not influence the shoreline.

Remaining east of East Link Bridge, the development of the modern port – the most significant interaction between the city and the river since 1800 – began, tentatively in the 1850s, and vigorously with the commencement of the construction of the North Wall Extension in 1871. This development has continued, although with some intervals, through to the present day, and has totally changed the north bank of the river and estuary between Clontarf and Ringsend. In the process it has channelled the Tolka (which showed its displeasure in December 1954), and formed extensive areas of new land around its mouth in Fairview. It has also led to the formation of new land along the Clontarf shore and in the port precinct, burying Clontarf

Island and obliterating the route of the mysterious Nightingale Ford. Several new open tidal basins have been formed, graving docks constructed, and new industries as well as storage and handling facilities established. The work is still ongoing, and one must now surely accept that the accommodation of the port in the city at Grattan Bridge, so cogently urged in the 18th century, would have been impossible.

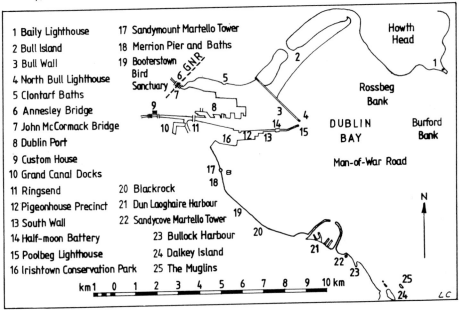

1 Baily Lighthouse	17 Sandymount Martello Tower
2 Bull Island	18 Merrion Pier and Baths
3 Bull Wall	19 Booterstown
4 North Bull Lighthouse	Bird Sanctuary
5 Clontarf Baths	
6 Annesley Bridge	
7 John McCormack Bridge	
8 Dublin Port	
9 Custom House	
10 Grand Canal Docks	
11 Ringsend	20 Blackrock
12 Pigeonhouse Precinct	21 Dun Laoghaire Harbour
13 South Wall	22 Sandycove Martello Tower
14 Half-moon Battery	23 Bullock Harbour
15 Poolbeg Lighthouse	24 Dalkey Island
16 Irishtown Conservation Park	25 The Muglins

Figure 4: Liffey shoreline in the estuary, today

On the south bank, east of East Link Bridge the city and its suburbs began quite early to encroach on the South Bull sands. In the 19th century the Rathmines and Pembroke sewer embankment enclosed the area between Irishtown and the South Wall that became Ringsend Park. During the 20th century the road along the shore from Irishtown to Merrion Gates was completed, and new land was formed on the sands where once Robert Emmet had walked of an evening to view the defences of the Pigeonhouse Fort. This intake was used for residential areas and industry, and for a new park named for Sean Moore, lord mayor of Dublin in 1963–4. The main sewage treatment plant for the city was developed close by in the Pigeonhouse precinct, and that area became also the city centre for the generation of electricity, with the Poolbeg Twins replacing the Tramway Twins of an earlier time.

A pleasing feature of this south shore development has been the raising of a high grassy headland between the Liffey and Sandymount Strand from which there are new views of the city and port and of the Dublin and Wicklow Mountains seen across the sands. This headland covers an extensive refuse disposal area of the middle 20th century, and the decision to landscape it and cultivate it as Irishtown Conservation Park is an imaginative use of new intake which will flourish as it is further planted.

One now walks to this park from Irishtown by a path at the edge of the strand, past a new unnamed monolith at the east end of Sean Moore Park and close to the spot where Gerty

MacDowell 'was seated near her companions, lost in thought, gazing far away into the distance' (27) out towards the mouth of the bay, where the text ends.

FINALLY

In the sense that this book is primarily a descriptive index of the metropolitan Liffey and its interaction with the people of Dublin, it will be appreciated that comprehensive treatment of individual topics is necessarily beyond its scope. So many areas are covered that further study and syntheses to whatever depth or breadth may be desired must be left to the reader. The texts in the bibliography will be found of value, and the more specialised works mentioned in their own bibliographies open access to most of the existing body of knowledge in the relevant areas. The author recognises only too well inadequacies in this work that arise from the limitations of his study, and asks the indulgence of readers for these shortcomings. Clearly there is considerable scope for more intensive studies in many of the topics that are discussed. To take a random example, identification and detailed analyses of the several riverside precincts into which the Liffey in Dublin may properly be divided is just one subject awaiting research. The evolution of deep-sea trading in Dublin and the development of the bridge system are others. The list is endless. It is hoped, however, that the material offered here may in itself convey some useful impression of the dialogue between the Liffey and the city during the last 1,100 years, and that it may demonstrate the part played by each in moulding the river and modulating Dublin's growth.

Acknowledgments

The author acknowledges his use of the books, journals and other records listed in the bibliography. He is grateful to those authors whose work is finished and those who are still writing for what they have caused to be available to him, and trusts that they may accept his sincere thanks. He thanks in particular the many authors whose works comprise the journal of the Old Dublin Society.

He is privileged to have had access to the archives of Dublin Corporation, Dublin Port and Docks Board, the Institution of Engineers of Ireland, the Irish army, and Messrs Arthur Guinness, Son and Company, and acknowledges the invaluable help of their archivists, Mary Clark, Gerry Daly, John Callanan, Commandant Peter Young and Peter Walsh.

He has also been privileged to use many libraries, and thanks, for their courtesy and help, the National Library, the National Archives, the Gilbert Library, the Linenhall Library in Belfast, the Dublin libraries of the King's Inns, Religious Society of Friends, Representative Church Body, Royal Dublin Society, Royal Irish Academy, Royal Society of Antiquaries of Ireland, Trinity College and University College, as well as the British Library, the National Maritime Museum at Greenwich, the Port of London Authority Library, and the Public Records Office at Kew.

The author is grateful for the opportunities given to him to view and study so many of the huge numbers of maps, charts, drawings and illustrations that have built up around the tidal Liffey since the end of the 16th century; and he thanks those institutions already named, and also the National Gallery, the National Museum and the Irish Architectural Archive, as well as the National Portrait Gallery in London and the Museum of London, for the material they contain. He also acknowledges with thanks the permission given to him to view pictures and maps in private collections, and in particular in the Proby Collection at Eldon Hall and the Burghley Collection at Hatfield House.

In addition to these silent sources, the author is conscious of the many individuals who, over several years, have encouraged him and given him information in areas which the literature appears to have left unclear. In the whole exercise, he recognises that in attempting a synthesis of the interaction of the river and the city over a period of 1,100 years, he must risk entering into many disciplines in which he is not professionally trained. He recognises further that within these disciplines there exist many single areas of study, medieval, renaissance and modern, and indeed locational, that in themselves constitute long-term programmes for individual scholars. If then the obvious inherent limitations for a single writer are combined with some necessary level of brevity, it will be realised that many entries in the text must be ripe for useful development at other, more expert hands. It is the sincere wish of the author that this will occur, and that any errors, omissions or gaucherie, for which he can hold only himself responsible, will be made good. In the meantime, he acknowledges most sincerely the information and help he has received in conversations and correspondence over many years from more than 100 individuals, who represent a wide range of scholarship and whose observations have greatly enriched this text. Their names are in his records and he trusts they may accept this very brief and anonymous tribute as a mark of his grateful thanks to each and every one.

The preparation of the text for publication has been assisted considerably by the draftsmanship of Larry Clarke, and by the photography of Myles Christian of the Department of Civil Engineering in University College, Dublin, for the interest of which the author is most grateful. The help, encouragement and advice of the publishers and of Jonathan Williams is warmly acknowledged, as are the skills and unending good humour of Angela Rohan, whose contribution as editor has been invaluable.

The author thanks his son and daughters and their families for their generous assistance at various stages of the study. And finally and totally he offers tribute to the limitless patience and word-processing achievements of his wife, without whose heroic co-operation this work would surely have vanished like a river in a desert of unfulfilled aspirations.

Abbreviations

AD	Anno Domini
Add. MS	Additional manuscript in British Library
BC	Before Christ
BL	British Library
BP	Before present
c.	*circa*
CARD	*Calendar of the Ancient Records of Dublin* (ed. Gilbert et al.)
DGIN	Directors General of Inland Navigation
DHR	*Dublin Historical Record* (the journal of the Old Dublin Society)
DNB	*Dictionary of National Biography*
FRS	Fellow of the Royal Society
FTCD	Fellow of Trinity College, Dublin
ha	hectare(s)
HWOST	High-water ordinary spring tide
ICE	Institution of Civil Engineers
ICEI	Institution of Civil Engineers of Ireland
IEI	Institution of Engineers of Ireland
JRSAI	*Journal of the Royal Society of Antiquaries of Ireland*
km	kilometre(s)
LWOST	Low-water ordinary spring tide
m	metre(s)
mm	millimetre(s)
n.d.	not dated
NGI	National Gallery of Ireland
NLI	National Library of Ireland
NMM	National Maritime Museum (Greenwich)
NPG	National Portrait Gallery (London)
N.S.	New Style (calendar)
OD	Ordnance datum
O.S.	Old Style (calendar)
OS	Ordnance Survey
Proc. RIA	*Proceedings of the Royal Irish Academy*
PRO	Public Records Office (Kew)
RDS	Royal Dublin Society
RIAI	Royal Institute of the Architects of Ireland
RN	Royal Navy
UM	Ulster Museum
UNESCO	United Nations Educational, Scientific and Cultural Organisation
WSC	Wide Streets Commissioners

Notes on the use of the metric system of measurement in this book and on the relation of statute measure to Irish measure

Modern international practice urges the general use of Système International (SI) units of measurement rather than the imperial system. Thus for lineal and area dimensions the metre is preferred to the foot or yard.

Relevant conversion factors include the following:

1 mile = 1.6093 kilometres (km)
1 foot = 0.3048 metres (m)
= 304.8 millimetres (mm)
1 inch = 25.4 millimetres (mm)
(the centimetre is little used in SI)
1 acre = 0.405 hectares (ha).

In those entries in this book in which both systems are quoted as alternatives, the conversions generally given are close approximations which are convenient to use and sufficiently precise for all usual comparisons. Thus 1 mile is taken as equivalent to 1.6 km (i.e. 5 miles = 8 km), 1 foot as equivalent to 0.3 m or 300 mm, and 1 inch as equivalent to 25 m. Furthermore all dimensions in metres are given to one place of decimals unless there is a special reason to do otherwise, and large dimensions are usually given to the nearest whole metre. More accurate calculations can be made by using the conversion factors, but the author believes that they are rarely necessary.

The difference between statute measure and Irish measure lies in the fact that 1 perch (statute) = $5\frac{1}{2}$ yards (statute) whereas 1 perch (Irish) = 7 yards. Hence 1 square perch (statute) = 30.25 square yards (statute) and 1 square perch (Irish) = 49 square yards = 1.62 square perches (statute). From these relations, 1 Irish mile = 1.27 statute miles, and an Irish acre = 1.61 statute acres.

A

ABBEY GREEN
See LITTLE GREEN.

ABBEY STREET OLD
See SHIP BUILDINGS.

ADAM AND EVE'S
See IMMACULATE CONCEPTION, CHURCH OF THE.

ADAM AND EVE'S LANE
See MERCHANTS QUAY.

ADMIRALTY CHARTS OF DUBLIN
In 1977 a chart of Dublin Bay (no. 1415), made to a scale of 1:25,000, was published at Taunton under the superintendence of Rear-Admiral D. Haslam, hydrographer of the British navy. A new edition was issued in 1979. The soundings are confined to the bay and offer no information inside the mouth of the Liffey. Depths are given in metres below Lowest Astronomical Tide level (LAT). An alteration of 9° 50' is noted in the magnetic variation from 1875 (Kerr) to 1979.

The chimneys at Poolbeg generating station (height 210 m) and the gasometer at Rogerson's Quay (height 70 m) are seamarks that are described as 'conspicuous'.

A companion chart for the Liffey (no. 1447), made to a scale of 1:7,500, was published in 1977 with a new edition in 1979. Minor revisions were made to this map in 1985.

ADMIRALTY PREROGATIVES
From early times the control of the waters and profits of the harbour and bay at Dublin lay, with some contention, between the city and the Crown.

The subject is complex and one for specific research. It involves ownership of treasure, fishing, ballasting, jurisdiction over causes of accidents and death, and charges for use of the harbour facilities, as well as the right to levy customs and other duties on imported merchandise.

Already in 1280 Hugh de Kersey was claiming to be chief sergeant 'of the seashore of the city of Dublin', probably in the name of Edward I, and in 1306 Geoffrey de Mortoun was defendant in an action brought by the Crown, which claimed that he had not paid the king's 'prise' on a cargo of wine. At the same time Henry III had in 1250 given Dublin permission to levy 'of every great ship sixteen pence', the income to be applied to the fortification of the city.

Clearly, both the king and the city expected to benefit from levies on merchandise brought in to the port, but agreement could not always be reached on who was entitled to what. The city held that charges for the anchorage of vessels in the harbour and for quayside facilities, which involved quayage, slippage, plankage and cranage, should be paid to it, as it had to bear the costs of maintaining perches and buoys in the approaches to the harbour and of making and operating the quays in the city.

Two controversial aspects were the function of the Admiralty and the 'threepenny customs'. Part of the royal prerogative was exercised through the Court of Admiralty, said to have been erected by Edward III in 1357, and the Admiralty Office, established by Henry VIII in 1512; and there was in Dublin a vice-admiral as well as a marshal and a judge of the Admiralty. The threepenny customs were an ancient imposition. In 1631 the Assembly recorded that the city had taken 'tyme beyond the memory of man for the space of these many hundreds of years three pence for every twenty shillings worth . . . from every merchant tradinge hither out of England or any of his majesties dominions or from any other foraine contrie'. This levy was used to provide perches, buoys and beacons, as well as a proper channel and safe landings. The charge was not imposed on freemen of Dublin.

On 25 January 1582 Elizabeth I granted by charter to the Corporation of Dublin 'the office of Admiralty and all things thereunto belonging between Arklow Head and Nannie Water' (the Nanny or Nenny River enters the sea between Balbriggan and Drogheda). Despite this grant, however, the Admiralty prerogatives and the collection of customs at Dublin were generally in some confusion during the 17th and 18th centuries.

The Crown was continuing to collect its own levies. In 1604 the Assembly complained that the king's 'customers of this porte of Dublin doe exacte their dueties contrarye to the lawes of the realme'. In 1608 Thomas Bolton, the recorder of Dublin, reported from London that a legal action, in which he had argued that the city was the owner of the river and was maintaining it 'with perches and the Crane', had been settled with a decision that while Dublin should continue to receive the threepenny customs levy from all vessels belonging to strangers, the Crown also should have three pence in the pound on all vessels entering the port, whether used by freemen or by strangers.

In 1623–5 the Assembly claimed that abuses were being committed at Ringsend by the vice-admiral, who should have been its nominee but who was holding his own court and sending pursuivants to arrest freemen of Dublin; and it summoned William Ellsworth, 'who pretended to have some jurisdiction at Ringsend', to appear before it, at the same time ordering the city sheriffs to continue their courts in that area. In 1660 the Assembly appointed Owen Jones, a merchant, to be 'marshall of the Admiralty for the bay and porte of this cittie of Dublin' with all perquisites and profits 'during the pleasure of this city'; but in 1677 the city was fending off the king's Court of Admiralty, which was claiming a right to the fishing of Salmon Pool and within the city liberties. Between 1683 and 1688 the vice-admiral, Colonel Cary Dillon, had seized 'a parcel of silver coin found covered with sand at the strand near Ringsend and put it to his own use', despite the disapproval of the city; and two inquests by city coroners on persons drowned or killed near Merrion and Ringsend had been interrupted and

taken over by the judge of the Admiralty. Where all of this left Elizabeth's charter of 1581–2 is unclear.

In 1707 the city did recognise the superior jurisdiction of the lord high admiral, Prince George of Denmark, in the control of all ballast offices, and it did agree to a yearly gift to him of 100 yards of sailcloth in return for permission to establish a ballast office in Dublin. In 1706 the collection of customs and quayage in Dublin had plainly been in confusion and unauthorised persons were attempting to collect port dues; and in 1708 the Assembly was again proclaiming the right of the city to exercise its chartered admiralty jurisdiction in the port to the exclusion of other claimants. It is not surprising then that merchants trading to Dublin resented the many charges imposed upon them at the port and took whatever action they saw fit to avoid paying any of them.

The city did continue active, if not very effectively, in collecting the threepenny customs. In 1695 the Assembly appointed William Alcock to 'collect and receive at the Custom House the threepenny customs duty of keyage and of Chapman Guild belonging to this citty'. (It is not clear what the Chapman Guild, or Yeald, was, other than that it formed part of yet another port levy. A chapman was a pedlar, perhaps trader, and the term 'chapmanysmesure' was known in the 15th century in England as a measure for barley.) In 1703 it was recognised that only a small part of the threepenny customs was being collected. In 1730 the Assembly was not certain 'how far the city's right to the threepenny customs extends and upon what sums the same is to be taken', and in that year the total amount collected under that head was less than £131. This need not be wondered at, since in 1721 the Ballast Office, a city committee, 'discovered one Edward Edwards who is appointed by the Anchorage Office to look after the buoys and take the soundings of the bar once a week'. Edwards presumably was paid, but not by the city, since its committee did not know him.

In 1752 the Assembly yet again affirmed its right to anchorage payments and to the 'fines, forfeitures and profits belonging to the office of Admiralty'; but only a few years later, in 1760, it was seeking the protection of the king against the Privy Council for Ireland, which was proposing a parliamentary bill for 'securing ships coming into and going out of the port of Dublin, and for the more convenient ordering their anchorage within the said harbour and the quays of the said city'.

In the middle of these new complications the Assembly granted at this time a lease to Alderman John Taylor to collect anchorage levies and other monies accruing to the city from Elizabeth's charter. As part of his responsibility he was to keep the buoys in the harbour in repair, a function that throughout the centuries had been associated with the threepenny customs. This lease would remain with Taylor and his descendants into the 19th century.

Payments for slippage and anchorage would continue to be exacted, despite the autonomy of the Ballast Board but arguably still within the framework of the threepenny customs, until 1828, when their annual value was assessed as £800. In that year the Assembly decided that there should be no further leases, but that the city's share of the income should thenceforward form part of the lord mayor's salary. At this time the operation of the river and port had passed largely into the responsibility of the Ballast Board; and, following the Act of Union in 1800, the customs function at the port had been substantially reduced.

[158, 181, 239, *Calendar of the Justiciary Rolls* (1305–7), *CARD*, I–VII, X, XIV, XV, XVIII, map (Petty 1654)]

ALBERT QUAY

See WOLFE TONE QUAY.

ALDBOROUGH HOUSE

Aldborough House was built for Edward Stratford, second earl of Aldborough. The name of the architect has not been recorded. When first conceived in 1792, the site, scenically, was fine, situated as it was on the eastern toe of the ridge separating the Liffey from the Tolka, where it sloped down in ancient times to meet the north strand of the bay. It faced directly out to sea across the flat and almost totally undeveloped North Lotts. By the time the house was completed in *c.* 1798, the Royal Canal was curving across its vista

Aldborough House, c. 1800 (W. Skelton)

only some 250 m from the front door, and the sweep of the North Strand was being broken by the rise required to cross Newcomen Bridge.

Aldborough House, which has been described as the last major aristocratic house to be built in Dublin, was not a very successful residence and was little lived in until 1813. A contemporary verse is suitably depressing.

> Where once the billows roared along the strand,
> Now, far from billows, spreads the thirsting land.
> There on a flat, in all the pride of taste,
> A pompous palace beautifies the waste.

In 1813 Professor von Feinagle (Feinaigle) from Luxembourg (one account describes him as a monk from the German town of Salem, near Constance) acquired the premises, with support in Dublin, and founded there a school which he called the Feinaglian Institution, adding some new buildings and renaming the house as the Luxembourg. The education offered was his own development of a system based on the use of mnemonics, with special emphasis on memory. The school was successful, and several notable figures in Dublin life were educated there. Feinagle died in 1819 and the school closed down about ten years later.

Aldborough House was then used as a military barracks for many years. Troops were stationed there at the time of the Crimean War (1854–6) and up to the Fenian rising in 1867, and in the days leading up to Daniel O'Connell's proposed Repeal meeting at Clontarf in 1843. In 1862 the barracks had accommodation for 7 officers, 276 men and 4 horses, and it is recorded that it could hold in its stores 145,600 barrels of powder, an enormous quantity.

In modern times the premises have been used as a storehouse for the Post Office.

[3, 134, 182, 195, 197, *DHR* (Bowen, O'Donnell, Quane), maps (Rocque 1760, Wilson 1798, OS)]

ALDBOROUGH MAN-OF-WAR

In 1725 the man-of-war *Aldborough* sank in the pool of Polebegg in the mouth of the Liffey. The commander, Captain Lawrence, sought the aid of the lord lieutenant, who in turn desired the lord mayor to send five gabbards to help in raising the ship. The work was achieved in 12 days with the assistance of these boats, manned by 15 Ballast Office crewmen.

[*CARD*, VII]

ALEN, JOHN, ARCHBISHOP AND LORD CHANCELLOR

Also Alan, Allan, Allen. John Alen, formerly canon of Lincoln, came to Ireland in February 1529. He had been appointed to the Council of Ireland as an anti-Geraldine, and he was nominated by Cardinal Wolsey in 1529 as archbishop of Dublin, an office he held until 1534, and as lord chancellor of Ireland. He was a man 'of turbulent spirit' but also hospitable and learned, and 'a diligent enquirer into antiquities'. He accumulated debts readily and had to be warned by Thomas Cromwell regarding monies he owed to the king that 'Henry VIII is no person to be deluded or mocked withal'. He was removed from the Chancery by the king in 1532, but retained the 13 titles associated with his archbishopric, including that of 'regular abbot of the cathedral church of Holy Trinity of the Arroasian Order'.

He was 'an enemy of the Geraldine family' and fled to Dublin Castle for sanctuary when Lord Offaly (Silken Thomas) rose against the English in 1534. Fearing capture, however, he tried to escape to England by boat from the harbour at Dames Gate, but was stranded at Clontarf by contrary winds or by the carelessness of his crew. He then fled to the house of a friend, Hollywood, at Artane, where, according to the account given by Ware, he was captured by Silken Thomas with a party of his followers. His men

dragged the old man out of his bed and led him half naked to [their] master. Alan fell upon his knees in his shirt, barefooted and bareheaded, and begged him to spare his life. But in vain labouring to bend the headstrong youth to mercy, he betook himself to Divine Meditations and while he was on his knees pouring out his Soul to God in prayer he was villainously murdered in the presence of his enemy near Artane castle, and his brains scattered about.

He died on 27 or 28 July and was then 57 years of age. Another account maintains that Silken Thomas did not order the murder of the archbishop.

The old castle remained in the hands of the Hollywood family until the 19th century, when it was pulled down in *c.* 1825 and the stones used to build a new house. Purchased by the Irish Christian Brothers as a novitiate in 1875, it became instead an orphanage at the request of Cardinal Cullen, developing a comprehensive trade school which was active for much of the 20th century. It is now St David's Secondary School.

The site of Archbishop Alen's murder and burial-place is still identified at the ancient chapel and cemetery that stands near the junction of Kilmore Road and Pinebrook Drive. Henry replaced him as archbishop with another English cleric, George Browne, who has been remembered for ordering the public burning in Dublin of St Patrick's crosier, the ancient and venerated relic known also as Baculum Jesu.

[16, 22, 36, 159, 160, 189, private communications]

ALEXANDRA BASIN

In general terms the new port of Dublin lies east and north of East Wall Road and, south of the Liffey, between Ringsend and the Pigeonhouse precinct.

During the time of the Ballast Board, the only work east of East Wall Road consisted of two graving slips, the first graving dock and much of the large pool known as North Wall Basin or Halpin's Pond. These works are mentioned elsewhere in the text; see Graving and Halpin's Pond.

Shortly after the Dublin Port and Docks Board replaced the Ballast Board in 1867, the construction of the North Wall Extension or North Quay Extension began in 1871 under the direction of Bindon Stoney, chief engineer to the Board. This was a quay 700 m in length extending the Liffeyside section of the North Wall downstream. It was in this work that Stoney used the 360-ton precast concrete wall units for which he won international fame (*Min. Proc. ICE*, vol. 37, 1873–4, part 1). This new quay, together with the embankments started by George Halpin in 1836 to the east and north of Halpin's Pond, would form Alexandra Basin, which might be seen as the heart of the new port.

The basin was named after Alexandra, princess of Wales, who with her husband, the future Edward VII, formally opened the completed work in 1885.

The eastern embankment to the basin would begin to be transformed into a formal quay in 1940, and would be named Ocean Pier. The northern embankment had from 1860 incorporated the first graving dock and from 1869 incorporated a jetty known as Goulding's Jetty, leased to WHM Goulding Limited, the fertiliser manufacturers; and it gradually developed to have its principal waterfront become Alexandra Quay, completed in 1931.

The northern edge of the northern embankment, speaking broadly, was demarcated by a retaining wall built prior to 1860 and running for 700 m west–east from the sharp corner on East Wall Road along the present Tolka Quay Road. An effect of this retaining wall was to deflect the River Tolka, and, as a result, the wall came to be known as Tolka Quay. This quay has now been incorporated into later land reclamation extending northward, and covering in its spread the former Clontarf Island.

In projects following the Second World War the port complex was continued downstream with the formation of Alexandra Quay East and Alexandra Basin East, and, to their north and east, extensive oil, freight and cross-channel ferry facilities.

A comprehensive account of the port will be found in Gilligan's *History of the Port of Dublin*. [129, 180, map (Dublin Port 1987)]

ALEXANDRA BASIN EAST

See ALEXANDRA BASIN.

ALEXANDRA QUAY

See ALEXANDRA BASIN.

ALEXANDRA QUAY EAST

See ALEXANDRA BASIN.

ALFIE BYRNE ROAD

See JOHN MCCORMACK BRIDGE.

ALICE OF HARWICH

In 1292 a vessel named the *Alice of Harwich* was trading into Dublin. This is possibly the earliest-named ship to use the port.
[181]

ALL HALLOWS PRIORY

Also known as All Saints Priory. In *c.* 1162 Diarmait Mac Murchada, king of Leinster, vowed that if he survived a serious illness he would erect a religious house at Dublin in honour of all the saints. In 1166 he built All Hallows Priory and installed there the Augustinian canons of the Order of Arrouaise. In his charter Mac Murchada granted lands at Baldoyle (Baldoil, Ballidubgail) to the priory. These lands are described as being granted 'to his spiritual father and confessor Edan, Bishop of Louth, for the use of the canons of the church of the daughter of Zola and their successors'; and they are also recorded as granted by charter (*c.* 1162) to the Augustinian priory of All Hallows.

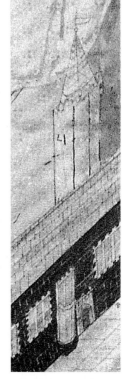

The priory steeple, c. 1592 (detail from the Hatfield Plan of Trinity College)

The priory was located at the east side of Hoggen Green, immediately to the east of the River Stein and close to the south shore of the Liffey. Its main gate, known as 'the dore next the sea', faced north and opened on to a road along the shore that ran from Hoggen Green to Lazars Hill. The priory had its own mill 'without ther yet [gate] betwyx the gren banke and the Lang sten in the Steyn'. In 1303 the prior was granted 'four great oak trees from the King's forest at Glencry for the repair of his mill and the bridge towards the Steyn'. Four years later, in 1307, Robert Bagot of Bagotrath gave the prior permission to make a conduit from the Dodder to 'the mill at the gate of the Priory', on condition that the mill would 'grind 2 crannocks of corn weekly for him free'. This was a remarkable watercourse, which one may speculate left the Dodder between Ballsbridge and Donnybrook to flow either by Mount Street towards the priory, or direct to the Stein near St Stephen's Green to augment its flow. A comparison between it and the 'old canal' drawn off the Camac in or before the 12th century is of interest, with the Dodder conduit being the more surprising.

All Hallows came to enjoy the goodwill of the Anglo-Norman rulers of Ireland. Its prior was one of those who sat in parliament as a spiritual peer, and in 1380 it was enacted by parliament that 'no mere Irishman should be permitted to make his profession in this priory'. This patronage continued, and in 1478, at a time when the king's admirals of Ireland were seeking increased jurisdiction over the coastal waters near Dublin, the priory appealed for protection of its rights at its lands of Baldoyle. The matter was resolved by the parliament, which established the prior as 'Admiral of Baldoil' with his own authority.

On 16 September 1538 All Hallows was formally dissolved and two months later on 16 November the last prior, Walter Hancoke, with the sub-prior and four canons signed a deed of surrender of the priory and its possessions. In February 1539 Henry granted it to the mayor and citizens of Dublin in recognition of the part that the faithful citizens had played in resisting the attack of Silken Thomas in 1534.

The buildings and lands then lay idle for about 50 years except for a short period during an outbreak of plague in 1575–6 when the great garden of All Hallows 'was appointed to buyld lodginges in for the releife of the infected', a gate being built and a guard posted to prevent their escape back to the city.

At the end of the 16th century Trinity College was established on the site by Elizabeth I. Key dates in this new foundation were as follows:

December 1591   Elizabeth instructs the lord deputy to erect and make the corporation of a college.

January 1592   The City Assembly passes a resolution saying 'the city herby agree and order that the scite of Alhallowes and the parkes therof shalbe wholly gyven for the ereccion of a collage there'.

3 March 1592   Elizabeth issues her charter.

13 March 1593   Foundation-stone laid by Thomas Smyth, mayor of Dublin, who was just then finishing his one-year term of office.

9 January 1594   Buildings in use by staff and students.

Early in this process, Archdall records that, the priory site having been granted 'for the founding of the university, the whole building, the steeple excepted, was for that purpose immediately demolished', thus substantially completing the obliteration of the 400-year-old monastic foundation. Mahaffy comments that the steeple was preserved as affording 'a feature in the view from the city or a landmark for ships coming up from the sea, and upstairs in it was the porter's lodge of the College'. The Hatfield Plan of the college, probably made for its first chancellor, Lord Burghley, in 1592, shows the steeple as a square structure, some four storeys high, with a steep-pitched slated or leaded roof, and names it as a 'sea marke'.

The new college remained liable to occasional damage from storm waters in the Liffey until William Hawkins built his river wall in 1662–3. This work substantially removed the danger, although a storm in 1670 did bring water up to the walls of the college. At about this time the site of the buildings of All Hallows/Trinity College ceased to be directly affected by the Liffey.

[21, 22, 53, 147, 150 (Ryan), 244, *CARD*, I, *DHR* (Boylan, O'Connor), map (Hatfield Plan *c.* 1592)]

AMIENS STREET
See NORTH STRAND.

AMIENS STREET RAILWAY STATION
See CONNOLLY RAILWAY STATION.

AMORY GRANT
In January 1675 Jonathan Amory, a merchant, was granted a lease for 299 years by the city 'of that part of the Strand on the north side of the Liffey, situate betwixte the wall of the Pill, in the possession of the Lord Sangtry, and the water mill lately built by Mr Gilbert Mabbott'. It was a significant feature of the lease that 'All which strand and premises are Covered every tide at full sea with water and is part of the river Analiffy'.

It appears from de Gomme's map of 1673 that there was a small cluster of buildings near the north bank of the Liffey, close to where the Abbey Theatre is today, and the dimensions in the lease suggest strongly that a length of about 100 m of the river-bank at around this place was excluded from Amory's lease, although he was given space to continue his highway past it as his lease required him to do. It is possible that this ground, whether by its original profile or by earlier protection, was not 'Covered every tide at full sea' and was not therefore part of the strand. In this context the cluster of buildings shown by de Gomme may be relevant. One does not erect buildings where they will be submerged by the tide twice a day. Brooking shows this area heavily built up in 1728 with no thoroughfare on the river-bank. The city recorded its ownership of this short stretch of land in 1733, noting significantly that its holding was bounded 'on the south by the river Anna Liffey, and on the north by the land granted to Jonathan Amory'.

If this area was not part of the Amory grant, then the land leased to him appears to have been (i) a

strip of strand up to about 99 m wide and 794 m long from near Arran Street East to Ferryboat Lane (near the modern Abbey Theatre), (ii) a strip of strand up to 110 m wide and 378 m long from the vicinity of modern Liberty Hall to the junction of modern Store Street and Amiens Street, and (iii) a narrow strip of land along the modern laneway known as Abbey Street Old, which was necessary to enable Amory to complete the 60-foot-wide roadway to which his lease committed him. Thus it is suggested that a parcel of land about 100 m long and 50 m wide, north to south, remained in, or at some time prior to 1733 reverted to, the possession of the city, to be used by it in that year to form the Iron Quay and some yards between the land leased to Amory and the river. It is recognised here that this interpretation does not accord with Thomas Mathews's map, now held in the city archives, in which he records that 'I have endeavoured to lay down a parcel of ground let to Jonathan Amory for 299 years in 1674 taken from a Description in the Town Clerk's office and surveyed in April 1781 by T. Mathews'.

The northern boundary of strip (i) followed generally the line of Little and Great Strand Streets and Lotts. The northern boundary of strip (ii) was roughly a straight line from Liberty Hall to the Store Street–Amiens Street junction. The location of this strip is shown on Bolton's 1717 map of the North Lotts as Amory's Ground, and a large part of the New Custom House was built on this site in 1781–91.

Part of Ormonde Quay Upper, the whole of Ormonde Quay Lower and Bachelors Walk, and part of Eden Quay were built on ground reclaimed from the river in the area of Amory's lease, as were the building developments along those quays. The remainder of Eden Quay was made on land owned by the city. It should be mentioned that the precise extent of the Amory grant may still be seen as a matter for conjecture.

[*CARD*, V, VIII, *DHR* (Bowen), Dublin Corporation Archives (Ancient Revenue no. 16), maps (de Gomme 1673, Bolton 1717, Brooking 1728, Rocque 1756, OS various)]

Amory's Ground

See Amory Grant.

Anchorage Office

See Admiralty Prerogatives.

Andrews Folly

See Fort at Lazars Hill.

Anglesea Street

See Aston Quay.

Ankisters Parke

An area known in the 17th century as Ankisters Parke appears to have been located on the River Bradogue south of Little Green. It is mentioned that a 'little bridge' spanned the Bradogue in this vicinity, and this bridge may be represented by the discontinuity shown in the river on Speed's map near the southern gateway to St Mary's Abbey, or it may be near the intersection of St Mary's Lane and Boot Lane on Rocque's map.

[CARD, V, XI, maps (Speed 1610, Rocque 1756)]

Annesley Bridge

Annesley Bridge

In April 1792 an act was passed in the Irish parliament under the title, 'An Act for enabling the Trustees for making, widening, and repairing the road from Dublin to Malahide, and the other Roads leading to Dublin over Ballybough-Bridge, pursuant to several Acts of Parliament, more effectually to carry the said Acts into Execution'. The bill had been brought before the Irish House of Commons in February 1792 by three members, the Honourable Richard Annesley, Sir John Blaquiere, Bt, KB, and Sir William Gleadowe

Newcomen, Bt; and it was brought to the House of Lords by Annesley.

The act (32 Geo. III, c. 37) stated 'that it would be of advantage to the public, if that part of that space of ground overflowed by the sea at high water, lying eastward of Ballybough-bridge, between the wall enclosing the ground formerly taken in from the sea, called the north-lots, and the weir-wall on the north strand, were enclosed and taken in'.

This reclamation is almost precisely the triangle enclosed today by Fairview Strand, Annesley Bridge Road and the present channel of the Tolka. The exact location of the weir wall is uncertain, but it may be the unnamed feature that appears in an appropriate position on the Rocque/Scalé map of 1773.

Later in the act it was said that,

whereas it is intended that the said new communication shall be made nearly in a direct line from the strand road leading from his Majesty's custom-house to the said ground overflowed by the sea and across the same to the road adjoining the said weir-wall on the north-strand, nearly at the end of the place called Fairview on the said strand . . . it will be necessary to build, erect and make a new bridge and causeway, eastward of Ballybough-bridge aforesaid.

The new bridge was Annesley Bridge, and the causeway consisted of two parts: the short portion of the North Strand Road extending from Annesley Place to Annesley Bridge, and the site of the present Annesley Bridge Road from the bridge to Fairview. The first of these parts, prior to that time, was a simple embankment where there were sea-water baths reported to have been frequented by the earl of Charlemont.

A contract for the construction of Annesley Bridge, under that name, was let to William Pemberton – surprisingly in March 1792, before the act was passed – and the bridge was recorded as complete in 1797. It was described by D'Alton in 1838 as 'a handsome erection of granite consisting of three semicircular Arches and exhibiting in the centre of the parapet the Annesley Arms'. In 1928 a new widened Annesley Bridge was completed. Designed by M.A. Moynihan in 1924 with advice on the foundation system from Sir John P. Griffith, the new bridge is a three-span steel beam structure with a concrete deck supported on steel troughing and surfaced with asphalt, and with concrete piers and fascia beams and metal parapets. The contractors were Orr, Watt, and Company, Lanarkshire Bridge Works, Glasgow.

It is of interest to mention that the 1792 act introduced to Ireland, quite possibly for the first time, the organisation of traffic lanes. It stated that,

> whereas great inconveniencies hath arisen on the said roads, by drivers of carriages going or driving different ways, keeping the same side of the said roads; be it enacted, That it shall and may be lawful for the said trustees, or any seven or more of them, to make such rule and order for compelling drivers of all coaches, chaises, carts, cars and other carriages going from Dublin to keep such carriages on one side of the roads, and coming towards Dublin to drive or keep such carriages on the other side of the roads, as they shall think proper.

The penalty for non-compliance was to be five shillings or, in the event of non-payment, three days in gaol.

[4, 80, 87 (vol. 3), 94, Statutes of Irish Parliament (vol. 16), Dublin Corporation Archives, maps (Rocque/Scalé 1773, OS 1963)]

ANNESLEY BRIDGE, BATHS AT

See ANNESLEY BRIDGE and SHALLOWAY'S BATHS.

ANNUAL CALENDAR

See CALENDAR, OLD STYLE AND NEW STYLE.

APOSTLESHIP OF THE SEA, THE

In c. 1893 the Society of St Vincent de Paul, which had established its first Conference in 1833, started active work among seamen in several English and French seaports; and in 1893 the first Catholic Seamen's Club in the world was founded in Montreal. In 1895 a Jesuit priest, Fr Gretton, inaugurated the Apostleship of the Sea as a confraternity for seamen. In 1910 the Stella Maris Conference of the Society of St Vincent de Paul in Dublin opened the Catholic Seamen's Institute at Sir John Rogerson's Quay. In 1962, as a branch of the worldwide Apostleship or Apostolatus Maris,

the SVP Conference moved to 3 Beresford Place to establish the Stella Maris Seafarer's Club; and from that centre it continues to observe the traditions and serve the objectives of the international organisation and of the Society.

In June 1995 the centenary of the Apostleship of the Sea was commemorated in Dublin by the celebration of mass on the north steps of the Custom House, the principal celebrant being the archbishop of Dublin, Dr Desmond Connell.

[303; Peter F. Anson, *Apostleship of the Sea in England and Wales*, London, Catholic Truth Society, 1947; private communication (R. Kearney)]

ARCH LANE

A narrow lane of the 17th and 18th centuries running north through the King's Inns lands from Inns Quay beside the Charitable Infirmary. It is shown by Rocque (1756). Pool and Cash (1780) name it as Pursictor Alley. The origin of this name is obscure. O'Meara suggests, particularly because of its location near the King's Inns, that it may be a corruption of the Latin verb 'persector', signifying eager pursuit and investigation.

Arch Lane was later absorbed into the Four Courts complex.

[Maps (Rocque 1756, Pool and Cash 1780), private communication (J. O'Meara)]

ARCHBISHOP ALAN

See JOHN ALEN, ARCHBISHOP AND LORD CHANCELLOR.

ARONS BRIDGE

See MELLOWES BRIDGE.

ARRAN BRIDGE

See MELLOWES BRIDGE.

ARRAN LANE

In the 18th century, and probably in the 17th when it was built, Arran Quay did not extend along the river-bank as far as the present Fr Mathew Bridge; neither did the earlier Inns Quay. The link between these two quays was a narrow thoroughfare, which crossed Church Street about 16 m away from the river wall, with houses between it and the river on both sides of the bridge. This was Arran Lane. Its location is reflected in the break or step in the building frontage that can be seen today near the east end of Arran Quay at Church Street. Arran Lane appears to have passed through an archway between the bridge and Inns Quay.

[16, *CARD*, XI]

ARRAN QUAY

In 1637 Sir Gerard Lowther, lord chief justice, was granted a small parcel of land beside a stable which he already possessed. The letting was described as 'extending and abuttinge on the east to the peticioners stable and wall, on the south to the river of Annalyffee, on the west to parte of the strande of the said river, and on the north to the highway which leadeth by the river side from Hamon's lane'. In the same year Charles I, proposing to build a mint house, was granted a plot beside Lord Lowther's holding, 100 yards long from east to west and extending south to north 'from the lowe water marke [to] within a yard of the high waie next to the Strand', a distance of 79 yards. These may be the earliest documentary references to a general development of the river-bank as we now know it, west of the Old Bridge (now Fr Mathew Bridge). The highway 'next to the Strand' was Hamon's Lane, known earlier as Hangman's Lane and now Hammond Lane.

Recent archaeological excavation shows that waterside protective works incorporating timber revetments and stone walls had been carried out in the 14th century between Lincoln Lane and Church Street. The association of this area with the earlier Áth Cliath may be relevant.

In 1674 the king's holding, still underdeveloped, was granted to John Greene, a carpenter, who apparently also left it underdeveloped. In 1682 William Ellis was given a grant of the whole of the strand from near the Old Bridge westward to the park gate. This Ellis grant is mentioned in the entry on Ellis Quay.

Ellis went quickly to work, making a quay and filling in the land behind it. As a result, in 1692,

St Paul's Church

Arran Quay, which extended from near the Old Bridge to Mellowes Bridge, was ready to be designated formally as one of the four quays in the city at which coal might legally be unloaded. The quay was probably named after Richard Butler, earl of Arran (died *c.* 1685), second son of the duke of Ormonde, and his deputy in Ireland from 1682 to 1684.

In 1728 Brooking showed that the whole frontage of Arran Quay had been built up. The parents of Edmund Burke were early residents, and a letter from him, written in 1746, discussing flooding on the quay is quoted in an entry under his name. This inundation came from the combination of a very high tide and flash-flooding in the Liffey, and it soon abated, as Burke wrote in a later letter.

The relationship of Arran Quay with the Old Bridge is mentioned in the entry on Arran Lane. This short dog-legged thoroughfare shown by Brooking in 1728 and in more detail by Rocque in 1756 probably reflected the need to allow access for wheeled vehicles from the quay to the bridge; and the houses between it and the river, which were pulled down in the period 1770–80, may have included the site of Lowther's stable. The step in the house frontages on modern Arran Quay, which marks the end of Arran Lane, may still be seen.

In 1835–7 St Paul's Catholic church was built on the quay to a design of Patrick Byrne. The Catholic parish of Arran Quay had been constituted in 1707. Ten years earlier an old warehouse had been converted into a chapel, but on a Sunday in December 1708 'a Beam in the Mass house on Arran's Key gave way which occasioned three persons killed and several others wounded'. A new chapel was built on the same site in 1730, rebuilt in 1786, and continued in use until the present church was opened in 1837. The earlier building still existed as a winestore early in the 20th century. Arran Quay parish became part of Halston Street and Arran Quay parish in 1974, and St Paul's now serves as one of the two churches of that parish.

A narrow laneway, shown first on OS 1838 as Lincoln Lane, runs north from the quay beside St Paul's Church. This passage was named as Pudin Lane by Brooking in 1728 and as Pudding Lane by Rocque in 1756. The name of Lyncolns Lane was, however, already in use in 1730, when its corner was designated as one of the stands for the night-watchmen of St Michan's parish.

In 1850 Charles Haliday (1789–1866), merchant and consul for Greece, antiquary and author of *The Scandinavian Kingdom of Dublin*, had his places of business at 35 Arran Quay and at 13 Arran Street close by; and to the east, at no. 24, was located the Western Lying-in Hospital with the Revds Thomas

Scott and W.R. Smith as secretaries. This building had previously been Agar House, the residence of the Ellis family. At the present time many of the early houses on the quay have been demolished and new office and residential development is in progress, extending back from the quay to the old highway from Hammond Lane to the west.

[3, 34, 40, 146, 196, 198, 200, *CARD*, III, XI, XII, maps (Brooking 1728, Rocque 1756, Pool and Cash 1780, OS 1838, Walsh 1977), private communication (A. Hayden)]

ARRIVAL OF A LORD LIEUTENANT
See CEREMONIAL IN DUBLIN.

ART GALLERY ON LIFFEY
See LIFFEY BRIDGE.

ARTICHOKE ROAD
See SOUTH STRAND.

ARTISTS OF THE RIVER AND BAY
See ILLUSTRATORS OF THE LIFFEY.

ASDILL'S ROW
Asdill's Row, which marks the west end of Crampton Quay, appears on modern maps as a substantial street connecting Temple Bar to the quays. It appeared first as an unnamed laneway on Brooking's map of 1728, and Rocque showed it in 1756 as a narrow gated passage leading from Temple Bar to the bank of the river. Neither it nor nearby Bedford Row, to which it is parallel, lies at right angles to the quay; and the original layout of the contained building plots with their sides parallel to Asdill's Row may offer the reason for Merchants Hall having its front skewed to the line of the quays.

[Maps (Brooking 1728, Rocque 1756, OS current)]

ASSAULT BY UA RUAIRC ON DUBLIN
In September 1171 Tigernán Ua Ruairc, prince of Breifne, knowing that Strongbow and Raymond le Gros were away from Dublin, attacked the city for the third time that year. At first his attack looked like succeeding, but after a sudden turn of fortune,

he was driven off by Miles de Cogan. Tigernán lost his son in this battle and in the following year he himself was killed near Athboy, County Meath.

It would be nearly 400 years before the Irish would make their next armed assault on the power centred in Dublin; and then it was led by a Norman lord, Silken Thomas Fitzgerald, against Henry VIII, the last English lord of Ireland.

[35]

ASSEMBLY, CITY

See MUNICIPAL GOVERNMENT OF DUBLIN.

ASSOCIATION FOR THE SUPPRESSION OF MENDICANCY IN DUBLIN

See MOIRA HOUSE.

ASTON QUAY

Using the evidence of maps, the topography of Aston or Aston's Quay is as follows. The modern names are given first, and the corresponding name on the earlier map is given in parentheses.

Ireland on College Green. The land had a northern frontage of 77 m along the bank of the Liffey, which at that time lay close to the line of Fleet Street. It was a condition of Carey's lease that the river-bank would not be developed for commerce. This may be the earliest development of this part of the south bank, and it may be the reason for Speed's showing of it as a walled bank in 1610.

In 1641 Richard Bamber was granted a lease of 300 m of the river-bank east of Newman's development, and he was to build a quay wall there with a carriageway 7 m wide. Little, if anything, seems to have come of this enterprise. In 1657 Arthur Annesley was granted a lease on 'that parte of the Strande unto the lowe water marke which abutteth and meareth unto severall houses and gardens belonginge to him, scituatt on the Colledge Greene, adjoyneinge to the seaside there'. This lease, which had a river frontage of 61 m, indicates the position of the high-tide shoreline at future Westmoreland Street at the time.

In 1662–3 William Hawkins took the important initiative of building a river wall on or close to the

Year	Map	Western end	Eastern end
1610	Speed	not in existence	river shown walled
1673	de Gomme	do.	do.
1685	Phillips	do.	no reference
1728	Brooking	Bedford Row (Anglesea Street)	Hawkins Street
1756	Rocque	Bedford Row (Porter's Row)	Hawkins Street
1780	Pool and Cash	Aston's Place (Lee's Lane)	Hawkins Street
1797	Faden	Price's Lane (unnamed)	Hawkins Street
1838	OS	Bedford Row (do.)	O'Connell Bridge (Carlisle Bridge)
Current	OS	Bedford Row	O'Connell Bridge

As time passed, Burgh Quay was laid out to the east and Crampton Quay to the west; and the change-over from Crampton Quay to Aston Quay shifted as noted.

In 1602 Sir George Carey was given a lease of land to build a hospital near the modern Bank of

line of the present quay wall. Hawkins's Wall extended from east of Hawkins Street to the line of modern Temple Lane, if de Gomme's map of 1673, on which he described the consequent reclamation as 'ground taken in from the sea', is to be accepted. In 1666 Sir George Rawdon could report 'the new project of walling out the sea goes on between the Custom House and Lazy Hill being abetted more than formerly . . . a double wall and a fair bank between'.

It seems probable that in *c.* 1680 Major Henry Aston was given permission to develop this river frontage. It would be recorded by the City Assembly 80 years later, when his grandson, Henry Aston, sought renewal of a lease for a holding on Aston Quay in 1760, that the renewal should be granted, seeing that 'his grandfather, Major Aston, was the first person who took in and enclosed the said premises from the sea and laid out a considerable part of his fortune in improving and building thereon'.

Haliday records that the quay was known as Aston's Quay in 1708; and in 1735 a set of beams and scales was erected on the quay for commercial use, even though it appears that there was little demand for them.

In 1757 Aston Quay was seen as 'a place of considerable trade', but was very cramped, with the buildings in poor repair and ripe for demolition and reconstruction. A committee, probably already influenced by the principles that would guide the Wide Streets Commissioners, reported to the Assembly in 1760 regarding the necessary redevelopment.

> The houses to be built in a uniform and regular manner, that is to say that each and every house be at least three stories high, besides cellars; the first or shop story to be nine feet in height, the second or middle story to be ten feet in height, the third or garret story to be eight feet in height, the front and rear walls to be of an equal height and range with each other.

In addition, a 40-foot width was to be provided for the quay and a width of 19 feet for each of the lanes leading off it.

The Aston family retained a substantial property on the quay during the 1760s. Other householders in that decade included Blair, Foot, Manning, Darquier, Rudd, Dignam, Donnelly, Gorman and Carmichael. None of these names would still be on the quay in 1850.

In 1794 Francis Tunstall was instructed by the Ballast Board to rebuild the quay wall from the west end of Carlisle Bridge (O'Connell) to Price's Lane, which at the time was the western end of Aston Quay. This short wall was to be the prototype for the reconstruction of all the Liffey quay walls west of Carlisle Bridge; and it was probably in this work that the step in the wall of this quay, shown on the earlier maps, was removed.

The narrow and crowded precinct between Aston Quay and Fleet Street was served by four lanes. Using their modern names, these were (i) Bedford Row, named as Porter's Row on Rocque (1756); (ii) Aston's Place, named on Brooking, Rocque and OS 1838 as Lee's Lane; (iii) Price's Lane, named on Brooking and unchanged since then; and (iv) Fleet Alley, shown but not named on Brooking, named on Rocque, and now contained in Westmoreland Street.

The construction of Burgh Quay to the east of Aston Quay, and of Crampton Quay to its west, are mentioned in separate entries.

[3, 6, 87 (vol. 3), 146, 160, *CARD*, II–IV, VIII, X, maps (as named)]

ASTON'S PLACE
See ASTON QUAY.

ÁTH CLIATH
The *Annals of the Four Masters* relate that on the night of the birth of Conn of the Hundred Battles in about AD 100 there were 'discovered five principal roads to Teamhair which were never observed until then. These are their names: Slighe Asail, Slighe Midluachra, Slighe Cualann, Slighe Mór, Slighe Dála.' While it is most probable that these Slighthe Móra were known before that time, there is little doubt that they existed before AD 900, when this record begins.

It appears that Slighe Midluachra, running south from Ulster, followed the east coast and crossed the major barrier of Dublin Bay and the Liffey estuary at the ford that was already known in AD 770 as Áth Cliath. Close to the south bank of the river, Slighe Midluachra met with three others of the great roads, Slighe Mór from Connaught, Slighe Dála from Limerick and north Munster, and

Slighe Cualann from south Leinster and Waterford. The crossing-place of Áth Cliath was just upstream of Fr Mathew Bridge. It may well be represented today by St Augustine Street, where Usher's Pill was, on the south bank, and by Bow Street or Church Street or some track between them, now built over, on the north.

At the site of Áth Cliath the effect of spring tides was twice each day to transform a low-water channel perhaps 5 m wide and, in dry weather, 0.5 m at deepest into a tideway perhaps 90 m wide and 4 m deep at the centre. At neap tides the tideway would be narrower, but because of the smaller tidal range the low-tide channel would be deeper. In normal weather conditions these tidal variations controlled the viability of the ford. In flash-flood conditions, however, it was the volume of water flowing to the sea from the Liffey catchment that determined the depth of both the channel and the tideway.

The term Áth Cliath, on which the Irish name for the city, Baile Átha Cliath, is based, signifies a ford with hurdles. The hurdle by definition is a mat or sheet of interwoven saplings, or possibly saplings at close centres in one direction bound together at intervals to transverse pieces without interweaving. It is not known what the hurdles at Áth Cliath were nor how they were used. It may be that they were simply mats laid down and perhaps spiked into the mud and shingle slopes of the strand and into the bed of the channel, more or less in the manner of securing thatch. Such mats have been discovered in the Somerset levels and in the bog toghers at Annaghbeg and Derryoghil in Longford, where, however, the lateral force imposed by fast-flowing water would not have been significant.

Were the Áth Cliath in use today, the ford would be passable or open at spring tides for about 10 hours in each 24, provided the user, assumed to be 1.75 m tall, was prepared to wade knee-deep at midstream for much of the open time. At neap tides the open time would be reduced to about 8 hours and the user would be waist-deep at midstream for most of this period. In times of storm flooding from the river upstream the ford could be closed for 24 hours or more on end, and fast-flowing water was always dangerous. The account of the battle of Áth Cliath in AD 770 records that members of one of the armies 'were drowned in the full tide'.

This book proposes that the tidal conditions in AD 900 were sufficiently similar to those today to expect that a ford at that time, depending on the use of the river bottom as it was, would have been impassable for very much more than half of each 24-hour period; and of its open time about half would be during the night. Even for an uncosseted people these time limitations and the degree of immersion required during the nominally open periods may have been intolerable. For these reasons the possibility should be considered that a submerged stone causeway, perhaps 1 m high and similar to those used for access to crannogs but wider, was laid down in the deep part of the channel, with the hurdles fixed down on the sloping banks of the strand and on the top of the causeway. It seems unlikely that we shall ever know precisely the nature or dimensions of Áth Cliath.

[120, 147, 235, *Proc. RIA* (vol. 90C: de Courcy)]

AUGUSTIN MONASTERY
See St Augustine's Friary.

B

BACHELORS LANE
See BACHELORS WALK.

BACHELORS QUAY
See BACHELORS WALK.

BACHELORS WALK

known as Bachelors Quay in 1766. The origin of the name is uncertain. One record suggests that it derived 'from some long deceased capitalist named Batchelor'. Others suggest that it was a popular promenade for unattached males. One or other is probably correct. It is, however, unlikely by the nature of the terrain and by its difficulty of access that it would have been a popular walking-place before 1674; and it quite soon afterwards became a bustling quay.

Phillips indicates that the quay existed in 1685, and it was already a busy commercial quay when its name appeared on Brooking's map in 1728. At this quay in December 1738 'a Bristol man fastened [a ship] and the ship came down on another ship, the current being very strong, they went adrift

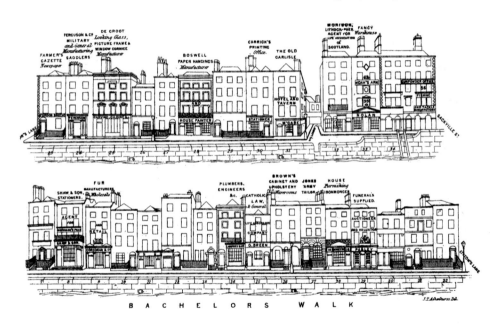

Bachelors Walk in 1850

The lease granted to Jonathan Amory in 1675 entitled him to reclaim the strand on the north bank of the Liffey east of the Pill. The stretch of quay from the Halfpenny Bridge down to the Abbey Theatre, to use modern landmarks, was developed as Batchelours Walke (Brooking 1728), Bachelors Walk (from 1838) and The Bachelors Walk (records of 1723 and 1728). It was also

both and broke loose six or seven other vessels which all came to damage, which damage in all probability cannot be repaired with less than one hundred pounds'. In 1756 John Rocque, who would have known the quay because he lived there from 1754 to 1760, shows the river between it and Aston Quay crowded, with shipping moored at both quays and passing along the channel.

The importance of this quay emerges also from the evidence given at an inquiry held before 1774 into proposals for building a new custom house downriver. Hamilton, the secretary to the Commissioners for Customs, testified that 'merchants seek leave to unload and load their ships at Batchelors Walk' rather than at the old Custom House. Graydon, the haven-master, said that 'the best lying for ships in the river is from Batchelor's lane to the graving bank'. Bachelors Lane is the narrow laneway known in 1850 and today as Williams Row, which now links Bachelors Walk to Middle Abbey Street some few yards west of O'Connell Street. The graving bank was on the north shore, possibly at or near the North Wall Slip. Another witness, Dempsey, said 'the deepest water between the walls is from the old glass house to Batchelors Lane and there also the ground is softer'. This glass house is probably that shown by Rocque on the site of the future George's Dock.

During all this time the eastern end of Bachelors Walk was at Union Lane near the present Abbey Theatre. It was linked to the main east–west artery of Abbey Street only at its extremities – Liffey Street at the west, and Union Lane – and there was no direct connection between it and the south bank except by ferry. Also, on the north side of the Liffey, the splendid, newly developed Sackville Street and Mall stopped short near the present General Post Office, and was continued southwards as the narrow Drogheda Street, which stopped at Abbey Street. As a consequence, Bachelors Walk remained largely isolated from the expanding north city, and would not become a full part of the city street system until Carlisle Bridge (now O'Connell) was opened in 1795, and Drogheda Street was extended southward to meet it, at about the same time. The new circumstances possibly led to the action taken by the residents of Bachelors Walk in 1817 to seek status symbols considered appropriate for other quays. In that year they petitioned the Ballast Board for kerbs and a gravel walk along their quay to have 'this side of the water placed in the same stile of elegance as the opposite'.

In 1813 the Ballast Board announced that it was about to open Eden Quay to the public. Earlier, in 1791, the formation of Eden Quay had been planned as part of Beresford's development, but the old extent of Bachelors Walk continued to be shown by Faden in 1797 and by Wilson in 1803. It may then be suggested that Drogheda Street finally became the eastern limit of Bachelors Walk in c. 1813, with the remainder becoming part of Eden Quay.

With the intervention of Carlisle Bridge, Bachelors Walk ceased to be a quay for seagoing vessels and joined the other quays 'west of Carlisle Bridge' as riverside city streets with little maritime function. General city activity continued, however, with shops, offices, hotels and small industries flourishing. Mr d'Esterre, a former English naval officer, lived on Bachelors Walk as a provision merchant until February 1815, when he was killed in a duel – which he seems to have provoked – by Daniel O'Connell. It was observed that for several years afterwards O'Connell, on his way along the quays to the Four Courts, would raise his hat when passing d'Esterre's house. In 1850 the influence of the proximity of Bachelors Walk to the courts and its central position in the expanding city was reflected in there being 22 solicitors named as having their rooms in the 34 houses listed along this quay at the time.

In a horrifying incident in July 1914 a detachment of soldiers of the King's Own Scottish Borderers, returning to barracks after an abortive attempt at Fairview to seize guns landed by the Irish Volunteers at Howth, fired on a crowd of Dublin people that blocked its passage on Bachelors Walk, killing 4 and wounding 38 others. In 1915 Jack B. Yeats would offer his own recognition of the occasion with the painting 'Bachelors Walk, In Memoriam', in which he illustrated a specific incident he had mentioned in his diary, that of 'a flower girl placing her own offering on the scene of a killing'.

A narrow street, now named Litton Lane, was first shown, unnamed, by Brooking in 1728 and as Littin's Lane by Rocque in 1756, connecting Bachelors Walk to the Lotts. The origin of the name is uncertain.

[16, 31, 58, 87 (vol. 8), 103, 146, 203, 204, 205, 206, CARD, V, VII, VIII, X, maps (Phillips 1685, Brooking 1728, Rocque 1756, Faden 1797, Wilson 1803, OS 1838)]

BACK QUAY

See ELLIS QUAY.

BAGNIO LANE

The name of Bagnio Lane is used by Gilbert (A History of the City of Dublin, vol. 1, p. 370) and later repeated by M'Cready. The implication is that Bagnio Lane existed in 1559 or 1560, but this may be erroneous. The corresponding entry in Gilbert's edition of the Calendar of the Ancient Records of Dublin (vol. II, 1560) refers not to Bagnio Lane but to Rame Lane, which, as both of Gilbert's quotations indicate, was at Merchants Quay; and a built slip in 1559, the year quoted, is more probable in this location than at the Bagnio Slip, where the river-bank at that time was still undeveloped.

See also Bagnio Slip.

[18, 39, CARD, II]

BAGNIO SLIP

Before the construction of Wellington Quay, the street now known as Fownes Street, Upper and Lower, continued downhill to run into the Liffey as a slip. This was the Bagnio Slip, and it was also a ferry terminal. When Wellington Quay was built in 1816 and the ferry was superseded by the Halfpenny Bridge, the slip was built up to become Lower Fownes Street.

The Bagnio Slip is said to have derived its name from a bagnio or brothel which existed nearby on Temple Bar in the reign of Queen Anne (1702–14). The slip was a busy but somewhat murky appendage to Temple Bar. On the one hand, notable citizens, including William Coats, a merchant and one of the wardens of the Holy Trinity Guild, the Merchants' Guild, lived along it during the 18th century. On the other, Gilbert found it appropriate to describe it at that period as a lane in which 'the houses were the resort of the lowest characters connected with the shipping in

the river and the scene of frequent brawls and occasional murders'.

John Rocque, the cartographer, would have used the slip quite frequently to travel from his lodgings and shop, which after 1754 were immediately across the Liffey in Bachelors Walk, to his agent in Essex Street.

See also Bagnio Lane.

[18, CARD, XI, DHR (Bowen), maps (Rocque 1756, OS 1838)]

BAILY LIGHTHOUSE

Baily lighthouse

It is recorded that there was a warning beacon on Howth Head from the ninth century. Eight hundred years later, in 1686, Greenvile Collins shows a lighthouse that had been built at the green bayley high on the Head by Sir Robert Reading in 1665. This is noted also by Scalé and Richards in 1765 (Green Baily). In 1790 Thomas Rogers built a new lighthouse, again high on the Head, and this was included by Bligh in 1800/3.

Since these lights tended to be obscured by fog or cloud, the Ballast Board instructed George Halpin in 1811 to build a new light closer to water level. This lighthouse, on the present site, was brought into operation in 1814, and is shown by Taylor in 1816 as the 'new lighthouse'. The Baily lighthouse is due to be automated, and left without keepers in residence in 1997, thus ending the history of manned lighthouses around the Irish coastline.

This account is taken largely from Long's study of the Irish lighthouses, in which further details of the Baily light are given.

[268, maps (Greenvile Collins 1686, Scalé and Richards 1765, Bligh 1800/3, Taylor 1816, Kerr 1875)]

BAKERS' TOWER

Two of the riverside buildings were at different times occupied by the Bakers' Guild, known as the Guild of St Anne. See FITZSYMON'S TOWER and NEWMAN'S TOWER.

[2, 18, CARD, I]

BALDOIL, ADMIRAL OF

See ALL HALLOWS PRIORY.

BALLAST

Material placed in a ship to supplement or substitute for cargo to ensure stability. In the context of this book, the material used as ballast was for many centuries generally sand, gravel or stone.

BALLAST BOARD

See CORPORATION FOR PRESERVING AND IMPROVING THE PORT OF DUBLIN.

BALLAST CORPORATION

This name was used in 1833 in the title of a critical appraisal of the work of the greater Dublin port area. The anonymous publication, which declared its policy as 'nothing extenuate nor aught set down in malice', dealt principally with the Corporation for Preserving and Improving the Port of Dublin, otherwise known as the Ballast Board, then nearly 50 years in existence, but makes reference also to the work of the earlier Ballast Office.

[73]

BALLAST OFFICE

The need for a ballast office in a seaport in earlier times arose from two factors. First, there had to be control of the places from which ballast was excavated and where unwanted ballast was dumped, and secondly, there had to be a sound legal background, which a ballast office duly established by act of parliament could provide, for the prosecution of offenders and for the imposition and collection of port charges. It was clearly profitable to control a ballast office, and in the 26 years from 1676 to 1702 three different private groups of entrepreneurs petitioned the reigning monarch for letters patent to enable them to establish a ballast office at Dublin. Two of them offered the inducement of providing a lighthouse on the South Bull. The Corporation resisted these applications on the grounds that nearly 500 years earlier King John had, by royal charter, granted the citizens of Dublin all the strands within the liberties and franchises of the city and that therefore the city had the sole rights to profits arising from the supply of ballast material from those strands.

The city also, from 1676 onwards, had been seeking an act of parliament to enable it to establish a ballast office, but there was a dilemma. Although an act was necessary, Prince George of Denmark, lord high admiral of Great Britain and Ireland, and husband of Queen Anne, refused when asked to support a bill to be put before parliament. The grounds for his refusal were that an act of parliament would infringe the rights and authority of the Admiralty. He agreed, however, that if Dublin was prepared to make a proper application 'to him and to him only', he would not 'refuse the granting of a lease of a Ballast office to the city . . . for a term of years'.

This attitude appears to have been seen in Britain as constitutionally unsound. Nevertheless, the matter was at length resolved by the Corporation's offer to give all profits of an office established by act of parliament to the boys in 'Blew Coate Hospitall . . . whereby they are instructed in navigation to qualify them for her majesties sea service', and by the city's acknowledgment that the disposal of the ballast office was indeed in the hands of the lord high admiral. As an earnest, it offered to the lord high admiral annually for ever 'a hundred yards of the best Hollands duck sayle cloath as shall be manufactured within the realm of Ireland which will be a lasting evidence of our holding the office under the admiralties tytle'. The status of the Admiralty was established in the act by a statement in the preamble that, as a result of a humble petition made by Dublin to the lord high admiral, 'his Highness would interceed with Your Majesty for your Gracious Approbation of a Bill for Erecting a Ballast Office'.

The Ballast Office Act was passed in 1707 and was entitled 'An Act for cleansing the port, harbour and rivers, of Dublin, and for erecting a Ballast Office in the said city'. It was to come into effect on 1 May 1709. The city then moved quickly. It is recorded that on 20 January following, some members of the Corporation met at the coffee-house in the Custom House to discuss a location for the Ballast Office in the city as there was none to be found at 'Cock leake' or at Ringsend. They asked first for permission to use a coach-house and stable behind the Custom House, but this was refused. They then agreed with Mathew Hacken, who later and until 1718 was to be a supervisor of the Office, to lease part of his house and a slip at Essex Street and forthwith ordered that 'the city arms with the words "Ballast Office" should be painted on a board and set over the Door'.

During the following months a committee of directors of the Ballast Office was elected from the City Assembly, and arrangements were made to establish charges for ballast and to license and to identify with numbers all privately owned gabbards, lighters and wherries. The function of cleansing began to expand. Not only was the Ballast Office to keep the shipping channel free, but it was to repair the banks and to take steps to improve the port and harbour generally. This extended role would lead it to two of its outstanding historic achievements: the embankment of the north shore of the Liffey along the North and East Walls, and the construction of the Great South Wall from Ringsend to a new lighthouse at Poolbeg.

The directors of the Ballast Office, who in 1781 comprised 10 aldermen and 20 common Assembly members, continued their work as a committee for 79 years. Throughout most of its time of office, the committee had to contend with much of the high cost of making the Great South Wall and with the overall running of the port, a large commercial undertaking, acting at all times as a body not in control of its own finances.

In 1786, mainly through recognition of this difficulty, a bill was brought before the Irish parliament to replace the Office with an independent port administration. The bill, which became law in May of that year, established the Corporation for Preserving and Improving the Port of Dublin and gave to it the functions of the Ballast Office, which then became defunct. The new corporation adopted the name of the Ballast Board as a short title, not to be confused with the earlier Ballast Office.

The port authorities that succeeded the committee appointed under the act of 1707 went on using the term 'ballast office' both for that purpose and as a title for their headquarters. The Ballast Board took premises at 6 Lower Sackville Street (now O'Connell Street) in 1793 and established a Ballast Office there. In 1801 it moved to a new site on the corner of Westmoreland Street and Aston Quay and built there the third Ballast Office, which continued in its function until 1976. Shortly afterwards, in 1981, the Dublin Port and Docks Board – which had replaced the Ballast Board in 1867 – moved its headquarters to new premises at Alexandra Road. At this time, the old title of Ballast Office was discontinued and the new offices were given the name of Port Centre.

[129, *CARD*, V–VII, XIII, private communication to Alderman T.C. Harrington, lord mayor 1903]

BALLAST OFFICE WALL, THE

The part of the South Wall lying between the Pigeonhouse precinct and Ringsend. See THE SOUTH WALL.

BALLIBOGHT

See BALLYBOUGH.

BALLYBOUGH

It is likely that there was a fishing hamlet of Ballybough or Balliboght around the mouth of the Tolka from the earliest times, and that much of the fighting in the battle of Clontarf in 1014 took place nearby. It lay on the boundary of the city liberty in 1324 when the riding of the franchises passed 'by the middle way of the town of Ballyboght'. Eleven years earlier, in 1313, John Decer had built Ballybough Bridge (now Luke Kelly Bridge) as close as was convenient to the mouth of the Tolka as it was then, and by 1488 a gate had been built to command the bridge and the road through the village from Clontarf and Howth. How long it lasted is not clear. Following the Malahide Road Act (26 Geo. III, c. 30), turnpike toll-gates were erected at the bridge and at the east end of the village at the junction of modern Fairview Strand and Annesley Bridge Road. These remained until 1855.

The village was not shown by Petty, Phillips or Collins in the 17th century, but is shown densely built by Rocque in 1760. In the 18th century the main road through Ballybough ran on from the bridge towards Fairview Strand. It was at that time built up on one side only. The other formed the high-water shoreline with, at low water, a strand, and the Tolka flowing by. This part of the road would be known in the 19th century as Phillipsburg Strand, although by then the former strand, still a waste space, had been cut off from the tide by the building of Annesley Bridge Road. At the beginning of the 20th century this area had been fully built up and was served by two new streets, Addison Road and Cadogan Road.

The Ballybough district contained in 1787 a mill for making iron implements, and from early in the 18th century a thriving flint-glass factory. These were replaced by vitriol works, which were in production during the 19th century. These factories were on the city side of the Tolka in Poplar Row, rather than in Ballybough proper.

Kingston records that there was an unconsecrated burial plot 'beside the bridge' but does not offer dates.

[4, 9, *CARD*, I, maps (Petty 1654, Phillips 1685, Greenvile Collins 1686, Rocque 1760, OS 1838, 1912)]

BALLYBOUGH, JEWISH CEMETERY AT

See JEWISH CEMETERY AT BALLYBOUGH.

BALLYBOUGH BRIDGE

See LUKE KELLY BRIDGE.

BALLYBOUGH ROAD

This street that runs north today from Summerhill to Luke Kelly (formerly Ballybough) Bridge is part of one of the ancient thoroughfares of Dublin. It was mentioned in 1488 as the 'hye wey that goeth to Balliboght'. It is named by de Gomme in 1673 and shown by him as falling from 'the top of the hills' down towards Ballybough Bridge. The quite steep gradient from the ridge of the watershed between the Liffey and the Tolka down to the shoreline can still be appreciated, if one ignores the man-made slopes introduced in the 18th century to carry Clarke's Bridge over the Royal Canal.

Ballybough Road, or Lane, was the principal highway to the Howth–Malahide coast until Annesley Bridge was built in 1797. It is shown, for instance, as 'the road to Baldoile' by Greenvile Collins in 1686.

[*CARD*, I, maps (de Gomme 1673, Greenvile Collins 1686)]

BALLYBOUGH WEIR

See TOLKA RIVER.

BANK OF IRELAND

In 1602 Sir George Carey (Carye, Carie, Cary) was given a lease for land in Hoggen Green 'to build a hospital for the relief of poor, sick, and maimed soldiers'. The site had a frontage of 85 yards (76.5 m) along the river but Carey 'was not to engage in river merchandizing and was not to build a watergate or slip or other place for landing of goods'. The south shore of the Liffey lay at that time near modern Fleet Street.

The hospital was built and appears on Speed's map of 1610 as 'Hospitall'. It was known also as Carye's or Carew's Hospital. Its use as a home for soldiers was short-lived. Carey served as lord deputy of Ireland from 1603 to 1604, and the house was being used for lawcourts in 1605. In the following seven years it was occupied by Sir

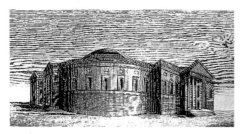

The Bank of Ireland in 1790, showing the east portico on its podium (Myers)

Thomas Ridgeway and later by Sir Arthur Bassett 'as a large mansion'; and in 1612 Sir Arthur Chichester (1563–1625), baron of Belfast and lord deputy from 1604 to 1615, acquired it as a 'capitall messuadge or house neere the cittie called the Hospitall, together with the gatehouse, court, and wall about the same', paying the city a yearly rent of four pence, Irish. Following the death of Chichester, the house, already known as Chichester House in 1613, passed first to Sir Samuel Smith and later to Sir John Borlase, lord justice, who received it in a 'much decayed and ruinous' condition.

The first parliament held in Ireland after the restoration of Charles II opened in Chichester House in May 1661. In 1673 the Crown took a lease of the property for use as a parliament house (a title acknowledged in de Gomme's map) and William Robinson was appointed as its keeper in 1677. The main house, a building 33 m square in plan, still known as Chichester House, continued to deteriorate, reaching a state of gross decay in 1728.

In that year the Commons agreed that a new parliament house should be built, and appointed as designer Edward Lovett Pearce, architect, army captain and member of parliament for Ratoath, County Meath. The foundation-stone was laid in 1729, and the work proceeded sufficiently rapidly under Pearce's direction to permit the parliament to assemble there in 1731. Pearce had been appointed director-general and overseer of fortifications in Ireland in 1730–31, but died in 1733 at the early age of 34. The work then continued under the superintendence of Arthur Dobbs (later to be governor of North Carolina) and was finally completed in 1739.

In 1778 the Irish peers decided to build additional accommodation for the House of Lords, and in 1785 work began on this extension at the east of the existing building, to the design of James Gandon. The project included the east portico facing Westmoreland Street, which in its original form rose from a podium approached by four steps. With the raising of the street level, however, this podium has been buried. It is shown, as built, in a print of March 1790 by Myers (NLI, 598 TA), and with the podium buried, by Petrie in 1821 (NLI, 722 TA). In 1792 a fire gutted the House of Commons, collapsing its dome, and leaving it, as Craig observes, to be 'meanly rebuilt'. At about this time also, the buildings were extended to the west, using a design prepared by Robert Parke.

In January 1799 a proposal for legislative union between Ireland and Great Britain was introduced in the parliament. In June 1800 Castlereagh, at his second attempt, carried a bill implementing the union through the House of Commons. On 1 August that year the royal assent was given and the Parliament House ceased to exist as such.

In 1802 the Bank of Ireland, which had been established in St Mary's Abbey in 1782 or 1783 and had occupied four houses there on the corner of Boot Lane in 1786, purchased the parliament buildings. Fourteen years earlier it had tried unsuccessfully to acquire the Old Custom House site for a new headquarters, and in 1799 it had negotiated to buy a large site in the triangle formed by Westmoreland Street, D'Olier Street and College Street. This deal, however, fell through when the parliament buildings became available. Following an architectural competition for the adaptation of the buildings for use in banking, in which the first premium was awarded to Henry Aaron Baker, an associate of Gandon, the work of adaptation was started in 1804 under the superintendence of Francis Johnston, and the bank opened for business in 1808.

Until 1663, when William Hawkins completed his river wall, the high tide reached Chichester House. Thus in 1657 several houses and gardens belonging to Arthur Annesley were described as 'scituatt on the Colledge Greene, adjoyneinge to the seaside there'. The association of this area with the river would continue for many years. In 1734 the surveyors Cave and Stokes made a map naming the east boundary of the Chichester House lands as 'the old shore', in a position corresponding to the east portico of the bank as it stands today. In 1800 Sherrard made a map for the Wide Streets Commissioners (no. 384) showing a plot including Westmoreland Street and Hawkins Street and naming its south-west corner as 'the corner of Chichester Garden now the Parliament House'. The title of this map was 'Map of a piece of ground formerly called the South Strand'.

[3, 6, 55, 77, 192, 208 (vol. 15), 279, CARD, II–IV, Dublin Corporation Archives (WSC maps), maps (Speed 1610, de Gomme 1673)]

BANQUETING HOUSE IN BARRACK STREET

This banqueting house is referred to in 1724. It is not named on any map, although it was sufficiently prominent to be used as a lease landmark. Francis Place, in 'Dublin from the Wooden Bridge' (1698/9), shows a substantial well-designed building in the left foreground, but does not identify it. Rocque (1756) shows a large structure built into the corner of the city pipe yard in Barrack Street, and this appears again in slightly different form on the Pool and Cash map of 1780. The three locations described are all roughly on the line of Ellis Street, and they may be showing what was the Banqueting House.

[206, CARD, VII, maps (Rocque 1756, Pool and Cash 1780)]

BAR, CLONTARF

See CLONTARF BAR.

BAR, DODDER

See RINGSEND.

BAR, RINGSEND

See RINGSEND.

BAR OF DUBLIN, THE

The Bar of Dublin is a submerged sandbank, connecting the South Bull sands, now known as Sandymount Strand, and the North Bull sands, particularly that part known today as Bull Island. Its position has changed slightly from time to time over the centuries, but in broad terms it lies north-east to south-west across the mouth of the Liffey and is about 1 to 1.5 km east of the Poolbeg lighthouse. It appears that at no period in the time-span of this book has there been less than a nominal depth of 1.5 to 2 m of water over the highest point of the Bar. In moderately rough seas the depth in the trough of a wave could have been considerably smaller, perhaps 0.5 m.

It is probable that the Bar first became a problem for mariners when the Norse knarr or merchant ship began to use the new harbour at Wood Quay during the tenth century. These vessels and their successors for many centuries faced three serious problems. Two of these were the Bar at low tide and the exposure of shipping to onshore and offshore gales as far up as Ringsend.

It should be realised that at high tide at that time, and for some 700 years to come, there would have been an unbroken expanse of water in Dublin Bay extending from Blackrock to Clontarf, with the river entrance to the port of Dublin somewhere on its western side. There may not have been any marker indicating the Bar for the first 500 years. Even when the vessels reached the river-mouth safely, the third problem arose, this being to find secure anchorages in the labyrinthine estuary in which to ride out storms. It would not be until the 18th century, 700 years after the beginning of significant maritime trade in Dublin, that this third problem would begin to be alleviated by the construction of the South Wall.

The Bar, then, can never be seen as the sole obstacle to the development of the port of Dublin; and in fact Bligh in 1801 would say that it was not the Bar but the estuary and harbour generally that damaged Dublin's maritime trade.

The three problems led in 1358 to an appeal by the 'merchants and others of the commonalty of Dublin' to Edward III, in which they sought exemption from parts of statutes that had recently been promulgated to regulate trade (the Ordinance of the Staple, 1353). They pleaded

> that owing to the dangers of the harbour of the city of Dublin, no large ships laden with cargo will venture thither and that consequently merchants have usually sold their goods on shipboard within a distance of six leagues [about 29 km] from the city; but that this course being prohibited under the recent ordinances of the Staple, traders have ceased to come to Dublin and now bring their goods for sale to safe ports, thus causing loss to His Majesty and injury to the city.

The cargoes were generally wines, iron, salt and other merchandise. The king granted the exemption.

The Bar was to be blamed many times for the loss of shipping attempting to enter or leave Dublin. In 1562 Fytzwylliams, vice-treasurer of Ireland, advised William Cecil, secretary of state for Queen Elizabeth I, that 'the ship with the artillery and munition was wrecked on the bar in Dublin Bay on 10 September. All drowned but two'; and a few years later, in 1574, a Captain Piers reported 'all his plate and household staff [stuff?] cast away on Dublin bar'. In 1580 it was complained that 'the "Handmaid" cannot pass the bar in Dublin Bay'. These are random examples, and one is probably thinking of some thousands of such incidents from the 10th to the 19th century.

The city took what steps it could. In 1582 it was agreed

> that Richard Condren, waterbalyve shall have a lese of three score and one yeres uppon the proffytes formerlie appoynted and layde downe by assemblie uppon all shipps, barques and botes that shall com into the porte or haven of this cittie, in consyderacion wherof he shall presentlie set upp, uppon his proper costes and chardges, a strong and sufficient beoie or perche uppon the barr, and shall sufficientlie repayr and mantayne the same during his lese.

The practice of marking the Bar with floating buoys continues to the present time.

Gerard Boate, writing in *c.* 1641, classified Dublin as one of the 'lesser havens and the barred havens of Ireland', saying that 'Dublin haven hath a bar in the mouth upon which at high flood and spring tide there is fifteen and eighteen feet of water, but at the ebbe and nep tide but six'. Greenvile Collins showed the Bar very simply but graphically in his map of 1693.

The establishment of the Ballast Office in 1707 led to the start of a programme for the improvement of the harbour; and this initiative by the city and later by the government, which is still ongoing, would have as one of its successes the mastery of the problem of the Bar about 120 years later. There were two schools of thought about the Bar. One was that the problem was, by its nature, insuperable in practical terms. This group, which would come to include many eminent engineers, held that the Bar should be left in position, and the problem circumvented by forming a new channel from the bay to the river near Ringsend. The other group, which in the end prevailed, believed that an adequate channel could be made across or through the Bar.

Much depended upon understanding the nature of the Bar, and the reasons for its formation. One opinion offered, for instance, by Thomas Burgh in 1707 was that the Bar consisted of sand brought down by the Liffey in times of flood and deposited where the current in the river met the tidal current. It is now generally accepted that this theory was wrong, and that, whatever the origin of the sand, the formation of the Bar had been predominantly influenced by the currents induced in the bay by the rise and fall of the tide, with the flow in the river through the city an insignificant secondary factor.

Various proposals made for circumventing the Bar are mentioned in the text. They commenced in 1725 with Captain John Perry and include subsequently the opinions of William Cubitt, Joseph Huddart, William Jessop, John Killaly, Alexander Nimmo, Thomas Hyde Page, John Rennie, Thomas Rogers and George Semple. Other complementary entries discuss ship canals proposed for the same purpose at Dunleary and Sandycove, along the shore of Clontarf (see Perry's Canal and his Other Harbour Proposals) and through the Sutton isthmus.

During the 18th century the Great South Wall was built from Ringsend to the Poolbeg lighthouse. While the main function of this wall was to provide safety from storm for vessels lying in the estuarine pools, it was hoped that one of the incidental effects of this work would be to reduce the Bar. This hope was not realised. Some slight increase in the depth of water did occur on the main shipping route, in what has been called the North or East Channel over the Bar, but Bligh was still recording depths as low as 1.5 m at low-water spring tides in that channel in 1800.

An unexpected improvement did, however, occur as a result of the building of the South Wall, through the formation of a 'gut' caused by enhanced tidal flow around the end of 'The Piles' and later around the Poolbeg lighthouse platform. This gut developed into a South Channel between the Bar and the South Bull sands. It is shown formally by Rocque (1760) and by Scalé and Richards (1765). In 1801 Bligh stated that the depth of water in the South Channel of the Bar was greater than in almost any other part of the harbour; and as late as 1832 it was mentioned by Nimmo in his instructions for entering the port 'to sail in by the South Channel, bring Irishtown Church to the right of Saint Patrick's steeple . . . and round the lighthouse at a cable's length'. One cable is approximately equivalent to 180 m.

In 1804 the Directors General of Inland Navigation in Ireland submitted a report to the lord lieutenant, Hardwicke, dealing with the improvement of Dublin Harbour. They were seeking a long-term solution, saying, 'we must not limit our views to alterations of the Harbour calculated for ships of particular build or burthen, for particular times of tide or for particular winds'. They would have found difficulty with the proposal of Sir Thomas Hyde Page, who suggested in 1801 that

a portion of the bar in the bay might be raised above high water by means of fascines and stones with some small old vessels filled with the same kind of materials and sunk into the body of the work to form an island, which would be attended with great advantage, confining the current to certain lines of direction, and causing deeper water.

The Directors General had invited John Rennie to advise them. He had already told them in 1802

that 'The improvement of Dublin Harbour is perhaps one of the most difficult subjects which has ever come under the consideration of the civil engineer.' He reviewed the works and proposals of the 18th century. He endorsed the provision of a sea wall extending from the Clontarf shore to the Spit Buoy about 300 m north of the Poolbeg lighthouse. This proposal had first been made by William Chapman in 1786 and had been advanced again by Messrs Maquay and Crosthwaite, members of the Ballast Board, in 1801, receiving at that time the support of Captain Daniel Corneille, the engineer for the Directors General.

It had become recognised that if the Bar were to be removed by artificial scour, that is to say by the action of flowing water deliberately channelled by man for that purpose, then this action should occur on the ebbing tide, and the quantity of water bearing on the Bar at that time should be as great as possible. For this reason Rennie proposed that, in addition to the wall from Clontarf, an embankment should be built across the South Bull from the Half Moon battery on the South Wall to a point near Blackrock. This would create a huge reservoir that would fill during rising tides through arches in the South Wall near the Pigeonhouse precinct and discharge in the same manner during the ebb. The volume of water represented by this reservoir, in addition to the tidal water impounded on the North Bull by the Bull Wall and contained in the river in the city, would maximise the volume of water that could be directed against the Bar.

An alternative proposal had been offered by Bligh in 1801. He, the naval officer, tended to dismiss the Bar as the major disadvantage of the port, and was in favour of improving the channel of the Liffey westward from the Poolbeg lighthouse as the most significant need of the harbour. Accordingly he recommended building a wall roughly parallel to the South Wall to form a north wall to the river channel from opposite Ringsend to the Spit Buoy, and then concentrating on the improvement of the channel. As matters developed, neither Bligh's proposal, which would have reduced the volume of water available for scour at the ebb and which it was thought might on occasions lead to dangerous bore conditions reaching up into the city, nor Rennie's reservoir, would be built.

One may say that the decision to build the wall from Clontarf to the Spit Buoy, a wall which would become known later as the Great North Wall or the Bull Wall, had been taken in principle by 1804. The finance for its construction did not, however, become available until 1814 when the government purchased from the Ballast Board buildings and land at the Pigeonhouse precinct for approximately £100,000. With this money in hand the Board, in 1818, invited the engineer Francis Giles to work with its own inspector, George Halpin, senior, to advise on the construction of the Great North Wall.

During these years the Bar had remained stubborn. Some slight amelioration did follow the completion of the South Wall, but in 1819 the depth of water at low spring tide over the highest point of the Bar on the main shipping route was still the same 1.8 m, more or less as it had been for the preceding 800 years.

In 1819 the building of the Great North Wall, or Bull Wall, was commenced. One of the purposes of the wall was declared to be 'to admit as great a body of tide water as possible into the harbour and to return the same past the lighthouse within such limits and in such direction as will produce the best scouring power to deepen the bar with the least obstruction to the navigation'. The intention seems to have been to build the wall throughout to a height of 1.8 m above high water. However, in 1822, following consultation with Thomas Telford and possibly as a result of his influence, it was decided to build only the northern section, 1,700 m long from the Clontarf shore, to the full height, and to form the remainder as what Mann has described as a 'submerged mound, the height varying from high water level to about 0.3 metres above low water, from which at its extreme end it slopes down to a sandy bottom 7.5 metres below low water'. This important decision was not based on shortage of money. It recognised the relationship between tide levels and the direction of currents in the bay, and it dictated the length of the period before low tide during which the full force of the ebb flow would be directed against the

Bar through the constricted river-mouth between the Spit Buoy, now the North Bull light, and the Poolbeg lighthouse.

The effect of this work was considerable. During the 19th century the minimum depth of water over the Bar at low water of spring tides increased without dredging from 1.8 m in 1819 to 4.8 m in 1873; and during the period from 1820 to 1880 the registered tonnage of shipping that entered the port of Dublin annually increased from 350,000 tons to 2,000,000 tons, this increase being due in large measure to the reduction of the Bar. Mann illustrates the progressive increase in depth in bib. ref. 118.

Since then the greater draught of the ships using the port has made it necessary to deepen the channel through the Bar and to maintain it at the increased depth by dredging. Thus a channel 150 m wide and 7.8 m deep below low water now exists through the Bar, approximately following what was in former centuries the north or east passage. The south passage formed by the building of the South Wall still offers a depth of about 2.2 m below low water, but it is not now described as a formal channel.

[15, 17, 70, 75, 118, 157, 158, 160, *CARD*, I, II, VI, maps (Greenvile Collins 1693, Rocque 1760, Scalé and Richards 1765, RN Hydrographic Chart, no. 1415 of 1977)]

BARR-FOOT
See REINELAN.

BARRACK BRIDGE
See RORY O'MORE BRIDGE.

BARRACK STREET
See BENBURB STREET.

BARRAGES ON THE LIFFEY
The concept of forming barrages or weirs on the tidal Liffey is of long standing. Shortly before 1220 the monks of the hospital of Kilmainham built a weir at Islandbridge near the furthest point to which the tide flowed in the river. The obvious purpose of this weir was to provide water to turn a mill-wheel. It may be suggested, however, that the monks also recognised that a weir at that place

would substantially separate the fresh water in the Liffey above the weir from the brackish water of the estuary, thus ensuring a permanent source of fresh water for the hospital and its community. This is the only barrage that was ever built. It is still in existence and indeed in the 18th and 19th centuries was used by the city in works augmenting the Dublin water supply. This weir is mentioned in a separate entry.

In the early 18th century Thomas Burgh and John Perry, working in the same years and sometimes in collaboration, proposed a barrage on the Liffey near Ringsend. Burgh's main intention was to impound a large volume of water in the Liffey behind the barrage and to release it through sluice-gates at low tide to scour out the Bar at the mouth of the river. Perry's main intention was to transform the river into a linear deep harbour, using lock-gates to release vessels at high tide to the estuary or, possibly, to his canal. These matters are mentioned in more detail in entries on Burgh and Perry; and Perry's proposal would be brought forward again by a Mr R. Richards in 1837.

During the 19th century, the navigation problem at the Bar being largely overcome, the stench in the river at low tide became the new reason for proposed barrages. In 1853 the viceroy approached the Ballast Board through the Commissioners of Public Works to have something done to maintain a sheet of water between the quay walls at all states of the tide. George Halpin, in his reply to the Board, dismissed damming as unsuitable. He pointed out that 'the Liffey is still the great main drain into which the sewerage of Dublin opens'; and he commented that, since 1830, nine schemes incorporating either damming or interceptor sewers had been proposed. He accepted the finding of the 'King's and Queen's college of Physicians' which said that 'the deposits left when the tide ebbs taint the atmosphere to a great extent with the most offensive effluvia', but he observed that the river-bed itself was clean and that the smells were coming from the discharge of sewers into the river; and he added that the Ballast Board removed hundreds of tons of deposits each year in an attempt to control the problem.

The discharge of domestic sewage directly into the Liffey in Dublin, so serious in the late 19th century, ceased at the turn of the century. For many years in the 20th century, however, industrial effluents reaching the river through its tributaries, particularly the Camac, continued to produce unpleasant conditions at low tide.

The most recent proposal for a Liffey barrage in the city was made during the 1970s when the Talbot Memorial Bridge was being planned. It was urged then that the river crossing required should incorporate a dam which would maintain a constant minimum depth of water in the river upstream at low tide. The primary purpose of this latest proposal was the provision at low cost of a public amenity in the city, a waterway pleasant to view and available for water traffic at all tides.

The construction of any barrage in the Liffey in Dublin will always present problems for the city, due perhaps to the substitution thereby of a constant minimum water-table level along its course for that now existing in conditions of tidal fluctuations, and perhaps to some difficulty in keeping the bed of the river clean upstream of the barrage. New proposals for barrages will undoubtedly be made from time to time. The last one was built nearly 800 years ago.
[87 (vols. 16, 21)]

Barrington's Bridge (Proposed)

In 1823 William Barrington sought permission to build a cast-iron bridge in front of his premises on Essex Quay to connect the quay to Upper Ormonde Quay at Arran Street. Permission was granted subject to the agreement of the ferry leaseholders, but the project was abandoned.

In 1822 Barrington had taken over the long-established leasehold of Cooke's holding on Blind Quay.
[CARD, XVII, XVIII]

Bartlett, John, and his House

Before Hawkins built his wall occasional inundations flooded the area at the Long Stone. The only main route from the city to Lazars Hill

to pay rents due for properties leased to him near Temple Bar; and he remained a member of the Ballast Board until 1843. He died later that year at the age of 77.

[50, 87, 117, 145, 185, 208, 246; BL, Add. MS 35673 (Hardwicke Papers), vol. 325, ff. 185–7]

BERESFORD PLACE

Beresford Place, 1846

The Custom House was built to the design of James Gandon, in the period from 1781 to 1791. In 1790 the Wide Streets Commissioners accepted Gandon's design for an imposing residential crescent, built close to the 17th-century shoreline, to define an elegant space to the north of the Custom House. In 1797 the crescent, given the name of Beresford Place, had been built. The title must be associated with the Honourable John Beresford, the principal promoter of the Custom House and a strong supporter of Gandon.

The crescent extended at first from Lower Abbey Street to the waterside at the Old Dock, but in 1838 the curve at the west end had been extended to the river at Eden Quay. Early in the 20th century the Old Dock was filled in, but it was not until 1952–3 that the encirclement of the Custom House was completed by the construction of Memorial Road as an extension of Beresford Place to join the quays at the site of the future Talbot Memorial Bridge. The practical purpose of the extension was to improve the road connection between Amiens Street and the north quays, and generally to meet the increasing traffic demands of the port.

[209, maps (Rocque 1756, Faden 1797, OS 1838, Dublin Port 1987)]

BERESFORD SWING BRIDGE

See BUTT BRIDGE.

BETAGH, DR THOMAS

Dr Thomas Betagh (W. Brocas)

Dr Thomas Betagh, a Jesuit priest who became vicar-general of the diocese of Dublin, was appointed parish priest of St Michael's and St John's parish in *c*. 1790. He worked there from the parish church in Rosemary Lane until his death in 1811 at the age of 73. Gilbert records his 'indefatigable zeal in the promotion of religion and education among the lower orders of his parish, many of whom he gratuitously educated and clothed out of his private resources'.

His death was greatly mourned and he was given a public funeral. Maxwell relates that 'his fellow citizens gave expression to their feelings by shutting up their shops'.

[18, 30]

BIG WIND, NIGHT OF THE

The night of the big wind, known throughout Ireland as a marker in its social history, occurred on Sunday, 6 January 1839. It led to one of the major inundations of Dublin by the River Liffey, with the flood waters overflowing the quays at several places.

[173, *DHR* (Dixon)]

BIRD SANCTUARIES

The two bird sanctuaries on the estuary and bay came about through man's modification of the shoreline, the North Bull Island by the building of the Bull Wall (1819–24), and Booterstown Marsh by the formation of the causeway for the Dublin and Kingstown railway (1834).

Booterstown Marsh, 4 ha in area, contains both freshwater and salt-water habitats. During the winter months, waders including snipe, curlew and lapwing, oyster-catcher and dunlin can be seen on the marsh. Small wildfowl such as the teal and widgeon may also be found feeding. The curlew and snipe are occasional visitors. Birds to be seen throughout the year include also the heron and moorhen and land-based songbirds. A feature of Booterstown Marsh is the use that was made of part of it for cultivation during the Second World War. The ridges formed at that time may still be identified.

The very much larger North Bull Island sanctuary extends for 5 km from Bull Bridge to the north-east point of the island near Sutton, and, for various species as appropriate, from the shore road across the island to the low-tide shoreline. It is a known resting-place for wintering and migrating wildfowl and waders. Notable among the several variations of wildfowl are the brent-geese; they congregate to feed, mainly at the north-east point of the island. Other species tend to gather to the north of the causeway constructed in 1964. Large flocks of waders of different species will be found in winter feeding in the sanctuary or elsewhere on the shoreline of the estuary and bay, and commonly roosting between the causeway and the Bull Bridge. Seabirds including shags, cormorants, gulls of many varieties and, occasionally, gannets are found along and off the seaward side of the island. Land-based songbirds and some hunting birds may be seen in the dunes and the golf-links that form the island proper.

[38, *Booterstown Marsh* (Dublin, An Taisce, n.d.)]

BISE'S TOWER

A three-storeyed tower in the city wall between Buttevant Tower and Dames Gate. Perrot's survey recorded in 1585 that the walls of Bise's Tower were 4 feet thick and 26 feet high and that it was 16 feet square within the walls. It was not shown by Speed in 1610, but according to his representation of the walls, it would have risen straight out of the western channel of the Poddle/Liffey confluence.

The tower was owned by Robert Bise in 1585 and continued in the possession of the Bise (also Byse or Bysse) family during the 17th century, the owner in 1662 being John Bysse, lord chief baron of His Majesty's Court of Exchequer.

The tower, also known as Bysse's Tower, was located in the centre of modern Parliament Street and was demolished when that street was being laid out in 1762.

[97, *CARD*, II, IV, map (Speed 1610)]

BLACK DANES BRIDGE
See Fr Mathew Bridge.

BLACK DEATH, THE
See The Plague.

BLACKHALL PLACE
See Ellis Quay.

BLACKROCK

The district of Blackrock is of significance in the development of the coastline of Dublin Bay and the Liffey estuary. While the vast sands of the South Bull would at very low tides have been uncovered as far as Sandycove, early maps, e.g. Rocque (1760), show the south-eastern limit of the South Bull at Blackrock. There also begin the rock outcrops that continue intermittently as a feature of the coastline as far south as Greystones, County Wicklow. Westwards towards Dublin the high-water mark was a shingle or sand bank, along which the road ran through Booterstown, and which then continued without a road towards Irishtown and Ringsend. The present bird sanctuary in the slob at Booterstown and Blackrock Park indicates clearly the extent of the tidal area as it existed prior to the building of the Dublin–Kingstown railway in 1834. The position of the high-water coastline in this vicinity made only

The shore at Blackrock, 1744 (W. Jones)

too appropriate the use of the 'burying place' shown by Rocque at the roadside in Booterstown for the interment of a number of those drowned in the wrecking of the *Prince of Wales* in 1807.

A painting by Will Jones, 'A View of the Black Rocks' (1744), shows a small horseshoe strand with bathing-places framed with low rock cliffs above which the houses of Blackrock stand. In the centre of the strand, rising out of the sand, there is a massive outcrop of rock, some 6 m high. This is named as 'The Black Rocks'. Some 20 years later Rocque on his map would describe presumably the same outcrop as 'the Black Rock from whence the town takes its name'. Today this outcrop appears to lie in the vicinity of the Blackrock Baths. Early records suggest this outcrop as the south-eastern limit of the city of Dublin, and its visibility and dominance as a landmark, seen across the expanse of the South Bull, are plain. In 1603 the cavalcade riding the franchises of the city, leaving Reinelan at the north-east tip of the South Bull, 'beat their course southward as directly as they could to the Black-stone, now called the Black-rock, opposite against the place, where the sheriffs of Dublin did keep court, upon the land on the west side of the new stone of the Strone'. A century earlier, in 1488, this part of the route had been described as being from a point near Reinelan to 'the blak stone be Este Myrrionge'.

Ball, in 1902, recorded the stone cross that now stands in the centre of Blackrock as the termination of the ancient jurisdiction of Dublin Corporation. Was this perhaps the 'new stone of the Strone' in 1603?

During the 18th century, while the Ballast Office committee was building the South Wall, enormous quantities of stone were needed for masonry work and – in the form of very large shingle, cobbles and small boulders – for filling. The shores at Clontarf and Blackrock were seen as main sources, with Blackrock being preferred because the material was cheaper. In 1726 the Ballast Office was given permission by the city to use Blackrock. However, the weather, which could be 'excessive bad' even in October, made loading and transport dangerous in the sudden storms that could sweep the bay. Permission was given to make first a form of timber jetty and then in 1730 a stone pier. There seems to be no record of the actual construction of either, but stone was still being taken from the Blackrock shore in 1731 and probably continued to be used until the South Wall was finished.

When the Dublin and Kingstown railway was opened, Blackrock was the principal town between the termini. Blacker has recorded, from a survey prepared by the promoters of the railway, the 'numbers of cars, carriages, etc. passing to and from the Rock [Blackrock] from the 12th February 1831 to the 13th February 1832 between six o'clock in the morning and nine at night':

	Total	Daily average
Private carriages	36,287	99
Hackney coaches	7,272	20
Private cars	133,537	365
Public cars	186,108	508
Gigs	24,175	66
Saddle-horses	46,164	126
Carts	69,133	189

(The daily averages are not given by Blacker.)

This traffic would have travelled the Booterstown road, now Rock Road, along the high-tide waterline at that time, and would undoubtedly have been interrupted on occasions by storm-driven water from the bay in the stretch between Booterstown Avenue and Merrion Gates.
[56, 57, *CARD*, I, VII, map (Rocque 1760)]

BLAK STONE, THE
See BLACKROCK.

BLESSED VIRGIN MARY DEL HOGGES, CONVENT OF
See ST MARY DE HOGGES, CONVENT OF.

BLIGH, CAPTAIN WILLIAM

Admiral William Bligh, c. 1803 (J. Smart)

Born in England in 1754. In 1772 he sailed with Captain James Cook on his second voyage of exploration to the South Seas, and he later commanded two expeditions, on the *Bounty* in

1787 and the *Providence* in 1791. He commanded the *Glatton* in Nelson's attack on Copenhagen in 1801. He was reprimanded for tyranny in 1805 when captain of the *Warrior*. Later that year he was appointed as governor of New South Wales. He was gazetted as vice-admiral in 1814 and he died in 1817. His tomb may be seen in London, in the churchyard of St-Mary-at-Lambeth.

Bligh had great skill as a marine surveyor and hydrographer, and on the direction of the Admiralty he visited Dublin in 1800, as a captain in the Royal Navy, to survey and sound the bay and the river estuary. His report was made on 12 January 1801 and was accompanied by a map (see separate entry).

It was Bligh's opinion that many ships were wrecked in Dublin Bay because they carried too little cable and inadequate ground tackling and could not therefore safely anchor in the bay to ride out storm conditions. In his report he drew attention to the need to strengthen the South Wall 'from the Lighthouse to the Battery' (presumably to the Half Moon battery) and he proposed a north wall for the Liffey channel from Ringsend to the Spit Buoy. His report did not propose a wall from Clontarf shore to the Spit Buoy: that is to say, it did not propose the Bull Wall.
[44, map (Bligh 1800/3)]

BLIGH'S MAP OF DUBLIN BAY
Bligh's map of Dublin Bay, a work of extremely high quality, was prepared to accompany his report of January 1801 and was published commercially by him in London in 1803. It shows in fine detail the coastline from Baldoyle to Dalkey Sound, reaching up the Liffey to Ringsend and sketching the channel up to the New Custom House. Three improvements proposed by Bligh are shown. They are (i) the construction of a north wall to the river channel from the North Wall House opposite Ringsend to a point near the Spit Buoy (roughly the present North Bull lighthouse), (ii) a short length of new wall extending the Pigeonhouse harbour wall upstream to merge smoothly with the South Wall, and (iii) walls for a refuge harbour at Dunleary.

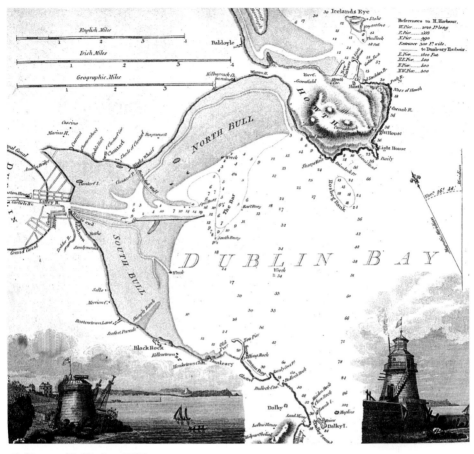

Bligh's map of Dublin Bay, 1800/3

It seems in the literature that Bligh's map has been developed by others, for example in Warburton, Whitelaw and Walsh (p. 436), where it illustrates a proposal for what was substantially to become the Bull Wall. This was not a proposal shown by Bligh.

Among the significant details on Bligh's map are the Grand Canal Docks, the Pigeonhouse precinct, the White Bank, the Battery (later to be the Half Moon), Ballybough Bridge, Clontarf Island, the East Wall development, the Furlong of Clontarf, Weekes's Wharf, the Rossbeg Bank and the Bar.

It should be noted that the grid on Bligh's map is based on magnetic north, which at the time of making was 26° 48' west of true north.

Bligh's map, or chart, drawn to a scale of approximately 1:19,900, was made at the desire of the viceroy, Marquis Cornwallis, and by the direction of the lords commissioners of the Admiralty of Great Britain. After commercial publication, it was sold by W. Faden, who had in 1797 published a general map of Dublin.
[29, map (Bligh 1800/3)]

BLIND GATE
See DAME STREET.

BLIND QUAY
Speed (1610) shows a wide strip of open ground inside the city wall running east from modern Wood Quay to Isolde's (Newman's) Tower and then south to the gate of Dublin Castle. The development of this strip in the ensuing 300 years is complex.

In 1577 Stanihurst located a lane named Scarlet Lane or Isolde's Lane in this strip and called the Wood Quay end of it Tullock's Lane. Clarke (1978) identified this lane as the whole of modern Exchange Street, Lower and Upper, from Fyan's Castle to Cork Hill (or Lorimers Street). By 1639 Scarlet Lane had become known as the Blind Quay and this name was shown by de Gomme in 1673. This route was the direct thoroughfare from the quays to Dublin Castle, and through Dames Gate to the eastern suburbs and the sea coast.

Only the northern part of Blind Quay, later to be called Blind Quay Lower, from Wood Quay to Smock Alley had any pretensions to being a quay. The part later to be called Blind Quay Upper, from Smock Alley to Cork Hill, had little right to be described as a quay. It is clear from contemporary records that, at the start of the 17th century, the northern side of Blind Quay Lower was built up with houses and plots generally about 41 feet deep, backing on to the Liffey in a haphazard pattern, although Speed in 1610 does not suggest this to be so. Fyan's Castle and the Buttevant Tower lay at the ends of this series of houses and Case's Tower and Newman's Tower punctuated it. It appears that in 1605 there was pedestrian access along the bank of the Liffey behind the Blind Quay plots as far as the Poddle estuary, because in that year a lease granted to Jacob Newman for ground near Isolde's Tower referred to the property being 'scituate on the Wood Key'. There was, however, no quay proper north of Blind Quay at that time, and it may be that Blind Quay was so called because the houses on it had their backs turned to the river and had no direct public access to it by way of slips. Nearly a century later the construction of Essex Quay would begin.

During the period 1606–20 Newman reclaimed the land in the Poddle estuary, and in 1674 Essex Street and Essex Gate were constructed, taking advantage of the new intake to improve the access from Custom House Quay to the centre of the city. In 1684 a petition was addressed to the Assembly 'that the street leading from Essex Gate to the Wood Key, commonly called Blind key, was very narrow and inconvenient for the great number of coaches and carrs that pass that way dayly, it being a very great thoroughfare and the way soe narrow that two coaches can hardly passe by each other'; and it was suggested that a new route be made, part of which would become Essex Quay.

This was done, but Blind Quay Lower remained, as indeed it does to the present day, a very narrow and awkward street. Constantly during the 18th century efforts were made to control building along the Blind Quay, to remove old encroachments by householders and to keep existing houses from falling down. The gradually disintegrating structure of Newman's Tower at the corner of Kennedy's Lane was a case in point.

During the 17th and 18th centuries Blind Quay Lower was ceasing to be a quay in any sense, becoming instead a busy commercial and residential street. Immediately after the restoration of the monarchy, there were four titled noblemen living on the quay, and during the ensuing century eight taverns and half a dozen printers and publishers could be found there. In 1767 a master of the Merchants' or Holy Trinity Guild and the masters of the Barber Surgeons' Guild (St Mary Magdalen's) and of the Glovers' and Skinners' Guild (St Mary's) all resided on the quay. In 1776 the inhabitants of Upper Blind Quay, disturbed by the gradually worsening reputation of the name of the Blind Quay, had their street name changed to Exchange Street. It later became Upper Exchange Street, and by 1780 Blind Quay Lower had become Lower Exchange Street.

During the 19th century Exchange Street was curtailed at its southern end by the opening of Lord Edward Street in 1886, while at the Wood Quay end the building of the new parish church of Sts Michael and John began in 1810. In the middle of the century the street had become one of small industries and was showing signs of decay. Of the 54 houses listed in Upper and Lower Exchange Street, there was only one private residence. Thirteen houses were vacant, two had fallen down, nine were tenements and two were stables. Two industries predominated, with four cork manufacturers and five jewellers and watchmakers recorded.

It is arguable that of all the streets today in the vicinity of the Liffey in Dublin, Lower Exchange Street most closely reflects the layout and appearance of its 16th-century counterpart.

[3, 18, 29, 39, 146, CARD, II, V, VII, IX, maps (Speed 1610, de Gomme 1673, Pool and Cash 1780, Clarke 1978)]

BLOCKHOUSE

See PIGEONHOUSE: A PRECINCT.

BLOODY BRIDGE

See RORY O'MORE BRIDGE.

BLUE-COAT SCHOOL

See ELLIS QUAY.

BOATS ON THE LIFFEY

See SHIPS AND BOATS ON THE LIFFEY.

BOLTON'S MAP

See NORTH LOTTS.

BOMBING ATTACK ON NORTH STRAND

See NORTH STRAND.

BOND, OLIVER

Born in Ulster in 1760, Bond began trading as a woollen merchant in Pill Lane near the north bank of the Liffey in 1782, and from 1786 lived at 13 (later renumbered as 9) Bridge Street, near the south bank.

He became a member of the Society of United Irishmen on its foundation in 1791, and rose to be one of its leading members in Dublin. In 1793 he was imprisoned for five months in Newgate, with the Honourable Simon Butler, for attacking the 'inquisitorial proceedings of Parliament'.

In 1797, with Lord Edward Fitzgerald, he accepted Thomas Reynolds into the Society. In March 1798 Reynolds, who had risen in the Society to the rank of colonel and delegate for the province of Leinster, gave information to Dublin Castle about the imminence of rebellion and Bond's involvement in it, and this led to the arrest of Bond and 14 others for high treason. In July 1798, the rebellion then being at its height, Bond was tried and after a jury deliberation lasting seven minutes was found guilty and condemned to death. He was subsequently given 'a conditional pardon' but died in the Newgate prison. The cause of death was given as apoplexy, and John Beresford in a letter of 6 September 1798 to Lord Auckland wrote, 'We got rid of one enemy last night. Oliver Bond after playing ball all the evening died suddenly of apoplexy.' In more sinister vein Mitchel has recorded that 'friends of this gentleman believe that he was murdered at night by one of the jailers or turnkeys – for what cause or at whose instigation was never known'.

He is now remembered in Dublin by the name Oliver Bond House, given to one of the largest residential complexes in the inner city, situated in the angle of Bridgefoot Street and Usher Street.

[18, 54, 185, 246]

BOND ROAD

See CLONTARF ISLAND.

BOOT LANE

See ST MARY'S ABBEY.

BÓRUMA, BRIAN, HIGH KING OF IRELAND

See BATTLE OF CLONTARF and CHRONOLOGY OF RULERS IN DUBLIN.

BORUMBORAD, ACHMET

Sir Jonah Barrington (1760–1834) records that late in the 18th century Dr Achmet Borumborad, coming to Ireland as a Turkish exile, established hot and cold sea-water baths in Dublin. The bathhouse included an immense cold pool that communicated with the Liffey and was renewed at every tide. The establishment prospered for several years, being greatly favoured by, among others, many members of parliament. It went into decline, it is said, only when Dr Borumborad shaved off his beard to win his wife, and declared himself no Turk but rather Patrick Joyce from Kilkenny.

[278]

BOTHE STREET

See FISHAMBLE STREET.

BOW BRIDGE

Bow Bridge crosses the River Camac at Bow Lane. It is a very early bridge site, and was a key landmark in the riding of the city franchises. The record of this event in 1488 mentions the bridge, and in 1603 the account states that the mayoral party came 'down the Murdring Lane' from Mount Brown to Bow Lane 'to the water of Camacke and under the west arch of the bridge called Bowe Bridge and tornid uppon the left hand under the high grownd of Kilmainehame to a deep ford thre wher it was said the Annlyffe came of ould tyme'.

Bow Bridge appears also under the names Bowe Bridge and Bowbridge.

[CARD, I]

BOW STREET

See LOUGH BUOY.

BOWBRIDGE (BOWBRIGE)

See BOW BRIDGE.

BOWEN, E.: MAP OF HARBOUR AND BAY

Bowen's map is an edited version of Stokes's map of 1725. It is dated 1728 and is entitled 'A New and Correct Map of the Bay and Harbour of Dublin: with a Small Plan of the City Curiously Engraved'. It carries an advertisement for Charles Brooking's map of 1728, and it appears that Bowen's 'Small Plan of the City' is taken from Brooking. It may be that Bowen was published to complement Brooking, by extending his city map out into the bay as far as Dalkey Island and the head of 'Hoath'. Interesting features on Bowen include (i) a textual description of the harbour, the bay and the Bar, (ii) Perry's canal and the entrance to it at Sutton, (iii) a proposed breakwater across the North Bull, to protect the canal, (iv) early details of Clontarf, which is called Clondaf, (v) Clontarf Island in a different location to that shown on Stokes, who

places it along the high-water shoreline, (vi) Cock Lake, which Stokes calls Cork Lake, and (vii) the extent of the South Wall piling as of 1728.

See also Gabriel Stokes: Map of Dublin Harbour and Bay.

[Maps (Stokes 1725, Bowen 1728)]

BOWLING ALLEY

See HOGGEN GREEN.

BOWLING GREEN

See OXMANTOWN.

BRADOGUE BRIDGE

See ANKISTERS PARKE.

BRADOGUE LANE

The continuation southward of Halston Street to Mary's Lane was known in 1756 as Bradogue Lane. The name Littlegreen Street has also been used.

[39, map (Rocque 1756)]

BRADOGUE RIVER

The River Bradogue has a short course and is today largely underground. It rises near the angle of Faussagh Road and Quarry Road in Cabra and passes under the North Circular Road near the top of Grangegorman. It then flows past St Loman's Hospital and bears eastward to pass under Constitution Hill near the former Royal Canal basin at Broadstone. From there it flows under Halston Street and Arran Street East to join the Liffey at Upper Ormonde Quay.

While now controlled and of little significance overground, this river played its own important part in the early development of the north bank of the Liffey. Speed shows that in 1610 the mouth of the Bradogue, a name that was known at the time, was a confusion of creeks and inlets which together with the stream proper formed a 'pill' or pool, probably overflowed at high tide and marshy at low tide. Tradition has held that the Bradogue was navigable, but the Speed configuration suggests that it may be that the channels provided

Green Island. In 1914 the island was closed to the public for some time and used as a rifle-range.

In 1964–5 a causeway was built to the island at Watermill Road and the tidal channel from Sutton Creek to Crablake Water was blocked.

A very full description of Bull Island is given in the 18 chapters of *North Bull Island Dublin Bay: A Modern Coastal Natural History*, published by the Royal Dublin Society in 1977.

In 1981 the island was designated as a Biosphere Reserve by UNESCO, and in 1988 it was designated as a National Nature Reserve.

[38, 87 (vols. 10, 11), *DHR* (Corry, Hammond), Dublin Corporation Information Sheets, maps (Cowan 1800, Bligh 1800/3, Giles 1819, OS 1838, 1869)]

BULL LIGHT

See NORTH BULL LIGHTHOUSE.

BULL WALL, THE

The Bull Wall, or, as it was officially known, the Great North Wall, extends about 2.7 km from the Clontarf shore near Seafield Road to the North Bull lighthouse, which is built near the site of the earlier Spit Buoy. It is a stone structure some 25 m wide at the base. It is 7 m high for 1.7 km of its length, in this portion standing about 3 m over normal high water. For the remainder of its length, it is overtopped at about half tide, and is narrower at the base.

Flood records that the idea of building this wall originated with William Chapman in 1786, but his name was not subsequently associated with the work. Early in 1801 Bligh proposed making a wall along the north edge of the Liffey channel from the North Wall opposite Ringsend out to the Spit Buoy, which lay across the channel from the Poolbeg lighthouse. Later in that year the Ballast Board proposed to the Directors General of Inland Navigation in Ireland the building of a pier 'on the west of the North Bull from the Point of the Sheds of Clontarf to the Point of the Spit'. The Directors General asked Captain Daniel Corneille, who was or would become their engineer, to report on this proposal, and in September 1801 he replied, supporting the concept, although he expressed

anxiety that the construction of such a wall might lead to enlargement of the Rossbeg Bank. He recommended that the wall start from Crablake House, rather than from the Point of the Sheds, and run in a straight line to the Spit Buoy. During the next two years the matter was clearly being discussed, as one may judge from correspondence. The rival merits of a curved and a straight wall were considered, another attempt was made to have a wall built 'from the eastwardmost point of the present North Wall' (opposite Ringsend), and controversy arose over the closing off or retaining of the Sutton Creek gut at the north end of any proposed wall. By 1804 the Directors General were in favour of the building of the wall, attributing the proposal to Corneille and to Rennie, who, with his friend Huddart, had endorsed the idea in 1802.

Although one can say the decision to make the Bull Wall had been taken in 1804, it was not until 1814, when the Ballast Board sold its site at the Pigeonhouse precinct, that funds became available to build it. In 1818 the Board engaged Francis Giles, an English engineer, to prepare a scheme. He appears to have collaborated with George Halpin, senior, who has been variously described as inspector of works for the Ballast Board and engineer for the port of Dublin; and in 1819 Giles produced his map of the North Bull showing the proposed wall.

In 1819 the controversy about the north shore gut was terminated by the erection of Bull Bridge (although it would flare up again in 1964 when the causeway was built to the east). The Bull Wall was started in 1819 and completed in *c.* 1824.

A major purpose of the wall was to eradicate the Bar by concentrating the power of the ebbing tide through the narrowed gap of the river-mouth. The entry on the Bar of Dublin deals further with this matter.

[38, 70, 75, *DHR* (Flood)]

BULLOCK AND ITS HARBOUR

There is a narrow sea creek opening to the north-west in the granite coast at Bullock. In 1307 Sir Thomas Asyk is recorded as being lord of 'Boulek' but before then the monks of St Mary's Abbey

Bullock Harbour and Castle, c. *1699* (F. Place)

owned the fishing rights there and had built Bullock Castle to defend their property. Despite its exposure, the creek was a valuable landing-place for cross-channel vessels and a local fishing fleet. It is recorded that the young lord lieutenant Thomas of Lancaster landed there in 1402, as also did the earl of Sussex, returning as lord deputy in 1559.

On the dissolution of the monasteries, the castle, village and creek at Bullock were seized from St Mary's Abbey, and passed through the Talbot and Fagan families to be acquired by the Allens, later earls of Carysfort, in 1703.

In 1660 Bullock, with about 100 adults, was the largest centre of population along the south shore of Dublin Bay, and exhibited what Cooper would describe 100 years later as a 'complete walled town in miniature'. It had a certain reputation for smuggling, and a revenue officer was stationed there early in the 17th century.

With the upsurge of marine works at the port of Dublin in the 18th century, Bullock with its own granite sources and those close by at Dalkey Common (or Dalkey Quarry) became the principal south shore loading-place for stones and slabs to be used in the South Wall and Poolbeg lighthouse. Later this trade would be extended to the supply of paving-stones for the city.

The exposure of the creek to open bay conditions continued, however, to hamper its use, and this defect was not reduced until in 1819 the Ballast Board appointed George Smith as the contractor to build a quay across much of its mouth, thus converting the creek into a narrow triangular harbour. The maps of Taylor (1816) and Kerr (1875) illustrate the conversion.

The importance of Bullock to the early authorities at Dublin Port may be gauged from a plea made by Revd Samuel Grier to the Ballast Board that it contribute to the building of a school there, particularly for the children of pilots and other employees of the Board. 'Convinced', he wrote, 'of the gross ignorance of that part of [Monkstown] parish including Bullock, Dalkey, and the adjoining vicinity and as a necessary consequence the deplorable moral degradation of the inhabitants thereof in the lower walks of life,' he felt it his duty 'to endeavour the removal of this spiritual darkness and to advance their moral, social and religious improvement'.

Bullock in the early 19th century is illustrated by G. Holmes, 1799 (NLI, 791 TA), and G. Petrie, 1820 (NLI, 792 TA).

[4, 56, 77, 87 (vols. 7, 10, 13), 195 (Smyth), 221, *CARD*, XI, maps (Taylor 1816, Kerr 1875)]

BULL'S HEAD TAVERN

See FISHAMBLE STREET.

BURFORD BANK

Nimmo, in 1832, locates this bank roughly south of the Baily, and extending from north to south across the mouth of the bay for about 1.6 km. It was then 2½ fathoms below low-water level. He records that it was named after the man-of-war *Burford*, which was wrecked there in 1770. The name appears as Burfort on Cowan's chart of 1800. He shows it in the same general position as does Nimmo, but suggests it is about 500 m long from north to south and 200 m from east to west.

[17, map (Cowan 1800)]

BURGH, LIEUTENANT-COLONEL THOMAS

Born of Irish parentage in 1670 and died in 1730. He entered Trinity College at the age of 15, and then joined the English army, serving in Ireland during the Williamite campaign and later in the Low Countries. During his service he was trained as an engineer, and in 1699 he joined William Robinson's staff in Ireland. In 1700 he was appointed surveyor-general in succession to Robinson and subsequently he also became lieutenant of the ordnance of Ireland and barracks overseer for Ireland, a post he held until 1721.

While he was primarily a military engineer and held rank as the chief engineer of Ireland, his posts led him also into the practice of architecture. In this sphere his works along the Liffey included the Royal Barracks (now Collins), begun in 1701, the Old Custom House at Essex Bridge, begun in 1707, and in 1721 the pedestal structure in the river for the equestrian statue of George I at Essex Bridge. As an engineer of note working in Dublin, he was inevitably drawn into the baffling civic debate, then already 400 years old, about the making of a safe harbour for the city. In 1707 he presented a paper to the Dublin Philosophical Society entitled 'Some Thoughts for Improveing the Harbour of Dublin'. He saw, as Rennie would 100 years later, the difficulty of the problem. 'This place', he wrote, 'has none of the natural advantages that might be improved to make it a convenient harbour.' He

subscribed to the incorrect belief, as several would later, that the Bar was formed substantially by sands and silt carried down by the river, and he was the first to recommend that the channel of the Liffey be dammed to 'keep up the river at high water till it be dead low water below the [dam] and then by opening flood-gates made in the said work to let down the upper waters which by the violence of the stream must necessarily cleanse all before them', especially, he added, if the bottom were loosened by harrowing. He believed also that the silt and sand deposited upstream of the dam could be removed and that the old Custom House Quay would continue to be readily accessible.

In addition to the dam, he proposed the building of a large basin, although he did not say where,

> sufficient to hold such a number of shipping as the trade of this town may seem to require, the tops of which bason rise about twenty feet above high water mark which will sufficiently secure ships from any danger of weather, and that it should be well fortified to defend against any enemy, and have a high house at each end of it in a direct line with the channel that ships might with safety go in the said bason in the night if it should be found necessary.

Burgh's proposals were received with interest, but little more. Within a few years the city would start building the South Wall; and it would be that wall and the 19th-century Bull Wall which would at last show the way to a solution of the ancient problem. In 1711 he gave advice on the embankment of the river at the North Wall.

In 1721 John Perry made proposals to the Ballast Office that mirrored aspects of Burgh's 1707 paper. They were welcomed but not pursued. In 1725 he made a new proposal, his scheme for a ship canal from Sutton along the Clontarf shore. He enlisted Burgh's help in taking soundings in the bay and estuary of the Liffey, and these were recorded on a map prepared by Gabriel Stokes in 1725. Perry submitted a report on this matter to the Ballast Office, only to have it rejected again, this time with some asperity. Burgh's interest appears not to have gone beyond the soundings.

It is clear that Burgh was much admired by his building teams and by the communities in which he worked. His relations with the craftsmen who worked with him were mutually respectful. The city made him a freeman and, in 1723, presented him with a gift of plate to acknowledge his 'services for public works'. He represented Naas, where he lived, as its member of parliament for the final 17 years of his life.

[3, 66, 285, *CARD*, VI, VII; BL, Add. MS 35931 (Hardwicke Papers), Sloane MSS (vol. 90H: 3329, vol. 4)]

BURGH, THOMAS

See BURGH QUAY; see also the entry on LIEUTENANT-COLONEL THOMAS BURGH, who lived 100 years earlier.

BURGH QUAY

Throughout the 18th century the eastern end of Aston Quay lay just east of Hawkins Street, where there was a ferry connecting it to the east end of Bachelors Walk at Union Lane.

In 1795 Carlisle Bridge (now O'Connell) was opened for traffic and by 1797, according to Faden's map, the two new south bank arteries, Westmoreland Street and the future D'Olier Street,

had been opened in some rudimentary form from the quay to College Green and to Townsend Street. These works effectively broke the continuity of Aston Quay, and led to the idea of a separate quay with its own name, east of Carlisle Bridge.

Already in 1802 the Wide Streets Commissioners were planning for the extension eastwards of this separate quay to connect it to George's Quay; and they were proposing to purchase from its owner, William Sweetman, a brewery that stood on the river-bank between modern Corn Exchange Place and Tara Street and blocked the route for the connection.

In April 1805 Thomas Sherrard, surveyor and clerk to the Commissioners, laid before them 'the map of the ground and quay from Westmorland Street and D'Olier Street to Hawkins Street laid out in plots for building'. At their meeting on 17 May 1805 the Commissioners resolved formally that the buildings and quay were to be called Burgh Buildings and Burgh Quay. No reason was given for the choice of name. Thomas Burgh, an active member of the body, did not attend this meeting, but he acted as chairman at their meetings of 5 April and 31 May in that year.

Burgh Quay, 1820, showing also the Corn Exchange (S.F. Brocas)

The whole of Burgh Quay was under reconstruction at this time. The earlier buildings shown by Rocque in 1756 were to be replaced, and new levels were to be determined for the quay to suit the new Carlisle Bridge. It was proposed that a two-level quay be built, comprising an upper main thoroughfare connected to the bridge, and a lower waterside strip 3 m wide to be established close to high-tide level for loading and unloading vessels. This concept was not pursued.

The process of reconstruction of the quay was slow and was complicated by the need to build a new quay wall, a work to be done by the Ballast Board. Complaints were made that, because of the building works generally, the quay was impassable, and it appears that the works were not finally completed until 1808–9.

Sweetman's Brewery still stood as an obstacle to the extension of the quay eastward. In 1810 William Sweetman offered the Commissioners '236 feet of my ground fronting the river Liffey and 75 feet in depth in order that they have it in their power to open a passage from Burgh Quay to George Quay'. His financial demands were, however, considered unacceptable, and it was not until 1816 that the Ballast Board could report that the junction between the new wall at Burgh Quay and George's Quay had been completed.

The construction and profile of Burgh Quay continued to give trouble. In 1845 the Ballast Board raised the height of the river wall by up to 600 mm to enable parts of the quay surface to be raised; and in 1865 a length of 118 m of the wall, founded 1.2 m below low tide and 3.3 m thick at the bottom, had to be strengthened to avoid collapse.

Notable buildings on Burgh Quay have included Conciliation Hall and the Corn Exchange. A fine impression of the bustling activity on the quay in 1820 is given by S.F. Brocas in his drawing 'View of the Corn Exchange, Burgh Quay and Custom House', published in that year.

[87 (vols. 6, 9, 18), 90 (vol. 9: Mann), 208 (vols. 18–20, 22), *CARD*, XVI, map (Faden 1797)]

BURKE, EDMUND

Orator, statesman, political philosopher. He was born in January 1729 at 12 Arran Quay, and died in

Edmund Burke, on right, in conversation with Charles James Fox (T. Hickey)

1797. Maxwell records that in January 1746 Burke described in a letter one of the more serious floods to inundate the city:

No one perhaps has seen such a flood here as we have now, the quay wall which before our door is I believe about [?] feet high is scarce discernible serving only as a mark to show us where the bank once bounded the Liffey. Our cellars are drowned ... the water comes up to the first floor of the house threatening us every minute with rising a great deal higher, the consequence of which would infallibly be the fall of the house ... From our doors and windows we watch the rise and fall of the waters as carefully as the Egyptians do the Nile, but for different reasons.

Six days later Burke commented that the water in their house had soon abated but said that it was 'melancholy to see the poor people of the other parts of the town emptying their cellars ... for as fast as they turn out the water so fast does it, through some subterraneous channels, return again'.

It is probable that there was no parapet wall along Arran Quay at the time, so Burke's description would imply a water level perhaps 200–300 mm above the actual quay surface; and

his first floor would have been what today would be called the ground floor.
[30]

BURNELL'S LANE
See MERCHANTS QUAY.

BUTLER, JAMES, FIRST DUKE OF ORMONDE

James Butler, first earl of Ormonde (P. Lely)

Born in 1610. He entered the Irish parliament in 1633 as earl of Ormonde, and from 1641 to 1644 led the army of Charles I against the rebels in the Ulster rising. He was appointed lord lieutenant of Ireland in 1644 and in the following five years was involved in complex negotiations with the Ulster rebels, the Kilkenny Confederates, the Royalists and the Parliamentarians. In 1649, after the beheading of Charles I, Butler, now marquis of Ormonde,

proclaimed Charles II as king in Ireland. Later that year he was defeated by Colonel Michael Jones in the battle of Rathmines and retired to France, where he lived in exile during Cromwellian rule.

In 1662 he returned to Ireland as duke of Ormonde and again as lord lieutenant. He would retain this office until 1685, except for the years from 1669 to 1677, when he was in royal disfavour and was replaced by Lord Robartes (1669–70), Lord Berkeley (1670–72) and then Arthur Capel, earl of Essex. Butler retired from public life in 1685, on the accession of James II, and died in 1688.
[50, 54, 190]

BUTLER, RICHARD, FIRST EARL OF ARRAN
See ARRAN QUAY.

BUTT BRIDGE

Butt Bridge (Swivel Bridge)

In 1837 a committee of Dublin merchants, who were already dissatisfied with the effectiveness of Carlisle Bridge, advised the Ballast Board that a new bridge to the east was imperative. By 1852 the pressure had increased, and a New Bridge Committee, with the earl of Charlemont as chairman, again approached the Board. Its request was turned down in favour of widening Carlisle Bridge. The Board had decided to 'abandon the idea of erecting a bridge to the eastward [since the difficulties were] almost insurmountable'. Lord Charlemont begged to disagree.

The present Butt Bridge

While, then, the Board continued to plan for the improvement of Carlisle Bridge, the agitation for a new bridge to the east persisted. Hindsight shows clearly that the remedies were complementary and that both were necessary. Not surprisingly, then, the two projects came to maturity together.

In 1876 a parliamentary act provided for the altering, widening and improvement of Carlisle Bridge, and for the construction and maintenance of an opening bridge. The opening span of the new bridge was to allow ships to lie at Burgh Quay and Eden Quay. A design was prepared by Bindon Stoney for a four-span bridge consisting of a fixed masonry arch approach span of 11.1 m at each end and a central span consisting of a double-cantilever plate-girder iron bridge structure. This metal structure, 38 m long, could rotate horizontally on a central pier, thus opening simultaneously two navigation spans, each 12 m wide. The bridge, for which William Doherty was the main contractor, with Skerne Ironworks of Darlington supplying the metalwork and machinery, was opened for traffic in 1879. It was named for Isaac Butt (1813–79), barrister and parliamentarian; and was popularly known as the Swivel Bridge, and, perhaps less popularly, as the Beresford Swing Bridge.

The building of the Loopline railway bridge downstream of Butt Bridge in 1888–90 meant that access for shipping to Butt Bridge was stopped, and the swivelling structure became in effect two stationary spans.

Butt Bridge had quite steep approach gradients and its carriageway was only 5.6 m wide. As early as 1912 there was agitation for its alteration, but negotiations and general debate dragged out, and it was not until 1925 that the Dublin Port and

Docks Board lodged a bill for the reconstruction of the bridge. A parliamentary committee was later established to decide 'whether the erection of a new bridge in the place of the present Butt Bridge would in any way prejudice the proposals which are or may be made for the solution of the traffic problem in the centre of the City'. The unanimous opinion of the committee was 'that if the proposals in the bill are combined with the proposal to erect a transporter bridge at Guild Street, other proposals for dealing with traffic problems in the City will not be prejudiced'. An act giving permission for the reconstruction of the bridge and embodying this proposal was passed in 1929. The transporter bridge has not been built.

The new Butt Bridge was designed by Joseph Mallagh, who consulted Pierce Purcell and, for visual aspects of the design, Messrs O'Callaghan and Giron. It was opened to traffic in 1932. The width of the river at the site is 65 m. The bridge, which was the first Liffey bridge in Dublin to be built with reinforced concrete, has three spans. The centre span, which is 33.6 m long, was constructed as two separate cantilevered half-spans of 16.8 m, with this arrangement enabling one-half of the river to be kept open for barge traffic at all times. Pedestrian traffic was accommodated throughout the construction period on a footbridge spanning the supports of the adjacent Loopline Bridge. The width of the new bridge between parapets is approximately 19 m and the maximum depth of water at HWOST under the bridge is about 7 m.

An inscription on the bridge in Irish and in English reads as follows:

Testing Butt Bridge, May 1932

BUTT BRIDGE
BUILT 1879
REBUILT 1932 BY
THE DUBLIN PORT AND DOCKS BOARD
THE YEAR OF THE 31ST INTERNATIONAL
EUCHARISTIC CONGRESS
CHARLES E. MC GLOUGHLIN P.C.
CHAIRMAN
THE RIGHT HON ALFRED BYRNE TD
LORD MAYOR
JOSEPH MALLAGH B.E., M.INST. C.E.I.
ENGINEER
GRAY'S FERRO-CONCRETE (IRELAND) LTD
CONTRACTORS

[87 (vols. 16, 20), 90 (vol. 59: Bond; vol. 65: Mallagh), 180]

BUTTER CRANE

A centre for the butter trade, presided over by a weighmaster or craner, existed on Usher's Quay in the mid-18th century, and possibly for 100 years before. It was the responsibility of the weighmaster to provide 'at his own expense a convenient weigh house and also beams, scales, weights, branding irons, and other necessaries'.

The centre continued in service in the 19th century with Robert Usher, a cooper, being appointed in 1812 as craner.

[*CARD*, XI, XII, XVI]

BUTTEVANT TOWER

'The tower called Le Botavant' was in the possession of Fromund le Brun in 1327. In 1585 Perrot's survey described 'Buttevantes tower' as an 'ould sqware ruenus towre with one vawt [vault] and the wall 4 foote thick, 30 foote hie from the chanell and 12 foote sqware within the walles and the grounde 8 foote hie within the said towre from the chanell'. At this time the tower, which lay in the line of the city wall and in the area of the modern street called Essex Gate, was owned by the Byse family.

In 1674 Buttevant Tower was demolished to make way for Essex Gate. The name, however, was still recorded in 1705 for 'a piece of ground' in the vicinity of the former tower.

[*CARD*, I, II, V, VII]

BYSSE'S TOWER

See BISE'S TOWER.

C

CADSLOUGH

A lane off Moore Street. The name suggests the existence at one time of a pond or lough (see also Lough Buoy). Cadslough is not shown by name on Rocque's map (1756) but may there be contained in what he calls the Old Brick Field. The name was still in use in 1850. Rocque does show ponds at the corner of Marlborough Street and Henry Street, now North Earl Street, and at Mabbot Street, now Corporation Street. The possibility of these ponds being connected to the Liffey by creeks in early times is strong. Compare, for instance, the pond or marsh in the 'moraghe' near Sandymount.

[31, 146, map (Rocque 1756)]

CALENDAR, OLD STYLE AND NEW STYLE

(i) The Gregorian calendar was adopted in England and Ireland by act of parliament in 1751. The change-over was made in 1752, when the day that in the earlier reckoning would have been 3 September was declared to be 14 September.

(ii) By the same act, the first day of the year was declared to be 1 January, commencing with 1 January 1752. Prior to this, the first day of the year, from early times, had been 25 March. Thus 1751, the final year in the old dating, lasted formally only from 25 March 1751 to 31 December 1751. This change accounts, for instance, for such works as Gilbert's *Calendar of the Ancient Records of Dublin* giving dates for events in January, February and early March in years before 1752 which appear to refer to the previous 'calendar year'.

All dates in this book from 1 January to 24 March, whatever year they refer to, should be read as New Style, unless otherwise stated.

CALENDAR OF THE ANCIENT RECORDS OF DUBLIN

The Calendar of the Ancient Records of Dublin in the possession of the Municipal Corporation of that City, to give the work its full title, consists of 19 volumes as follows. The date in parentheses is the year of publication.

Vol. I (1889)	Royal Charters and governmental grants to the City of Dublin
	Liber Albus: The White Book of the City of Dublin
	The Chain Book of the City of Dublin
	Rolls of the City of Dublin
	(i) Assembly Roll (AR) 1447–61
	(ii) AR 1461–85 and Franchise Roll 1468–85
	(iii) AR 1485–1504
	(iv) AR 1530–47
	(v) AR 1547–53
	(vi) AR 1553–8 plus Appendices (including Riding of the Franchises in 1488)
Vol. II (1891)	(vii) AR 1559–75
	(viii) AR 1575–9
	(ix) AR 1579–94
	(x) AR 1594–1607
	(xi) AR 1607–10 plus Appendices (including Description of Dublin, 1577, by Richard Stanihurst)
Vol. III (1892)	(xi) AR 1611–25
	(xii) AR 1625–49
	(xiii) AR 1649–51 plus Appendices
Vol. IV (1894)	(xiii) AR 1651–60
	(xiv) AR 1660–69
	(xv) AR 1669–71 plus Appendices
Vol. V (1895)	(xv) AR 1672–87
	(xvi) AR 1687–9
	(xvii) AR 1690–92 plus Appendices

Vol. VI (1896) (xvii) AR 1692–1706
(xviii) AR 1706–14
(xix) AR 1714–16 plus
Appendices (including
correspondence on the
establishment of the Ballast
Office)

Vol. VII (1898) (xix) AR 1716–26
(xx) AR 1726–30

Vol. VIII (1901) (xx) AR 1731–40 plus
Appendices (including Port and
Harbour of Dublin: 1721–31)

Vol. IX (1902) (xxi) AR 1740–51 plus
Appendices

Vol. X (1903) (xxi) AR 1752–6
(xxii) AR 1756–60 plus
Appendices (including Calendar:
New Style, 1752)

Vol. XI (1904) (xxii) AR 1761–9 plus
Appendices

Vol. XII (1905) (xxii) AR 1769–70
(xxiii) AR 1771–8 plus
Appendices

Vol. XIII (1907) (xxiii) AR 1778–9
(xxiii A) AR 1780–86 plus
Appendices (including Ballast
Office)

Vol. XIV (1909) (xxiii A) AR 1787
(xxiv) AR 1788–95
(xxv) AR 1796 plus Appendices

Vol. XV (1911) (xxv) AR 1797–1802
(xxvi) AR 1803–6 plus
Appendices (including Port of
Dublin; and On impressing men
for the Navy)

Vol. XVI (1913) (xxvi) AR 1806–7
(xxvii) AR 1808–14 plus

Appendices (including Port and
Harbour of Dublin)

Vol. XVII (1916) (xxvii) AR 1814
(xxviii) AR 1815–21
(xxix) AR 1822 plus Appendices
(including Port and Harbour of
Dublin)

Vol. XVIII (1922) (xxix) AR 1823–31 plus
Appendices (including Port and
Harbour of Dublin; and a note
on the Liber Albus)

Vol. XIX (xxix) AR 1832–41

Volumes I to VII were edited by Sir John Gilbert and volumes VIII to XVII by Lady Gilbert, with the assistance of John Francis Weldrick for volume XVII. Lady Gilbert died during the preparation of volume XVIII and it was edited by Weldrick. He and his daughter Mary Weldrick edited volume XIX. John Weldrick died during its preparation and Mary died when the book was at proof stage; and in that unfinished form it was printed by Dollard of Dublin and issued by Dublin Corporation. The other 18 volumes were published by Dollard.

The *Calendar of the Ancient Records of Dublin* (*CARD*) is probably the most extensively quoted of all sources for the history of the city of Dublin.

CALENDAR OF THE ANCIENT RECORDS OF DUBLIN: PERSONS NAMED BUT NOT INDEXED

The *Calendar* is a valuable source for the names of some 1,200 Dubliners and others who had some association with the Liffey and the harbour between the years 1200 and 1841, but who are not mentioned individually in the present book.

CAMAC RIVER

The River Camac rises on Knockannavea Mountain near Brittas and flows through Slade, by Saggart to Clondalkin. It then flows east past Fox and Geese and Bluebell towards Drimnagh. It passes under the Grand Canal and Davitt Road at Blackhorse

be of particular interest to the building profession today. Firstly, the last clause, which allows 'for day labourers and incident charges which cannot exactly be computed, aboute £5,000'; and, secondly, the use of the 'flower' as the unit of site levelling and filling, the flower being '18 foot square and one foot deep'.

In 1685, the year in which de Gomme died, Phillips was in Dublin again, and put forward his own proposal for a great citadel. He did not favour the Ringsend site but instead proposed a location that would have sprawled across the modern city from Merrion Row to Mount Street Bridge and from Sandwith Street to Mespil Road. Phillips's draft map of 1685 suggests that, from a citadel in this position, the whole of the city from Ringsend to Bloody Bridge, and including the Castle, was within the range of mortar fire, while cannon shot could reach Clontarf and the Phoenix Park.

Fortunately, perhaps, for the future of the city, neither scheme was realised and the provision of a fortress had to await the development of the Pigeonhouse precinct over 100 years later when Napoleon menaced. Then, it would be built on ground which in de Gomme's day did not exist.

[160; *CARD*, V; BL, Add. MS 16370; maps (de Gomme 1673, Phillips 1685, Rocque 1760)]

CITY ARCHITECT

There are early references in the Assembly records to a 'master of the city's works', and this title continues as 'master of the works' or 'of the city works' throughout the 17th century. The works appear to have included municipal and other public buildings and bridges, and some interest and skills in building must have been involved. In 1559 the Assembly appointed John Dympse and John Venables to this position for that year.

In 1666 Thomas Kirkham and William Brookes, described as 'late masters of the citty works', asked the Assembly for monies due to them in that they were 'imployed for the building of the pesthouses on Clontarf Island'. Their role may have been as overseers or, possibly, designers, as it was later recorded that Brookes was a brewer, and the actual builder may have been William Harvye.

In 1702 Richard Mills was appointed as assistant to the master of the city works (he has also been described as 'the first Master of the City Works in Dublin'). In 1719 he was succeeded in this post by James Nelson. Both of these men are included by Loeber in his dictionary of architects in Ireland. It is not known whether either designed any buildings.

In April 1842 the newly established Dublin City Council, in one of its earliest decisions, appointed a city architect. It appears that until that time, works for the Corporation requiring the services of an architect were executed by private practitioners on a fee basis. The post of city architect has continued to the present day, although between 1974 and 1988 the functions were shared between a chief civic and amenities architect and a chief housing architect; and in recent decades the duties of the post have been influenced by the evolving role of the City Planning Department.

The succession of city architects is generally as follows:

1842	Hugh Byrne
1866	John S. Butler
1880	Daniel Freeman
1893	Charles J. McCarthy
1922	Horace T. O'Rourke
1947	C. Mac Fhionnlaoich
1959	Daithí Hanly
1966	Thomas Randall (as deputy)
1974	Christopher Dardis (civic and amenities)
	J.F. Maguire (housing)
1985	Christopher Dardis (civic and amenities)
	John McDaid (housing)
1988	Christopher Dardis
1994	James Barrett

[66, 121 (*Minutes*, vol. 1), 224 (various), 275 (various), *CARD*, II, IV–VII]

CITY ASSEMBLY

See MUNICIPAL GOVERNMENT OF DUBLIN.

CITY COUNCIL

See MUNICIPAL GOVERNMENT OF DUBLIN.

CITY FRANCHISES

See FRANCHISES, CITY.

CITY GROUND

A small triangular area on the riverside at the west end of Dublin Key (North Wall Quay) shown on Bolton's map in 1717. The south-east corner of the Custom House is built on the City Ground.

[Map (as named)]

CITY OF DUBLIN STEAM PACKET COMPANY

See CROSS-CHANNEL PACKETS.

CITY QUAY

The Seamen's Memorial

In 1712 the city faced a problem regarding the embankment of the Liffey along part of the south side of its channel. The Croft lease taken over by John Mercer in that year required Mercer to complete a river wall from the Hawkins wall to a point eastward of modern Creighton Street. At the

same time Sir John Rogerson was negotiating the grant that he was to be given in 1713. One of the terms of this was that he would build a river wall from the east end of Mercer's wall to the mouth of the River Dodder at Ringsend. It appears that in 1712 the city realised that Mercer was not going to complete the wall in his lease. Not wishing to leave a gap in the wall system, it decided to take into its own hands the construction of the remainder. Precise dimensions are not available, but in 1715 the city began work along a length of river wall incorporating the part now known as City Quay, eastward from Moss Street.

In 1719 the actual quay wall and a parallel back wall were approaching completion, as was the filling in of the quay between the two walls 'built even with the first floor' of the Fountain Tavern on Sir John Rogerson's Quay. City Quay was substantially complete in 1720 and the ground was ready for what later became the South Lotts project.

City Quay developed in parallel with George's Quay as a busy shipping area during the 18th and 19th centuries, and it is recorded that in 1850 the harbour-master, Captain John Duniam, had his office near the east end of the quay at Creighton Street.

Earlier, in the unsettled period around 1800, an ordnance store and yard with a small artillery barracks had been established at the west side of Creighton Street, then called Ordnance Lane. This appears on the Faden and SDUK maps, but is not marked on the 1838 Ordnance Survey map, the thoroughfare there being called Creighton Street. In 1811 Campbell described this barracks as a 'recruiting depot'.

The parish church of the Immaculate Heart of Mary was built in 1861–3 near the west end of the quay, and the district has in the last 20 years been revitalised by extensive and imaginative housing development. In 1988 a memorial, sculptured by James Power, was erected on the quay for the Venerable Matt Talbot. It is inscribed: 'Matt Talbot 1856–1925. Presented to the citizens of Dublin by the Dublin Matt Talbot Committee for the Millennium year 1988.'

A memorial based on a large bronze sea anchor, unveiled by President Patrick Hillery on 6 May 1990, is 'in honour of the seamen lost while serving in Irish merchant ships, 1939–1945'. The men are named and the ships which were lost are also listed, as follows:

1940   *City of Limerick, Kerry Head, Ardmore, Innisfallen,* also the lighthouse tender *Isolda* and the trawler *Leukos*
1941   *Saint Fintan, Clonlara, City of Waterford*
1942   *Irish Pine*
1943   *Kyleclare*
1944   *Cymric*
1945   Fishery vessel *Naomh Garbhan*

The circumstances of the building of City Quay suggest that the city authorities were building the quay wall because its earlier sponsors withdrew. The name was of little significance, and it may be noted that both Harris in 1766 and Rocque in his map of 1756 ignored it and connected Sir John Rogerson's Quay directly with George's Quay.

[16, 146; *CARD*, VI, VII; maps (Rocque 1756, Faden 1797, Campbell 1811, SDUK 1833, OS 1838); PRO, MP HH682 WO 55/2306(8)]

CITY STABLES
See BENBURB STREET.

CITY SURVEYORS AND ENGINEERS
The formal office of city surveyor for Dublin dates back at least to the appointment of John Greene, junior, in 1679. It has continued to this day under various titles.

Until 1851 it is probable that the appointments were part-time or that emoluments consisted of fees paid for particular works. The Assembly records contain several requests from city surveyors for payment; and in 1842 an early decision of the Corporation, newly reconstituted in 1841, appointed Charles Tarrant, junior, as an engineer 'without salary but to be paid the usual professional fees for any work which he shall be called on by the Pipe Water Committee to perform'.

A letter written in 1851 by Parke Neville shows that he had been appointed as joint city surveyor

in 1845, probably with Arthur Neville, and possibly with Tarrant still sharing the position; and it is evident that he had been paid on the basis of fees for work done. In 1842 the Pipe Water Committee had, at the request of the Corporation, considered the office of an engineer for Dublin, and had reported that 'there is no necessity for a regular salaried Engineer to the Corporation; but that incidents may arise in which the services of such an officer may be required and that therefore it is expedient to appoint an Engineer to be paid for such occasional duty as he may be required to perform'. At that time both the Pipe Water Committee and the Paving Board did have their own skilled staffs, although not at professional engineering level.

In 1847 an 'Act for consolidating in one Act certain conditions usually contained in Acts for paving, draining, cleansing, lighting and improving Towns' became law, and, following that and the Dublin Improvement Act of 1849, the Corporation decided in 1851 that a borough engineer and local surveyor should be appointed to deal with all these topics, an officer who would be required to 'devote his entire time to the services of this Corporation'. Parke Neville was elected to this post. He had practised both as a civil engineer and as an architect, and would be elected president of the Institution of Civil Engineers of Ireland in 1881–2. In 1878 Neville, reporting on his work, included all the responsibilities of the 1847 act in his remit, as well as tramways and the treatment of dangerous buildings.

Between 1679 and 1851 those appointed were known generally as city surveyors. Until the 19th century their function was primarily as land surveyors for the Corporation, mapping the property of the city to protect its interests. Some of the early city surveyors worked also on maps of the river and its estuary, but it is not clear that any was ever consulted on, or supervised, specific engineering projects. The expanded function in 1851 brought with it the new title of borough engineer. This would change over the years to city engineer and borough surveyor, and then to chief engineer. From the time of Parke Neville there have generally been also one or more deputy city engineers, under various titles and dealing with particular topics, especially in recent times with roads.

The succession of officers from 1679 with the date of appointment of each is as follows:

1679	John Greene, junior, who may have served again later
1687	Barnaby Hackett
1698	Joseph Moland, possibly with others
1718	James Ramsey
1735	Roger Kendrick
1764	Thomas Mathews
1782	Samuel Byron
1795	David Worthington
1801	Arthur R. Neville
1828	Arthur Neville, possibly with others including John Semple
1842	Charles Tarrant, junior
1845	Parke Neville, Arthur Neville (and perhaps Tarrant)
1851	Parke Neville
1887	Spencer Harty
1910	John G. O'Sullivan
1913	Michael J. Buckley
1927	Michael A. Moynihan
1936	Norman A. Chance
1950	Edward J.F. Bourke
1973	Kevin C. O'Donnell
1991	James Fenwick

[121 (*Minutes*, vols. 1, 15; Gen. Purposes Com. 1878), 224 (various dates), 259, 275 (various dates)]

CLANCY BARRACKS

In 1757 an artillery corps was created in the Irish establishment of the British army. In *c.* 1760 it became the Royal Irish Artillery, and was housed in a barracks at Chapelizod. In 1797 the *Dublin Journal* reported that the arsenal yard in Dublin Castle had become too small to accommodate the Irish ordnance and that 'a piece of ground contiguous to the Royal Hospital at Kilmainham is preparing as a general park or repository of artillery'. This area was on the south bank of the Liffey downstream of Sarah Bridge. It would later be named the Ordnance Depot, which name still

appears on maps current today. In 1798, the barracks at Chapelizod having become too small, the Royal Artillery moved to the new site, manning it in 1799 with 6 officers, 87 non-commissioned officers and men and 8 additional gunners. In 1803 it was one of the targets selected for attack by Robert Emmet, but it is not clear that this attack was ever launched.

The OS map of 1838 shows that by that time the establishment at Islandbridge consisted of two elements, the Ordnance Depot near the river and the Royal Artillery Barracks beside it to the south. At that time neither group of buildings had a frontage to the Circular Road. In 1862 the establishment was considerably enlarged, bringing much of its western boundary on to the Circular Road. The whole area was now known as the Islandbridge Cavalry Barracks, and it included also extensive ordnance repair shops. At that time there was accommodation available for 18 officers, 589 men and 435 horses. There was also a horse hospital in the complex, located near the laneway now called Hospital Lane. In 1896 the cavalry moved to Marlborough (McKee) Barracks, and Islandbridge became a general support area.

In December 1922 the barracks was handed over to the Irish government; and in 1942 it was renamed Clancy Barracks in honour of Peadar Clancy, vice-commandant of the Dublin Brigade of the Republican Army, who had been shot dead in Dublin Castle in November 1920.

[134, 216, 217, *An Cosantóir* (O'Donnell), Irish Army Archives (Egerton), map (OS 1838)]

CLAR RADE
See CLARADE.

CLARADE

For several hundred years the Liffey from Ringsend upstream to the Long Stone had several channels meandering at low tide through sandbanks. Below Ringsend there appears to have been one principal channel at low tide that flowed through the Poolbeg pool to the sea. This was regarded as the 'clear road' for shipping and is mentioned as such in the riding of the franchises, as Clarade or Clar Rade.

[Maps (de Gomme 1673, Phillips 1685, Greenvile Collins 1686)]

CLARE ROCK

See LAMB ISLAND.

CLARKE'S MAP

In 1978 medieval historian Howard Clarke prepared a map of the city of Dublin for the Friends of Medieval Dublin. Using part of OS map 18, section 11 (scale 1:2,500) as a base, he shows, superimposed in colour, a view of 15th-century and earlier Dublin. The map illustrates the Liffey from Rory O'More Bridge to Butt Bridge, showing also the Stein, Poddle and Bradogue tributaries, and it suggests the location of the high-tide shoreline. Accompanied by an extensive index, the map, entitled 'Medieval Dublin', is printed by the Ordnance Survey.

CLENMTHORP

A name used for Clontarf in the 13th century, in the granting to the Brothers of the Temple (the Knights Templars) 'a vill near Dublin called Clenmthorp with its appeartenances'.

[181]

CLOCK ON BRIDGE GATE

See BRIDGE GATE.

CLONLIFFE

In 1838 the area known as Clonliffe consisted of two townlands, Clonliffe West to the west of Drumcondra Road, and Clonliffe East between that road and Ballybough Road and bounded on the north by the River Tolka. The combined area of the two townlands was 200 statute acres or 81 ha. The then new artery of Clonliffe Road, which had recently replaced the shorter Fortick's Lane (see Wilson's map of 1798), ran east–west through Clonliffe East, ending at Ballybough Road, where it was submerged in the flooding of the Tolka and the inundation of the East Wall district in December 1954.

In the 12th century Clonliffe (Clunlif, Clunlith, Cluenlyff, Clonclyffe) corresponded more closely with its name, pasture-lands or meadows of the Liffey. It may be proposed that Clonliffe then covered much of the north shore of the river, extending from the Bradogue in the west to the Tolka estuary 2.9 km to the east, and from the shore of the Liffey northward to modern Glasnevin.

In 1200 it is recorded that 'the king grants to the Cistercian monks of Saint Mary near Dublin the following lands etc.: Clunlith in which lies the site of the monastery with the adjoining plain near the sea'. While this implies that the abbey lands extended to the shore, the charter of John in 1192 speaks of an area known as Crinan and refers to a 'mear between Clunlith and Crinan so far as Tolekan'. This boundary may have lain along Ballybough Road, with the land between there and the shore being Crinan. But the actual extent of Crinan seems uncertain and it is possible that it was not distinct from but formed part of the greater area known as Clonliffe.

The statutory independence of the community of St Mary's Abbey from the city liberties, and the difficulties arising from this in identifying the city boundaries and describing the riding of the franchises in the centuries prior to the dissolution of the monasteries, make the precise location of early Clonliffe harder to determine. Further specific research, beyond the scope of the present work, would be required in the matter.

[29, 181, *CARD*, I, maps (Wilson 1798, OS 1838)]

CLONTARF, BATTLE OF

See BATTLE OF CLONTARF.

CLONTARF, BRICKMAKING AT

See BRICK AS A BUILDING MATERIAL.

CLONTARF, PROPOSED REPEAL MEETING AT

During 1843 Daniel O'Connell addressed many very large meetings throughout Ireland, on behalf of the Loyal National Repeal Association, and in furtherance of the campaign for the repeal of the

Act of Union of 1800. On 8 October he was to speak at a 'monster meeting' at Clontarf. The location for the speakers' platform was at Conquer Hill, a mound separated from the shore by the Back Strand road, which followed the shoreline between Vernon Avenue and Seafield Road.

The government, increasingly concerned by the growing momentum of the campaign, and possibly taking advantage of a spurious anonymous notice in the *Nation* newspaper on 30 September 1843 which called for the mustering of a corps of Mounted Repeal Volunteers to ride through the city to Clontarf, prohibited the meeting in a proclamation posted up in Dublin late on Saturday, 7 October. The proclamation, signed by the Irish secretary, the privy councillors and the commander of the forces, called on all magistrates and officers 'and others whom it might concern to be aiding and abetting in the execution of the Law in preventing that meeting'. In support of this proclamation a large contingent of troops was brought to the site. O'Connell recognised the physical dangers associated with holding a banned meeting and succeeded in cancelling it and turning back the tens of thousands who were already converging on Clontarf.

The *Nation*, in an editorial on 14 October, describes the army in position on the strand of Clontarf, probably along the high-tide shoreline, and 'the merriment of the infantry who smoked, drank, and probed for cockles'. More seriously, it noted 'the jaded listlessness of the 7th Hussars, the steady soldier-like appearance of the 5th Dragoon Guards, and the startling spectacle of artillery men with unlimbered guns and lighted matches'.

The wisdom of O'Connell in cancelling the meeting quite possibly prevented serious riot and bloodshed at Clontarf, consequences which it had been suggested, perhaps unjustly, might have suited the purposes of the government.

[177, *DHR* (Flood), *Nation,* vol. 1]

CLONTARF BANK
See KERR'S CHART OF DUBLIN BAY.

CLONTARF BAR
This is a name for part of Clontarf Strand, and as such is mentioned in two *CARD* references in the 18th century as a source for shingle for filling kishes and building sea walls. In the context of the Pool of Clontarf and the small harbour at the Sheds, the Bar probably represents an obstruction which existed to the free flow of the Tolka on its old course, north of Clontarf Island, to the bay. It would have been formed by tidal action, by the deposition of silt carried down by the river, and possibly by a hard gravel or rock ridge in the channel.

[*DHR* (Moore), *CARD*, VI, VII]

CLONTARF CASTLE
See VERNONS OF CLONTARF.

CLONTARF FURLONG
See THE FURLONG OF CLONTARF.

CLONTARF GUT
See CRABLAKE WATER.

CLONTARF HEAD
Maps of the 17th and early 18th centuries (de Gomme 1673, Phillips 1685, Greenvile Collins 1686, Price 1730) show a narrow spit of land some 300 m long projecting south-west from near the Sheds of Clontarf and called Clontarf Head. It formed a small inlet which probably acted as a mooring for the fishing-boats. Rocque ignored this feature in 1760, as did Scalé and Richards in 1765. Bligh, in 1800/3, while showing its stump as Clontarf Point, implied that the spit no longer existed as dry land above high tide, although its outline remained at low water; and this was repeated by Taylor in 1816. This alteration over 100 years is quite possibly due, as has been suggested, to the removal of shingle and small boulders from the strand, and perhaps the Head, for use in the construction of the South Wall.

See also Clontarf Strand and Weekes's Wharf.

[Maps (as named)]

CLONTARF ISLAND

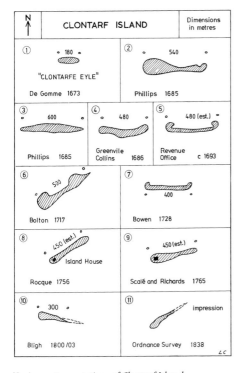

Various representations of Clontarf Island

If, today, one were to leave the East Wall Road and walk north-east for about 200 m along Bond Road, one would be standing on top of what was, for 1,000 years or perhaps very much longer, Clontarf Island. Men will have stood on this island in 1014 and perhaps fled out to sea in boats beached on its shore during battle. In 1538 it was included in a lease of lands by the prior of Kilmainham to Matthew King, and the Kings, who had fishing interests along the north shore of the bay, would be concerned with the ownership of the island until it passed into the hands of the Vernons in the 17th century. The city claimed jurisdiction over it, awarding a lease of the island to the city recorder in 1621, and including in the route taken in riding the franchises in 1603 a passage 'from the furlonge to the Island of Clontarfe and so by the river of Anlyffe alongst westward' to St Mary's Abbey. The eastern sections of the franchises were ridden at very low tide, and it appears that the island could

then be approached on horseback across a strand. It would of course have been necessary to cross the channels of the Tolka, which at that time passed principally north of the island.

The shape and size of the island, as might be expected with what was in part a sandbank, has varied; and it has been shown in several forms. Generally, however, it appears that until perhaps the middle of the 18th century it was a strip of land about 450 m long east to west and about 120 m north to south at widest. Some maps show its main axis north-east to south-west, and the dominant portion would seem to have been at the west or south-west end.

In 1665 the lord deputy and his Council, being concerned about 'the great perill and danger which might cause to this citty of Dublin [due to] the infection of the plague in the citty of London . . . if persons of all sorts should be suffered freely to resort hither without controul', ordered that 'two howses' convenient for storing merchandise 'and for receaving and entertaining of passengers, be forthwith erected a convenient distance from this citty'. It was agreed 'that the island of Clontarffe be appointed as the most convenient place'. In 1666 the houses, described as the 'pesthouses', were built.

During the 18th century the building of the East Wall started the process that was to divert the channel of the River Tolka to flow south and west of the island, rather than to its north and east, a process that was completed in the 20th century. The more recent land intake, which buried the remains of the island, has now, however, caused this channel to be relocated, to pass again north of the island site.

When Bligh prepared his survey map (1800/3) he found Clontarf Island smaller than shown earlier. The shrinkage clearly related in a high degree to the removal of sand, gravel and boulders for the South Wall and for the North Lotts reclamation. One sees for instance on the Bolton map of 1717 the strand north of the island described as 'quarry reserv'd in common for the work'. And this whittling away of the island would continue through the 19th century, to obtain material for the new substance, concrete, so widely used in the port developments of the second half of the century, and to provide shelly sand as a fertiliser for gardeners.

During the 18th and 19th centuries Clontarf Island was a place of recreation for Dubliners. Ferry-boats took parties out from a wharf known as the Smoothing Iron at the corner of the East Wall Road, and the island was known to many as the Bathing Island. Early in the 19th century Christopher Cromwell, a publican of Beaver Street, owned a house on the island which he used for fishing. On a night in October 1844, during a very severe storm, Cromwell and his son were drowned at the island. The name Cromwell's Island will sometimes be seen. Cosgrave has recorded that in 1909 the outline of the island could still be identified at low tide, and a reference to it in 1875 will be found in Kerr's Chart of Dublin Bay.

Geomorphologically, one cannot overlook the remarkable similarity between the spit of Ringsend south of the river, and the conjunction of Clontarf Island and Clontarf Head, seen for instance on the maps of de Gomme and Bligh, north of the river. The River Tolka quite possibly in prehistoric time flowed south and west of the island, with the island being the point of a spit. Conversely, had the Dodder ever forced a passage across the peninsula south of Ringsend, Ringsend too would have been an island.

Clontarf Island has also been known as Clontarfe Eyle, Clontarf Hard and Clandaf Island.
[31, 38, *CARD*, I, III–V, *DHR* (Bowen), maps (Bolton 1717, Bligh 1800/3, Kerr 1875)]

CLONTARF LEAD MINE

A lead mine was located on the shore at Clontarf near the swimming-baths. It had at least two shafts, one on the shore and the other a short way inland. Mentioned in a list of Irish mines prepared in 1497, it continued in production for about 300 years. Kane notes that it was abandoned 'when the tide broke in on the workings and the mine became filled up with water'.

Taylor's map shows its location in 1816, and it may be associated with an abrupt change of

location in the road shown by Rocque/Scalé in 1773. Much more recently, the shaft on the shore still appeared as a tall stone tower with thick masonry walls, containing rusted pithead gear. When the promenade wall was built, this shaft was cut down to become the base for a shelter on the city side of the swimming-baths.
[10, 160 (vol. 2), 176, maps (Rocque/Scalé 1773, Taylor 1816)]

CLONTARF POOL, THE
See POOLBEG.

CLONTARF QUARRIES
See CLONTARF STRAND.

CLONTARF SALT-WORKS

Greenvile Collins shows, on his map of 1686, a series of roughly rectangular beds just above 'high water marke' about 2 km east of Clontarf Head. He describes them as 'salt work's'. It is probable that they were employed for the recovery of salt by evaporation for use in preserving fish landed at Clontarf.

[Map (as named)]

CLONTARF SHEDS

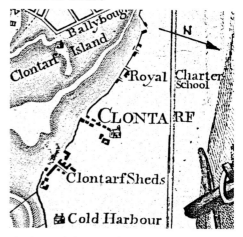

The district of Clontarf, 1765

During the 12th and 13th centuries a castle and a Commandery of the Knights Templars were

Clontarf Sheds, 1796, showing what may be Weekes's Wharf (J. La Porte)

founded at Clontarf, and a village built up along the road leading to the castle from the shore. This village, which may have antedated the castle, is shown on the earliest maps of the district, as for instance on Phillips's map of 1685. About 1 km south-east of the castle, near the present junction of Vernon Avenue with Clontarf Road, lay the harbour for the village. It was protected from the east by Clontarf Head, then more prominent than it is now, and it had reasonable access to the deep water of the Pool of Clontarf, and thence to the bay. The little inlet became the most important place for landing fish on the north shore of the Liffey estuary and the bay.

As such, the area acquired its own identity. Greenvile Collins names it as Herringtowne on his map of 1693, and Phillips, more simply, calls it 'Fish House'. Buildings were erected here from some early date for the processing and storage of fish; and until the 19th century these, and consequently the area, were known variously as the sheds, shelds, shade, shades, sheads of Clontarf. In riding the franchises in 1767 the procession passed by 'the Shades of Clontarff'.

Rocque/Scalé shows in 1773 a substantial village which it names Clontarf Sheds; and it adds in along the shoreline road the title Clontarf Shade, which perhaps suggests that the 'shade' was something

separate, notionally the protection of the inlet from east and south-east gales.

During the 18th and early 19th centuries the shore at the Sheds and the inlet beside them was a popular seaside spot, in which Weekes's Wharf was a particular attraction. The place provided a favourite subject for artists. Works by King, Wheatly and O'Connor are held in the National Library of Ireland, and a robust coloured engraving by La Porte is in the British Library (King's Topographical Collection, vol. 53, 21.c).

The village of Clontarf Sheds lasted into the 19th century, being named as such by Taylor in his map of 1816, and shown therein as containing a precinct called Rutland Place. But the fishing industry at Clontarf had declined greatly and D'Alton in 1838 recorded the demise of the village as such: 'A few houses, once of fashionable resort, still maintain the name, though the Sheds have long since vanished with the good days of the fishermen.'

[4, 77, 162, *CARD*, XI, maps (Phillips 1685, Greenvile Collins 1693, Rocque/Scalé 1773, Taylor 1816)]

CLONTARF STRAND

This area, which generally could be said to consist of the Furlong of Clontarf, Clontarf Island and Head, and the sand shoals around the mouth of the Tolka from Ballybough Bridge to the sea, was a major source of shingle and small boulders for the South Wall and other harbour works in the 18th century. Material was excavated for filling kishes and as stones for walling. Local residents were removing 'peble stone to pave' their yards. This source of material was described as 'the quarries on Clontarffe strand' in some references. There was probably no quarrying in the sense of detaching pieces from bedrock faces, but it is clear that the dressing of boulders to form walling stones was a standard process. See for instance the abstract in *CARD*, vol. XI, pp. 404–10. Some such stones were included in the Poolbeg lighthouse. [*CARD*, VI, XI, *DHR* (Moore)]

CLONTARF SWIMMING-BATHS

The Clontarf Baths and Assembly Rooms were first built in 1864. In 1884 Clontarf Swimming Club was founded, and in 1886 a private company formed by W.L. Freeman bought the premises and recon- structed the baths to meet the needs of the club. Hot sea-water baths were installed, and, as at Merrion, the main bathing area was divided by a central wall into two pools, for men and women. In 1945 the premises were purchased by Clontarf Baths Limited. The hot baths were closed and the main bathing area was converted into one large pool.

This note is based on the account given by McIntyre in his general work on the district of Clontarf.

[296, private communication (A. Delany)]

CLUNLITH

See CLONLIFFE.

CLUT, RADULF AND RICHARD

See STEIN, DISTRICT OF.

COAL QUAY

See WOOD QUAY.

COAL QUAY (BELOW RINGSEND)

See PIGEONHOUSE: A PRECINCT.

COAL QUAY BRIDGE

See ORMONDE BRIDGE.

COASTING PILOTS

See CAPTAIN GREENVILE COLLINS; MACKENZIE'S CHART; ALEXANDER NIMMO; SCALÉ'S AND RICHARDS'S CHART, and accompanying descriptive text (bib. ref. 161).

COCK LAKE

From the earliest times, it seems probable that, just east of Ringsend, a small secondary channel of the Liffey branched to the south of the main stream and flowed to the bay in a tortuous, possibly fluctuating, course through the South Bull. This became known in the 17th century or earlier as the Cock Lake, Cockle Lake, Cock Leake or Cork Lake. It appears to have been of sufficient size to permit the passage of small fishing-boats at most stages of the tide, and the rate of flow through it, in either direction depending on the state of the tide, could be considerable.

When the Ballast Office was piling along the line of the South Wall, it found difficulty in 1717 in getting piles long enough to block the junction of the Cock Lake and the main river, but this had been achieved by 1733.

The watercourse, thus blocked, did not disappear but instead formed itself into a great loop with two mouths, both at the east of the South Bull between the new South Wall and the Merrion shoreline. Thus while Bowen's map of 1728 shows Cock Lake flowing into the Liffey, Rocque (1760), Scalé and Richards (1765) and other contemporary maps show the loop.

Bligh's map of his survey of 1800 shows what can only be the Cock Lake, but does not record the loop. Instead it meanders westward through the Bull to peter out just east of Ringsend.

Once this channel lost its connection with the main river, it ceased to be useful for boats. It has continued to exist in a modified form to this day, following as far as it can the course mapped by Bligh, and it still acts as a feeder from which the rising tide inches its way across the sands; in Joyce's words, 'In long lassoes from the Cock Lake the water flowed full covering greengoldenly lagoons of sand, rising, flowing.'

Until the 19th century a large pool, some 8 ha in extent, known as the Marsh and located in the vicinity of modern Park Avenue, filled and emptied with the tide through a gut or channel that connected it to the Cock Lake near the Sandymount Martello tower. The subsequent reclamation of the pool and blocking of the channel has led to the reshaping of the looped Cock Lake.

[27, maps (Bowen 1728, Rocque 1760, Scalé and Richards 1765, Bligh 1800/3, Taylor 1816)]

COCKLE LAKE
See COCK LAKE.

COCKLE POINT
Bligh shows on his map a minor headland on the Clontarf shore roughly midway between the Sheds and the Royal Charter School, and gives its name as Cockle Point.

[Map (Bligh 1800/3)]

CODLING ROCK
The Codling Rock was a group of three rocks near the shoreline between the old harbour of Dunleary and the Martello tower at Sandycove. The name is given by Scalé and Richards (1765) and by Bligh (1800/3), and the group appears to have been that named The Three Churls by Rocque in 1760. Following the construction of the new harbour of Dunleary, the name no longer appears on maps, as the rocks are largely incorporated in or lie close to the landward end of the East Pier of the new harbour.

These rocks are not to be confused with the Codling Bank, which lies east of Wicklow Head.

[Maps (Rocque 1760, Scalé and Richards 1765, Bligh 1800/3)]

COGAN, MILES AND RICHARD DE
Miles de Cogan led the assault on Dublin in 1170 that seized the town for the Anglo-Normans. Strongbow later made him its governor. In 1171 de Cogan defeated Tigernán Ua Ruairc, who had laid siege to the town, and later that year, with his brother Richard, he defeated Askulv Mac Thorkil and his allies at the battle of Hoggen Green. He was joint ruler in Cork with Robert FitzStephen for five years from 1177, but was killed near Lismore in County Waterford in 1182.

[35]

COLD HARBOUR
This was a house near the shore at the end of modern Seafield Road and near the land end of the Bull Wall. It is shown as a seamark by Scalé and Richards in 1765 and is shown also by Bligh (1800/3) and by Taylor (1816).

[Maps (as named)]

COLLEGE GREEN
See HOGGEN GREEN.

COLLINS, CAPTAIN GREENVILE
Greenvile Collins was a captain in the Royal Navy and a hydrographer, and was a 'younger brother' of Trinity House in 1679. Acting, according to Flood, on a commission of Charles II, Collins carried out the survey and charting of the coasts of the kingdom in the period 1681–8. In 1693 he published his work as *Great Britain's Coasting Pilot*. In November 1686 he published, possibly as a draft, his 'map of the bay and harbour of Dublin', and in 1693 what is probably the same map in its final form appeared with a dedication to the duke of Ormonde.

Rennie records in a letter in July 1802 to the Directors General of Inland Navigation that Collins took soundings in Dublin Bay in 1711 at the behest of the Ballast Office.

Collins's first name is also recorded as Grenville, Greenville and Greenvil.

[6, 29, 55, 73, 162, *CARD*, XVII, *DHR* (Corry, Flood)]

COLLINS, CAPTAIN GREENVILE: MAPS
There are records of two maps of Dublin Bay and Harbour by Captain Greenvile Collins.

(i) 'A map of the bay and harbour of Dublin surveyed by Capt. Greenvil Collins November 1686' (BL, King's Topographical Collection, vol. 53, 5).

(ii) A map of the bay and harbour by Captain Grenville Collins in 1693 'humbly dedicated and presented to his Grace James Duke of Ormond' (BL, Add. MS 35931, Hardwicke Papers, vol. 583, ff. 5–6).

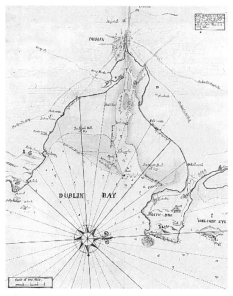

Dublin Bay and Harbour, 1686 (G. Collins)

Haliday includes a version of the 1686 map printed by Morrison and Co., Dublin, in bib. ref. 6.

The sheets are close to one another in content. The first map is probably an early draft for the later one, which was included in *Great Britain's Coasting Pilot*.

The 1686 map shows the Doney River (the Dodder) flowing through Doney Brooke and offers a sketchy view of Lazars Hill as a well-established district. The detail of the city is poor and inaccurate. Salt-works are shown near Booterstown and Dollymount.

The 1693 map gives the Clontarf Sheds the name of Herringtowne and suggests that the bar across the mouth of the Liffey is dry at low water.

Both maps show the small fort in the village of Ringsend.

The divergence between the two Collins maps in their representation of the Bar and the considerable difference between these two sheets and the almost contemporary de Gomme map of

1673 show the difficulties which the various surveyors of the time must have found in illustrating their understanding of the Bar; and they underline the severe problems that mariners must have faced in navigating past it.

[162, maps (as named)]

COLLINS BARRACKS

See ROYAL BARRACKS.

COLMANS BROOK

In the area bounded by the River Camac on the west, the River Liffey on the north, James's Street and Thomas Street on the south, and Winetavern Street on the east, there has since the earliest times been a confusing pattern of man-made watercourses. They have been associated with the supply of drinking-water and the provision of water power for mills, and they have contributed to the formation of Usher's Island.

One of these was Colmans Brook. Jackson (*DHR*: 'The Glib Water and Colmans Brook') has argued that Colmans Brook was part of a watercourse drawn off the River Camac in antiquity to provide water, untainted by estuarine salt water, for early dwellers between the High Street ridge and the Liffey.

A recent archaeological excavation has shown, however, that in the 13th century a defensive ditch with its invert level at approximately 1.0 m OD (Poolbeg) was cut north–south along modern Bridge Street. Its course cut the line of Colmans Brook at right angles near Gormond's Gate. One must assume that from that time onwards, Colmans Brook was blocked at the east side of the defensive ditch and existed only as a short dead-end channel from there to the Liffey. Its course would have run first eastward, and then turned north between Cook Street and Merchants Quay to flow into the Liffey at right angles a little to the west of Skippers Alley. The western part of the watercourse may have flowed into the defensive ditch, or may have joined the south–north stream, known in 1696 as Glib Water, to flow with it into Usher's Pill.

The name of Colmans Brook, which possibly relates to the name of a landholder, is of great antiquity. It appears in a deed dated 1258–9, and is noted again by Gilbert in the 15th century. In the 16th century it was an open tidal watercourse for part of its length, passing at Merchants Quay either through a space between houses or under a house; and it was used both for boat access and for the disposal of 'filthred'. In 1605 it was recorded that 'the housse of Christopher Blacknye, merchaunt, is supported with manye postes in the brooke, annoyeinge the passage of every boate that might come into the baksydes of the inhabitantes housses, as of ole tyme have bene accustomed'; and the cleaning of the brook and removal of the posts were ordered.

The watercourse was clearly navigable, if only for a short distance. During the uneasy years at the end of the 16th century, when the postern gates in the city walls were being blocked up 'with lime and stones', it was ordered for increased security that 'a grate of stone or tymbre shalbe fensyblie made upon the gate of Colmans brooke next the river'. In 1641, at the start of the insurrection, Conor Maguire, baron of Enniskillen, one of its leaders, was apprehended on 22 October in Cook Street, where he was plotting the seizure of Dublin Castle. It was recorded afterwards that he had been offered a chance to escape arrest by being 'conveyed by Colmans Brooke', but had not had time to do so. His fellow leader Rory O'More did in fact escape by water on the following day, being rowed up the Liffey from the city to Kilmainham Bridge, where he took horse for Leixlip.

Later in the 17th century the city authorities, probably in the interests of hygiene, put the watercourse into a culvert which then discharged 'into the Liffey by the mouth of the great shore on Merchants'-quay', as reported by Perry in 1721 (CARD, VII). Sweeney describes this culvert, which now flows into an interceptor sewer on Merchants Quay, as egg-shaped in section, 2.4 m high and 1.8 m wide near its discharge point.

Throughout the period in which Colmans Brook was an open watercourse, it will have formed a break on Merchants Quay, which does not appear to be mentioned in the literature. One must suppose that this break was bridged by a wooden drawbridge, or by a stone arch similar to those proposed for the waterfront near Lazars Hill in the late 17th century.

[18, 184, *CARD*, II, V, VII, *DHR* (Jackson, Hughes), private communication (A. Hayden)]

COMMISSIONERS OF IRISH LIGHTS

The statutory authority for providing aids to navigation for shipping around the coast of Ireland. The Commission was established in 1867 by act of parliament and took over its function from the Corporation for Preserving and Improving the Port of Dublin, which had also been the national Lighthouse Authority since 1810. There are 21 Commissioners on the board. These are the lord mayor of Dublin, 3 aldermen of Dublin Corporation and 17 co-opted members, filled by the board as vacancies occur.

In the context of this book, the Commission operates the two Dún Laoghaire lighthouses and the lighthouses at Baily and the Muglins. The Poolbeg and North Bull lighthouses and those within the Walls are operated by the Dublin Port and Docks Board.

[Service Information (Comm. of Irish Lights), June 1990]

COMMONS STREET
See NORTH LOTTS.

CONCILIATION HALL
Conciliation Hall was built on Burgh Quay, between the Corn Exchange and Corn Exchange

Conciliation Hall, following its conversion for use as the Tivoli Theatre

Place, as a meeting-place for the Loyal National Repeal Association, and was given its name by Daniel O'Connell, with what Mitchel described as a peculiar taste in nomenclature. The name was intended to indicate the necessity to unite all classes and religions in Ireland in a common struggle for the independence of their common country.

The hall was opened in October 1843 in great form and amid high enthusiasm. The chair was taken by John Augustus O'Neill of Bunowen Castle, a Protestant gentleman who had been early in life a cavalry officer and member of parliament for Hull in England. The hall was described as a large oblong building, not beautiful externally but inside spacious, handsome and convenient. It was lit

> by twelve bronze candelabra, each containing two lamps of ground glass, ranged around the panels of the gallery, and a row of twelve or thirteen more, each having one lamp, extended around the walls above the gallery. Upon the ceiling were three very large and beautiful rosettes of pale green and gold containing the shamrock in low relief with a harp in the one in the centre.

The elevation to the quay was ornamented with pilasters, the harp and Irish crown cut in stone and, over all, a balustrade.

The building was used as stores during the 1870s, was converted into the Tivoli Theatre, a music-hall, in 1896, and became offices for the *Irish Press* when that newspaper was first published in 1931.

[113, 177, 210]

CONNIVING (CONIVING, CONNIVEING) HOUSE

An inn near Irishtown that flourished in the 18th century, the landlord at one time being Johnny Macklean. It is shown on Scalé's and Richards's chart of 1765 as a two-storey house near the water's edge; and it appears on Rocque's map of 1760 and on the Rocque/Scalé map of 1773 in such a position that it would today be at the junction of Beach Road and Marine Drive. Ball records that it was thatched, and that its specialities were 'fish dinners and excellent ale'.

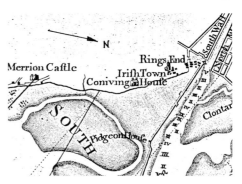

The Conniving House, showing also the Cock Lake on South Bull sands, 1765

An account of the inn and its services in 1725, quoted by Joyce, is given in Thomas Amory's book *The Life of John Buncle, Esq.*

[56, 65, *DHR* (Hussey), maps (Rocque 1760, Scalé and Richards 1765, Rocque/Scalé 1773)]

CONNOLLY RAILWAY STATION

In 1838 an act was passed enabling the building of a railway from Dublin to Drogheda, for which William Cubitt was the engineer. In 1846 a terminus for this line, then the Dublin and Drogheda railway, was built at Amiens Street on ground taken in from the Liffey in the 18th century. The architect was William Deane Butler. The station was built high above street level, and Sheriff Street, which had already been detoured to avoid the Inner Dock, passed underneath it to join Amiens Street.

In 1876 three railway companies, Ulster, Dublin and Belfast Junction, and Dublin and Drogheda, merged to form the Great Northern Railway Company, and the Amiens Street station became its Dublin terminus.

On Easter Sunday in 1966 the station was renamed Connolly Station in memory of James Connolly (1868–1916), signatory of the Proclamation of the Irish Republic and military commander of the republican forces in Dublin in 1916.

[3, 190, 226, *Engineers and Architects Journal*, vol. 1, 1837–8]

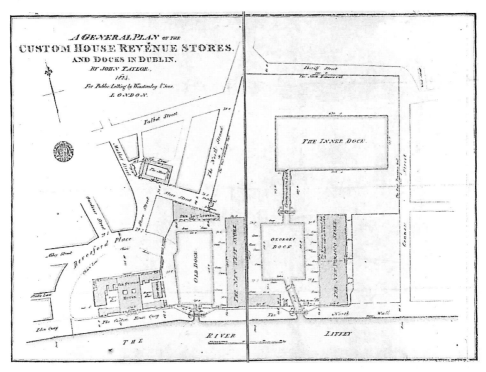

Taylor's plan of the Custom House Docks, 1824

70 degrees to the main channel of the Liffey. George's Dock is 96 m long north to south and 72 m wide. At the north of this dock a channel 86 m long and 11 m wide leads north to the Inner or Revenue Dock, which is 89 m wide north to south and 195 m long. The continuity of the North Wall quay was preserved during the 19th century by a narrow swing-bridge but this was replaced prior to 1935 by twinned Scherzer bridges similar to those built earlier at the Liffey entrance to the Royal Canal.

George's Dock is named after George IV, the first of the Georges to come to Ireland and only the sixth king of England to do so in the history of the city; and the dock was to have been formally opened by him during his brief and somewhat idiosyncratic visit in 1821. However, as Gilligan records, 'A social engagement at Slane over the preceding weekend delayed his return to the city and the dock was opened in his absence by Lord Castlecoote.'

In 1851, responsibility for the Custom House Docks having, some 20 years earlier, passed from the Revenue Commissioners – who had neglected their maintenance – to the Ballast Board, it was found necessary to replace the wooden structure of the entrance gate with stone and cast iron. The contract for the iron work was let to the firm of John and Robert Mallet (see separate entry).

In 1856 the Tobacco Store, now called Stack A, was used as a venue for the banquet given to the Irish regiments returning from the Crimean War. No other covered space in Dublin at the time would have been large enough to fit the 3,600 guests (*The Irish Times*, 18 October 1986) who attended.

As part of a comprehensive redevelopment of the Custom House Docks area, to the design of Burke-Kennedy Doyle & Partners, the planning of an international financial services centre began in 1988. The building programme has been continuous since then and five buildings with a combined floor area of about 50,000 sq. m. have already been brought into use. These buildings cover part of the Old Dock.

The general development of the area under the direction of the Custom House Docks Development Authority will convert George's Dock and the Inner Dock into freshwater lakes, and will include residential, shopping, hotel, museum and entertainment elements. It is an aspiration of the scheme that the east end of Custom House Quay from Memorial Road to Commons Street will be closed to traffic to become a formal waterfront for the new precinct.

[57, 68 (vol. 2), 87 (vol. 20), 90 (vols. 38, 62), 129, map (Taylor 1824)]

Custom House Quay, c. 1830, showing the entrance to the Old Dock

CUSTOM HOUSE DOCKS DEVELOPMENT AUTHORITY

The Custom House Docks Development Authority was established by the government in 1986 under the Urban Renewal Act of that year. It has eight members, including Professor Dervilla M.X. Donnelly, who chairs the Authority. Its general duty is to secure the redevelopment of the Custom House Docks Area, which is now about 30 ha in extent, stretching downstream from Talbot Memorial Bridge to Guild Street and, south to north, from the middle of the Liffey to Sheriff Street.

In its final form, the development proposed will contain the following approximate floor areas:

Offices:	111,500 sq. m.	Residential:	79,000 sq. m.
Retail:	4,600 sq. m.	Hotel:	7,400 sq. m.
Cultural use:	6,500 sq. m.	Community facilities:	2,000 sq. m.

The anticipated working population in the area will be about 7,000 and the residential population 2,400.

This note is based on the Report of the Authority for 1994, and on its published Planning Scheme, 1994.

CUSTOM HOUSE LANE

See CRANE LANE.

CUSTOM HOUSE QUAY, NEW

The north side of the Liffey in the vicinity of the new Custom House was first embanked by the Ballast Office in *c.* 1715–25. Gandon recorded that the quay wall on the south front of the Custom House was an old embankment made about the year 1725; it was 60 feet wide at the top and badly constructed; the walls of black stone; its foundations laid on the surface of the strand; on the side next the river it was 12 feet high but on the inside only 8 feet; the filling between the walls was a sand used for ballast; the base of the foundations stood at least 6 feet above the bed of the river; the tide not only soaked under them but filtered in several places through the joints of the masonry.

Some of this embankment was evidently made before 1725. In 1716 it was recorded that 'we are carrying the Kishes up towards Mourney's Dock' and in 1717 Bolton's map of the North Lotts shows the bank built at the future Custom House site and forming part of what he named Dublin Key. The Ballast Office did, however, turn to walls rather than banks built with kishes while it was building the North Wall, and Gandon's reference to black stone walls may represent the strengthening of an earlier embankment.

In 1786 Gandon proposed that the quay wall be altered to lie parallel to the Custom House, and this change was accepted by the Ballast Board. The completed quay is shown by Malton in his view of the Custom House drawn in 1792. It has timber fenders and a timber kerb secured to a stone retaining wall. It does not have a parapet wall.

Faden shows in 1797 that the Custom House Quay extended westward from the narrow swing-bridge at the entrance to the Old Dock to a line roughly 40 m west of the Custom House building. There was access to it from Lower Abbey Street, but access along the river frontage to Bachelors Walk would not become available until 1814 when Eden Quay was completed.

It appears that all or part of Custom House Quay was enclosed in the interests of security. In 1814 the Commissioners of Customs referred to their new gateway on the quay, and invited the Ballast Board to join them in providing new riverside protection where the junction of their quay and Eden Quay was open to the public. Part of this protection was to be an iron railing and part a stone parapet wall similar to that on Eden Quay. In *c.* 1816 an undated anonymous letter warned the Commissioners that 'individuals and small groups of both male and female held communication with the daily watchman and quay porters' and were receiving stolen property from them.

Custom House Quay, c. 1885, looking upstream

A plan prepared by John Taylor in 1824 to show the Custom House Revenue Stores and Docks indicates a boundary to the western end of the quay, but does not make it clear that it is a gateway. However, some security was enforced, as a drawing by S.F. Brocas in 1828 shows quite firmly a soldier in red coat and busby guarding the entrance to the Old Dock. In 1838 all obstructions to public traffic had been removed, and in 1842 Bartlett showed in his drawing that a timber railing had been constructed along the riverside of the quay. In 1912 the east end of Custom House Quay had been established at Commons Street, and it remains there today.

Custom House Quay was active as a shipping quay late into the 20th century, being used extensively by the Guinness Brewery. In 1978, however, the construction of Talbot Memorial Bridge across the Liffey at the eastern end of the Custom House closed the quay permanently to seagoing vessels.

[77, 87 (vols. 8, 9), 102, 153; *CARD*, VII; BL, Add. MS 40258, f. 298; maps (Bolton 1717, Faden 1797, Taylor 1824, OS 1838)]

CUSTOM HOUSE QUAY, OLD

James I (D. Mytens)

In 1620 James I ordered his lord deputy, Sir Oliver St John, to take a lease of ground in the newly reclaimed Poddle estuary from Jacob Newman. This was to be for 'a place in the port of Dublin which is found to be convenient for erecting a crane and making a wharf'. The crane was to replace the former Crane near the foot of Winetavern Street. The plot to be taken was 'lying in or near Dame-street in the suburbs of the city of Dublin containing from the river on the north side in length southward 160 feet and at the south side in breadth 106 feet'. The plot was to have access to Dame Street through 'a lane containing in breadth 18 feet'. This lane would become known as Crane Lane, and the plot appears to have extended north–south from the high-tide shoreline of the Liffey to the south side of modern Essex Street,

Old Custom House Quay, showing also the old Custom House, Essex Bridge and Ormonde Quay, Upper, c. 1753 (J. Tudor)

and east–west from Crane Lane to a line east of modern Crampton Court.

In 1621 the lord deputy and his Council announced that 'We have caused a Custome house, Crane, and Wharfe to be builded' on the plot described, and thenceforth it was to be 'the onely, sole and proper Crane and Wharfe for the loading, landing, putting aboard or on shore, any goods, wares, merchandise, or commodities whatsoever, to be by sea exported or imported into or forth of this said Port of Dublin'.

What precisely was built at this time is not certain, but a wooden quay named 'newe keay' existed in 1625. It is clear that 16 years later, in 1637, the Dublin merchants were dissatisfied with the customs facilities available to them at the 'New Custom House' and the 'New Crane' and were seeking better accommodation for their goods in transit; and it appears that Charles I, then king, was prepared to enlarge the wharf and build better premises.

There is no indication when that work was done. The wharf had, however, in 1651 become the 'Custom House Key' and was so described in a commonwealth order of that year. De Gomme suggests in 1673 that the quay extended along the river-bank from the line of Crane Lane at the west to the new channel of the Poddle, still an open stream, to the east. Pooley's Wood Yard extended east from

there along the bank to Dirty Lane (now the line of Temple Lane). It is likely that some additional building was done between 1621 and 1660, for on the formal occasion of celebrating the restoration of Charles II to the monarchy, it was decreed that 'the commissioners of the government of the nation are to meet at the councell chamber at the Custome House' to join in the celebratory procession.

This Council Chamber, which de Gomme shows in 1673 as 30 to 35 m long, was used as a meeting-place for the Privy Council of Ireland, and it was usually there that lords lieutenant were sworn into office upon their arrival in the country (e.g. Henry, Viscount Sydney in 1692). The Irish parliament had commenced sitting at Chichester House in 1661, but committees of the House of Commons and of the peers occasionally met at this time in the Green Chamber and the Garden Chamber in the new Custom House; and these rooms, according to a record of 1682, were located 'over the Council Chamber'. This observation would suggest that the Council Chamber was located in whatever Custom House existed in 1660.

On the other hand, if the 1682 record can be questioned, there is a case to be made for the Council Chamber being a separate building close to the Custom House, for it continued to be used by government until 1711, four years after the building of the next Custom House, when it and its

DE RIDELISFORD, WALTER

See RIDELISFORD, WALTER DE.

DECER, JOHN

John Decer or le Decer was mayor of Dublin for four years between 1302 and 1309 and for the two years from 1324 to 1326. He built Ballybough Bridge in 1313. During his mayoralty in 1308, he played a part in the provision of a water supply for the city. In 1304 the church at the Priory of St Saviour was destroyed by fire. It was rebuilt in 1308 with considerable help from John Decer, who always maintained a close association with the priory.

[16, 29, *DHR* (Culliton), Dublin Corporation Archives]

DEER PARK

See PHOENIX PARK.

DEIGHAN, PAUL

In his book *A complete treatise on the geography of Ireland on a new plan never before attempted by any writer, adapted to the Merchant, the Gentleman, the Politician, the Antiquarian, the Naturalist, the Scholar and the Artist*, for which he wrote the preface in 1810, Paul Deighan praises the South Wall, noting the 'beautiful Pharos' at its eastern end, and the 'commodious house in the nature of a hotel' in the Pigeonhouse precinct. He describes also in some detail the development of both shores of the Liffey from the 17th to the 19th century.

[*DHR* (Little)]

DELVIN'S TOWER

There is a single reference in 1615 to the widening of 'the wharfe betwixt Fions Castell and the buildinge of William Shelton, near Delvins Tower'. It is not clear where this tower was, but it may have been along Wood Quay in the vicinity of Prickett's Tower.

[*CARD*, III]

DENMARK, PRINCE GEORGE OF

See BALLAST OFFICE.

'DERMOT AND THE EARL, THE SONG OF'

A poem of about 3,500 lines describing the events of the Anglo-Norman conquest of Ireland, with extensive references to the capture and subjugation of Dublin in 1170–71. One of the very few written descriptions of the time, it has been suggested that it represents the journal of Morice Regan, secretary to Diarmait Mac Murchada, the Dermot of the title. The earl is Richard de Clare, earl of Pembroke, known as Strongbow.

[49]

DEVONSHIRE WHARF

Devonshire Wharf was named by Robert Emmet as one of the two points from which the Pigeonhouse Fort was to be attacked in 1803. The wharf quite possibly lay to the west of the fort as it was then, and south of the then causeway from Ringsend. A drawing 'Le Fort de Pigeon House dans la Baie de Dublin' (NLI, 622 TA) shows in this location a broad slip which was subsequently covered by the later buildings in the Pigeonhouse barracks complex.

[60, 77]

DIRECTORIES OF DUBLIN

The main uses of the Dublin directories in the context of this book lie in the records of persons living or working near the Liffey, of bodies and industries related to it, and of quays, streets and alleys existing at various times.

From the early 18th century the *Gentleman's and Citizen's Almanack* was the principal directory in Dublin. It was produced by members of the Watson family, and would continue to appear, either alone or as part of a composite publication known as the *Treble Almanack*, until 1844. In 1751 *Wilson's Dublin Directory* appeared, and it also continued in publication, sometimes with a map, and either alone or as part of the *Treble Almanack*, into the early years of the 19th century. The *Treble Almanack* appeared first *c.* 1796. Its constituent directories varied from one year to another, the *English Court Registry* and the *Post Office Annual Directory* sometimes being included.

In 1832 the *Post Office Annual Directory*, 'printed for the letter carriers of the General Post Office', was published independently, and would continue to appear, under slightly varying titles, until *c.* 1849. During this time, from 1834 to 1847, the broad function of a Dublin directory was served by *The Dublin Almanac and General Register of Ireland*, compiled by Pettigrew and Oulton.

In 1844 *Thom's Irish Almanac and Official Directory* was introduced. This directory and a succession of Thom's almanacs or directories, with variations in their detailed titles, have continued to the present day.

A useful directory, published once only, in 1850, and an important source for mid-19th-century Dublin, is the *New City Pictorial Directory 1850*, compiled by 'Henry Shaw, 40, Lower Ormond Quay'. This work was reprinted by the Friar's Bush Press, Belfast, in 1988 under the title *The Dublin Pictorial Guide and Directory of 1850*, with an introduction by Kevin B. Nowlan.

These notes are not a complete record. The complex sequence of the Dublin directories with their changing titles for the last 300 years is outside the scope of the present work.

[146, 222, 223, 224, *Wilson's Dublin Directory, Treble Almanack*]

DIRECTORS GENERAL OF INLAND NAVIGATION

In 1729 the Irish parliament passed an act establishing Commissioners of Inland Navigation for each of the four provinces to encourage the development of rivers for communication and the construction of canals. In 1751 the four boards were amalgamated into a single navigation board. In 1787 the Commissioners were dissolved and their responsibilities passed to local bodies. In 1800, shortly before its own dissolution, the Irish parliament appointed a board of five Directors General of Inland Navigation; and this board carried on its work until 1831, when it was dissolved and its duties taken over by the Commissioners of Public Works.

While the title of the body suggests that rivers and canals inside Ireland were its remit, the Directors General issued an open report to the Irish public, undated but probably in 1802, inviting comment on the several problems influencing the development of the port and harbour of Dublin and in particular on dealing with the bar at the mouth of the Liffey. They followed this in December 1804 with their *Representation for the Improvement of Dublin Harbour submitted to his Excellency the Lord Lieutenant and the Lords of His Majesty's Treasury*. These actions were taken 'in pursuance of the Act of the 40th year of His Majesty's reign' under which 'the Improvement of the Harbour of Dublin is committed' to the Directors General.

It is not easy to reconcile this authority with that given to the Corporation for Preserving and Improving the Port of Dublin (the Ballast Board) by the Irish parliament in 1786, although with the eastern terminals of both the Grand and the Royal Canals connecting to the Liffey in the port area, the Directors General could properly have sought a role in organising the Dublin port.

The first years of the 19th century were a confused period in the history of the estuary, with many experts 'proclaiming with no little heat their various opinions'. The two bodies, however, appeared to work in harmony, with the Directors' *Representation* of 1804 agreeing with the Ballast Board proposal for a wall or pier from the Clontarf shore to the Spit Buoy, and the general development of the port remaining in the hands of the Board.

[70, 75, 282]

DIRTY LANE AT BRIDGEFOOT STREET
See BRIDGEFOOT STREET.

DIRTY LANE NEAR DAME STREET
See TEMPLE BAR.

DISSOLUTION OF RELIGIOUS HOUSES
In 1534 the English parliament of 1529–36, described as the Reformation Parliament, passed an Act of Supremacy, which declared the king (Henry VIII) to be Supreme Head of the Church of

Henry VIII, c. 1542

England. In 1536 this parliament passed an act suppressing the smaller monasteries. In 1537 or 1538 Henry extended his prerogative to include also the larger religious houses.

In 1536 the Irish parliament, again known as the Reformation Parliament, met under the lord lieutenant, Lord Grey. A bill prepared between Thomas Cromwell, English secretary of state, and the Irish Council was moved in Dublin in that year for the suppression of the Irish religious houses, and this was passed in 1537.

Notes on the implementation of this measure will be found in the entries on All Hallows Priory; St Augustine's Friary; St Mary's Abbey; St Mary de Hogges, Convent of; St Saviour's Priory; and in reference to the Priory of the Knights Hospitallers of St John of Jerusalem in the entry on the Royal Hospital, Kilmainham.

DIVELIN
See DUIBHLINN.

DOCKS, GENERAL
Entries relating to the docks connected to the Liffey will be found under the following headings: The Custom House Docks; George's Dock; Grand Canal Docks; Graving; The Inner Dock; Marney's Dock; Mercer's Dock; The New Docks; The Old Dock; Pigeonhouse Dock; Royal Canal Docks; Spencer Dock.

DOCKWRA, LORD
Sir Henry Dockwra, who fought in the Irish wars in

the reign of Elizabeth, was created Baron Dockwra of Culmore in 1621. He married and had five children, two boys and three girls, the youngest of whom, Elizabeth, married Sir Henry Brooke, governor of Donegall. They had two sons, George and Henry. Lord Dockwra died in 1631, his heir, the second baron, died unmarried, and the title became extinct.

In the 17th and 18th centuries the Dockwra estate and George Brooke became legally involved with the city authorities in actions to determine the ownership of lands at Lazars Hill.

[148]

DODDER, PROPOSED DIVERSION OF
A proposal made first in the 18th century. See RINGSEND.

DODDER, WOODEN BRIDGE PROPOSED AT MOUTH OF
In 1812 a proposal for a wooden bridge across the estuary of the Dodder from Rogerson's Quay to the end of the South Wall at Ringsend Point was favourably received by the Ballast Board. It would have had 'a portcullis for the admission of vessels into the Dodder'. Five tenders were received in 1813, and it was proposed that Thomas Colbourne, who had quoted £6,840, be awarded the contract. Due, however, to representations from the Grand Canal Company, made through its acting engineer, John Stokes, the Corporation had second thoughts about the problems which could be caused for vessels wishing to use the new Grand Canal Docks. The project was abandoned and Colbourne was compensated for the trouble he had taken.

Some years afterwards, in 1819, the Board was to state quite firmly that the interior of the mouth of the Dodder was not within its jurisdiction, but rather a matter for the attention of Lord Pembroke or the Grand Canal Company.

[87 (vols. 8, 10, 11)]

DODDER BAR
See RINGSEND.

DODDER RIVER

'Ringsend from Beggarsbush (before 1813)' (F. Danby), showing the Dodder delta

The Dodder, like the Liffey, rises on a shoulder of Kippure. Because it rises to the north of the summit plateau, it has, unlike the Liffey, a direct northern course, tumbling down to join the Liffey at Ringsend. On its course, it passes through Glenasmole, Bohernabreena, Templeogue, Rathfarnham, Milltown, Clonskeagh, Donnybrook and Ballsbridge. On some early accounts it is known as Rathfarnum water and on others Dodir, Dother and the Doney River, or the Doney Brook, Donnabrook, Donebrook or Donney Brook River. Because of its short course and mountain catchment it was, until the reservoirs were built in Glenasmole, and indeed occasionally afterwards, a fast-rising river, capable of sudden flooding and widespread destruction. The inundation of August 1986 was particularly severe. The vicissitudes of the bridges at Ringsend and Ballsbridge are mentioned elsewhere.

Boate, writing in c. 1641, records the drowning in the Dodder of 'Mr John Usher, father to Sir William Usher that now is, who was carried by the current, no body being able to succour him, although many persons, and of his nearest friends, both a-foot and horseback, were by on both the sides'. John Usher should be instead Arthur Usher. (See entry on this family.)

In the context of the Liffey, the interesting stretch of the Dodder is Ballsbridge to Ringsend.

The first representation of this area is on the de Gomme map of 1673. A comparison of this with the Phillips map of 1685, the Rocque map of 1760 and the Ordnance Survey map of 1838 suggests the following.

In 1673 the 'road to Donnybrook' started at Sandwith Street, which was the east extremity of Lazars Hill. Its route then followed Grand Canal Street, and Shelbourne Road to Ballsbridge, from where it would have run south through Herbert Park to Donnybrook. That thoroughfare as far as Bath Avenue, and including Sandwith Street, was the high-water shoreline of the tidal Liffey; and one can therefore understand the wrecking of a collier in c. 1690 in what would later be the forecourt of Sir Patrick Dun's Hospital. Roughly along the line of Bath Avenue, however, the twice-daily tidally submerged strand through which the Dodder delta passed, ended; and from there south to Ballsbridge the Dodder (and the Swan) made various channels through 'marsh ground' that was nearly 1 m higher than the strand. This marsh ground or river meadow was subject to freshwater flooding, but not generally to tidal submersion. It included such future places as the Lansdowne Road football grounds, and Havelock and Vavasour Squares. To the east of the strand and marsh, the narrow spit of Ringsend, with Irishtown at its root, lay between the Dodder delta and the South Bull.

The spit was said to be about '4 feet heigher as the marsh ground'. The 1673 map did not indicate any formal road across the strand or across the marsh. The Phillips map of 1685 adds little to the picture as presented in 1673 although it is more graphic in showing the complexity of the western edge of the Ringsend-Irishtown spit and in depicting the web of channels through which the Dodder, and the tide ebbing from the strand, may have flowed.

In 1760 Rocque shows that Sir John Rogerson's quay wall was complete and was providing a 'horse road to Ringsend', and that a road had been formed and named as 'road to Ringsend' along the line of the present South Lotts Road. Thus, Sandwith Street and Grand Canal Street were no longer at the edge of the tide. The whole expanse of former strand bounded by these four roads had been nominally taken in from the sea and was becoming known as the South Lots or Lotts. A 'foot road' now crossed this area from Ringsend to Lazars Hill. The strand containing the Dodder delta was reduced to the area between South Lotts Road, a line approximately along Bath Avenue and the Ringsend spit. The marsh between the future Bath Avenue and Ballsbridge had probably changed very little, but there was now a roadway meandering across it, generally following that part of Lansdowne Road from Shelbourne Road to New Bridge. In both the 1673 and 1760 maps the easternmost channel of the Dodder below New Bridge appeared to have flowed closer to Irishtown than the river does today.

When the Ordnance Survey published its first 6-inch map of the area in 1838, the Dodder from Ballsbridge to Ringsend had been firmly confined to a single channel, including a straight line from New Bridge to the Liffey, and the Grand Canal Docks had been built on the south bank. New streets such as Barrow Street, Cardiff's Lane and Great Clarence Street (now Macken Street) now crossed the new land north to south and Great Brunswick Street (now Ringsend Road) followed roughly the route of Rocque's 'foot road' east to west from the new Ringsend Bridge towards the city. Bath Avenue had been made, and crossed the Dodder by London Bridge, which was at first a wooden structure. The road meandering across

The confluence of the Liffey and the Dodder, from East Link Toll Bridge

the marsh had become Haigs Lane (now part of Lansdowne Road). It led to a crossing of the one remaining channel of the Dodder at the New Bridge site, where there was a weir, related probably to the nearby distillery on the site of the present Marian College. The Dublin and Kingstown railway, completed in 1834, traversed the whole original Dodder delta area from the terminus at Westland Row and Sandwith Street to a crossing of the river a little south of the New Bridge.

It seems clear that there were three land routes from Ringsend to the city in the 17th century:
(i) at low tide across a ford near Ringsend and then across the strand to Lazars Hill;
(ii) across the marsh ground quite probably along the line of Lansdowne Road or perhaps along its northern verge, that is roughly along Bath Avenue, and then into the city along Grand Canal Street, called in the past the Artichoke Road;
(iii) along the high ground of the Ringsend spit through Irishtown to the ford or bridge at Ballsbridge and so into the city through Baggot Street, passing the gallows on the way near the headquarters of the Bank of Ireland.

All these routes would have been impassable if the Dodder were in flood and the current Ballsbridge in ruins, as it often was. It was indeed partly the frequent inaccessibility of the parish church at Donnybrook to many residents of Ringsend and Irishtown that led to the creation of St Matthew's Church at Irishtown in 1706.

Travellers on the second and third of these routes had an additional hazard to face and this would persist well into the 19th century. The district between the Dodder, Bath Avenue and Northumberland Road became known as Beggarsbush, and it and the surrounding areas were notorious as a haunt for footpads and highwaymen; many voyagers out of England were 'wrecked' on this, the last lap of their journey to Dublin. The isolation and rusticity of the general district may be gauged from contemporary illustrations. See for instance 'Ringsend from Beggars Bush' by F. Danby (before 1813), 'A View of Ringsend etc.' by N. Jones (c. 1746), and 'Beggarsbush 1802', reproduced by Ball and showing what is quite possibly the New Bridge at the time. The painting by J. Campbell 'Ringsend and Irishtown from the Grand Canal Dublin' (1809), while the title may rely somewhat on artist's licence, also shows quite clearly the nature of the Beggarsbush terrain.

The embankment of the lower Dodder, carried out by William Vavasour, is noted in an entry under his name.

[15, 56, 81, maps (de Gomme 1673, Phillips 1685, Rocque 1760, OS 1838)]

DODSON, WILLIAM
See PHOENIX PARK.

DODWELL, GEORGE: PROPOSAL FOR HARBOUR
Dodwell served in the navy and later commanded a ship in the service of the East India Company. Writing to Lord Hardwicke in 1804 from 10 Dorset Street, Dublin, his proposal to overcome the difficulty of the Bar was to bypass it by making a new channel for the Liffey. He wrote, 'I struck off my line from the Pigeon-house in a direction pointing to Sandycove Bay.' His proposal included a new embankment on the South Bull, and the blocking off of the existing river channel by driving piles 'from Sutton Creek to the South Bull' (with a

floodgate for emergencies). He would then have built a fortification on the enlarged North Bull. The recently completed South Wall and the Poolbeg lighthouse would presumably have become redundant.

[BL, Add. MS 35747, ff. 183–6]

DOG AND DUCK YARD
See USHER'S QUAY.

DOLDRUM BAY
See CANDLESTICK BAY.

D'OLIER STREET
See WESTMORELAND STREET.

DOLOCHER, THE
The *Dublin Penny Journal* in its issue of 24 November 1832 described a gruesome creature in the form of a black pig that terrorised women by night for some years during the early 19th century. One incident in a lane near Wood Quay was mentioned. Fear of this creature, known as the Dolocher, led to the wholesale slaughter by groups of young men of all pigs found wandering in the streets during the hours of darkness; but the mystery was compounded, as the carcasses of the slain pigs had always vanished by the following morning.

It was noised abroad that the Dolocher was the spirit of a man who, being sentenced to death for the murder of a woman, had committed suicide in the Black Dog prison in the Cornmarket at the end of the 18th century. Eventually the mysterious creature was challenged and unmasked. It was a man who dressed in the skin of a black pig for his nocturnal activity. He had been a warder who had connived in the suicide of the prisoner, and who had then created a mystery which, properly manipulated, had led to a handsome untaxed income from pork for himself and his accomplices.

DOMINICAN SCHOOL AT USHER'S QUAY
The Dominican Order established the Priory of St Saviour in 1224 on the north bank of the Liffey on

A second pier, which lay along the landward end of the present West Pier, is shown by Mackenzie in his chart of 1776. It is possible that this was built in an attempt to prevent the silting in the harbour, which was not controllable by 'drudging' or 'dredging'.

The harbour nevertheless continued in use. The pier of 1768 was shown by Jukes in 1799 in an illustration entitled 'The Pier at Dunleary Five Miles from Dublin'. Bligh recorded it in his report of 1801. Strangely, he did not include it in his map (1800/3) although he did show on that map 'the proposed plan of a new pier' at Dunleary, which would have started from the vicinity of the present East Pier. At that time the building of an asylum harbour at Dunleary had not been mooted, although John Killaly was already working on the first project for a ship canal from a basin at Dunleary to the Liffey at the Grand Canal Docks.

In 1809 the Assembly in Dublin, distressed by the calamitous loss of the *Prince of Wales* and the *Rochdale* in 1807, proposed the construction of a pier on the south side of Dublin Bay to shelter vessels in times of storm. In 1812 a formal petition was sent to the prince regent, asking that a pier and lighthouse be built. On 20 June 1816 an act for the erection of an asylum harbour at Dunleary received the royal assent. John Rennie, FRS, was appointed as the design engineer, and eight harbour commissioners were nominated. They replaced the Ballast Board, which from 1786 had controlled the existing harbour. In 1819 the Board would be invited, nevertheless, to agree the building of the new West Pier, probably because its construction required the removal of the old pier shown by Mackenzie in 1776. It would again be consulted in 1834 about the causeway required for the possible extension of the Dublin and Kingstown railway, a work that would cut off a useful part of the existing harbour.

On 31 May 1817 the first stone in the new East Pier was laid by the lord lieutenant, the earl of Whitworth. In 1820 permission was given for the construction of the new West Pier and work began in that year. The East and West Piers would be, respectively, 1.14 km and 1.49 km in length. The new harbour would be 102 ha in area, making it the largest artificial harbour in the world at that time.

Dún Laoghaire Harbour, late 20th century

Building proceeded quickly. In 1817 a contract was let to George Smith for the supply of stone. It was quarried mainly in Dalkey quarry but also in the present People's Park and in Moran Park near the Mariners' Church. The stone from Dalkey quarry was transported to the work site in small wagons which, on descending, drew empty wagons up to the quarry, basically on an endless rope system. Grooves cut by the rope into the rock at the trackway can still be seen. The numbers working on the contract have been recorded variously as 600 and 1,000. Smith had had long experience in providing prepared stone for public works. He was by repute a hard employer, but one might offset against that the praise given him in a ballad published in 1825 entitled 'The Praises of Kingstown Harbour'. For 12 verses of 8 lines, the poet lauds 'our grand employer, brave noble Smith'. The sixth verse begins:

Kind fortune prosper our honest master
By land and sea for his contracts sure.
He's a friend and credit to the Irish nation
And a Benefactor to all the poor.

In the final verse he is exalted exceedingly; the last line reads, 'Long live brave Smith and God save the King'.

The East Pier and its lighthouse were completed in 1842, and the West Pier and lighthouse some six years later. Within the harbour two short piers were built, Carlisle Pier and Traders Wharf. Carlisle Pier, close to the East Pier, was completed in 1859, and has been in use since then as the mailboat pier. Traders Wharf was built in 1855 close to the old harbour of Dunleary, later to be known as the inner coal harbour, which lay in the south-west corner of the new Kingstown Harbour. The new wharf lies parallel to the old pier of 1755–68, with the water between them being known as the outer coal harbour; and the two coal harbours are now the fishing harbours of Dún Laoghaire.

Kingstown Harbour was deemed to be complete in 1860, and in fact no significant addition was made to it for over 100 years until St Michael's Pier, parallel to Carlisle Pier, was built in 1969. Further development to expand the use of the harbour for increased vehicle traffic and as an amenity is at present in progress, without, it is clear, unanimous popular approval.

A general and comprehensive account of the growth of Dún Laoghaire as an urban centre from the 18th century towards the present time is given by Pearson in *Dun Laoghaire Kingstown*.

[4, 19, 26, 29, 56, 87 (vols. 2, 10), 161, 165, 173, 190, 195 (Smyth); *CARD*, XVI; *DHR* (Murray); *Dún Laoghaire* (Dept of Marine, *c.* 1990); *Saunders Newsletter*, 26 June 1816; BL, *A Book of Ballads* (1825), 11622.6.43 (15); maps (Greenvile Collins 1686, Price 1730, Rocque 1760, Scalé and Richards 1765, Mackenzie 1776, Bligh 1800/3)]

DUNCAN'S MAP

A map of the county of Dublin to a scale of approximately 1:44,100 which was made in 1821, probably for military use, by William Duncan, principal draftsman to the Quartermaster General's Department in Ireland. It is possibly the best map made of the city, harbour and bay before the Ordnance Survey.

It is of particular interest in showing the new harbour at Dún Laoghaire completed, although the battery had not then been built on the east pier; and it shows the coastline from Merrion Gates to Dún Laoghaire before the railway was built in 1834. It emphasises the emptiness of the Liffey estuary by linking Poolbeg lighthouse with Shalloway's Baths as a navigational bearing; and it pinpoints three wrecks on the North Bull. It indicates the extension of the title of South Lotts to a far larger area than originally was the case; and it names the river as the Anna Liffey.

DUNLEARY, PROPOSED SHIP CANALS AT

See SHIP CANALS PROPOSED AT DUNLEARY AND SANDYCOVE.

DUVENOLBROC

Donnybrook.

DYFLINNARSKIRI

The Norse kingdom centred on Dublin that extended in the tenth century along the coast from Skerries to Wicklow or Arklow and inland from the sea along and around the Liffey valley to Leixlip. This territory has been known also as Dublinshire. [150]

E

EAST LINK TOLL BRIDGE

East Link Toll Bridge

Traffic studies made in Dublin during the decade from 1960 to 1970 identified the need for a major Liffey bridge east of the city. In partial response to this, Talbot Memorial Bridge would be opened to traffic in 1978. In 1976, however, the Dublin industrialist Tom Roche saw a role for another bridge well downstream in the port area. He proposed that it should be a toll bridge. In 1979 the government stated that it would be prepared to consider toll schemes generally, and expressed its hope 'that the private sector will respond to this opportunity to participate in the development of the country's road system'. Against this background, Roche was given permission in 1982 to build a bridge from near the end of Thorncastle Street in Ringsend to the junction of North Wall Quay and East Wall Road, on the condition that access was maintained for shipping to the river quays. This was to be the third toll bridge in the history of the city.

The construction of the East Link Toll Bridge began in April 1983 and the bridge was opened to public use on 21 October 1984.

The bridge has four fixed prestressed concrete spans and one opening steel span. It has a clear length of 210 m between the walls of the river, and its width between parapets is 10.5 m. The clear width of the navigation channel at the opening span is 33 m. The structure at this span is a single-leaf cantilever bascule with a total weight, including the counterweighting elements, of 500 tonnes. The Scherzer principle is employed, and under normal climatic conditions the deck can be raised in under one minute, with the estimated time for suspension of traffic to permit the passage of a single vessel being three and a half minutes.

By February 1985 1,000,000 vehicles had passed over the bridge, and since then the maximum weekly number of crossings that has been attained is 137,000 vehicles. The highest intensity of use occurred on the occasion of a taxi strike in Dublin in August 1992 when over 25,000 vehicles crossed the bridge in one day.

The designers of the bridge were McCarthy and Partners, and the main contractors were Irishenco Limited. The Dorman Long Bridge and Engineering Company collaborated in the mechanical design of the opening span.

The maximum depth of water under the bridge (HWOST) is approximately 11 m; and a tunnel under the river, completed by Dublin Corporation in 1928, passes under the main pier of the bridge at a depth of about 32 m below the deck.

The existing Pigeonhouse Road and York Road on the south side of the river could not accommodate the bridge traffic, so a new road, named the Southern Approach Road, was constructed to connect the bridge to South Link Road. This road was built on new ground taken in from the tideway of the river. Because of this reclamation, the earlier South Wall ceased to be a river wall in that vicinity, and the flight of steps with two landings known as Cromwell's Steps, leading through the wall down to the strand a little way east of the end of Cambridge Road, was buried.

[90 (vol. 110: McMahon and Faherty), private communication (C. Blair)]

EAST QUAY
See THE NORTH WALL.

EAST ROAD
See THE EAST WALL, and note two different applications of this name.

EAST WALL, THE

The programme of new land formation on the north shore of the Liffey east of O'Connell Bridge that was carried out by the Corporation in the first half of the 18th century is described in the entries on the North Wall and the North Lotts. The enclosing wall extended downriver to a point opposite Ringsend and that section was named the North Wall. It then turned first north, then north-east, and then north-west at the Bathing Wharf to finish below Ballybough Bridge (now Luke Kelly Bridge). These three sections were called, in general terms, the East Wall. The road which follows their line is now called East Wall Road (Port and Docks Board map, 1987) and the contained precinct, particularly the area north of Sheriff Street, is often described today as East Wall.

The first map to show the completed wall is the Rocque survey of the County of Dublin (1760). It shows a road along the whole length of the wall from the North Strand to the North Wall, and names the first two sections as East Quay, leaving the third, north-west section unnamed. In 1838 the OS map named the whole of this road along the wall as East Road. In 1909 it was known also as Wharf Road, probably because it passed by the Bathing Wharf.

As early as 1760 the three roads running north-east across the East Wall precinct to join modern East Wall Road had been named as West Road, Church Road and East Road (a second application of that name). These names are still in use, although West Road has been divided into two parts by 19th-century railway works.

[31, maps (Rocque 1760, OS 1838, Dublin Port and Docks Board 1987)]

EAST WALL ROAD

See THE EAST WALL.

EDEN GARDENS

Rocque shows that in 1756 the North Strand, as a newly developing road, ran in nearly a straight line from, to use modern names, Abbey Street Old to the junction of Store Street and Amiens Street. In this stretch, it had underdeveloped slob land to its south and four streets joining it from the north. These streets were:
(i) an unnamed lane which was called Eden Gardens on map 241 prepared for the Wide Streets Commissioners in 1792
(ii) Mabbot Street, now Corporation Street
(iii) Cazer's Lane
(iv) Lime Street, which would later become part of Gardiner Street, connecting the North Strand to Frenchman's Lane.
Cazer's Lane and Eden Gardens disappeared in the development of Beresford Place.

[Dublin Corporation Archives (WSC map 241), map (Rocque 1756)]

EDEN QUAY

In 1782 it was possible to take a wheeled vehicle along the quays on the north bank of the Liffey from John's Street near Rory O'More Bridge to the present Abbey Theatre, and similarly to travel westwards from the end of the North Wall, opposite Ringsend, to the present Liberty Hall. However, to pass from Liberty Hall to the Abbey Theatre, it was necessary to go north on to Abbey Street and then south again to the east end of Bachelors Walk. The intervening river-bank consisted of the Iron Quay and some yards and buildings owned by the city.

In that year the Irish parliament approved development plans, promoted by John Beresford, to build a bridge across the river, the future Carlisle Bridge, and generally to open up the north bank street system around that bridge. In the previous year of 1781 the foundation-stone had been laid for another Beresford promotion, the new Custom House, which would be substantially complete in 1791. In 1795 Carlisle Bridge (now O'Connell) was opened for normal traffic.

In 1802 the Wide Streets Commissioners advised the Ballast Board that they proposed to extend the north quays eastward towards the Custom House from the end of Bachelors Walk. In 1814 the Ballast Board reported that the new lengths of wall and parapet needed to complete the extension of the quay had been built. The name of the new quay, which now began at Carlisle

In 1684 the city received a petition criticising the inadequacy of the Blind Quay as a commercial thoroughfare and urging that inconvenience might be prevented 'by a very commodious way that might be made on the north side of the building on the Blind Quay from Essex Bridge to the Wood Key, by takeinge downe some part of the encroachments there, and adding but ten or twelve foot to the same out of the river'. Later that year Sir William Sands offered to build this quay, provided he might have 'the benefits of the vaults to be under the said key and encroachments upon the river'. The city turned down this offer and recommended instead that the work be done collectively by the tenants of properties on the Blind Quay having a frontage to the river, with the tenants to make a quay 30 feet wide and to have the benefit of the vaults and cellars beneath it. The tenants were clearly unenthusiastic, and ten years later, in 1694, the city authorities decided to organise the work themselves. A river wall was to be 'continued and built from the Wood Key to Essex Bridge and filled up and paved' by the lord mayor and citizens. 'All incroachments that stood in the way or should hinder the finishing of the said quay [were] to be taken down and removed as nuisances.'

As late as 1726 the city was still urging that this new quay should be, now, 25 feet wide, and Brooking would suggest in 1728 that it was substantially complete and in use.

William Mossop, senior (1751–1804), the internationally known medallist, lived at 13 Essex Quay; and in 1850 the quay had become a centre for engravers, watchmakers, jewellers and gilders, with 18 of the 32 houses along it being occupied by craftsmen in these trades.

[146, *CARD*, I, V, VI, maps (Speed 1610, Phillips 1685, Brooking 1728)]

ESSEX STREET

See ESSEX GATE.

EUCHARISTIC CONGRESS, 1932

The 31st International Eucharistic Congress was held in Dublin in 1932 from Wednesday to Sunday,

Final benediction of Eucharistic Congress on O'Connell Bridge, 1932

22 to 26 June. Large numbers gathered from many parts of the world.

Seven ocean liners moored in the port basins and along Sir John Rogerson's Quay. These were *De Grasse, Doric, Dresden, Duchess of Bedford, Marnix van Sint Aldegonde, Rio Bravo* and *Sierra Cordoba*. Five others, *Antonia, Laconia, Lapland, Samaria* and *Saturnia*, anchored in or near Scotsman's Bay. The liners ranged in gross tonnage from about 6,000 to 24,000 tons, and they provided floating hotel accommodation for their passengers during their stay, with the numbers ranging from about 130 on *Lapland* to 1,500 on *Saturnia*.

The final public mass of the Congress was held in Phoenix Park at 1 p.m. on Sunday, and was celebrated by Dr Curley, archbishop of Baltimore. It was attended by roughly one in every four of the population of Ireland, with 127 special trains bringing members of the congregation from every part of the country. After the mass, four processions left the Park to bring approximately 500,000 people together around O'Connell Bridge, where the concluding benediction of the Congress was given at 6.30 p.m. by the papal legate, Cardinal Lorenzo Lauri. The processional routes were by Thomas Street and Dame Street, along the south quays of the Liffey, along the north quays, and by North Circular Road and O'Connell Street.

G.K. Chesterton, who was present, observed later that 'there flashed through my mind as the illimitable multitude began to melt away towards the gates and roads and bridges the instantaneous thought "This is Democracy"'; and he commented that it was quite certain that the 'General Will' of a population 'walked about the streets of Dublin for a week' at that time.

On the following day, at a ceremony in the Mansion House, the title of honorary freeman of the cities of Dublin and Kilkenny was conferred on Cardinal Lauri.

[129, 237, *Irish Independent*, 23–8 June 1932]

EXCHANGE, PROPOSED

See WOOD QUAY.

EXCHANGE STREET

See BLIND QUAY.

F

FACTION-FIGHTING

John Edward Walsh (1816–69), attorney-general for Ireland, wrote in 1847 about life in Dublin in the late 18th century. He described, from the memories of witnesses, fighting that could break out between rival gangs, the Liberty Boys, whose leaders were tailors and weavers from the Coombe, and the Ormond Boys, who were led by butchers from the Ormonde Market. The boundary between their territories was the Liffey, and conflict could rage all along the quays from Essex Bridge to Island Bridge. The bridges would be taken and retaken, and defenders could be driven back as far as Thomas Street or the Broadstone before rallying.

Battles could last for a day or more, and one observer reported seeing over 1,000 men milling around Essex Bridge. The rules of engagement were probably few, but some did exist, for Walsh describes that on a Saturday in May 1790 there was fighting all day along Ormonde Quay, which, as the issue had not been resolved by nightfall, was then suspended, for resumption on the following Monday morning.

[116]

FADEN'S MAP

On 2 January 1797 a map entitled 'A plan of the city of Dublin as surveyed for the use of the Divisional Justices to which have been added plans of the canal harbour and its junction with the Grand Canal and the Royal Canal and every projection and alteration to the present time, 1797' was published in London by W. Faden at Charing Cross.

Made to a scale of about 1:7,500, it includes the River Liffey from Island Bridge to Ringsend. The new Custom House and the adjacent Old Dock and Beresford Place are shown, as are the 'New Courts and Offices' at 'Kings Inn Quay'. The map is in error in showing a continuous quay from Aston Quay to George's Quay and, by modern usage, in naming the east end of Rogerson's Quay as the South Wall. It is of interest in naming Sandwith Street as The Folly, and modern Hogan Place and Grand Canal Street west of the canal as Artichoke Road.

FAGAN'S ORCHARD

Fagan's orchard, which is mentioned in Jacob Newman's land reclamation lease of 1606, appears to have lain close to the high-tide shoreline near the junction of modern Essex Street and Sycamore Street.

[CARD, II]

FAIRVIEW STRAND

Before Annesley Bridge and Annesley Bridge Road – which connects it to Fairview – were built in 1792–7, the River Tolka flowed through Ballybough Bridge (now Luke Kelly Bridge) and at once widened into a tidal estuary. The road along the high-tide shoreline immediately to the east of Ballybough Bridge was named as Phillipsburg Strand (OS 1838) and later as Fairview Strand.

When the Tolka became confined to a walled channel between the two bridges, the area between this channel and Fairview Strand was filled in and two residential roads, Addison Road and Cadogan Road, were built on the new ground. Fairview Strand, which contains the old Jewish cemetery, the Catholic Church of the Visitation and the junction of Phillipsburgh Avenue, then ceased to be at the water's edge. It has, however, retained the name of Fairview Strand. The junction of Fairview Strand and Annesley Bridge Road marks the west end of the road named Fairview.

See also Annesley Bridge.

[Maps (various)]

FR MATHEW BRIDGE

The bridge that crosses the Liffey from Church Street to Bridge Street is now formally called Fr Mathew Bridge. It and its three predecessors

Fr Mathew Bridge

have shared 15 names in the last 1,000 years. In its earliest form it was known as Droichet Dubhgaill, Danes Bridge, Ostmans Bridge and Black Danes Bridge. In the 13th and 14th centuries the name of King John's Bridge was added. Also at that time or from then until the early 19th century it was the Bridge of Dublin or Dublin Bridge, Great Bridge, Old Bridge, Friars Bridge, and more simply the Bridge or the Brydge. From 1816 to the present time it has been Whitworth Bridge, or more recently Dublin Bridge, and it is now Fr Mathew Bridge. It will always tend to be known locally as Church Street Bridge.

It is probable that by the year 1000 a bridge, almost certainly a wooden bridge, existed across the Liffey beside the quite inefficient Áth Cliath. In 1014, in the closing hours of the battle of Clontarf, it is recorded that 'the household of Tiege OKelly followed these [nine Dublin Norsemen] and slew them at the head of the bridge of Áth Cliath, that is Dubhghall's bridge'. O'Donovan's suggestion that the Droichet Dubhgaill was over the River Tolka should not be overlooked, but the probability of the location being beside Áth Cliath is strong.

In 1214 John granted 'to the citizens permission to make a bridge beyond the water of Avenlith, wherever they consider may be most convenient for the use of the city; and that they may, if advisable, cause the bridge previously constructed to be destroyed'. It is not clear when the citizens

built their bridge, or when they destroyed the earlier one. A wooden bridge existing in 1000 would have had to be repaired frequently, to the extent of being largely rebuilt more than once during the ensuing 200 years, and would have been ripe for replacement in 1214.

Several records of the 13th century mention a bridge as existing, substantially on the site of the present Fr Mathew Bridge; and one can argue strongly that it was a new bridge rather than one developed from the earlier pre-1214 construction.

Already in 1240 a tower had been granted to Randulf le Hore 'At the south end of the Ostmans Bridge'. From then on there are references to buildings and a fortified bridge gate being made at that south end, while in 1307 it is recorded that there were shops and other buildings on the bridge. What structural form this bridge took is a matter for conjecture, but it can be suggested that in accordance with practice elsewhere, it may have been a structure of about twelve 5-metre spans with stone piers and a wooden deck.

Related entries for this period include Edward Bruce, John and Alice de Grauntsete, Little John his Shot, Ostmans Gate, St Mary on the Bridge and St Saviour's Priory.

In 1385 the bridge was destroyed by floodwater, and it was not replaced for 40 years. After the collapse, Richard II gave permission for the tolls of the ferry to be applied to the making of a new bridge. In 1428 this bridge was completed at the particular entreaty of the Dominicans of St Saviour's, and with their support, and under the supervision of a committee headed by the abbot of St Mary's Abbey; and a toll, formal or informal, was taken from users for some time afterwards.

The new bridge, of four unequal stone arched spans, would be kept in service for nearly 400 years and was always heavily used (it was the only bridge across the Liffey in the city until 1670). During the late 16th century and the early 17th, it was falling into disrepair. In 1603 two of its arches were described as 'ruynated and decaied', and the wooden piles, whose function must have been the protection of the stone piers, were in urgent need of replacement. Between 1640 and 1660 the city was twice fined for its failure to repair the bridge, and in 1666 the civic authorities appealed to the 'honour of this antient citty' to carry out the necessary repair works.

In 1717 permission was given to a William Oakley to build a house on the south end span arch; and it emerges from the reports of the Wide Streets Commissioners and from Rocque's map (1756) that by the middle of the 18th century both ends of the bridge were encrusted with houses either on or beside the bridge proper.

Related entries for the period from 1428 to 1816 include The Sundial on the Bridge.

At the beginning of the 19th century the old bridge was approaching the end of its useful life. It was judged in 1805 to be a 'crazy dirty wretched pile of antiquity'. In 1814, however, it was still being deemed to be safe, although those who had given this opinion, namely Francis Johnston, architect, George Halpin, as an engineer, and George Knowles, builder, did say that

> to do away any apprehension of danger and enable the heaviest loads to pass in perfect safety, we recommended that long timber be laid over [the north arch], the ends to rest on the quay and first pier, the timber to be covered with earth and then paved over, this will afford a safe passage should the arch ever fall in or be taken away.

Shortly before then Knowles had, in 1812, begun the construction of the three-span Richmond Bridge at the foot of Winetavern Street

to a design by James Savage, and in 1815, in the face of the clearly increasing deterioration of the bridge at Church Street, he was invited to tender for a bridge there to replace it. The new structure was to be generally similar to Richmond Bridge. His offer of the same price as for Richmond Bridge was accepted; and he commenced work in 1816, the bridge being completed and opened to traffic in 1818, under the name of Whitworth Bridge.

Some years earlier the Old Bridge had been seen as being 'devoid of any architectural embellishment'. However, in 1796 the new Four Courts building had been largely completed and there was a civic policy for the general visual enrichment of its setting. For this reason, the parapets of both of Savage's bridges and the linking Inns Quay were balustraded, the materials used being painted cast iron for the balusters, and granite for the plinths and coping.

The 1818 bridge was named in honour of Earl Whitworth, who was lord lieutenant from 1813 to 1817. On 2 January 1922 the civic authorities decided to change the name to Dublin Bridge, but in 1938 it was again changed to become the Fr Mathew Bridge. An inscription on the bridge in Irish and English reads as follows:

Fr Theobald Mathew, OFM Cap. (1790–1856) (detail from painting by J. Haverty)

DROICEAD AN ATAR MAITIÚ
MAR CUIMNE AR TÚIS ASBOLACT AN ATAR
TIOBÓLD MAITIÚ
OM CAP. IN AGAID AN ÓLOCÁIN CÉAD
BLIADAIN Ó SOIN.
IS EAD TUGAD AT-AINM AR AN DROICEAD SO
1838 + 1938

FATHER MATHEW BRIDGE
+
THIS BRIDGE HAS BEEN RENAMED
TO COMMEMORATE THE
INAUGURATION 100 YEARS AGO
OF THE APOSTOLATE OF TEMPERANCE
BY FATHER THEOBALD MATHEW OM CAP.
1838 + 1938
[6, 18, 22, 82, 87, 106, 120, 133, 181, *CARD*, I–IV, VII, XII,
map (Rocque 1756)]

FEINAGLIAN INSTITUTION

See ALDBOROUGH HOUSE.

FERRIES ACROSS THE LIFFEY

*The last day of the public ferry system, 20 October
1984, showing also a ticket for the crossing*

It is reasonable to assume that ferry-boats first
plied for hire on the Liffey in Dublin over 1,000
years ago.

In 1385 the Great Bridge of Dublin (now Fr
Mathew) fell down, and Richard II granted 'to the
mayor, bailiffs and citizens for four years the city

ferry over the Liffey' with permission to take a toll
of a farthing from each person carried. The profits
were to be used in rebuilding the bridge. This
appears to be the first formal reference to a ferry in
Dublin, although the wording could imply that an
official ferry was already known. The bridge was
reconstructed and in use again in 1428, but it
seems probable that a ferry continued in operation
under the control of the city, perhaps near the
future Bloody Bridge (now Rory O'More) at
Watling Street.

After a silence of nearly 200 years, the City
Assembly decided in 1624 that Richard Golburne
'shall alone be licenced to keep a ferrie dureing his
naturall life on the river of Annaliffe'. This
prerogative passed to his widow, Elizabeth, in
1629, and to Thomas Dongan in 1632, with the
condition that he was not to charge more than a
halfpenny for each person crossing.

By now, the city apparently regarded the ferry as
an ancient right, and the Assembly protested in
c. 1633 when Lord Deputy Wentworth, on his own
authority and acting on behalf of Charles I, granted
the ferry over the head of the Assembly to 'one
Amby'. A case was immediately threatened by the
Assembly for trial of its title by common law 'if his
lordship shall deny to settle the citty in theire
antient possession'. Obviously the issue became
clouded, for in 1641 the city granted the lease of
the ferry to Alderman Charles Foster, provided
that he recovered 'the said ferry for the citties use
from such person or persons as detaine the same
from the said cittie'.

Larger events resolved this problem. Cromwell
came, and in 1652 the city was able to grant 'the
ferries over the Liffey' to Nathaniel Fowkes, a
member of the Guild of Tailors and captain of the
city militia, for the term of his natural life. Fowkes
was to provide a boat.

In March 1665 Charles II wrote to the City
Assembly, thanking it on his own and on his
father's behalf for its services over many years and
promising it gifts, including the right to the ferry.
In May of that year he confirmed his gift, decreeing
that as

it is very expedient and necessary for the common
good and utility of our subjects . . . of Dublin, and the

suburbs of the same, and that it will always conduce much to the safety of the public and the security of our said city that the ferry over the river of Annaliffy should be committed to the charge and oversight of the mayor sheriffs commons and citizens, [he granted] unto the mayor . . . for ever the said ferry or passage over the river of Annaliffy, together with free liberty and privilege of transporting carrying and recarrying all manner of passengers over the said water . . . with the fee of a halfpenny or less if less hath been accustomed to be taken . . . together with free liberty and power to provide and erect one or more ferryboat or ferryboats [and he ordered] that the said mayor . . . or his servants, from sun-rising and an hour before and until sun-setting and an hour after, give due attendance upon the execution of the said office with sufficient boats and other things necessary [and] that no other person . . . shall at any time hereafter erect . . . any ferryboat . . . or carry over any person or persons whatsoever for gain or hire over the said river Annaliffy at any place or places between the bridge of Dublin and the Ring's End, other than the said mayor . . . or such person authorised under them.

Following this, Nathaniel Fowkes, in 1668, surrendered his lease of 1652, and in 1669, now an alderman, was granted a lease for 96 years for 'the ferry or passadge over the River Annaliffy . . . from the Old Bridge to the Ring's End', all in accordance with the king's charter. The condition governing the daily duration of the service would remain in place right through to the 20th century.

Fowkes's selection would seem to have been resented, perhaps by unsuccessful competitors for the monopoly, for already in 1669 he was seeking the support of the Assembly for legal action against harassment because his boats were being 'dayly stopt and interrupted by Mr Mabbott and colonel Carey Dillon and others'. He survived, however, and is recorded as continuing in his lease in 1694.

Rocque (1756) was the first mapmaker to show the locations of the ferries. He described the ferry from Hawkins's Wall to Ferryboat Lane as the Old Ferry. A ferry at this crossing is mentioned in the Amory lease of 1675, and this was possibly the only ferry being operated by Fowkes at that time. It is unclear whether another ferry, said to have been located near Watling Street before Bloody Bridge (Rory O'More) was built in 1670, and perhaps the inheritor of Richard's grant of 1385, was the one

that featured in the legal altercations of 1633–41. It did of course lie upstream of the Old Bridge and so would not have been covered by Charles's charter or by Fowkes's lease of 1669.

Two names, Singleton and Jones, are predominant in the ferry leases of the 18th century. It is not known why Fowkes surrendered his lease, but in 1707 Michael Hamcock or Hancock was named as lessee in his place. His lease was for the Old Ferry and lasted less than one year. In 1708 Thomas Singleton was granted a lease, specifically for the Old Ferry, and held it until 1729. The city was then expanding quickly downriver from Essex Bridge, and the Assembly found it timely to offer a comprehensive lease for all city ferries existing or likely to come into use. A committee was appointed in 1729 'to set up at cant . . . the liberty to ferry persons, horses, cattle, goods and carriages on the river Anna Liffey from the end of Dirty Lane to Ringsend Point'. The successful bidder was to 'procure slips and landing places as he shall think necessary'. This lease appears to have given the lessee the power to erect new ferries if he saw fit. However, the only ferry existing across the lower river at the time was the Old Ferry, and, as it later transpired, it was effectively the rights to this single ferry that were let in 1729. The new lessee was John Jones and he in turn demised it to his son John in 1745.

In 1756 Rocque showed four ferries on the lower river, the Old Ferry from Ferryboat Lane at the east end of Bachelors Walk to Hawkins Street, and new crossings from terminals on the south bank at Porter's Row (now Bedford Row), the Bagnio Slip (now Lower Fownes Street), and Temple Lane (or Dirty Lane), now buried under Wellington Quay. It is not known when these three ferries started operating. John Jones, junior, formally became lessee of the Dirty Lane ferry in 1753. In 1762 two other names, Tuke and Breadin, appear as ferry operators.

In 1768 Jones obtained a lease or leases for 31 years for the 'ferry or passage . . . from the end of Dirty Lane inclusive to Rings End point', including specifically 'the ferrys at Dirty Lane Slip and Crampton Quay opposite Bedford Row'. There were to be 'two or more good substantial and staunch boats' at each ferry, and he was to provide 'two able and sufficient men for the manning of each boat and a sufficient number of lights at each ferry with an additional man to trim the lights'. He was to maintain all existing slips and to erect and maintain any new slips needed. He was not to demand 'more than one penny for every horse' and he was to have a monopoly from Dirty Lane to Ringsend. Jones's lease of 1768, although it is to some degree overwritten, was to be the model for future lettings. The same formula was used when the lease of the ferries was given to John Claudius Beresford and William Walsh in 1800, and again in 1814 when William Walsh became the sole lessee.

Walsh and his legal successors were to dominate the 19th-century ferry system. In 1815 the city agreed to Walsh replacing the ferry at the Bagnio Slip with the Halfpenny Bridge. In 1818 he surrendered his lease of 1814 and was given a new lease for 70 years that embraced both his taking tolls from the bridge and his monopoly of the river ferries. In 1835 he was granted a new lease that extended his entitlement to the bridge and river tolls until September 1916. The terms of the 1835 lease revealed that all of the ferries above Carlisle Bridge (now O'Connell) had been discontinued, but before 1837 Walsh had established two new ferries downstream, one at the Old Dock east of the Custom House and one linking Creighton Street and Commons Street. It is not precisely clear when the Old Ferry stopped working, but there is evidence to suggest that it was in 1814.

Walsh was still restricted to charging not more than one halfpenny per foot passenger; and, surprisingly, the 1835 lease required him to accept a halfpenny for 'every horse that shall be ferried over or across the said river or for permitting pass over the said bridge during the said term'. In all other ferry leases the permitted toll for a horse was a penny.

The main ferry system developed downstream during the century, away from the bridges; and with the expansion of industry along the lower quays, it became overloaded. In 1881 a report prepared for the Corporation dealt with complaints that were being made about the service. The timber merchants Messrs Martin and other employers on the quays wrote that the boats, which were still rowing-boats, could be dangerously overcrowded, often with 30 people aboard on dark winter nights. 'In winter the evening boat is rarely provided with a light, nor have the steps a lamp, and as they are covered with slime from the river, people frequently slip and fall in.' The report listed the five ferries then operating in the lower river. They were:

(i) 14 City Quay to Transit Shed at east side of Custom House dock,

(ii) Creighton Street to Commons Street,

(iii) 29 Rogerson's Quay near Cardiff's Lane to west side of Royal Canal,

(iv) Messrs Kurtz, coal tar distillers between Forbes Street and Benson Street, to near Wapping Street,

(v) east point of Rogerson's Quay or Ringsend Point to Messrs Martin's sawmills.

Messrs Kurtz and Company were operating at 73 Rogerson's Quay as Keightley, Kurtz and Company, manufacturing chemists, in 1856, and from 1866 to 1887, at the same address, as Charles Kurtz and Company. Charles's daughter, Lucy Cometina, married Douglas Hyde (1860–1949), later president of Ireland, in 1893, and died at the age of 78 in 1938, shortly after his inauguration to the presidency. Their graves are at Frenchpark in County Roscommon.

Shortly before the 1881 report, in 1878, the Walsh interest in the ferries and the Halfpenny Bridge had ceased, and in 1887 the franchise was in the hands of John Shanks, Alfred Killingley and Earnest (sic) William Harris. The 1881 routes continued in service during the 20th century, with engines replacing oars. The Creighton Street, Cardiff's Lane and Ringsend ferries were still being shown on the OS map of 1954.

On 21 October 1984 the East Link Toll Bridge was opened. On the previous day the last ferry on the river, from the east point of Rogerson's Quay to a landing near the end of East Wall Road, made its final journey, and brought to an end the long history of the city ferries. The fare was 10 new pence, nearly 100 times the rate in 1385.

Six other ferries on the Liffey in Dublin should be mentioned.

fish market for the city was transferred to the Ormonde Market north of the river.

[18, *CARD*, I]

FISH STREET (NORTH BANK)

See CASTLE FORBES ROAD and NORTH LOTTS.

FISH STREET (SOUTH BANK)

See FISHAMBLE STREET.

FISHAMBLE STREET

Fishamble Street, which joins Wood Quay at the Fish Slip near Fyan's Castle, was almost certainly a public thoroughfare in the tenth century. It is mentioned in the 14th century as Vicus Piscariorum and as Fish Street. It has also been named by Stanihurst in 1577 as St John's Street. The northern end of the street, where it is joined by Blind Quay, has been named as St Tullock's Lane, near which the church of St Tullock or St Olaf was said to have stood. The southern end has been named as Bothe Street, perhaps signifying a street with booths or stalls where fish was sold.

Fishamble Street, which some editions of Speed's map of 1610 call simply the Fish Shambles, remained as the official fish market for Dublin until the end of the 17th century when the city markets generally were removed to the north bank of the Liffey. The street, which was close to the centre of city activity and already an agreeable place to live, then came to be used for other purposes.

The General Post Office was located in Fishamble Street for some 30 years from *c.* 1680. A tavern on the street, the 'Bull's Head', was much in demand during the 18th century for anniversary dinners of the city guilds and other bodies, and provided accommodation for assemblies of the Grand Lodge of Irish Freemasons; and it was the Bull's Head Musical Society that undertook the building of the Music Hall, now so closely associated with Handel's *Messiah*.

This hall, 'executed under the superintendence of Richard Cassels' (*c.* 1690–1751), was formally opened in 1741, and it was here that Handel conducted *Messiah* on 13 April 1742 before an audience of more than 700. He had come to Ireland in November 1741 and remained until

August 1742. During his stay he lived in Abbey Street and gave numerous performances in the Music Hall. The hall continued in constant use throughout the 18th century for concerts, balls, debates, and professional and amateur dramatic productions. Its popularity declined in the 19th century, this being due in part to the change in pattern of Dublin society after the Act of Union.

If it be remembered that the ancient street, comprising Bothe Street, Fishamble Street and St Tullock's Lane, extended from Castle Street to Wood Quay, then the S-bend midway along that street is of interest. It has been proposed that the crookedness of the street may reflect a line of defence for the earliest Norse settlement around the future Dublin Castle, but the possibility should not be overlooked that the S-bend may also represent an ancient concession to the steepness of the direct gradient from the ridge to the shore of the Liffey, and the profile of the original spur or bluff between the Poddle mouth and Christchurch Bay.

[18, 29, 99, 305, *CARD*, II]

FITZGERALD, LORD EDWARD

Lord Edward Fitzgerald (H.D. Hamilton)

Born in 1763, Lord Edward was the twelfth child of the first duke of Leinster. He joined the Sussex militia in 1779, and saw service and was wounded in the American War of Independence. He became member for Athy in the Irish parliament in the 1780s, and after a short time spent in Canada was elected as MP for Kildare.

In 1792 he visited Paris, where he met and married Pamela, a ward of Madame de Genlis. His enthusiasm for the ideals of revolutionary France led to his being cashiered from the English army for supporting the abolition of hereditary titles. On his return to Ireland he did not seek a seat in parliament as he saw little hope for reform through parliamentary action. In 1796 he became a United Irishman and he quickly rose to leadership in Leinster. A price was put on his head by Dublin Castle and, after an encounter in Watling Street, he was captured in the house of a supporter, Mr Murphy, a dealer in feathers, in Thomas Street. The search-party was led by Major Sirr, and included Major Swann and Captain Ryan. In the attack, Lord Edward was wounded in the shoulder by gunshot, and he wounded Swann and mortally wounded Ryan. He was removed to Newgate Prison, where he died from his wounds on 4 June 1798.

A comrade in the United Irishmen, Charles Teeling, wrote in 1828 of Lord Edward 'sacrificing in this pursuit all the prospects to which rank, fortune, and an illustrious line of ancestry opened the way, he sought only in the ranks of his country that distinction which his talents and virtues could not fail to attain'.

[54, 190, 283, 284]

FITZGERALD, THOMAS (SILKEN THOMAS)

Thomas Fitzgerald, Lord Offaly, tenth earl of Kildare, was born in 1513. He was appointed deputy governor of Ireland by his father, the ninth earl, governor of Ireland, in February 1534. On receiving a report in June that his father had been killed in the Tower of London, he summoned the Council of State for Ireland to a meeting in the Chapter House of St Mary's Abbey on 11 June, and there he formally renounced his allegiance to England. Whether he forthwith led a troop of horsemen across a ford of the Liffey to attack the Castle, as has been conjectured, seems unlikely.

In July he led an army to besiege and capture Dublin, but was repulsed. Henry VIII would in 1539

acknowledge, with a material gesture of gratitude, 'the great services, labours, famines, watchings, effusions of blood, cruel wounds, and lamentable slaughter which his faithful subjects in Dublin had undergone in strenuously and bravely defending the city against the traitorous siege and cruel attacks of Thomas Fitzgerald, his relatives and accomplices'.

From Maynooth and his other bases in Kildare, Silken Thomas fought against the Crown army, led by Sir William Skeffington, whom Henry sent to Ireland in late 1534, not eventually capitulating until October 1535, when, following negotiations with Lord Leonard Grey, who had come to Dublin as marshal of Ireland in July of that year, he surrendered his person to the king. He was later confined in the Tower of London and hanged at Tyburn in 1537.

Incidents of his rebellion include the assassination of Archbishop Alen, who had attempted to flee Dublin by boat down the river, and skirmishes at the Ballybough bridge and at a Liffey crossing at the narrow bridge at Kilmainham.

[36, 181, *CARD*, I, *DHR* (Mac Giolla Phádraig)]

FITZSYMON'S TOWER

This tower was leased to Robert FitzSymon in 1471. It was in ruinous condition and may have been first built in the 13th century. Perrot's survey of 1585 describes it as a small tower of 'Fitzsymon of Balmadroght' 43 m east of Fyan's Castle. It was 'a smale round towre withowte and square within, one timber lofte, with towe rowmes, 12 foot square one waye, and 14 foote the other waye, the walls 3 foott thick and 22 foot hie and the earthe hie within the said towre 8 foote as befor'. It is not clear whether each room was 12 x 14 or whether, as seems more likely, this was the combined size of the two rooms. Nor is it clear what height the tower was above its ground floor. It may be suggested, however, that the combined height of the rooms and the loft over them was 14 feet and that the ground floor stood 8 feet above the level of the river-bed at the face of the adjacent quay. This matter is discussed generally in the entry on Newman's Tower.

Early in the 17th century Fitzsymon's Tower became known as Case's Tower (1604) and Casses

Tower (1605). Later, the name of Casey's Tower was used. Under this name it was described in 1726 as a ruin with its south side facing on to the Blind Quay and projecting out of the building line in that street, and with the north side of the plot containing it bounded by Essex Quay. At the time, permission was given for it to be rebuilt 'on a range with the other buildings on the Blind Quay'. In that position in 1742 it had as its two closest neighbours to the west the taverns of the Sign of the Three Tuns and the Mermaid (or Mairmaid).

Harris identifies Case's Tower with the 'Baker's Tower' in his history of 1766. In support of this, Gilbert records that, following the sale of Casey's Tower as a forfeited estate in 1701, 'it afterwards became the Hall of the Guild of Bakers, thence acquiring the name of the Bakers Tower'. Gilbert notes that this tower was demolished in *c.* 1753.

[16, 18, 150, *CARD*, II, VII, IX, *DHR* (KM)]

FITZWILLIAM OF MERRION
See THORNCASTLE.

FITZWILLIAM QUAY
A quay on the east side of the River Dodder immediately upstream of Ringsend Bridge. It does not appear on Faden's map of 1797 but was probably constructed very shortly afterwards and associated with Vavasour's embankment of the lower Dodder. It appears unnamed on the OS map of 1838.

The quay is named after the Fitzwilliam family and possibly after Richard, seventh Viscount Fitzwilliam (died 1816) of Blackrock House, Mount Merrion, founder of the Fitzwilliam Museum at Cambridge.

[56, map (OS 1838)]

FIVE-GUN BATTERY
See HALF MOON BATTERY.

FIVE LAMPS
The junction of modern Portland Row, North Strand, Seville Place, Amiens Street and Killarney Street. The place is so called from a five-branched

The Five Lamps

lamp standard erected there during the 19th century, and is well known as a centre for public political meetings. The medieval high-tide shoreline passed through or very close to this junction.

During the early 19th century Portland Row and Seville Place were seen as part of the Circular Road, and there was a turnpike toll-house at the junction of the five roads in the angle between the streets now known as Amiens Street and Killarney Street. The Wide Streets Commissioners purchased the toll-house in 1817 for demolition to improve the street intersection, and completed the rearrangement of this corner in 1825.

[208 (vols. 29, 36)]

FLEECE ALLEY

A narrow laneway connecting Wood Quay and Fishamble Street. It appears unnamed on the maps of Brooking (1728), Rocque (1756) and Faden (1797). Strangways named it in his map of 1908. The name may be associated with the Fleece Tavern which stood there in 1666. During the 17th and 18th centuries a portion of the laneway was known as Molesworth Court. This contained, until 1777, the prison of the Four Courts Marshalsea, shown by Rocque; and it was in Molesworth Court that Jonathan Swift's *Drapier's Letters* were printed (1724). Part of Fleece Alley is named as Marshal Alley on the Wide Streets Commissioners map of 1757 for the opening up of Parliament Street.

Since 1791 the area served by Fleece Alley turned by degrees into yards and depots of the Corporation, and more recently to civic offices, and the laneway no longer exists.

[1, 18, maps (as named)]

FLEET ALLEY

See FLEET STREET.

FLEET LANE

See FLEET STREET.

FLEET MARKET

M'Cready records that Fleet Market formerly existed on the land where Tara Street was made, and that the name was no longer in use in 1892.

[39]

FLEET STREET

Fleet Street links Temple Bar and Townsend Street (Lazars Hill), both of which preceded it in age. Its construction became possible as a result of the building of Hawkins's Wall (1662–3), and the thoroughfare appears unnamed on Phillips's map of 1685. Prior to the completion of George's Quay, the eastern end of Fleet Street – near Hawkins Street – remained liable to occasional inundation from the river in storm conditions. The street is shown as fully built up on both sides by Brooking in 1728.

It appears that the 'fleet', which is found in names along the River Thames, is Anglo-Saxon and denotes a tidal inlet. It may be significant that the two passages, Fleet Alley and Fleet Lane, shown by Rocque in 1756 formed a route across Fleet Street from College Green to the bank of the Liffey along the line of the later Westmoreland Street. There was a ferry across the Liffey at the end of Fleet Alley before Carlisle Bridge (now O'Connell) was opened to traffic in 1795, and this ferry, if it preceded Hawkins's Wall, may have taken advantage of a tidal inlet in the river-bank. It is also possible, however, that the name echoes Fleet Street, the earlier London thoroughfare.

[94, 125, *CARD*, VI, maps (Phillips 1685, Brooking 1728, Rocque 1756)]

FLOATING BATTERIES

In 1778 two vessels, *Britannia* and *Hibernia*, were brought into service, to be manned by the Royal Irish Artillery as floating batteries in the defence of Dublin Bay and Harbour. Their period of service was short. Crooks records that

> in 1780 the Board of Ordnance having consulted Lieutenant Colonel Vallancey, he is of the opinion that the fear of opposition has prevented many privateers from attempting to cut out ships at Poolbeg, but that a King's cutter stationed in the bay

or harbour of Dublin would be of much greater use and not more expensive than the guard ships.

The vessels were withdrawn from this service in 1782.

[216]

FLOATING CHAPEL AT RINGSEND

Floating chapel at Ringsend

A pamphlet printed by M. Goodwin, Denmark Street, Dublin in 1823 gives the account of a public meeting held by the Port of Dublin Society for the Religious Instruction of Seamen on board its floating chapel at Ringsend in March of that year. The hull of a Danish vessel, the *Prince Christian*, of 250 tons' burden had been purchased and prepared for public worship in accordance with the Established Church. It had accommodation for 400 people, and it was reported that the congregation attending a service preferred to 'take their station in the rigging or gangways where they felt more at home than they could be in the most elegant cushioned pews on shore'.

An unsigned and undated engraving in the National Library of Ireland (954 TA) shows the vessel moored in the Grand Canal Dock at the corner of Hanover Quay and Grand Canal Quay. A flag depicting a dove bearing an olive branch flies from the mast and there is a naval ensign at the stern. Access to the chapel is through a doorway cut in the bow of the vessel below deck level.

The Ballast Board is recorded as making a contribution towards the maintenance of the chapel in 1832. The floating chapel was replaced by the Mariners' Church in Forbes Street, which was being built in 1832 and was sold to the Gas

Company in 1889. Its remains may still be seen on the west side of Forbes Street, quite close to the former berth of the floating chapel.

[77, 87 (vol. 14), private communication (R. Refaussé)]

FLOOD STREET
See ELLIS PLACE.

FLOODS IN THE LIFFEY
The metropolitan Liffey, by the nature of the catchment area of the whole river, aggravated by the combined influence of tide and wind storm, was for many centuries susceptible to sudden and severe flooding. It was this quality that earned it the ancient title of Ruirtech, which implied 'furious'. The significance of this flooding on the built environment of the city increased according as the tidal channel was progressively restricted by the continuing building of the city quays. It was not indeed until the construction of the hydroelectric generating stations and dams at Pollaphuca and Leixlip by the Electricity Supply Board in the period 1938–50 that the danger of the Liffey bringing flash-floods to the city was removed.

Many notable inundations have been recorded. Thus Harris describes that in March 1670 'a great storm happening at new moon with great winds and rain, the wind at SE, the water overflowed the bank at Ringsend, Lazers Hill and over Mr Hawkins' new wall up to the College and flowed very high into the city which overthrew some houses and laid many cellars and warehouses under water'; and again in 1687, in the deluge that caused the collapse of part of Essex Bridge, Harris reports that 'boats plied in the streets'.

It was generally inundations that brought the collapse of bridges in the city. Thus on 2 December 1802 floodwater caused the collapse of both Ormonde Bridge and the bridge over the Dodder at Ringsend.

That inundation was a constant menace may be suggested, for instance, by the reported occurrence of serious floods four times in 30 years, in 1735, 1746 (see Edmund Burke), 1761 and 1764; while the bizarre lengths to which high water might go may be illustrated by the wrecking of a collier in c. 1690 in what would later be the forecourt of Sir Patrick Dun's Hospital, and the sailing of a boat in 1792 through a breach in Rogerson's Quay to land at the end of the back garden of a Merrion Square house.

The inundation of 1687 was recorded by Rutty as the worst within living memory. He wrote, 'the lower parts of the city were under water up to the first floor, particularly in Patrick Street'. Consideration of relative levels must, however, indicate that this flooding in Patrick Street originated in the Poddle catchment and was not caused directly by high water in the Liffey.

It is important to distinguish between the overflowing of ground by high spring tides, storm-driven by gales at sea, and the deeper and more extensive inundation that could have been caused by a combination of such tides and torrential rain flooding from the Liffey catchment.

Inundations due to serious storm flooding of the Tolka and Dodder are noted in the entries for those rivers. See also Water, Tide and Ground Levels.

[3, 16, 30, 59, *CARD*, VIII, XI, *DHR* (Hammond)]

FLORENCE PLACE
See THE POINT.

FOLEY STREET
See WORLD'S END LANE.

FOLLY, THE
See FORT AT LAZARS HILL.

FOOTBRIDGE NEAR KILMAINHAM
See KILMAINHAM, NARROW BRIDGE AT.

FORD, NIGHTINGALE
See NIGHTINGALE FORD.

FORD NEAR SWIFT'S ROW
See STANDFAST DICK.

FORD OF KILMASTAN
See KILMEHANOC FORD.

FORD OF THE HURDLES
See ÁTH CLIATH.

FORT AT LAZARS HILL
In 1659 five inhabitants of Lazars Hill were given a lease of land extending eastward to a 'forte' which the dimensions quoted in the lease suggest was on the junction of Lazars Hill and its continuation, later known as Sandwith Street. This structure does not appear to be referred to later. Petty's map of the Half Barony of Rathdown in the County of Dublin, made in 1654, shows a construction of some form named Andrews Folly in the same location, and Faden's map 150 years later in 1797 refers to Sandwith Street as The Folly. The possibility that this fort may have been a customs post is suggested in the entry on Lazars Hill.

[106, *CARD*, IV, maps (Petty 1654, Faden 1797)]

FORTICK'S LANE
See CLONLIFFE.

FOUNTAIN TAVERN
A tavern built by Sir John Rogerson on his quay at some time between the years 1715 and 1718. It is said to have been the first building erected on the quay.

[*CARD*, VI, VII, *DHR* (Hammond)]

FOUR COURTS
Throughout the 17th and 18th centuries there was steady pressure, including a proposal by Lord Deputy Wentworth in 1636, to move the Four Courts to a site at Inns Quay, north of the Liffey, and for a short time from 1606 to 1608 the judges sat at that site. However, civic pressure was to keep the courts south of the river for nearly two further centuries.

In 1757 George Semple was invited to draw up plans for public offices and new courts, and in 1762, still against the wishes of the citizens, a

The Four Courts, showing also the Old Bridge, 1799
(J. Malton)

committee of the House of Commons recommended 'Inns Key' as 'the most proper place' for new offices and courts. In 1770 the King's Inns appointed a committee to arrange for new buildings on their site. Thomas Cooley, chosen as the architect, prepared a complete design for offices and courts, and in 1776 work began on the west wing of his design. The inscription on the foundation-stone laid in that year read:

> This First Stone of a Suit of Buildings containing the Public Law Offices, the Hall and the Law Library, for the use of the Society of the King's Inns, was laid by his Excellency Simon Earl Harcourt, Lord Lieutenant General and General Governor of the Kingdom of Ireland.

Cooley died in 1784, and James Gandon, whose work on the construction of the Custom House had started in 1781, was appointed to continue the project. In 1785 an act of parliament assigned £30,000 'towards building further offices for the public records and courts of justice adjoining'. Gandon's design, which did not receive universal praise, and which he was required to modify to meet objections raised, was adopted in 1785, and work began on the foundations in October. The foundation-stone was laid in March 1786 and incorporated an inscription on a copper plate that read:

> The first stone of this edifice erected for the realm was laid on the third day of March MDCCLXXXVI in the twenty sixth year of the reign of his most sacred majesty King George III by his grace Charles Manners, duke of Rutland, lord lieutenant and general governor of Ireland, James viscount Lifford being lord chancellor. James Gandon architect.

The buildings were sufficiently advanced in 1796 for the courts to sit there for the first time in November of that year. The construction was substantially complete in 1802. The great Liffey inundation in the December of that year, which caused havoc along the river, flooded the main entrance hall of the courts, causing Carr (who dates the flooding incorrectly as 1803) to liken the hall to an ancient Roman baths.

On 13 April 1922 the Four Courts were occupied by the Dublin Brigade of the anti-treaty Volunteers, who established there the headquarters of the Republican Army Council. At 4 a.m. on 28 June in that year the Provisional Government started a bombardment of the Four Courts with a field gun, first from the quay at Winetavern Street and later from the quay at Bridge Street. On 30 June the buildings took fire and were reduced to a shell. The siege of the Four Courts has been described by a senior member of the garrison, Ernie O'Malley, who in his account recalls watching from the roof the dawn breaking over the Liffey. A new dome to replace that destroyed at the time was completed in 1931.

The Four Courts complex has been illustrated by many artists. These include:

Ernie O'Malley, 1898–1957 (S. O'Sullivan)

James Malton	(1799): bib. ref. 76
S.F. Brocas	(1818): bib. ref. 77
G. Petrie	(1821): bib. ref. 77
W.H. Bartlett	(1832): bib. ref. 215
James Hore	(1837): bib. ref. 103
T.C. Dibdin	(1840): bib. ref. 100
James Basire	(1843): bib. ref. 77
W. Osborne	(c. 1901): bib. ref. 107
B. Coghlan	(1941): bib. ref. 77.

[3, 32, 82, 94, 182, 201, 217, *DHR* (Culliton)]

FOUR COURTS, OLD

Until the end of the 16th century the four courts of chancery, king's bench, common pleas and exchequer were housed in Dublin Castle, or, occasionally, in places elsewhere in Ireland.

Already in 1606 the present site at Inns Quay north of the Liffey was being considered as a suitable location for new courts, and in fact the courts sat there from 1606 to 1608. However, opposition by the citizens led to a site being chosen immediately to the south of Christ Church Cathedral and within its precincts, and in 1608 the courts were established there. During the following decades the adequacy of this accommodation was in constant question, and the development of the north bank of the Liffey after the restoration of Charles II saw a new move to take the lawcourts to join the new markets north of the river.

In 1684 and again in 1694 the lord mayors petitioned the lord lieutenant to keep the courts in the old city. As they said, 'Ever since the first conquest of this Kingdome the Courts of Justice have been constantly kept within the walls of this city.' They pointed out that the area surrounding the courts was of high value, the properties being 'sett to lawyers, attorneys and sollicitors' and generally used for accommodation and services linked to the courts; and they pleaded that 'if the courts be removed the heart of the cittie will be left destitute'.

These appeals were successful and in 1695 William Robinson was directed 'to rebuild the Four Courts of Justice' in the same location. Clearly, however, this site was too cramped, and despite the praise of 'a citizen of London' in 1732 that 'the

four courts is a large and fine building', and though attempts were made to improve it by rebuilding in 1744, the courts were falling into poor repair 12 years later when Rocque showed them on his map. They continued in service, however, until 1796 when their function was transferred to the new Four Courts north of the river.

[18, 69, 201, *CARD*, V, map (Rocque 1756)]

FOUR COURTS BRIDGE, PROPOSED

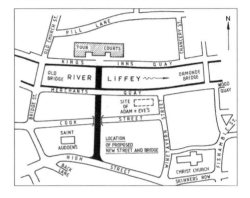

Proposal for street and bridge on axis of Four Courts (see entry on Inns Quay)

In *c.* 1813 a proposal was made to build a bridge across the Liffey on the axis of the recently completed Four Courts. See INNS QUAY.

FOUR COURTS MARSHALSEA

See FLEECE ALLEY.

FOWKES, NATHANIEL

See FERRIES ACROSS THE LIFFEY.

FRANCHISES, CITY

The formal visiting and affirming of the boundaries of the city by the civil authorities has been described since early times as 'riding the city franchises'. There was a general intention over the centuries that this should be done frequently, possibly every three years, but it was not always honoured.

The tradition is deep-rooted. In King John's charter and grant of 1192 he grants to his citizens of Dublin

G

GABBARD

Le Concorde, a Breton gabare of the 19th century

Also known as gabboate, gabboat, gabbart, etc. See Ships and Boats on the Liffey.

GALLOWS NEAR PARKGATE STREET

In 1200 there was a gallows close to the north shore of the Liffey, possibly near the modern junction of Parkgate Street and Infirmary Road. The approach to this place from the city was by the Old Bridge (now Fr Mathew Bridge) and Hangman's Lane (now Hammond Lane). From that time until the early 17th century the gallows or gibbet in Gibbet's Mead or Meadow continued to be mentioned in the riding of the city franchises.

Holinshed records that the notorious footpad Scaldbrother, who had a labyrinthine lair under Oxmantown Green, was accustomed to run past this gallows in derision as he went to ground after his robberies, but that he was eventually captured and hanged on it. D'Alton states that it was at this place that Dermot O'Hurley, archbishop of Cashel, was hanged in 1584 by order of Elizabeth I. Shortly after the restoration of the monarchy in 1660, the gallows was moved across the river to Kilmainham, where there was already a gaol.

The Parkgate gibbet is not to be confused with the better-known place of execution Gallows Hill or Gallows Green on Lower Baggot Street. This site was used by the Norse in the earliest times under the name of Hangr Hoeg, and was reputedly the place where the Normans beheaded Askulv Mac Thorkil after the battle of Hoggen Green in 1171. It continued in use as a place of execution until the early 18th century and the gibbet was still depicted on the Rocque/Scalé map of 1773.

[4, 6, 49, 56, 181, *CARD*, I, map (Rocque/Scalé 1773)]

GANDON, JAMES

James Gandon (T. Kettle and W. Cuming)

Born of Huguenot extraction in London in 1743. He entered the office of Sir William Chambers as a pupil in 1758, and in 1765 started his own practice in architecture. At about this time he was appointed by the East India Company as civil architect and assistant engineer in Sumatra. Later, during the 1770s, he was invited to Russia to work on the design of public buildings for Catherine the Great. He did not take up either of these positions. In 1781 he came to Ireland under the sponsorship of the Revenue Commissioners, to whom he had been recommended by Lord Carlow, and his practice appears to have been largely in Ireland from then on. Following the death of his wife in 1781, he lived in Mecklenburgh Street near the Custom House for many years. In 1808 he retired to an estate at Canon Brook in Lucan, where he died in 1823. He is buried at Drumcondra in the same vault as his friend Francis Grose, the antiquary.

In the context of this book, his major architectural works were at the New Custom House, the Four Courts, the Parliament House, Beresford Place and Carlisle Bridge. These are dealt with in separate entries. His portrait appears as the frontispiece in Mulvany's *Life* (bib. ref. 94) and in an oil painting in the National Gallery of Ireland (NGI, 1783; bib. ref. 107).

[55, 94, 182, *DHR* (Barrow)]

GARGET'S MEDUES

Garget's Mead, Meadows. In *c.* 1275 John Garget, a prominent citizen of Dublin, was granted land by the city which appears to have lain in the angle formed by the south bank of the Liffey and the east bank of the Camac. This would correspond today to the east part of Heuston railway station and the road system at the south ends of Sean Heuston and Sherwin Bridges. This land is described as having formerly included the site of a mill belonging to the canons of Christ Church. This may have been a mill on the tributary of the Camac mentioned in the description of that river, but the precise relationship of Garget's Meadows, which may have been only 1 acre in extent, and the Christchurch meadows is unclear. The name continued as Gargetismedes in 1504.

[189, *CARD*, I, *DHR* (Jackson, Moylan)]

GASOMETER, THE

The Alliance and Dublin Consumers Gas Company, established in 1866, built a new gasholder at the junction of Rogerson's Quay and Cardiff's Lane in 1934. With a capacity of 3,000,000 cubic feet (85,000 cu. m.) and a height of 82.4 m, it was a dominant feature of the Dublin city skyline until 1993–4 when it was taken down. It was not

'Gasometer 2' (M. Kane, 1993)

the only gasholder to be built near the river by the various undertakings that began to provide commercial town gas for Dublin in 1822, but its great bulk and prominent position beside the Liffey, and its mention as a seamark by RN chart no. 1415, suggest its inclusion in this book.

[*Engineers Journal*, vol. 41, no. 9 (de Courcy), map (RN Hydrographic Chart no. 1415: 1977)]

GATES NEAR THE LIFFEY

Healy shows ten gates in the ancient walls of Dublin. Four of these, Bridge Gate, Dames Gate, King's Gate and Ormond's Gate (or Gormond's Gate), are relevant in this book.

[150 (Healy)]

GEOLOGICAL DRIFT MAP OF DUBLIN

In 1917 the Geological Survey of Ireland published a map showing the surficial drift deposits in Dublin. It is based on sheet 18 (1:10,560) of County Dublin in the 1912 edition of the Ordnance Survey, and is overprinted Drift Edition 1915.

The map shows that the Liffey from the weir at Islandbridge to Grattan Bridge flows between banks of alluvium deposited by floods, overlying carboniferous limestone, with some terraces of river gravel south of Heuston railway station and along Steevens's Lane. From Grattan Bridge to Butt Bridge, where in medieval times the Liffey tideway widened, the level lands extending from the northern rise at Parnell Street to the southern rise at College Green and Nassau Street consist of alluvium overlying a raised beach, which in turn overlies the same limestone.

The map shows also the medieval shoreline indicated by de Gomme's map of 1673, and the intake from the beginning of the 18th century up to 1912.

GEORGE DUBLIN LIGHTHOUSE

See POOLBEG LIGHTHOUSE.

GEORGE'S DOCK

See CUSTOM HOUSE DOCKS.

GEORGE'S QUAY

There is little recorded official reference to George's Quay as such. It was being constructed in the early years of the 18th century as part of the development of Mercer's Ground and the slightly later construction at City Quay; and the erection of buildings along the quay paralleled the promotion by the city of the South Lotts project on City Quay. In 1728 Brooking referred to it as St Georges Quay but it is more likely to have been named for George I (1714–27).

George's Quay ended at the west end with a block of buildings that separated it from Burgh Quay until early in the 19th century. The quay may be taken as ending at the east end at Moss Street where it ran into City Quay. Access to George's Quay would have been by George's Street and Shoe Lane, later combined into Tara Street, and by Luke Street and Moss Street, all connecting it to the city by way of Lazars Hill (later Townsend Street).

The quay soon became an important link in the cross-channel passenger trade, whether as a direct berthing-place or as a terminal for ferries bringing passengers upriver from primary landing-places at and below Ringsend. Hammond, whose essay on George's Quay and Rogerson's Quay in the 18th century (*DHR*, vol. 5, no. 2), drawn in part from unpublished sources, offers a valuable insight of the area, mentions the arrival at George's Quay of Dean Swift in 1723 and of G.F. Handel in 1741, among other notabilities.

In that year of 1741 the ownership of the property on George's Quay and of lands behind the quay on both sides of Poolbeg Street passed by lease for ever to Grace Mercer, widow of John Mercer, and Luke Gardiner.

Appropriately, the commerce on George's Quay reflected the shipping trade, and in 1850 the 38 houses on the quay, when it was still considered to extend from White's Lane to Moss Street, included the following:

vintners and wine merchants	5 addresses
hotels and taverns	4
supplies of food, including	
ship's biscuit	4
ships' chandlers and rope stores	4
manufacturers of canvas, oilcloth	
and sailcloth	3
seamen's outfitters	3
coal factors	3
commercial agents and ship-brokers	2

The construction of terminals further to the east at the Pigeonhouse and at Howth and Dún Laoghaire later in the 18th and early in the 19th century largely brought to an end the south bank passenger traffic upriver in the city. George's Quay, however, continued to be very active well into the 20th century for cross-channel freight, with Bristol Seaway Limited maintaining its base at the quay until 1966.

The building of the Talbot Memorial Bridge at Moss Street in 1978 closed off George's Quay from significant river traffic, and the quay is now being developed as an office precinct.

[129, 146, 149, *CARD*, IX, *DHR* (Hammond), map (Brooking 1728)]

GEORGE'S STREET

See GEORGE'S QUAY.

GIBBET'S MEAD OR MEADOW

See GALLOWS NEAR PARKGATE STREET.

GILBERT, SIR JOHN T.

Irish historian and archivist, born 23 January 1829. He was at various times secretary to the Celtic

John Thomas Gilbert, antiquarian (J. Lavery)

Society, librarian and later vice-president of the Royal Irish Academy, fellow of the Society of Antiquaries, secretary to the Public Record Office of Ireland, trustee of the National Library of Ireland and governor of the National Gallery of Ireland. He was awarded the honorary degree of LL D by the Royal University in 1892 and was knighted in 1897. He died on 23 May 1898. In the context of this book, his most important works are the three volumes of his unfinished history of Dublin (vols. 1 and 2: 1854; vol. 3: 1859) and his programme for editing the *Calendar of the Ancient Records of Dublin.* He married Rosa Mulholland in 1891. She was to continue the editing of the *Calendar* until 1921, when she died.

[52]

GILBERT, ROSA MULHOLLAND, LADY

See SIR JOHN T. GILBERT.

GILES'S MAP

In 1818 the Ballast Board invited Francis Giles, an English civil engineer, to advise on the construction of the Bull Wall. Giles had been in practice since *c.* 1803 and had designed harbour works at Wexford. He would become active in English railway practice in *c.* 1830.

In February 1819 Giles sent the Board a map showing his proposal for the location of the wall. This basic map, made to a scale of approximately 1:25,000, was entitled 'A plan of the North Bull showing the land intended to be purchased and taken in by the Corporation for preserving and improving the port of Dublin'. He names himself as the surveyor. In March 1819 he forwarded to the Board his report, which is endorsed 'Report of Francis Giles relative Great North Wall'. This was to have dealt generally with 'improvements of Dublin Bar and the Channel of the River Liffey between Carlisle Bridge and Dublin Light House', but Giles considered that further study was needed on the river, and confined the report to 'the immediate subject of consideration', which he called the 'Great Embankment'. In May 1820 Giles sent a note to the Board from 4 Salisbury Street, Adelphi, London, and in August of that year he forwarded further plans intended to complete his commissioned work. A new proposal from him, however, to carry out a hydrographic survey of Dublin Bay was not accepted. Giles's association with the Board continued, and, for instance, he was consulted in 1840 about the design of wharves for steamers at North Wall Quay.

The construction of the Bull Wall began in 1819, and the wall, as built, ran in a straight line from its landward end west of modern Seafield Road (then called Green Lanes), as Giles had shown, to North Spit Buoy, the short curve depicted by him at the buoy being omitted.

A notable detail on Giles's map is the great increase in size, to a length of about 3 km, of Bull Island, or, as he named it, Sand Island or Green Island.

[68 (vol. 5), 87 (vol. 11)]

GLASLAWER

A stream in Blackrock. See THORNCASTLE.

GLIB WATER

The name probably derives from the word 'glebe', which is defined as a portion of land going with a clergyman's benefice. See COLMANS BROOK.

appears in volume VIII of the *Calendar of the Ancient Records of Dublin*, and the view along the bridge towards the Royal Exchange, drawn by Malton in 1797, is one of his six Liffey scenes. It is of interest to see in these illustrations how the northern end of the bridge was by then quite clear of houses on the riverside. It would be some time before a similar clearance was completed at the southern end of the bridge.

At this time the Essex Bridge had been for well over 100 years a focal point of Dublin, as Craig describes it, and had given its name to the whole surrounding area. It was the first crossing-point of the Liffey up from the sea and was at the official 'port' at the Old Custom House Quay. It had a commercially strategic position and this was jealously protected by the merchants of the city. Entries elsewhere on O'Connell Bridge and the New Custom House underline the determination, to put it mildly, of the business community to block any shift of the centre of gravity of the city's commerce downriver and away from its interests.

The bridge did of course attract all sorts of entrepreneurs. Already in 1756 the Assembly was urging the banishing of fruit-sellers who were setting up their stalls on the bridge, possibly using the arched alcoves as convenient shelters. More sinisterly, it was being complained by 1763 that 'Essex Bridge is subject to many mischiefs at night' and suggestions were made that improved policing 'would prevent many murders and robberies'. The bridge did have public lighting, installed in 1759, and it is possible that this was the earliest bridge lighting in Dublin to be maintained by the city rather than by the local parishes.

If we are to believe Zozimus, who often took his stand on Essex Bridge in the 1830s to declaim, among other things, about the wife of Dickey the Yeoman:

On Essex bridge she strained her throat,
And six-a-penny was her note,

we may suspect that the earlier campaign against the street traders had not proved a lasting success. In 1806 the Ballast Board instructed George Halpin to offer a proposal for lowering the centre of Essex Bridge. A new balustrade was to be similar to that proposed for the future Richmond Bridge (now O'Donovan Rossa). In 1808 a 'parcel of cast metal balustrades' arrived for use on Essex Bridge. In 1809 Halpin reported on 'preparing face and top of bridge' and 'flagging footway', and later that year he implied that the bridge was again ready for use. It is not known what exactly was involved in this reconstruction, but the expenditure of more than £1,000 suggests that it was major work.

In the second half of the 19th century it was decided to reduce the gradients across both Essex Bridge and Carlisle Bridge (now O'Connell) and to widen their carriageways to accommodate the increasing volume of traffic on the Dublin quays and to respond to its changing nature. A design was prepared for Essex Bridge by Bindon Stoney and in March 1872 a contract was let to William Doherty. The new bridge was to be made by rebuilding the three centre spans with flatter elliptical arches springing from Semple's piers and inserting a small semicircular arch at each end. These end arches had to be shorter than Semple's end spans and placed lower, to accommodate in the new bridge a local widening of the quays at both ends to permit the laying of main sewers if necessary. The carriageway of the new bridge was to be the same width as the whole of Semple's bridge, including the footpaths. New footpaths were to be formed by a system based on cantilevering wrought-iron beams out from both sides of the main arched structure. The carriageway was to fall uniformly from south to north, with no camber, to accommodate the difference in the quay levels, although the crowns of the three central arches were to be at the same level.

The work was to be completed in one and a half years. In fact the new carriageway was put into use in October 1874, although the footpaths and zinc-topped parapets were not completed until 1875. The bridge was then formally reopened and given the new name of Grattan Bridge. While the reconstruction was in progress a temporary timber bridge of 11 spans, which took nine weeks to build, was provided opposite Swift's Row, to carry all traffic. A pedestrian footbridge was provided immediately beside the main bridge site.

The plaque on Grattan Bridge reads:

Essex Bridge
Erected 1755
Rebuilt by the Dublin Port and Docks Board 1875
Renamed
Grattan Bridge
Right Honble Peter Paul McSwiney, J.P. Lord Mayor
Robert Warren, D.L. J.P. High Sheriff
Bindon B. Stoney, Engineer
W.J. Doherty, Contractor.

There is no mention of Sir Humphrey Jervis.

[3, 11, 16, 23, 66, 87 (vols. 6, 7), 90, 91, *CARD*, VI, X, maps (Phillips 1685, Brooking 1728)]

GRAUNTSETE, JOHN AND ALICE DE

Following the command of Edward II that houses built by Geoffrey de Morton on the line of the city wall at the south end of the Old Bridge (now Fr Mathew) be demolished because they made no provision for the movement of guards along the ramparts, John de Grauntsete and his wife, Alice, were given permission in 1317 to rebuild these houses on condition that they gave the citizens 'a sufficient passage on the wall with embattlements and well-built of the breadth of three feet and a half for crossing and returning through the two towers at the end of the bridge as often as requisite for the defence of the city'.

They were permitted also to retain 'a latrine already built with a drain through the middle of the open wall towards the water of Avenlyf near the tower at the head of the bridge'.

Thirty years later, in 1348, a John de Grauntsete was empowered to build a chapel at the north end of the bridge. (See St Mary on the Bridge.)

[*CARD*, I]

GRAVEL WALK

See GRAVEL WALK SLIP.

GRAVEL WALK SLIP

The pool at the Gravel Walk Slip began as a large inlet or bay on the north bank of the Liffey with its centre line approximately on the line of the present Blackhall Place. It is probable that it was to

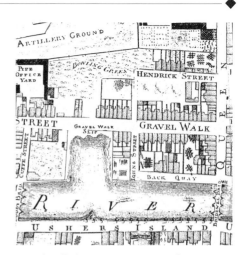

Gravel Walk Slip (J. Rocque's map, 1756)

some considerable degree shaped by man. It was first shown by Rocque in 1756, as a nearly rectangular area of water measuring about 75 m north to south and 70 m east to west. Its northern shore, which was probably close to the original high-tide shoreline of the river, lay along the south side of Barrack Street, now called Benburb Street, and it was that shore which was named as the Gravel Walk Slip. The continuation of Benburb Street to Queen Street was called the Gravel Walk in 1756, and in that year Rocque showed wasteland to the west of the inlet and a timber yard to its east. The proximity of the Smithfield market, the Royal Barracks and the city stores and pipe yard suggest that the inlet and slip, as well as being a watering-place for the army horses, formed a likely site for handling small commercial river lighters as well as timber from ships in the estuary, floated up the river as logs or roughly made rafts; and it is probable that it was used for the wet storage of pipe timber.

The pool at the Gravel Walk Slip was enclosed and filled in 1811.

See also Benburb Street, Ellis Quay and the Pipe Yard.

[Maps (Speed 1610, Rocque 1756, OS 1838)]

GRAVING

In earlier times it was a usual practice to careen vessels for cleaning or repair. For more extended

The first graving dock north of the Liffey, 1860

work and, indeed, for shipbuilding, a dry pit might be dug near the shoreline or river-bank and separated from it by an earthen bank or lock. See, for instance, Constable's painting 'Boat Building near Flatford Mill' (1815), mentioned elsewhere. Such a pit, which would be flooded on completion of the boat work, would have been the prototype of the modern graving or dry dock.

Marney's Dock, now largely buried under Eden Quay, appears to be the earliest recorded dry dock on the Liffey. It existed in 1716 and was shown by Brooking in 1728. Three other dry docks were built as annexes to the Grand Canal Docks in 1796 and these remained in service until the 1960s, being used by various companies – including Ringsend Dockyard Company – for building and repairing small vessels.

In 1826 the Ballast Board decided to develop the graving facilities in the port. Thomas Morton, a shipbuilder of Leith, had invented a patent slip for the graving of larger vessels. It consisted of a slipway inclined at about 1 in 16 with metal rails embedded in its surface. A carriage could be drawn up this railway by a winch and cable, and a vessel secured on the carriage could thus be hauled clear of the water. The Board ordered from Morton a slip suitable for vessels up to 300 tons, for the maintenance of its own fleet. This slip was built, and in 1827 was extended by 19 m, making it 'capable of receiving vessels of the greatest draft of water trading to the port' at that time.

In 1830 the Dublin traders and shipowners sought the Board's agreement to their using the patent slip for their trading vessels. This was granted, but, since it was recognised that larger vessels were coming into service, a second 'patent graving slip' was ordered from Morton to accommodate vessels up to 800 tons. In 1832 this slip was ready for public contracts. It was recorded that the equipment at the slip included blocks, shores, screws, a stove, boilers and a forge.

During the period from 1835 to 1850 there were persistent complaints about the inability of the patent slips to accept increasingly larger vessels. The Board attempted to meet these complaints, first by installing in 1835 a graving frame or 'gridiron' 30 m long at the end of the North Wall, and later, in 1847, by extending its length to 60 m. The gridiron was a heavy timber grillage fixed on a levelled area of strand, on to which a vessel to be serviced could be floated and secured. This was to be seen as a temporary solution, and in 1849 George Halpin was being instructed by the Board to prepare a patent slip suitable for vessels of 1,400 tons.

By then, however, it was realised that there had to be a limit to what such slips could accommodate, and the Board decided, with the advice of Halpin and Sir William Cubitt, that it would build a formal graving dock or dry dock to the east of modern East Wall Road. Halpin prepared plans and in 1853 William Dargan was appointed as contractor to build the graving dock in stone masonry, to be 120 m long and 21 m wide at the entrance. This dock was ready for use in 1860 and remained in service until 1989. In 1868 the construction of a second, larger graving dock was proposed, but obstacles – mainly financial – delayed the project and it was not until 1951 that work commenced. This second dock, designed by Nicholas O'Dwyer and 180 m in length, was built in concrete and completed in 1957.

[87 (vols. 12–14, 18, 19), 129, 180, 285, maps (Brooking 1728, Faden 1797, Dublin Port 1987)]

GREAT BRIDGE, THE

See FR MATHEW BRIDGE.

GREAT BRITAIN QUAY

The construction of an entrance to the Grand Canal Docks in 1796 necessitated the removal of part of the short length of river wall built 75 years earlier by Sir John Rogerson along the Dodder estuary from the Liffey to Ringsend Bridge. The new wall which was then made between the Liffey and the entrance was given the name of Great Britain Quay, and this name appears on the 1838 OS map.

In subsequent alterations this quay was widened, new buildings were erected on it and the original Great Britain Quay, or Britain Quay, became a street rather than a quay.

In 1803 Wilson, for no clear reason, used the name Great Britain Quay for the present South Lotts Road.

[Maps (Wilson 1803, OS 1838, 1963)]

GREAT BRUNSWICK STREET

See PEARSE STREET.

GREAT EASTERN STEAMSHIP

See SHIPS AND BOATS ON THE LIFFEY.

GREAT GALLEY OF DUBLIN

See SEAL OF DUBLIN and SHIPS AND BOATS ON THE LIFFEY.

GREAT NORTH WALL, THE

See THE BULL WALL.

GREAT ROADS OF ANTIQUITY

See ÁTH CLIATH.

GREAT SOUTH WALL

See THE SOUTH WALL.

GREEN, ABBEY

See LITTLE GREEN.

GREEN, COLLEGE

See COLLEGE GREEN.

GREEN, HOGGEN

See HOGGEN GREEN.

GREEN, LITTLE

See LITTLE GREEN.

GREEN, OXMANTOWN

See OXMANTOWN.

GREEN ISLAND

An early name for Bull Island, appearing on Giles's and later maps.

GREEN OF DUBLIN

Curtis records that, in 1036, the open country that lay south of the Liffey from Islandbridge to the Coombe was known as the Green of Dublin.

[DHR (Curtis)]

GREEN OF IRISHTOWN

See Irishtown. A monument on the green carries the inscription:

Irish Mercantile Marine Memorial
World War II
Emergency
1939–1946
Ar dheis Dé go raibh a n-anam
Unveiled by Captain D.P. Fortune and
Sean Moore Lord Mayor 1963–64
April 8th 1984.

It is recorded that the trees planted around this stone monument were chosen to represent the names of the vessels that served the country at the time. They include ash, poplar, spruce and pine.

[302]

GREEN OF THE STAINE

The district of Stein, described elsewhere, has been recorded by Stephenson as the Green of the Staine.

[DHR (Stephenson)]

GREEN PATCH, THE

About 1.8 km downstream from the Point of Ringsend there was an islet on the north edge of the South Bull. It was called the Green Patch and circumstances, and its name, suggest that it remained unsubmerged at high tide. It is shown on the Revenue map of 1694 and on Bowen's map of 1728. It is referred to as 'an anchoring place' by the Assembly in its application for a ballast office for the city, and is marked as an anchorage, but not named, by Greenvile Collins in 1686. It seems certain that it was cut off from Ringsend at high tide, but it has nevertheless been described as one of the places where ships, not willing or able to take their cargoes up to the city, offloaded.

It has been recorded by Flood that the cross-channel packet-boats left from the Green Patch in the early 18th century, and that this islet was the site on and around which the Pigeonhouse precinct began and developed.

During the 18th century, that part of the Green Patch which projected into the channel of the river was seen as a hindrance to shipping and in 1820 the Ballast Board gave final instructions that it be removed by being used as a source for ballast.

It is of interest that the Green Patch is not shown by Rocque in 1760 or by Scalé and Richards in 1765, and that it appears never to be named by the Ballast Office. One can surmise that the name, while generally known, was not a formal title.

[87 (vol. 11), CARD, VIII, DHR (Flood), maps (Greenvile Collins 1686, Revenue 1694, Bowen 1728)]

GREENHIDE CRANE, THE

A greenhide crane was in operation in 1819 at Bonham Street behind Usher's Island.

[29]

GREENS, GENERAL

Entries relating to the greens associated with the Liffey and its tributaries will be found under the following headings: Abbey Green, College Green, Green of Dublin, Green of Irishtown, Green of the Staine, Hoggen Green, Little Green, Oxmantown Green.

GREENVILE COLLINS, CAPTAIN

See COLLINS, CAPTAIN GREENVILE.

GRIDIRON

See GRAVING.

GROUND AND SHORE LEVELS

See WATER, TIDE AND GROUND LEVELS.

GUILD STREET

See NORTH LOTTS.

GUILDS OF DUBLIN

The 25 trade and craft guilds of Dublin, which played a leading role in the municipal government, are listed below in order of date of origin. Their rank in the order of precedence in the City Assembly is also shown.

Name	Origin		Rank in Assembly
Merchants	?	pre 1190	1
Tailors	Royal charter	1418	2
Cooks and Vintners	do.	1444	10
Barber Surgeons	do.	1446	4
Weavers (to which Combers were added in 1688)	do.	1446	14
Shoemakers	do.	1465	8
Smiths	do.	1474	3
Glovers and Skinners	do.	1476	13
Bakers	do.	1478	5
Carpenters, Millers, Masons and Heliers	do.	1508	7
Goldsmiths	Charter before	1557	16
Saddlers, Upholders, Coach and Coach-harnessmakers	Assembly charter	1558	9
Butchers	do.	1569	6
Tallow Chandlers, Soap Boilers and Wax-light Makers	do.	1583	12
Sheermen and Dyers	No charter but recognised in	1660	15
Coopers	Royal charter	1666	17
Feltmakers	do.	1667	18
Cutlers, Painters, Paper-stainers and Stationers	do.	1670	19

Bricklayers and Plasterers	do.	1670	20
Hosiers and Knitters	do.	1688	21
Tanners	do.	1688	11
Curriers	do.	1695	22
Brewers and Maltsters	do.	1696	23
Joiners, Ceylers and			
Wainscotters	do.	1700	24
Apothecaries	do.	1747	25

A full directory of the guilds is given by Clark and Refaussé and a detailed examination of the Merchants' Guild and the decline of the guilds will be found in Webb.

[2, 267]

Guinness barge with funnel down passing under O'Donovan Rossa Bridge

GUINNESS BREWERY

The Guinness jetty at Victoria Quay, 1955 (T. Cuneo)

In 1759 Benjamin Guinness leased 0.4 ha of land on the south side of James's Street and began to manufacture 'stout and porter which were already popular in England'. In 1875 his firm began to expand to the north of James's Street, buying up existing breweries and other industries, and coming to occupy much of the area known as Christchurch Meadows and Lord Galway's Walk down the hillside to Victoria Quay. This area forms the foreground of Malton's engraving 'The Barracks', published in 1796 when it was still pasture-land.

In 1873 the brewery built a jetty on Victoria Quay as a terminal for the transport of stout in barrels downstream to the Custom House Quay for transfer to seagoing vessels. This started a long association with the Liffey which would make Victoria Quay the only upstream quay in the city to be in active water-borne trade in the 20th century. The jetty system was developed up to 1913, and the steam barges with their funnels hinged to pass under the bridges at high tide were a familiar sight until 1961 when the use of the river was discontinued in favour of road transport and the jetties were removed. A full account of the use of the river by the Guinness barges is given by Walsh in bib. ref. 243, and a wall plaque on Victoria Quay commemorates the period.

An oil painting by Terence Cuneo, 'The Guinness Jetty, Victoria Quay', painted in 1955, shows the system in operation at the time. Photographs reproduced by Gorham show the jetty dressed for a visit by Victoria in 1900, and, more prosaically, stripped for action four years later.

[5 (McDowell), 24, 76, 110, 243]

GUNPOWDER EXPLOSION AT WOOD QUAY

See WOOD QUAY.

H

HAIGS LANE
See DODDER RIVER and WILLIAM VAVASOUR.

HALF MOON BATTERY
In 1793 the Board of Ordnance built a battery on the South Wall, about 800 m from the Poolbeg lighthouse. It was armed with five 24-pounder guns and it controlled the channel of the river and the water around the Poolbeg lighthouse. It appears as the battery on the maps of Bligh (1800/3) and Taylor (1816), and as the Half Moon or five-gun battery on the Ordnance Survey map of 1838. Frazer's map of 1838/42 shows the slip that was formed at the site but does not show buildings. The battery was subsequently dismantled and the site is now used as a swimming-place. A small structure was erected on the river side of the wall about 70 years ago to house experimental equipment for navigation in the port.

The name 'Half Moon' may come from the semicircular stone-built pit in the battery, which would have been associated with the placing of the guns. The profile of the South Wall changes at the Half Moon, being 1.3 m higher to the east than it is to the west. This difference is described in the entry on the South Wall. New stores have recently been built at the site and part of the original pit has been filled in.

[70, 87 (vol. 3), *DHR* (Hammond), maps (Bligh 1800/3, Taylor 1816, OS 1838, Frazer 1838/42)]

HALFPENNY BRIDGE
Also Ha'penny Bridge. See LIFFEY BRIDGE.

HALIDAY, CHARLES
See ARRAN QUAY.

HALPIN, GEORGE, JUNIOR
See GEORGE HALPIN, SENIOR.

HALPIN, GEORGE, SENIOR
When Francis Tunstall died in 1800, he was succeeded as inspector of works for the Ballast Board by George Halpin, senior, one of the most competent practical engineers in Ireland in the 19th century. The date of Halpin's birth is uncertain, but he must have been in his early twenties and a trained craftsman, probably a mason or carpenter, at the time of his appointment. He died in harness, inspecting a lighthouse, 54 years later at between 75 and 80 years of age. He never attained any academic qualification and was never a member of the Institution of Civil Engineers of Ireland, a body for professional engineers and architects, founded in 1835.

Halpin's work may be classified under four headings: the river, the port and estuary, lighthouses, and private design. His duties for the Ballast Board included design, supervision of construction, and maintenance of all the existing and new buildings and engineering works controlled by it.

The Board was responsible for the Liffey and for the structure of its bridges (except the Halfpenny Bridge) up to Rory O'More Bridge. In this context Halpin rebuilt completely the walls of the Liffey on both sides of the river from O'Connell Bridge to Rory O'More Bridge, and built the quay walls downstream at Eden Quay and Burgh Quay. He repaired Mellowes Bridge and remodelled the centre span of Grattan Bridge and the approaches to the Halfpenny Bridge. He oversaw the design and construction of Fr Mathew Bridge and O'Donovan Rossa Bridge, becoming involved in architectural controversy with the designer, James Savage, about details of their elevations. He pressed, from 1838, for the construction of a new bridge to replace Carlisle Bridge, and in 1839 proposed that a competition be held for the new design. He was critical of Gandon's bridge, saying in 1852 that 'many think it heavy and it is certainly not in accordance with the new idea held in bridge architecture at the present day. This may be said with every respect for the eminent architect who planned it, but whose practice lay in a different walk.' It was on Halpin's proposal that the parapet of Inns Quay was formed with a balustrade rather than a solid wall, but he failed to have this repeated, as he wished, along Merchants Quay.

In 1852–3 he sought funds to clean the river-bed through the city to remove its 'unpleasant smell' and he noted with regret that 'the Liffey is still the great main drain into which the sewerage of Dublin opens'. He was required to deal also with minor social irritations. Thus in 1818 he reported angrily, 'there is a number of people fishing from the Ballustrades on Richmond Bridge to the great annoyance of the public and injury of the bridge'; and in 1826 he had to urge the Board to curb the activities of disorderly fruit-sellers on several of the bridges.

Halpin's work on the port and estuary was extensive, involving him in visits to England and Wales to study new techniques in port organisation and marine building. Thus, in collaboration with Giles in the design of the Bull Wall, he went to Plymouth in 1816 to observe the construction of the breakwater there. Earlier, in 1810, he had spent more than a month in London and the south of England studying dock design, the new practice in steam dredging, tunnelling, and equipment for lighthouses. It was following this visit that he commented he 'would rather have 2 Irish than 3 English labourers', and dismissed a lantern-maker in London as 'the most trifling and unsatisfactory kind of man I ever had any dealings with'.

In this section of his career, Halpin, as well as sharing in the design and supervision of construction of the Bull Wall, made a new channel for the Tolka from Clontarf Island across Brown's Patch to the Liffey; raised parts of the South Wall east of the Half Moon battery to its present height and strengthened the base of the Poolbeg lighthouse; conferred with Vignoles on extending the Kingstown railway on a causeway across the old Dunleary harbour; consulted with Telford and Cubitt on the problems of deep-water berths at North Wall Quay; formed the large new berthing-pool in the earth-embanked basin east of East Wall Road that became known as Halpin's Pond and later was incorporated

in the Alexandra Basin; introduced steam dredging in the estuary in 1814; helped to ward off a proposal by the Tidal Harbours Commissioners in 1846 to divert the Dodder through Irishtown and form a new basin in the South Bull; designed the structure for the first patent slip to be built in the port; proposed in 1839 a bascule or swivel bridge where the Talbot Memorial Bridge would be built 140 years later; and steered the first graving dock project through to the appointment of William Dargan as contractor. This list is selective.

Halpin clearly maintained a high standard in his designs and their realisation. In 1849 Cubitt, writing to the Ballast Board, praised him, saying, 'it makes me feel as it were more a work of supererogation rather than necessity that I should report' on his proposals and work. The scale of Halpin's activity at Dublin may be gauged from a typical annual report made in 1823 that enumerated the 13 items to be dealt with that year at a total cost of £13,600. The Ballast Board did, of course, facilitate him by granting him, in 1802, a sum of £10 to buy a horse, and it defended his salary against a government charge of lavishness by pointing out that the house in which he lived, which formed part of his income, was 'in the storeyard at the point of the North Wall, where his residence makes a storekeeper unnecessary'.

In 1810 the Ballast Board was appointed to be the Lighthouse Authority for Ireland. The Board appointed Halpin as its inspector of lighthouses. In the following 44 years, he designed and built a lighthouse every 15 months, 35 in all, around the coast of Ireland. These included Inishtrahull (1813), Skellig Michael (1826), Tory Island (1832) and Fastnet (1854). As well, he largely rebuilt Poolbeg (1819–20), modified or was associated with the building of a further 8 lights, and maintained a steady programme of inspection of all the lighthouses in service.

In addition to his duties for the Ballast Board, Halpin appears to have found time for some private architectural work. The likelihood of his involvement with the Corn Exchange on Burgh Quay is mentioned in the entry on that building.

George Halpin, senior, collapsed and died during a lighthouse inspection in July 1854. His workload had been shared for many years by his son, George, junior, who was appointed by the Board as assistant inspector of works in June 1830. Already, between 1834 and 1840, Halpin junior had become involved in the works of deepening the river channel and building new quay walls east of the Custom House, and had held discussions in England with Telford, Cubitt and Giles. Later he carried through the design of the single-span metal-arched Rory O'More Bridge, and designed, probably among others, the lighthouse at Aranmore in Donegal, which was completed in 1865. George junior was elected as a member of the Institution of Civil Engineers of Ireland in 1847, and from 1848 to 1851 served as a member of its council. In September 1854 he was appointed to his father's post as inspector of lighthouses and works. He retired in 1862 due to ill health and was succeeded by Bindon Stoney, who had entered the service as his assistant in 1856.

[87 (vols. 4–7, 9, 13, 15, 16, 18–20, 22, 24), 129, 208 (vol. 28), 268, 276 (*Minutes*, vol. 1)]

HALPIN'S POND

Also known as Halpin's Pool. See THE NORTH WALL.

HAMMOND (HAMON'S) LANE

See ARRAN QUAY.

HANDSARD STREET

See PEARSE STREET.

HANGMAN'S LANE

Also known as Hangman Lane, Hankman's Lane. See ARRAN QUAY.

HANGR HOEG

See GALLOWS NEAR PARKGATE STREET.

HANOVER QUAY

See GRAND CANAL DOCKS.

HARBOUR COURT

Also known as Harbour Lane. See EDEN QUAY.

HARVYE, WILLIAM, BUILDER

William Harvye, or Harvey, was a public works contractor who, in 1665, was employed in making new ground and planting trees between the Bowling Green at Oxmantown and the roadway along the bank of the Liffey, and, in 1667, was building pesthouses for the city on Clontarf Island, and also remaking the road surfaces on the Old Bridge and under the city gates.

[*CARD*, IV, V]

HATCHES POINT

A definite place in the Liffey near Ringsend mentioned in 1852. Its precise position is unclear but it may have been one corner of the actual confluence of the Liffey and the Dodder.

[87 (vol. 20)]

HATFIELD PLAN OF TRINITY COLLEGE

A drawing in the collection at Hatfield House, pen and colour wash on vellum, 26" x 30½", undated, endorsed 'Plott of a colledg or hospitale and platts of howses'. It has been dated as *c.* 1592 and is described as showing what was probably a proposal for the new building at Trinity College submitted to Lord Burghley for his consideration as chancellor of the college. The buildings were built very much as shown, the first stone being laid in March 1593. The drawing shows the college buildings set around a quadrangle. To the west of the buildings are 'feeldes', with no indication of Lazars Hill. The 'Liffe Fluius', with a two-masted ship in full sail, flows past on the north side, its channel less than 15 m from the north-west corner. The area between the channel and the north block of the college is shown as tidal mud and perhaps river meadow, with what may be a proposed river wall at the meadow bank. The tidal mud and meadow are crossed by a large creek just west of the buildings.

This plan is possibly the earliest illustration to show the Liffey in relation to a city building, antedating Speed by some 18 years. A significant feature of the plan is the tower shown at the north-eastern corner of the buildings, and described as 'the steeple a sea marke'. This was the only part of

Hatfield Plan of Trinity College, c. *1592*

the earlier Priory of All Hallows to be left standing when the buildings of the priory generally were demolished, presumably because of its importance as a navigation mark for ships in the bay and river.

[Map (Hatfield Plan *c.* 1592)]

HAWKINS, WILLIAM
See HAWKINS'S WALL.

HAWKINS STREET
See HAWKINS'S WALL.

HAWKINS'S BRIDGE (PROPOSED)
In 1671, when Hawkins's Ground had been taken in from the sea by the building of his wall in 1662–3, and the development of the north shore of the Liffey was being actively pursued, a proposal

was made by seven citizens, including William Hawkins and Gilbert Mabbot, to build a bridge across the Liffey near the Old Ferry at Union Lane. It would have had an opening span or 'drawbridge', as the city had stipulated that 'vessels gabards and other boates shall have free passage, as now they have'. The proposal came to nothing, and it would be over 100 years before Carlisle Bridge (now O'Connell) would be built in the vicinity.

[*CARD*, IV]

HAWKINS'S GROUND
See HAWKINS'S WALL.

HAWKINS'S MILL
See HAWKINS'S WALL.

HAWKINS'S QUAY
See HAWKINS'S WALL.

HAWKINS'S WALL
In 1662 William Hawkins undertook to build a river wall eastward along the south bank of the Liffey from near Temple Bar. It is suggested in this book that the wall extended to approximately the present position of Corn Exchange Place and probably turned there at a right angle to extend southwards to Lazars Hill (modern Townsend Street). The wall was completed in 1663 and offered a potential for dry land unaffected by the tide over an area bounded by the present Aston and Burgh Quays on the north, College Street on the south and Tara Street on the east.

The area became known as Hawkins's Ground and in 1673 de Gomme was able to describe it as 'ground taken in from the sea', although it had, in 1670, been inundated by a Liffey flood which overtopped the wall and flowed up to the walls of Trinity College. The gradual reclamation of the area, on which Westmoreland Street and D'Olier Street would later be built, led to the culverting of the River Stein and to the obliteration of any traces that might have remained of a medieval harbour at the mouth of the Stein near the Long Stone.

In 1766 Harris referred to the wall where Burgh Quay now is as Hawkins's Quay. This may have been his personal choice, because Rocque in 1756 uses the name of Aston's Quay for the whole length of the present Aston Quay and part of Burgh Quay. De Gomme in 1673 did not show a street where Hawkins Street is now. In 1728 Brooking showed Hawkins Street in its modern position, but showed Aston Quay having its east end at Hawkins Street. This reflects the fact that the continuity of Burgh Quay (as itself or as part of Aston Quay) and George's Quay did not come until the 19th century. The de Gomme dimensions suggest that Hawkins's Ground did extend very roughly to Tara Street, but other evidence shows it more probable that it ended at Corn Exchange Place.

A Corporation lease map of 1683 letting lands to Phillip Croft shows 'Mr Hawkins windmill' on the river-bank at the north-east corner of Hawkins's Ground. This building does not appear to be mentioned at any subsequent date, but it may have been incorporated in the group of buildings forming the discontinuity mentioned earlier between George's Quay and Burgh Quay.

A contemporary observation in the *Calendar of State Papers* describes the construction of Hawkins's Wall as 'a double wall and a fair bank between'.

William Hawkins died in 1680.

[6, 16, 39, 149, 160, *CARD*, VI, Dublin Corporation Archives, maps (de Gomme 1673, Brooking 1728, Rocque 1756)]

HAWKSHAW FAMILY
On his map of 1673 de Gomme shows a quite isolated group of four houses close to the north shore of the Liffey, and directly opposite the east end of Hawkins's Wall on the south bank. These houses appear to be associated with the name of Hawkshaw in the lease given to Jonathan Amory in 1675. Two Dubliners named Hawkshaw are in the civic records: John, a merchant (Census, 1659), and Samuel, a heyler or helier – that is to say, a slater (Roll of Freemen, 1674).

The existence of the four houses so close to the shoreline in 1673 but presumably not affected by high tide, and so remote from any other building, is remarkable, and the matter may be significant in construing the Amory lease, which is mentioned elsewhere in this book.

[*CARD*, V, Dublin Corporation Archives, map (de Gomme 1673)]

HEAD OF THE PILES, THE
See THE SOUTH WALL.

HELGA, GUNBOAT
See LIBERTY HALL.

HEN AND CHICKENS
Also known as the Chickens. Rocks and a rocky shelf, now largely built over, on the shore of Dublin Bay west of the landward end of the west pier of Dún Laoghaire Harbour.

[Maps (Bligh 1800/3, Taylor 1816)]

HENRY II

Henry II was born in 1133 and was crowned as king of England in 1154. He came to Ireland in 1171, when the Anglo-Normans, under Strongbow, had subdued Dublin, landing at Waterford with his own army of 4,000 men on 17 October. He advanced to Dublin and established his court there on 11 November, building a 'magnificent royal palace outside the city near the church of Saint Andrew of wickerwork in the Irish fashion'. The location may have been on Dame Street, slightly east of the Olympia Theatre. There he celebrated Christmas.

> The princes [of Ireland] came to Dublin in great numbers to view the King's court. There they greatly admired the sumptuous and plentiful fare of the English table and the most elegant service by the royal domestics. Throughout the great hall, in obedience to the king's wishes they began to eat the flesh of the crane, which they had hitherto loathed.

While in Dublin, Henry, by charter, granted to his men of Bristol the city of Dublin, and he gave the city its first charter of municipal liberties. He appears to have left Dublin in February 1172, and he departed for England – because of disquiet there – from Wexford on Easter Monday. He died in 1189, never having returned to Ireland.

What kind of man was this, the first Anglo-Norman lord of Ireland? He

> had hair that was almost red in colour, grey eyes and a large round head. His eyes were bright and in anger fierce and flecked with red. He had a fiery complexion, his voice was husky, his neck bent forward a little from his shoulders, and he had a broad chest and powerful arms. His body was fleshy and he had a very large belly, naturally so, and not due to the effects of gluttony, which, by a kind of regulated superfluity, stopped short of extravagant obesity and all suggestion of an inactive life. For he was moderate and temperate in the matter of food and drink, and in all things inclined to be sparing, as far as this is possible for a prince.

[35, 36, 67]

HENRY OF LONDON, ARCHBISHOP

In the 13th century the pilgrimage to Santiago de Compostela in north-western Spain was drawing pilgrims from many parts of Europe to the shrine of St James, patron saint of lepers. Those who started from Dublin embarked, when vessels were available and winds favourable, from the south shore of the Liffey east of the mouth of the Stein, in the district that was probably already known at the time as Lazars Hill, the hill of the lepers.

Henry of London (Henri de Londres) was appointed archbishop of Dublin in 1212, and was granted the bishopric of Glendalough by John and appointed by him as justiciar, or royal representative, in Ireland in 1213. Archbishop Henry undertook at that time to build a hospital (or perhaps a hostel) for the waiting pilgrims near their place of embarkation. The date of the foundation has been given as c. 1220 and the building was later known as the Steyne or Stein Hospital. It is recorded that 'ten chaplains, dressed in black cloaks, were appointed to give the pilgrims when detained by stress of weather etc. all the necessary requirements during their stay in the hospice'. Walsh names this hospital as St James's Hospital. Henry ruled as archbishop until his death in 1228, acting again as justiciar under Henry III in 1221. During his time in Dublin he continued the building of Dublin Castle, which had been started in c. 1204, and he acted as promoter of the cause of Archbishop Laurence O'Toole, who was canonised in 1225.

[22, 29, 37, 147, 150 (Lawlor), 169, map (Walsh 1977)]

HERB AND ROOT MARKET
See ORMONDE QUAY.

HERBERT BRIDGE
See NEW BRIDGE.

HERRINGTOWNE
See CLONTARF SHEDS.

HEUSTON RAILWAY STATION
In 1845 a newspaper advertisement in the *Freeman's Journal* invited architects to submit designs for a railway terminus at Dublin for the

HOSPITAL FOR INCURABLES

Hospital for Incurables, Townsend Street

In 1743 the Charitable Musical Society of Crow Street, which had been instituted some years earlier for the relief of debtors and distressed families in Dublin, decided to offer help and nursing to persons suffering from incurable diseases. For this purpose it rented a house in Fleet Street in 1744, furnished it, and engaged a nurse. In 1753, needing more and better accommodation, the hospital was moved to a site on Lazars Hill at the corner of Luke Street. On this site a new building in classical style was started and, by 1771, was recorded as having 40 patients. The hospital was to complete its building in 1791, with the aid of generous private donations, to reach a final size of six wards capable of accommodating more than 100 patients. An illustration by J. Aheron showing the building as it stood in 1762 is held by the National Library (550 TA).

In 1792, on the recommendation of the earl of Westmoreland (lord lieutenant, 1790–95), the hospital was moved to an existing premises on Bloomfield Avenue off Morehampton Road, and the building in Lazars Hill became a hospital for venereal diseases, later known as the Westmoreland or Lock Hospital and as the Hospital of St Margaret of Cortona. This hospital was closed during the 1950s and the building was subsequently demolished.

[18, 113, 152, private communication (J.A. Irvine)]

HOSPITAL OF ST JOHN OF JERUSALEM

See ROYAL HOSPITAL, KILMAINHAM.

HOTEL ON NORTH WALL

See CROSS-CHANNEL PACKETS.

HOUSES OF EASEMENT

See PUBLIC LATRINES.

HOUSTMANEBI

Also Ostmanby. See OXMANTOWN.

HOWE, THE

See HOGGEN GREEN.

HOWTH: PROPOSED CANAL

In a letter of 7 September 1800, Hyde Page observed that he had proposed new docks at the Custom House some years previously and had in the same letter mentioned 'a ship canal from the shore to the west of Howth' to link Howth 'to the floating docks alluded to'. In 1818 Warburton et al. referred to this somewhat desperate proposal, noting that a link from the Inner Dock to the Royal Canal Basin might, if the increase in trade should require it, 'continue even to the harbour of Howth by means of a canal through the strand of Clontarf and across the isthmus'. Fortunately a growing awareness of the inadequacy of Howth Harbour as an all-weather cross-channel terminal scotched the proposal.

[29, 70]

HUDDART, JOSEPH, FRS

Born in Scotland in 1740. At an early age, Huddart commanded a sloop engaged in bringing Scottish herring to Dublin for sale. He later commanded an East Indiaman and on retirement became an Elder Brother of Trinity House, with a special interest in the establishment of lighthouses. John Rennie consulted Huddart about many of his important marine works. In 1802 Huddart wrote to the Directors General of Inland Navigation, dismissing Dalkey as a possible deep-sea harbour and supporting Rennie in many of his proposals for the bay and harbour. They agreed on the development of Dunleary Harbour, and Rennie at that time deferred to Huddart about some details for the proposed ship canal. Huddart also favoured the building of Perry's small asylum harbour at Sutton and recommended what appears to have been a proposed diversion of the River Tolka to flow along the Clontarf shoreline towards Sutton Creek. [68 (vol. 2), 70]

HUGUENOT INFLUENCES ON THE LIFFEY
When the French Huguenots first came to live in Dublin in the middle of the 17th century, they settled principally in the old city, around the Coombe and in Weavers' Square. The references in this book to Lord Galway, Daniel Corneille, John Rocque, James Gandon, Jeremiah (Jerome) D'Olier and William Dargan reflect associations that exist between the Huguenot community and the River Liffey. Others, whose influence on the river was less direct, would include the Latouche banking family and Elie Bouhereau, the French medical doctor who was Lord Galway's secretary and the first librarian at Archbishop Marsh's library.

HYDE, DOUGLAS, FIRST PRESIDENT OF IRELAND
See FERRIES ACROSS THE LIFFEY.

HYDE PAGE, SIR THOMAS
See PAGE, SIR THOMAS HYDE.

HYDROGRAPHIC DATA FOR DUBLIN
Information on Dublin Bay and the River Liffey is contained in the following maps:

1685	Phillips
1693	Greenvile Collins
1730	Price
1765	Scalé and Richards
1773	Rocque/Scalé
1800/3	Bligh
1816	Taylor
1821	Duncan
1823	Nimmo
1838/42	Frazer
1875	Kerr
1977	Admiralty (Bay)
1979	Admiralty (Liffey)

I

ILLUSTRATORS OF THE LIFFEY

Unlike the rivers of other European capital cities, the Liffey is not portrayed in any early illustrations. If it is accepted that such works as the Hatfield Plan (c. 1592) and Speed's map (1610) are maps rather than views, then Francis Place was the first artist to draw the river. His three, accurately observed ink-drawings, 'Dublin from the Wooden Bridge' (now Rory O'More Bridge), 'Dublin from Phoenix Park' and 'Dublin Bay and Howth from Ringsend', all drawn in 1698/9, are now held in the National Gallery of Ireland (nos. 7515, 7516 and 7518). Their interest includes showing the river and the estuary as they then were, and, in particular, the shores above Arran Bridge before the quays were made.

In the 300 years which have elapsed, some 110 to 120 named artists, and many unnamed, have made, at a conservative estimate, over 350 illustrations of the Liffey or of buildings on its banks or persons associated with it. It is outside the scope of this book to provide a comprehensive catalogue. A short list is offered with just one work from each artist, arranged chronologically.

F. Place (1647–1728)	'Dublin from the Wooden Bridge': 1698/9 (NGI, 7515)
W. Jones	'A View of the Black Rocks': 1744 (NLI, 785 TC)
J. Tudor	'The Custom House and Essex Bridge': 1753 (NLI, 377 TB)
G. Ricciardelli (fl. 1745–77) (attributed to)	'View of Dublin from the Sea': 1759 (bib. ref. 103)
J. Fisher (publ.)	'View of the Lighthouse in the Harbour of Dublin': c. 1780 (NLI, 623 TC)
J.J. Barralet	'The Old Custom House at Essex Bridge': 1782 (NLI, 965 TC)
C. Machell (1747–1827)	'The River Liffey in Flood at Islandbridge, Dublin': 1784 (NGI, 6773)
F. Wheatly (1747–1801)	'The Sheds at Clontarfe': 1785 (NLI, 447 TB)
W.H. Barnard	'Island Bridge after the Flood': 1788 (NGI, 19183)
J. La Porte (1761–1839)	'Dublin from Sarah's Bridge': 1796 (NLI, 966 TC)
J. Malton	See separate entry
W. Ashford (c. 1746–1824)	'A View of Dublin from Chapelizod': c. 1794 (NGI, 4138)
T.S. Roberts (1760–1826)	'South View of the River Liffey Showing the Ruins of Coal Quay Bridge': 1802? (NLI, 565 TD)
Wm. Sadler (1782–1839)	'A View of the Pigeon House Dublin' (NGI, 633)
W. Brocas (c. 1794–1868)	'Moira House': 1811 (NLI, 577 TA)

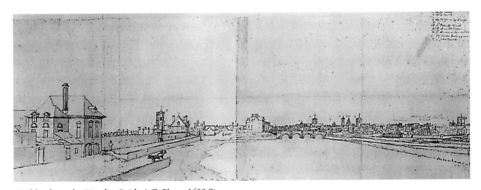

'Dublin from the Wooden Bridge' (F. Place, 1698/9)

George Petrie (J. Petrie)

C.M. Campbell (1791–1857)	'Cabins on Mud Island': c. 1817 (NLI, 1969 Tx [41])
S.F. Brocas (c. 1792–1847)	'Four Courts Looking Downstream': 1818 (NGI, 2440)
J.H. Brocas (c. 1790–c. 1846)	'Sarah Bridge' (NLI, 1961 Tx [1])
M. Connor	'Barrack Bridge': c. 1825? (NLI, 410 TA)
W.H. Bartlett (1809–54)	'The Cloth Mart, Homes Hotel, Queens Bridge, Ushers Quay': 1831 (bib. ref. 105)
G. Petrie (1790–1866)	'The King's Bridge and Royal Barracks': 1832 (NLI, 552 TA)
F. Danby (1793–1861)	'Ringsend from Beggars Bush' (UM, 2095)
E. Hayes (1819–1904)	'An Emigrant Ship, Dublin Bay, Sunset': 1853 (bib. ref. 103)
R. Barton (1856–1929)	'View up the Liffey with the Metal Bridge' (bib. ref. 103)
W. Osborne (1859–1903)	'The Four Courts Dublin': c. 1901 (NGI, 1916)
W. Orpen (1878–1931)	'Merchants Arch Dublin': c. 1909 (NGI, 2954)
Jack B. Yeats (1871–1957)	'Bachelors Walk, In Memoriam': c. 1915 (bib. ref. 103)
F. Mitchell (1890–1973)	'O'Connell Bridge' (bib. ref. 101)

This list of necessity omits many significant artists and many important works of those who are listed. Unattributed work, much of great interest, has been excluded. The list does not extend to artists born in the 20th century, and so does not incorporate such names as Brian Coghlan, Stephen Conlin, Brian Lalor, Pat Liddy, Nora McGuinness and John Piper, all of whom have made valuable illustrations of the river and bay. The Lawrence photographs, which surprisingly include little on the Liffey, are not mentioned, but what few there are, together with the many fine commercial photographs that have appeared in recent years from several sources, should be seen. The bibliography suggests some important sources, although not all have been used explicitly in this entry.

[77, 95, 96, 100, 101, 102, 103, 105, 110, 111, 112, 113, 115, 271, 272, 273, 274]

IMMACULATE CONCEPTION, CHURCH OF THE

When the Franciscans returned to Dublin early in the 17th century, one of the houses where the sacrifice of the mass was offered, as early as 1615, was in the warren of buildings between Merchants Quay and Cook Street. The order had a friary in Cook Street, from which one of its members, Dr Thomas Fleming, was ordained archbishop of Dublin in 1623. The mass house was approached from Cook Street by a lane on the corner of which there was a tavern named Adam and Eve's.

Early in the 18th century the mass house was replaced by a chapel on the same secluded site. Throughout that period it was safer politically to visit a tavern than a mass house, and it appears that those on their way to mass often said that they were visiting Adam and Eve's.

In 1756 Rocque indicated the chapel by a cross on his map, and named its gated approach from both Merchants Quay and Cook Street as Chapel

Yard. It seems that Adam and Eve's tavern had gone by that time, but in 1797 Faden named the approach to the chapel as Adam and Eve's Lane. In c. 1830 the chapel was replaced by the Church of the Immaculate Conception, designed by Patrick Byrne, and this was later extended to a frontage in Skippers Alley, from which there is today an entrance.

The church continues to be known popularly as Merchants Quay or as Adam and Eve's, a name introduced to literature by Joyce, who sets the scene for *Finnegans Wake* on the Liffey with his opening words, 'riverrun, past Eve and Adam's, from swerve of shore to bend of bay'.

[18, 19, 34, 173, 183, *DHR* (Mac Giolla Phádraig), maps (Rocque 1756, Faden 1797)]

IMPRESSMENT TO THE NAVY

A statute of Richard II in 1378 described the arrest of mariners and their retention for the king's service as a thing well known and practised without dispute. The right of the monarch to the service of his subjects when the state required it was indefeasible.

An early instance of impressment in Ireland appears to have been in 1678 when the lord lieutenant was instructed by the Privy Council to raise 1,000 men for the fleet. Similar directions were issued on several occasions during the 18th century. It is clear that there was a substantial pool of seamen in the country. A register prepared in 1697 listed 4,424 seafaring men, 2,654 being Catholics.

Dublin Corporation gave loyal support to enlistment in the navy. In 1755 George II issued a proclamation offering a bounty to those who enlisted voluntarily. The Corporation,

being truly sensible of the many blessings continued to them by his majesty's paternal care, and to demonstrate their firm and unshaken loyalty to his sacred person, family, and government, and their most sincere attachment to the welfare, liberty, and consequently the glory and honour of Great Britain, with which their duty and interest are so closely connected . . . the city of Dublin having at all times shown their zeal and firm attachment to his majesty's person and government,

thereupon offered an additional bounty of 30 shillings to each who enlisted.

In 1793 the Corporation allocated 2,000 guineas to encouraging enlistment 'in his majesty's navy in the port of Dublin'. The terms of the inducement suggest that this initiative was expected to raise upwards of 300 trained seamen and 400 landsmen.

While the principle of service by a subject might be a normally accepted royal right, impressment in practice could be harsh and unjust. Particularly during the 18th century, the press-gang was a rough troop to be avoided along the quays and at the riverside taverns. Merchant seamen could be shanghaied in port, thereby 'making it impossible for their own ships to sail'. The suspected presence of a press-gang in a port quickly reached sailors on their ships, even at sea. In 1726 a complaint made at the City Assembly noted, 'His majesty's ship-of-war "Lively" had of late a press warrant to press for seamen which occasioned great scarcity of coals in this city by coal ships not venturing to come in for fear of being pressed.'

The practice of involuntary impressment at Dublin appears to have faded out with the ending of the Napoleonic wars in the early 19th century.

[197, *CARD*, VII, VIII, X, XIV]

INLAND NAVIGATION, COMMISSIONERS OF
See DIRECTORS GENERAL OF INLAND NAVIGATION.

INLAND NAVIGATION, DIRECTORS GENERAL OF
See DIRECTORS GENERAL OF INLAND NAVIGATION.

INNER DOCK, THE
See CUSTOM HOUSE DOCKS.

INNS, THE
See THE KING'S INNS.

INNS QUAY
Until the end of the 18th century Inns Quay extended from the Old Bridge (Fr Mathew) to Ormonde Bridge, slightly downstream of Charles

Street. Since the completion of Richmond Bridge (O'Donovan Rossa) in 1816, following the collapse of Ormonde Bridge in 1802, Inns Quay stops at O'Donovan Rossa Bridge, and the east end has become part of Upper Ormonde Quay.

Inns Quay differs from most of the other Liffey quays in two ways. Firstly, it was dominated in early times by a single building complex which, as St Saviour's Priory or Blackfriars, was older than it. Secondly, the curvature of the river below the Old Bridge, and the fact that St Saviour's, built in the 13th century, lay close by the river, suggest that the north bank in that area was made of firm ground not normally overflowed by the tide. In this it would have formed a salient between the Arran Quay strand above it and the estuary of the Bradogue below it, and the development of a quay would not, consequently, have required such extensive reclamation as elsewhere. Even to the present day, the relative levels of Arran Quay and Inns Quay reflect this difference.

When the Society of the King's Inns received its first lease of the former Blackfriars in 1541, the first 50 m of the modern quay at its west end consisted of a narrow entrance lane from Church Street, separated from the river-bank by a cluster of buildings, and an open courtyard bounded by the priory buildings and the river-bank. The rest of the modern quay would have been a path between the walled garden of the priory and the river-bank, leading to the estuary of the Bradogue, east of modern Chancery Place. A slip near the courtyard gave access from the river, and was used by both St Saviour's and the King's Inns for water-borne traffic; and this slip and courtyard can perhaps mark the beginning, in the 13th century, of Inns Quay. It would have been the site of frenetic activity for a week or two early in 1317 when the stones from the priory chapel, demolished for the purpose, were being used to bolster the defences of the city against a threatened attack by Edward Bruce.

Speed shows this general arrangement in 1610. There is little changed in de Gomme (1673), although after 1638 Randall Beckett was active in building to the east of the King's Inns, under a lease which also compelled him to make a passage at least 20 feet (6 m) wide along the river-bank. Brooking in 1728 suggests that by that time building had been completed along the quay, which he called the Inns, from the King's Inns to Charles Street at Ormonde Bridge. By that time, also, three new arteries, Charles Street, Mass Lane and Arch Lane, had been made, running north from the quay; all are shown by Rocque in 1756.

Brooking also indicates that, by 1728, Inns Quay was a fully formed broad quay from the King's Inns to Ormonde Bridge. At its junction with Church Street, however, the narrow lane still restricted access to the quay. The lane had earlier been seen as the entrance to the King's Inns and had been blocked by a gateway, probably arched, controlled by the Society. In 1730 the gate had ceased to be an obstruction, as a record of the Watch of St Michan's Parish indicates: 'From Ormond's Bridge Watch-house: as soon as the clock strikes, the said inspector to turn out with four men westward and so along to the Inns turning into the arch, and so to the Old-Bridge.' This constriction of the quay, however, would remain until the 19th century, when the Wide Streets Commissioners reported in 1818 that they intended 'to pierce the dark and narrow obstruction through the very heart of the city' and had 'commenced on one side at Inns Quay and are opening from Church Street to the Four Courts'. It is probable that Faden was anticipating proposed work when his map showed in 1797 that this constriction had been removed.

Rocque in 1756 shows Inns Quay nearly as we know it today, and Malton's illustration of 1799 gives a lively impression of its use. After 1756 a new quay wall was built, increasing the width of the quay by 1.8 m at the east end and by 0.75 m at the west end, which by that time was located at Richmond Bridge. Also, the low plain parapet recorded by Carr in 1806 was replaced by an elaborate iron and stone balustrade, repeated on the flanking bridges, as an adornment for the Four Courts. These works appear to have been carried out between 1815 and 1825.

The building of Richmond Bridge, linking Chancery Place and Winetavern Street, in 1813–16 was prefaced by a controversy which could have altered the whole appearance and traffic pattern of Inns Quay and the parallel Merchants Quay. A memorial, signed by 22 influential persons, undated but almost certainly issued early in 1813, carried the title, 'Objections to the Intended Bridge Ormond Quay Dublin'. It claimed that the new bridge was to have been built on the axis of the Four Courts, and that a bridge at the foot of Winetavern Street could not be successful because 'the steepe at the west end of Christchurch is so great and the passage so narrow that no carriage can safely go up or down'. Furthermore, a new street carried down from High Street, crossing Cook Street on an arched viaduct and falling through Skippers Alley to Merchants Quay to extend as a new bridge on the axis of the Four Courts, would enrich the setting of that building. It should be stated that the primary purpose of the memorial was not to suggest the precise location of a new bridge in that vicinity, but rather to assert that any new bridge to be built at that time would be more useful if located where the King's Bridge was built shortly afterwards.

In another attempt to embellish the surroundings of the Four Courts, a proposal was made to form a stepped terrace in the river opposite the building. This was rejected on two grounds, namely that the river was too narrow for a terrace to add dignity to the Four Courts, and that a constriction of the river at that place could lead to flooding in storms.

Some influential citizens obviously saw the river as in some way unworthy of the Four Courts. In 1807 the Grand Jury approached the Ballast Board with a request to convey 'the river Liffey through arches from the scite of Ormond Bridge to the Old Bridge so covered as to form a great area or street' in front of the Four Courts. The Board demurred, and the matter was not raised again.

Inns Quay had also been called King's Inns Quay and the Inns.

[29, 76, 82, 87 (vols. 6, 9), 201; *CARD*, VIII, XI; BL, Add. MS 40196, f. 59; maps (Speed 1610, de Gomme 1673, Brooking 1728, Rocque 1756, Faden 1797)]

INSULA DE LE DAMES
See DAMES GATE PRECINCT.

INTERNATIONAL FINANCIAL SERVICES CENTRE
See CUSTOM HOUSE DOCKS.

Buildings in the International Financial Services Centre (architects: Burke-Kennedy Doyle & Partners)

INUNDATION FROM THE LIFFEY
See FLOODS IN THE LIFFEY.

La Rue Fabert, Paris, 1910

IRISHTOWN
The map prepared by de Gomme in 1673 is the first to give the positions of Irishtown and Ringsend. He shows them both on a threadlike peninsula no more than 70 m wide between the bay and the delta of the Dodder. Ringsend is near the tip, Irishtown is at the root and the distance between them is 270 m.

Human habitation at Ringsend (An Rinn) dates back almost certainly before 900. So far as this book is concerned, it has always been there. It seems likely that the area of Irishtown was inhabited at the same time, that the two were one community.

The origin of the separate name of Irishtown is obscure. As in other parts of Ireland, it may have arisen following the Reformation, and it is of interest to note that an early reference to the name is a census of 1659, which recorded that there were living in Ringsend that year 59 English and 21 Irish, and in Irishtown 23 English and 75 Irish. Shortly afterwards, de Gomme would name the two precincts as Rings-end and the Yrish Towne.

Nevertheless, when the time came early in the 18th century to build the church now known as St Matthew's, Irishtown, it was described officially as the Royal Chapel of St Matthew at Ringsend, and it continued under that name for more than 100 years. The name of Irishtown did, however, come into general use during the 18th century. Bolton in 1717 and Rocque/Scalé in 1773 called it Irish Town, and early in the 19th century it is named in the records as Irishtown.

The street pattern in Irishtown in the OS map of 1838 closely reflected the ancient precinct, with Bath Street running through the village along the spine of the original foreshore and continuing along the shoreline to meet Lancer Road, which is now Cranfield Place. There was no road at the time from Cranfield Place to Seafort Avenue West, which also ran onto the foreshore.

At the beginning of the 20th century (OS 1907/8) the area occupied today by the complex road intersection at the north end of Chapel Avenue had been named as the Green of Irishtown. There was still no road along the sea front from Cranfield Place to Seafort Avenue, but landfilling was in progress along the shoreline in that area. The Catholic church of Our Lady, Star of the Sea had been built, and an unnamed road (now Leahy's Terrace) ran past it onto the new landfill.

Thirty years later (OS 1935/6) the landfill on the seashore had been completed, and Beach Road ran in a straight line from Marine Drive (Seafort Avenue) to Cranfield Place to Bath Street. The old precinct of Irishtown is still identifiable in the Dublin Port map of 1987, but it is now far from the shoreline, with sports complexes, housing developments and large-scale industry occupying new areas of landfill north of the precinct and Beach Road.

[302, *CARD*, IV, VI, XVI, maps (de Gomme 1673, Bolton 1717, Rocque/Scalé 1773, OS 1838, 1907/8, 1935/6, Dublin Port 1987)]

IRISHTOWN CONSERVATION PARK
See PIGEONHOUSE: A PRECINCT.

IRON BRIDGE
See LIFFEY BRIDGE.

IRON POOL
See POOLBEG.

IRON QUAY
In 1733 the city ordered that a quay be built on its own land at what was then the east end of Bachelors Walk. Named as Iron Key on Rocque's map of 1756, this quay had a river frontage of about 30 m and its site now lies largely under the junction of Eden Quay and Marlborough Street. A document of 1781 refers to it as the Iron Yard. The quay was approached from Union Lane at the end of Bachelors Walk and also, according to Harris in 1766, from Ship Buildings.

[16, 58, 87 (vol. 5), *CARD*, VIII, map (Rocque 1756)]

IRON YARD, THE
See IRON QUAY.

ISLAND BRIDGE
From the earliest times, the ford of Kilmehanoc existed across the Liffey some 2.2 km west of Áth Cliath. A bridge stood near this ford in 1261 and this bridge site continued until the 16th century. (See Kilmainham, Narrow Bridge at.)

Island Bridge: Sidney's bridge of 1577 collapses in 1787 (W.H. Barnard)

In 1577 a stone bridge was built at the site on the orders of Sir Henry Sidney, lord deputy for Elizabeth I. It carried on the parapet his family crest and the date of construction. Place's drawing of 1698/9 (NGI, 7516) showed this bridge as having eight unequal arched spans. It was known at first as Kilmainham Bridge, but the name Island Bridge was in common use by 1725. From the middle of the 18th century the main pipe bringing water from Islandbridge to the city was embedded in the deck of the bridge, and in 1779 it was complained that 'the bridge is impassable by the frequent breaking it up for repairing the main that runs across the same'. In 1787 the area was, not for the first time, inundated by a great flood in the river. The six northern arches collapsed, and the two near the south shore were badly damaged. A makeshift arrangement was made with timber

Island Bridge (Sarah Bridge) (J.J. Barralet, 1793)

trestles and planking to accommodate hardy pedestrians and the water main, but the bridge was beyond repair. Its condition at that time was recorded by Machell (NGI, 6771 and 6779) and also in a drawing by Barnard in 1788 (NGI, 19183) and an illustration by J.J. Barralet in 1793 (NLI, 965 TC).

Planning for a new bridge began immediately and Barnard shows the piers for a new bridge of three arches just downstream of the older structure. This project was, however, abandoned, perhaps for fear of again obstructing a Liffey torrent; and, probably in 1791, Sarah, countess of Westmoreland, wife of the lord lieutenant, laid the foundation-stone for a new bridge, to be called Sarah Bridge. This structure, designed by Alexander Stevens, the elder, a Scot, has a single elliptical arch spanning 31 m. Completed in 1793, it was praised at the time as a 'monument of national taste', and still stands as possibly the most graceful bridge structure in the city. It has been illustrated by Petrie, among others.

On 2 January 1922 the Corporation decided to change the name of the bridge, reverting to the old style of Island Bridge. It is to be noted, however, that the name Sarah Bridge still appears on Ordnance Survey maps that have been revised since that time.

[12, 56, 79, 121, 215, 221, *CARD*, XIII, XIV, Dublin Corporation Archives, map (OS 1943/4)]

ISLAND BRIDGE, BATTLE NEAR
See KILMEHANOC FORD.

ISLAND IN MOUTH OF RIVER PODDLE
See DAMES GATE PRECINCT.

ISLAND QUAY
The group of the North Lotts, which was to have been located north of the rerouted Tolka River, was intended to be bounded on its east by a roadway running from the present junction of East Wall Road and Tolka Quay Road to join Clontarf Road west of the present Castle Avenue. This road, which would have cut across Clontarf Island and would have separated the Lotts from Clontarf Strand, is called Island Key on Bolton's map of 1717. The road was never built.

[Map (as named)]

ISLANDBRIDGE
Islandbridge, formerly written as Island Bridge, is a district west of Dublin with indefinite boundaries. Modern maps suggest that it lies south of the Liffey and west of the South Circular Road. It clearly includes the mills and other buildings along the river-bank west of the Circular Road and immediately to its east. The name is sometimes taken to include the area of the military barracks and depots east of the Circular Road, and the village that has grown up around the mills and the barracks. In more recent years the district has been taken as encompassing also the memorial park that extends westward along the south bank of the river. The possibility that there was an early Norse hamlet along the river in this area has been suggested by Curtis, and, given the importance of the ford of Kilmehanoc, this must be seen as likely.

The name of Islandbridge is of uncertain age. In 1210–20 the monks of Kilmainham dammed the Liffey with the weir that still exists today, and cut a channel for a mill-race, parallel to the river and about 390 m in length, thus forming the eponymous island. A narrow bridge, probably a footbridge, existed across the Liffey as early as 1261. Arguably, it was located near Kilmehanoc Ford just upstream of Sarah Bridge near the east end of the island. This narrow bridge was replaced by Sidney's stone bridge in 1577, and this in its turn was replaced by Sarah Bridge in 1791–3. Thus Islandbridge as a name can date back to the 13th century. In earlier history, however, the name of Kilmainham is generally used for this district, and one may possibly best look for a change of name to the late 16th or the 17th century. Here one may consider a legal conveyance of 1725 from William Fariss to Walter Griffith which spoke of the 'mills and weyres of Kilmainham commonly known by the name of Island Bridge', and also the use of this name by Captain Perry in a communication of 1721 to the city authorities.

The weir, islands, mills, fishery, bridge, barracks and memorial park which carry this name are dealt with in other entries.

[CARD, VII, DHR (Curtis), Dublin Corporation Archives, maps (OS 1838, current)]

ISLANDBRIDGE, ISLANDS AT
See THE SOMMER ILANDS.

ISLANDBRIDGE, ST JOHN'S WELL AT
St John's Well at Islandbridge is one of several holy wells in and around Dublin. It was located, according to Taylor (1816) and OS (1838), on the east side of the Circular Road south of Clancy Barracks. It does not appear on current maps, probably because of the cutting required for the railway lines entering Heuston railway station, but it is commemorated in the name of St John's Road.

The annual pilgrimage to St John's Well was on 24 June, the birthday of St John the Baptist; and a provision of the permission granted to Walsh in 1815 for the Halfpenny Bridge, which was to replace some ferry services, and of a lease granted to him in 1818 recognising that permission, was that he was to keep one or more boats available for a week each year to ferry those from the north side of the city who wished to cross the river near Steevens's Lane for the purpose of visiting St John's Well.

A spirited account of the pattern day at the well, which dates back at least to the first half of the 16th century, is given by Weston Joyce.

[34, 65, maps (Taylor 1816, OS 1838, current)]

ISLANDBRIDGE BARRACKS

See CLANCY BARRACKS.

ISLANDBRIDGE FISHERY

See ISLANDBRIDGE WEIR.

ISLANDBRIDGE MEMORIAL PARK

It was proposed in 1918 that a monument be created in Dublin to honour the memory of the Irishmen who had died during the war of 1914–18. Suggestions that Merrion Square should become a memorial park and that a monumental gateway should be built at Phoenix Park were rejected by the state during the 1920s. In 1933 agreement was reached with the Department of Finance that a memorial park would be built at Islandbridge on a sloping site between the present Colbert Road and the south bank of the Liffey immediately upstream of the weir. Sir Edwin Lutyens (1869–1944) designed the park, which covers 7.4 ha, and its buildings, and the work was carried out under the direction of the Irish Office of Public Works. The park was formally opened on 11 November 1940.

Book rooms in the park contain detailed Books of Remembrance listing those who died, and an inscription incised on a granite coping reads: 'I ndil-chuimhne ar 49,400 Éireannach do thuit sa chogadh mhór 1914–1918/To the memory of the 49,400 Irishmen who gave their lives in the Great War, 1914–1918'. A tall granite cross is inscribed with the dates 1914–18 and 1939–45. A fine feature of the design which was not built was a bridge to span the river and provide a formal entrance to the park from Chapelizod Road.

Work has recently been completed on the construction of a further element of Lutyens's design. Located on the main axis of the park near the Liffey, it is called the Temple and incorporates a covered bandstand.

During the middle of the 19th century, the southern part of the land on which the park was later made was found to contain several ninth-century Norse burial sites; and while the park was under construction in 1933 further sites were discovered. Items recovered from the graves included swords and a battleaxe, and one grave contained the skeleton of a tall man, with a two-handed double-edged sword lying across his body, a memorial to an earlier warrior. [86, 150, 305]

ISLANDBRIDGE MILLS

See ISLANDBRIDGE WEIR.

ISLANDBRIDGE VILLAGE

See ISLANDBRIDGE.

ISLANDBRIDGE WATERWORKS

See DUBLIN'S WATER SUPPLY AND THE LIFFEY.

ISLANDBRIDGE WEIR

Dublin from Chapelizod, showing Islandbridge weir (W. Ashford, c. 1794)

This entry discusses the weir, fishery and mills at Islandbridge under that name and under the name of Kilmainham. Separate entries deal with the general district of Islandbridge and other relevant topics.

From the earliest times, there was an S-bend in the Liffey, probably some 450 m west of Kilmehanoc Ford near modern Sarah Bridge, although the Rocque/Scalé map of 1773 contains a hint that it began further to the west.

At the end of the 12th century, Henry II granted to Hugh Tirrell 'the lands of Kilmahalloch together with the moiety of the River Liffey as far as the watercourse near the gallows'. Kilmahalloch is a variant of Kilmehanoc, and the gallows was on the north bank of the river near Sean Heuston Bridge. Tirrell, in his turn, bestowed the lands on the prior of Kilmainham, including 'waters and mills, pools and fisheries'. The priory had been established in c. 1174, and it is not clear whether it acquired this gift with mills already built. It is clear, however, that before 1220 an autocratic decision had changed the river for ever. In that year Henry III wrote to his justiciary, Geoffrey de Marisco:

the good men . . . of Dublin have informed the King that the city was always wont to have the Avelith in such a condition that any kind of victuals could be conveyed in boats up and down to the city; and the citizens and others always had a fishery on that river. The prior and friars of the Hospital of Kilmainham have however lately made a pool (stagnum) there, whereby the city and citizens are much damnified; their fishery is totally destroyed because the pool prevents the fish from ascending, and the boats can no longer pass up and down as they used to do.

Henry then ordered that de Marisco

cause the river to be so enlarged and the pool so rectified that ships and boats with every kind of victuals, with stones and wood, may have free passage up and down the river, and that fish may have free approach to the fisheries of the King and his subjects and free return therefrom.

The pool was made by the construction of Kilmainham weir or, as it would later be called, Islandbridge weir. Passage for boats was never restored.

The weir, about 250 m long, was built at the beginning of the S-bend in the river, and its introduction had four main consequences. First, the river ceased to be freely navigable at this point. In the 17th century Boate was to write that the Liffey 'would be navigable with boats some three or four miles further, but the Weyres made in her a little way above the bridge of Kilmainham do hinder that'. Second, the tide, which formerly flowed up towards Chapelizod, ceased almost totally to influence the river above the weir. Third, a valuable fishing-pool, later to be known as the Salmon Pool, was formed among the small islands immediately below the weir. This pool would become the focus of the Islandbridge or

Kilmainham fishery. Fourth, the mill-race, cut when the weir was made, formed with the river the large island that would give Islandbridge its name and that would be the site of the extensive mills and other industrial buildings erected during the 800 years that have since elapsed.

The restriction of the tidal flow was very significant. A survey in 1926 (P.H. McCarthy) showed that the crest of the weir stood then at a level of 19.51 feet OD (Poolbeg), and it noted that the highest water level in an ordinary spring tide that year reached 15.87 feet OD. This represented a freeboard of 3.64 feet, or about 1.1 m, below the crest of the weir. If, as may be argued, substantially the same conditions applied in 1220, the action of the community then was, in part, to create at the weir a clear line of demarcation which prevented the brackish tidal water in the city from adulterating the potable Liffey water upstream of the weir. This achievement, which one may believe was deliberate, although it does not appear to have been so recorded before now, provided the priory with an unlimited source of fresh water, and one that would be tapped by the city 500 years later in the expansion of its own water supply.

The weir and fishery were still in the possession of Kilmainham Priory when an inquisition was made concerning its estate in 1541, and it is probable that the priory still owned the mill or mills. At about this time, however, the whole property passed into secular ownership.

In 1641 a letter from the lords justices observed that a Mr (Francis) McAvoy, who was then in possession of the Kilmainham mills, was in open rebellion against the government and had allowed the property to fall into disrepair; and its confiscation was ordered. A series of leaseholders followed. Ball records that after the Restoration, the mills, which were the principal source of flour for the army, were let to Sir Maurice Eustace. In 1664 John Wolfenden conveyed to William Hawkins 'the great island scituate within the waters of Avon Liffey beyond Saint James his Gate Dublin, and the houses and buildings thereon'. In the ensuing 80 years the names of John Davies (1701), John Kendrick (1712), William and Ann

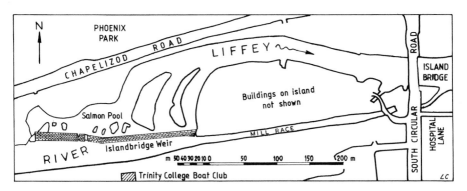

Islandbridge weir today

Fariss (1720), Walter Griffith, for 'the joint trade of buying selling and grinding of corn and flower and the salmon fishery' (1725), John Scott (1739) and Jonathan Darby (1741) appear as occupiers.

In 1741 the city began to explore the possibility of drawing off water from the mill-race to augment the municipal water supply, and in 1742 the Corporation purchased the entire property from Darby. For the development of the Liffey at Islandbridge as a municipal water source, see Dublin's Water Supply and the Liffey.

Finding the property as a whole to be unprofitable, the city again leased it, first to Robert Anderson in 1744, then to Timothy Mahon in 1766 and in 1774 to James Mahon. This letting included 'the dwelling house and stables together with the mills, mill races, weirs, floodgates, sluices, and sand banks situate at Islandbridge with their appurtenances . . . formerly known as the mills of Kilmainham . . . together with the right . . . to the fishery to the said premises belonging'. The city did, however, retain its water supply option.

The appearance of the weir and the islands below it at this period are shown by William Ashford in 'A View of Dublin from Chapelizod' (NGI, 4138), painted in *c.* 1794.

In 1783 the property, including the mills and fishery, was let to Alderman James Horan, and in that year also William Worthington, later to be Alderman Sir William Worthington, lord mayor (1795–6), was showing interest in Islandbridge. At first that interest aspired to the entire holding. During the 19th century, however, the Worthington

family concentrated on the fishery and on lands on both sides of the river but not including the mill premises or the island. During some of this period and into the 20th century, the family lived at Salmon Pool Lodge between the north bank of the river and Conyngham Road.

The extent of the buildings on the island increased sharply towards the end of the 18th century. In earlier times, the mill and ancillary buildings were clustered at its eastern end around the south end of the Kilmainham bridge of 1577. This grouping can be seen, for instance, from Place's drawing 'Dublin from Phoenix Park' (1698/9), and from the Rocque/Scalé map of 1773 and Samuel Byron's map in Alderman Horan's lease of 1783. Malton's view 'Dublin from the Magazine, Phoenix Park', published in 1795, and other contemporary illustrations show larger and more numerous buildings, and the OS 1838 map suggests that all the buildings now standing or in ruins on the island had been constructed by then. While the earlier mills had been built to make flour, the 1838 map described the large complex on the island as a calico-printing factory, and that same area was being described in the Plunkett lease of 1891 as Scotts Woollen Mills.

The eastern end of the island is close to the site of Kilmehanoc Ford, where, from the earliest times, the party riding the city franchises crossed the Liffey, this being then the farthest west point of the city liberties. In 1633 it was decided that the franchises should be ridden that year 'with certain permanent markers [to] bee set up in doubtfull places'. It is possible that one of these marks was at this western extremity. In 1773 the route taken by the civic party was 'across the Liffey Strand to the round stone by the Deer Park wall', and in 1815 this point was described as 'the large round stone in Sir William Worthington's ground south of Conyngham Road'. The likelihood is that the round stone was a millstone, for it is recorded that in 1795 'the fishing of the River Anna Liffey and Poolbeg from the millstone near Island Bridge eastwards within the city's liberty is the right and property of the Corporation'.

[15, 22, 56, 181; *CARD*, III, IX, XIV; BL, Single sheets relating to Ireland (1890.e.5, nos. 76 and 108), Add. MS 46296, ff. 18–20; Dublin Corporation Archives; maps (Rocque/Scalé 1773, OS 1838)]

ISLANDS WEST OF RORY O'MORE BRIDGE

In 1670 Henry Orson, a merchant, was awarded, on surrender of a former lease, 'a new lease of the small islands above the bridge of Dublin' for a term of 99 years at a yearly rent of £3 plus two 'sugar loafes'. The location and dimensions of those islands correspond closely with two islands shown by de Gomme in 1673, immediately upstream of Bloody Bridge (now Rory O'More Bridge), which was first built in 1670. In 1685 Phillips shows these islands as a single island with a house standing on it.

Speed had not shown the islands in 1610, and they do not appear on Brooking (1728), Rocque (1756) or OS (1838). It appears likely that they were sand and gravel banks formed in the river by storm flood conditions following construction of the bridge and that they were swept away in the course of later floods.

In 1683 William Ellis, who was then considering the development of that part of the north bank of the Liffey, argued that the terms of any lease given to him required prior negotiation with Orson regarding his interest. However, when the construction of Ellis Quay began some time later, little discussion would have been needed between the heirs of the parties. The islands had vanished.

[*CARD*, IV, V, maps (de Gomme 1673, Phillips 1685)]

ISOLDE'S GATE

See ESSEX GATE.

ISOLDE'S TOWER

See NEWMAN'S TOWER.

ISOLD'S SANT (FONT)

Also Isolde's Sante. A spring or well on the north side of the Liffey at Kilmehanoc Ford, probably within the wall of the Phoenix Park today.

ISOUD'S LANE

Also known as Isod's or Isolde's Lane. See BLIND QUAY.

IVORY, THOMAS

See HIBERNIAN MARINE SCHOOL.

IZOD'S TOWER

See NEWMAN'S TOWER.

J

JAUNTING CAR

A public transport vehicle used in Dublin from the 18th century. It was drawn by a single horse and was capable of carrying four passengers and a driver. The passengers sat, two on each side, back to back and facing sideways. Carr shows a jaunting car carrying two ladies with parasols along Merchants Quay.

This vehicle, with larger wheels and lighter construction generally, and with the passenger seats higher over the ground, continued in use as the side-car or jarvey car well into the 20th century.

[82]

JERVIS, SIR HUMPHREY

Humphrey Jervis, second son of John Jervys of Chatkyll in Staffordshire, was born in 1630. He was a Restoration figure, an entrepreneur active in the public and commercial life of Dublin. He became a sworn freeman of Dublin, served as a sheriff of the city for the year 1674–5, and was lord mayor for two years, from 1681 to 1683. He was already a titulado, a person of some importance, in St John's parish in 1659.

He negotiated, and caused to be built, the first Essex Bridge, commenced in 1676 and completed in 1678, the first Ormonde Bridge, a timber structure, in 1682, and the Ormonde Quays. He fell into vigorous disagreement with the city authorities and their officers about the real purpose of the two bridges and their cost. He had acquired, presumably from Lord Santry and Jonathan Amory, a considerable interest in the undeveloped lands of the 'Pill beyond the water' and in the whole of the north strand of the Liffey from the Bradogue confluence to the mouth of the river, that being taken at the time as near the present Abbey Theatre; and having secured the patronage of two successive lords lieutenant, Arthur Capel, earl of Essex, and the duke of Ormonde, he was planning new streets and quays and a major relocation of the city markets in those lands. Harris would later comment that Jervis promoted these works 'with great zeal and activity perhaps not without an eye to private interest'.

Sir Humphrey, for he had been knighted at the time of his mayoralty, continued to work on behalf of the city. In 1685 he was appointed by the lord mayor and aldermen to oversee the enlargement of Wood Quay, and the cost of this difficult engineering work became the cause of further civic investigation.

Arising out of his financial dispute with the city, Jervis lodged a legal petition which offended the civil authorities. This led to his being arrested on 23 December 1685 and held in confinement for four days through Christmas. His publicised incarceration increased his difficulties, for, as he himself recorded, 'his enemies in the city wrote immediately to all places that he was broke and in prison, which produced ill consequences, for the masters of all the ships he had abroad ran away with them'. It is clear that he had powerful enemies in the city who, as one reason for their enmity, did not wish to see the north bank of the Liffey developed, to the detriment of vested interest in the old city south of the river, certainly not while it was extensively in the possession of Jervis. His attraction towards speculative finance is exemplified in this episode by his listing, in the defence of his integrity, four ships then working on his instructions in European and American waters.

Further disagreements developed between Jervis and the city, one such arising from the cost and organisation of operating the drawbridge in the first Essex Bridge. His relations with the authorities and with the community generally deteriorated significantly when in 1690 he was charged with 'dealing with the Papists' in an improper manner by administering to them an oath of fidelity to William and Mary which omitted the word 'allegiance'. On that occasion he was able to show that his action was not in breach of the existing law. He was, however, unable to shed the embarrassment of having taken 'two guineas apiece from three or four Papists', they believing that 'he had favoured them in omitting the word allegiance which was really not in the oath'.

In 1695 Jervis, still seeking recompense for the cost of the two bridges, went over the head of the city authorities and sought from parliament that he should receive a payment for every ton of coal imported into Dublin. The city resisted this claim, but did find it possible, two years later, to grant Jervis an abatement of two years' rent on his leasehold of the Strand, the north shore of the Liffey, taking into account the troubled times through which the country had gone.

Some letters from Jervis at the beginning of the 18th century show his continuing concern with financial matters. One such matter, treated with diplomatic vigour in letters to John Ellis, former secretary to the duke of Ormonde, dealt with Jervis's interest in the Ormonde Market and his sale of a one-sixth share in it to William Ellis, brother of John.

In the closing years of his life, Jervis was again involved in a lawsuit. This was with John Cary, a merchant of Bristol, regarding one of Jervis's ships, the *Mary of Dublin*, a vessel of about 90 tons, which had been lost during its homeward voyage from Jamaica in 1689 or 1690. The hearing of Cary's complaint began in 1702 and in the November of 1707 Jervis applied for a rehearing. The case was reheard in June 1709, but during the 18-month interval 'Sir Humphrey dyed intestate', aged about 78 years. In later proceedings, Cary moved against the administrators of Jervis's estate: Dame Mary Jervis, Sir Humphrey's widow, Katherine White, his daughter, and her second husband, John White of Ballyellis, County Wexford. During an appeal to the House of Lords, which Cary won, the administrators deposed that, while Sir Humphrey 'had lost his credit by failing in the World' in 1686, he had when he died 'left assets sufficient to answer the appellant's demands'.

[16, 97, 132; *CARD*, VI; BL, Add. MSS 28875, 28877, 28878, 28892, 28893; House of Lords Appeals, 1707–13]

JERVIS QUAY

See ORMONDE QUAY, UPPER.

JERVIS'S LOTS

Prior to 1676 Humphrey Jervis and his partners bought 20 acres of land on the north bank of the Liffey. He later divided it into 28 plots to be leased for £10 each for development by others. These were known as Jervis's Lots. The street known today as Lotts, which is parallel to Bachelors Walk, may be associated with this development. It existed unnamed on a manuscript map of 1685 and on Brooking (1728), and is named by Rocque in 1756.

[*CARD*, VI; BL, manuscript map 10920 (1); maps (Brooking 1728, Rocque 1756, OS 1838)]

JESSOP, WILLIAM

Born in Devon in January 1745. He served John Smeaton, civil engineer, as an apprentice from 1759 to 1767, and as an assistant from 1767 to 1772. He established his own practice in 1773. In that year Smeaton, with the goodwill of the Grand Canal Company, which had consulted him on its work, invited Jessop to join him in a visit to Ireland. He was to undertake detailed work for which Smeaton did not have time of his own available. When this work was finished in c. 1773 Jessop returned to his practice in England. He was to become the greatest dock engineer of his day, and would be widely known also for his work on canal and river navigation and on land drainage.

In 1785 Jessop again visited Ireland and reviewed the proposal made by William Chapman in that year to build a canal along a circular line south of Dublin to connect the city terminus of the Grand Canal near James's Street to the Liffey at Ringsend. He favoured the proposal and recommended the formation of a pool at the end of the line in which canal boats could lie to have their cargoes discharged and lifted over a sea wall on to seagoing vessels berthed in the mouth of the Dodder. This modest scheme was superseded in a few years by the vastly more ambitious project of the Grand Canal Docks, which Jessop was commissioned to design in 1791 and which were built at a cost of £113,000, with Chapman as resident engineer, in the years 1792–6. This great basin, divided into two parts by a single-lane lifting bridge (now widened and known as MacMahon Bridge) on Great Brunswick Street (now Ringsend Road), was at that time the largest wet dock ever to have been built.

Also in 1791 Jessop was consulted by the Ballast Board about the proposed Pigeonhouse Harbour, and reported to it in July or August of that year on its practicability and its manner of construction. Slightly earlier, in 1786, he had been invited to design a wet dock beside the New Custom House, then in course of construction, but his design, while accepted by the Commissioners, was considered too extravagant and was not built.

Jessop is described as having been consulting engineer to the Grand Canal Company from 1790 to 1802, and it was probably in this role that he made his proposal in 1800 for a new harbour at Dunleary and a ship canal to link it to the Grand Canal Docks. Shortly afterwards, however, in 1801 or 1802, John Rennie was called in by the Ballast Board to advise on the Dublin port and harbour generally, and it was he who would design the new harbour at Dunleary (1817–21).

Jessop's last visit to Ireland was in 1806 in connection with the Barrow navigation works. He died in 1814.

[70, 73, 87 (vols. 2, 3), 171, 182, map (OS 1838)]

JEWISH CEMETERY AT BALLYBOUGH

In 1717 the representatives of the Jews of Dublin began to rent a plot of land on the Strand in the village of Ballybough for use as a burial-ground. They acquired a formal lease in 1718, and in 1748 they bought the land outright as a leasehold for 1,000 years at the annual rent of one peppercorn. In 1838 the plot was described as being surrounded by a high stone wall and having an area of about 1 rood (0.1 ha), and it appears on the Ordnance Survey map of that year with some suggestion of the layout being shown. It was guarded from 1798 to 1857 by a temporary caretaker's hut, replaced in 1858 by a caretaker's cottage, which still stands and shows over its doorway a stone inscribed in terms of the Jewish calendar, 'Built in the year 5618'.

It was the only Jewish cemetery in Dublin until the Dolphin's Barn cemetery was opened in 1900. Hyman gives a schedule of the inscriptions on 148 tombstones still standing at Ballybough in 1972, with the most recent interment listed in 1958.

[4, 9, 170, map (OS 1838)]

JINGLE

The jingle was a vehicle for passenger transport in use in Dublin in the 19th century. It is described as having a circular open body placed high upon springs and rolling on four wheels. It could accommodate six passengers and was drawn by a single horse. Its name derived from the jingling sound of the loose ironwork, presumably in the harness. The principal stand for jingles was at the St Stephen's Green end of Baggot Street, and the fare from there to the Pigeonhouse or to Blackrock was sixpence per person, provided that all the seats were occupied.

[29, 82]

JOHN McCORMACK BRIDGE

During the period from 1950 to 1980 Dublin Corporation reclaimed as parkland a broad belt of land south of the Belfast railway line and extending from the River Tolka at East Wall Road to the Clontarf shoreline at Clontarf Road, on what had been in earlier times the Furlong of Clontarf.

A new link, named Alfie Byrne Road after a former lord mayor of the city, was built on this land to join East Wall Road to Clontarf Road; and in 1984 the John McCormack Bridge, a two-span reinforced concrete structure, named in honour of singer Count John McCormack (1884–1945), was built across the Tolka as part of this link.

[Dublin Corporation Archives]

JOHN STREET NORTH

See ELLIS QUAY.

JOHN THE WODE

See BATTLE OF HOGGEN GREEN.

JOHN'S QUAY

Sir John Rogerson's Quay was so called in a Ballast Board reference in 1792.

[87 (vol. 3)]

JOHNSON'S ALLEY

Harris records two streets with this name in 1766, one connected with Mary's Abbey and the other with Wood Quay.

[16]

JOHNSTON, FRANCIS

Born in Armagh in 1760, Johnston came to Dublin in 1778 to train as an architect. He became, in Craig's words, 'after Gandon, the greatest name in Irish architecture'. In 1824 he was made president of the Royal Hibernian Academy of Arts, which had been founded in the previous year, and he provided headquarters for the Academy in Lower Abbey Street at his own expense. He died in 1829.

In 1811 or 1812 he designed the Richmond Guard Tower, which straddled the quay at the west of Usher's Island.

In 1814 Johnston joined with George Halpin, senior, and George Knowles in an examination of the north arch of the Old Bridge (Fr Mathew), which was believed to be in dangerous disrepair. They judged it to be safe, although 'to do away any apprehension of danger and enable the heaviest loads to pass in perfect safety', they recommended 'that long timber be laid over that arch, the ends to rest on the quay and first pier, the timber to be covered with earth and then paved over, this will afford a safe passage should the arch ever fall in or be taken away'.

Johnston and John Semple were consulted in 1815 about the proposed innovative cast-iron structure of the Halfpenny Bridge. Johnston found 'it is a practicable plan and it will be a secure and permanent one for the purpose intended'. Semple concurred.

Separate entries are given for the various individuals and structures mentioned above.

[1, 3, 54, 87 (vol. 9)]

JONES, JOHN

See FERRIES ACROSS THE LIFFEY.

JONES, MICHAEL

Colonel Michael Jones, one of four sons of the bishop of Killaloe, arrived at Dublin in 1647 at the head of a force in the Parliamentary army, and later became governor of the city. He defeated the marquis of Ormonde at the battle of Rathmines in 1649, thereby opening the way for Cromwell to land in Ireland with his army.

He accompanied Cromwell as his chosen lieutenant during the early months of the Irish campaign, but died with a fever at Dungarvan, County Waterford in December 1649. While his rank when he died was lieutenant-general, it is possible that the earlier mutual trust between Jones and Cromwell had by then diminished.

[47, 190]

JOYCE, JAMES

Born at Brighton Square in Dublin in 1882, died in Zurich in 1941. Joyce loved his city and its river. His final work, *Finnegans Wake* (1939), opens with the Liffey in the old town, 'riverrun, past Eve and Adam's, from swerve of shore to bend of bay', and returns to it to close and to begin again.

Ulysses (1922) smiles at pomp and ceremony along the quays in the city, and turns more than once to the vastness of the South Bull sands and the bay. *Dubliners* (1914) sets scenes on the old quays and in the newer lands and river-fronts at East Wall and Ringsend; and *A Portrait of the Artist as a Young Man* (1916) records a rich lonely day at Dollymount Strand on the North Bull, where Joyce moved away from his boyhood and became 'a hawk-like man flying sunward above the sea'.

References to the Liffey in Joyce's work will be found in this book. Many more await quotation and, perhaps, discovery.

[27, 62, 183, 306]

JOYCE, JAMES, TOWER MUSEUM

See MARTELLO TOWERS.

James Joyce (sculptor: M. Fitzgibbon)

JUSTICIAR, OFFICE OF

Shortly after the capture of Dublin in 1170, Henry II named Richard FitzGilbert, Strongbow, as his chief governor in Ireland. While Strongbow was out of Ireland in 1173 and after his death in 1176, William FitzAldelin held this position. He was succeeded by Hugh de Lacy, who served from 1177 to 1181. The title of justiciar was introduced during this period, and subsequent chief governors continued to use it at least into the 15th century. In 1308 Piers Gaveston, earl of Cornwall, was named by Edward II as his lord lieutenant to be chief governor in Ireland, and this title would remain in use until 1922, when for a few further years the form of governor general was substituted.

The titles of deputy and lord deputy were also used in late medieval Ireland; and the 'great earl' of Kildare, Gerald Fitzgerald, Garret More, of whom Henry VII said, 'since all Ireland cannot rule this man, this man must rule all Ireland', did in effect rule Ireland as the king's deputy, and the most powerful viceroy ever to occupy this position, for most of the period from 1477 to his death in 1513.

On occasions when a viceroy was away from Ireland – and indeed some of those appointed never visited the island at all – his duties devolved on, normally, three officers of state, the lords justices. In the 17th and 18th centuries these generally were the lord chancellor, the commander of the army in Ireland and the archbishop of Armagh.

[35, 36, 145]

K

KARNA
See CARNAN.

KAVANAGH, DONAL
Domnall Caomhánach was the illegitimate son of Diarmait Mac Murchada and was his right-hand man in military matters. He rode in the van with Miles de Cogan when the Normans went out from besieged Dublin in 1171 to attack and defeat the high king Ruaidhri Ua Conchobair. He was killed in 1175.
[35, 49]

KENNEDY'S LANE
See NEWMAN'S TOWER.

KERR'S CHART OF DUBLIN BAY
In 1875 the Admiralty published a map of Dublin Bay on the basis of a hydrographic survey made by Commander J.H. Kerr, RN, in 1874. The map is primarily to record the depths of water and directions of current in the bay, and shows the location and extent of the Bar, and Rossbeg and Burford Banks. The scale of this map is approximately 1:25,000 and the soundings are in fathoms, probably below low-water ordinary spring tide although this is not stated. A new edition of the map (c. 1903) shows a detailed survey of the bed of the Liffey from the Bar to O'Connell Bridge, which was made in 1889 by J. Purser Griffith, then assistant engineer to Dublin Port and Docks Board, and Commander W. Archdeacon, RN.

Some points of interest around the shoreline may be noted. Bull Island is named as Clontarf Bank. The area on the White Bank known as Costello's shows no buildings except the penstock station, here called an Engine House, but does contain a lifeboat station and rifle butts. Clontarf

Island is shown as a curved splinter of land 600 m long and tapering in width from 60 m to a point at its north-east end. The road from Ringsend to the Pigeonhouse precinct runs along the top of the South Wall, here called the Pigeon House Wall, and Cambridge Road runs directly on to the Wall. The three-arched stone bridge, now known as New Bridge, at the north end of Lansdowne Road is named on this map as Wooden Bridge.

KILKENNY, MV
The cargo container motor vessel *Kilkenny* collided with the motor vessel *Hasselwerder* about 2 km east of the Poolbeg lighthouse on 21 November 1991 and capsized. Three members of the crew of the *Kilkenny* died in the accident. The vessel was damaged beyond repair and was salvaged for scrap.

KILLALY, JOHN
Delany has described Killaly as Ireland's most successful home-trained engineer. He joined the Grand Canal Company as a young surveyor in 1794, and worked with it until the canal was completed. In *c.* 1803 he prepared a scheme for the construction of a ship canal through Dublin Bay from the little harbour of 'Dunlary' to the Grand Canal Docks, the purpose being to avoid the bar at the mouth of the Liffey. This project did not materialise.

In 1814 Killaly worked on the Royal Canal for the Directors General of Inland Navigation and, on their behalf, organised the construction of works outstanding, up to their completion in 1817. In 1831 an act was passed authorising the construction of the Dublin and Kingstown railway. Killaly was considered for the position of engineer for the railway company but was 'judged unduly favourable to canals', and the post went to Alexander Nimmo.

John Killaly died on 6 April 1832.
[48, 73, 74, 282, *DHR* (Murray)]

KILMAHENNOCKES HILL
See ENNOCNEGANHOC.

KILMAINHAM, NARROW BRIDGE AT

Before Sir Henry Sidney, the lord deputy, built his bridge at Kilmainham in 1577, it appears that not only was the ford of Kilmehanoc in use, but there was a bridge, at least a footbridge, crossing the Liffey in that vicinity. The following evidence is offered.

In 1535 Sir William Skeffington (see separate entry), returning from Trim, County Meath, with a party including archers and musketeers, was challenged by Silken Thomas as he attempted to cross the Liffey at Kilmainham by a bridge described as a 'narrow bridge'.

In the previous year, Ball records that the citizens of Dublin went out to intercept, at Kilmainham Bridge, a raiding party of O'Tooles who were crossing back to Wicklow after a foray into Fingal. On that occasion, the O'Tooles defeated the citizens at Sallcock's Wood some way to the north of the river.

Very much earlier, in 1261, a fishing dispute is mentioned in the White Book of the City of Dublin as existing between the city and the prior of the Hospital of St John of Jerusalem. In settling the dispute, it was agreed that 'saving the Prior's right to one draught of fish, free boat and net, the Major and commonalty are to have free fishing in the water of Avenelif from the bridge of Kylmaynan to the sea'.

It seems clear that a bridge did exist, but exactly where it was is not known. The practice is found in other estuaries, certainly in more recent times, of building a simple bridge for people and animals immediately beside a ford to provide a crossing there at all stages of the tide. This could suggest the bridge being at Kilmehanoc Ford, which must be the most likely location. However, the possibility cannot be discounted that such a bridge might have used as 'stepping-stones' the islands below the weir some half a kilometre upstream from the ford, in whatever form they then were.

[56; *CARD*, I; PROI (now incorporated in the National Archives), Carew MSS 1515–74, vol. 607]

KILMAINHAM, ROYAL HOSPITAL AT

See ROYAL HOSPITAL, KILMAINHAM.

KILMAINHAM BRIDGE

See ISLAND BRIDGE. Note that the bridge over the River Camac near Kilmainham Gaol is also known as Kilmainham Bridge.

KILMAINHAM MILLS

See ISLANDBRIDGE WEIR.

KILMAINHAM PRIORY

See ROYAL HOSPITAL, KILMAINHAM.

KILMAINHAM WEIR

See ISLANDBRIDGE WEIR.

KILMASTAN FORD

See KILMEHANOC FORD.

KILMAYNAN

Kilmainham.

KILMEHANOC FORD

Also known as Kilmayhane, Killmahennock, Kilmehenock, Kylmehanok, Kylmehanoc, Kilmohavoc, Kilmehafoch, Kilmahalloch, Kilmastan, Liffey-strand.

A ford across the Liffey, probably 50 to 100 m upstream of the present Island Bridge, it marked the westernmost limit of the city of Dublin and as such featured in the formal riding of the franchises from the time of John's lordship in 1192 onwards. In 1767 and 1818 the crossing-place was known as Liffey-strand. In 919 the high king of Ireland, Niall Glundubh, was defeated and slain by the Norsemen in a historic battle at this ford.

The ford is also referred to as Kilmastan and this may associate the area with Magh Maistean, about which the Book of Rights quotes, as a prohibition on the kings of Leinster, 'that it is forbidden to ride a dirty black-heeled horse across the Magh Maistean'. However, this name may relate instead to a place near Athy in County Kildare.

[29, 88, 147, *CARD*, I, XI]

KILMEHANOC FORD, BATTLE AT

See KILMEHANOC FORD.

KILMOHAVOC FORD

See KILMEHANOC FORD.

KING, SIR ANTHONY

Lord mayor of Dublin in 1778. It is recorded that when King was sheriff he pursued an escaping prisoner through the subterranean River Poddle and captured him, thus earning his knighthood. [34]

KING GEORGE THE FOURTH BRIDGE

See SEAN HEUSTON BRIDGE.

KING JOHN'S BRIDGE

See FR MATHEW BRIDGE.

KING'S BRIDGE

Also Kingsbridge. See SEAN HEUSTON BRIDGE.

KING'S CRANE, THE

See CRANES AND CRANERS.

KING'S GATE, THE

See WINETAVERN STREET.

KING'S INNS, THE

The King's Inns is, first, a society and, second, the premises where it functions.

In 1541, 17 named Irish lawyers were given by the commissioners acting for Henry VIII a 21-year lease at Blackfriars, the former Dominican priory of St Saviour, which had been taken by the king in 1539. Lawyers had been meeting there since that date. The lands and buildings, occupying about 3 acres (probably statute acres), lay in the angle of Church Street and the bank of the Liffey. The proposal was to establish there the Society of 'the Kinges Inn', one of the purposes of which was to provide education and training for those who wished to study law, and to enable this to be done in Dublin rather than London. It was a desirable part of this concept that the students should study in a community of lawyers, and that practising lawyers should themselves perceive a unity. Consequently it was also a purpose of the Society that lawyers of all categories be enabled 'to continue together at board and lodging like as his majesty's judges and serjeants of his realm of England termly usith to do'.

The quality of the buildings leased to the lawyers in 1541 was thus described: 'the priory church can be thrown down: the value of the timber, glass, iron and stones is not known. The other buildings in the site etc. with a cemetery and other accommodation, contain three acres and are worth nothing above repairs'.

By c. 1611 the Society of the King's Inns was firmly established, and at that time Blackfriars was conveyed to it to hold for ever. For the 70 years from 1541 to 1611 there are several records of leases relating to the property of St Saviour's. One of these was a renewal of the original 1541 lease. Others appear to have been related to different elements of the Dominican property, or to have represented conflict between government and the Society. Thus from 1588 to 1607 the King's Inns did not have possession of Blackfriars. In 1607 the state of the old buildings had so deteriorated that the only substantial structure held by the Society was the old priory hall and sleeping-quarters in a two- or three-storey building about 27 m long and 9 m wide.

A development of the premises of the King's Inns between 1630 and 1640 saw the construction of a court of wards and a record office close to the existing building. In 1638 the Society gave a lease of much of the eastern part of its land to its steward, Randall Beckett. The leased area already contained some houses, but Beckett was expected to develop it intensively and was required to maintain a public way at least 20 feet (6 m) wide along the bank of the Liffey.

A map first prepared by Gabriel Stokes in 1728, and developed in 1750, shows that there were in the 18th century nine substantial houses in a row parallel to the river, on the ground that had been leased to Beckett; and this map shows also the rather random development during the 17th century of the complex of the King's Inns' own buildings around a quadrangle at the west end of the site. In modern terms, the western edge of this complex would be parallel to Church Street and about 20 m east of the Fr Mathew Bridge. Its relationship to the river-bank is mentioned in the entry on Inns Quay.

Conservation of its buildings appears not to have been an important concern of the Society, and in 1730 a significant part of the complex was being occupied in squalid circumstances by impoverished persons not associated with the law. In 1742 the Society was exploring a proposal to dispose of the property completely with a view to building elsewhere, and in 1752 was given permission to do so if this were possible. Rocque shows the buildings as they remained in 1756, with their garden, which had also been part of the garden or orchard of Blackfriars, now being used as a timber yard. The reference on his map to a group of public buildings called the New Inn, near the north-east corner of the Society's property, is unclear.

In 1775 the government began a programme to construct a Public Record Office and Four Courts on the Inns Quay. The Society of the King's Inns acquired a new site on Constitution Hill about 1 km north of Blackfriars, and on 1 August 1800, the day on which the Irish Act of Union received the royal assent, the lord chancellor, John Fitzgibbon, laid the foundation for the new King's Inns as known today at Henrietta Street.

During its 250 years on the river-bank, the premises of the King's Inns became, in turn, 'The Inns of Court Dublin' during the period of the commonwealth, 'their Majesties' Inns' during the reign of William and Mary, and 'Queen's Inns' at the time of Anne.

It has been written that the premises of Preston's Inns, located on the Blind Quay near the future Essex Gate, were a forerunner of the King's Inns. It appears clear that from the middle of the 14th century some judges and lawyers lodged at Preston's Inns, which had been made available to them by Sir Robert Preston, chief baron of the Exchequer at the time, but that a purposeful Society, such as the King's Inns later was, did not exist.

A comprehensive account of the Society of the King's Inns and of its buildings, which is quoted extensively in this entry, is given by Kenny.
[29, 201, maps (Stokes 1728/50, Rocque 1756)]

KING'S INNS QUAY
See INNS QUAY.

KING'S LANE
See MERCHANTS QUAY.

KING'S MILLS
See DAMES GATE PRECINCT.

KINGSBRIDGE RAILWAY STATION
See HEUSTON RAILWAY STATION.

KINGSTOWN
See DÚN LAOGHAIRE, DUNLEARY.

KIPLING, RUDYARD
See ELLIS STREET.

KISHES, USED IN BUILDING
See THE NORTH WALL.

KNIGHTS HOSPITALLERS OF ST JOHN OF JERUSALEM
See ROYAL HOSPITAL, KILMAINHAM.

KNIGHTS TEMPLARS
See ROYAL HOSPITAL, KILMAINHAM.

KNOWLES, GEORGE
The building contractor who was awarded the contract for the Richmond Bridge in October 1812 and completed the bridge in the spring of 1816.

In August 1813 he reported, jointly with George Halpin, senior, to the Ballast Board on the state of the Old Bridge, and he made a further report on the same matter with Halpin and Francis Johnston in September 1814.

While these reports suggested that the Old Bridge was still usable, the Board decided to build a new bridge. In October 1815 Knowles was invited to quote a price for building this bridge, to be named the Whitworth Bridge, the design to be the same as for the Richmond Bridge. He quoted the same price, £25,800, and offered to complete the work in two years. This proposal was accepted.
[87 (vols. 8, 9)]

KYLMENAN

Also Kylmeinan. A variant of Kilmainham.

L

LAMB ISLAND

Three small rocky islets extend in a line north-west of Dalkey Island. These are Lamb Island, Clare Rock and Maiden Rock. They are named by Bligh (1800/3), and at about that time there was a proposal to form a breakwater from Dalkey Island to Lamb Island to improve Dalkey Sound as a refuge. It came to nothing.

[75, maps (Bligh 1800/3, RN Hydrographic Chart, no. 1415 of 1977)]

LANE, SIR HUGH

See LIFFEY BRIDGE.

LAT DATUM

See WATER, TIDE AND GROUND LEVELS.

'LAYER', THE

The 'layer' in medieval times was the surface of mud or shingle of a strand exposed at low tide. The term was used in the context that vessels that took ground at low tide were said to sit on the 'layer'.

[DHR (Corry)]

LAZARS HILL

In the year 837 there were large Viking fleets on the Boyne and Liffey Rivers, and in 841 the Norse established a harbour in Dublin. They used the mouth of the River Stein as a landing-place and set up a stone pillar, the Long Stone, to mark it, at what is now the meeting of six streets at the west end of Townsend Street. To the east of this place a low ridge of land extended eastward along the Liffey. The crest of the ridge was level and straight as far east as modern Sandwith Street, where it petered out, with the shoreline turning south-east

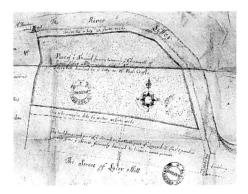

Part of Lazars Hill, 1683, showing also 'Mr Hawkins windmill'

to link up with the then high-tide shoreline on modern Denzille Street, Hogan Place and Grand Canal Street. To the north of the crest, which lay along modern Townsend Street, the ground sloped down to the strand of the Liffey, and to the south it sloped down, probably a lesser amount, to the marshy and sporadically inundated land which is now Pearse Street and College Park. It is probably because of these slopes and the fact that the ridge lay above high tide that the area was called a 'hill'.

Four hundred years later, in c. 1220, Henry of London, archbishop of Dublin, built a hospital or hostel on this ridge to provide accommodation for pilgrims, commonly lepers, who were on their way to Santiago de Compostela in north-western Spain. It is not clear how long the lepers or lazars had been using this embarkation area or whether there were other people living there, but the combination of the ridge and the presence of the pilgrims gave the area at some time the name of Lazars Hill.

Before the establishment of the hospital, the priory of All Hallows had been founded a little way south of the Long Stone by Diarmait Mac Murchada, and access to the ridge from the walled city to the west was by a roadway that passed from modern College Green to Lazars Hill, hugging the north boundary of the priory and occasionally closed by very high tides in the Liffey. The marshy estuary of the Stein further complicated this passage. At the east end of Lazars Hill, one could at low tide cross the Liffey strand direct to reach Ringsend, or at high tide follow the shore by Sandwith Street and Grand Canal Street to reach Ringsend eventually by way of Irishtown.

Little is recorded of Lazars Hill during the ensuing quiet centuries, although its subsequent history suggests that the use by leper pilgrims diminished and permanent dwellers began to occupy the area, so that by 1600 there was probably a significant settled population. Pool and Cash have recorded that 'about the year 1614, passengers from England used to land at Lazars Hill at the corner now leading to the low-ground where there was an house for the Surveyor and Custom-house officers'. This would have been the east end, at Sandwith Street, and is possibly what was later called the Fort at Lazars Hill. Despite this activity, the Hatfield Plan of Trinity College (c. 1592) does not hint at any land-based activity other than its own in the area, and Speed in 1610 shows nothing east of Trinity College.

The district had, however, been recognised earlier as part of the city, for in 1488 the riding of the franchises stated that the route lay 'owte of the Dameys Gate, and soe forth by the long stone of the Stayn levyng All Hallous on ther right hand, and soe by Ampnlyffy is side tyll they came to the Rynge's ende'.

The 17th century was a period of intense development for Lazars Hill. One might offer for its culmination the proud claim of John Hansard in 1702 that he had spent over £400 in 'fitting the mansion house on Lazy Hill for Alderman Loyd the Lord Mayor elect who afterwards declined the mayoralty'. This was before the acquisition of the present Mansion House in Dawson Street. Early in that century, in 1624, Edward Tanckard established a fishery on land at Lowsie Hill, and this is an early reference to the official use of the name of the district, and indeed to the use already at that time of a variation.

It may be mentioned in passing that there have been many variants of the name of Lazars Hill. It appears as Lazars, Lazers, Lazors, Lazy, Lazie, Lazey, Lasey, Lazoy, Lacy, Lousy, Lowsy and Lowsie Hill. Thus one reads that in 1649 the marquis of

Ormonde rode down to Baggotrath to inspect fortifications there before the battle of Rathmines, and was disturbed by the presence of strong parties of the enemy, some of whom were 'hiding themselves the best they could behind some houses at Lowsy Hill'. At that time, there would have been virtually no building between Lazars Hill and Pembroke Road, where Baggotrath Castle was located.

High tides and storm still caused distress in the area, in which by 1659 there were 237 people living, 180 English and 57 Irish. In 1651 the inhabitants of Lazars Hill and Ringsend complained that 'by reason of a greate breach of the highway leadeinge to Lazie Hill [and the water] floweinge from the sea into the sayd breach', they were enduring 'great losses not onely by theire longe stay, expectting the tide to goe forth, but also in daylie danger of looseinge theire goods by the river'. Analysis of this complaint leans towards the breach being near Trinity College, but it is possible that it was at Sandwith Street. This situation was almost completely remedied by the work of William Hawkins during 1662–3 in building a river wall from about Temple Bar downstream to roughly the present Corn Exchange Place. In 1673 de Gomme was able to describe all the land which is now D'Olier Street and Hawkins Street as 'ground taken in from the sea', and the threat of breaching 'the antient highway from Saint Stephens Green to Lazy Hill', as it was described in 1683, was largely lifted.

With this improvement of access, and with the work of Phillip Croft, John Mercer and Sir John Rogerson, and of the city authorities, in the construction of river walls at George's Quay, City Quay and Sir John Rogerson's Quay, all of which were made before 1720, interest became intense in acquiring new leases and defending ancient ownerships in the now expanding precinct. Land was leased along Lazars Hill, using the Long Stone as a fixed landmark. Conditions were imposed on new tenants of the city to provide space for new roadways and quays. In 1687 a new public market, to be called the Roscommon Market, was announced by the royal decree of James II, on the petition of Cary Dillon, fifth earl of Roscommon. Reference was being made to existing quays or wharves belonging to Captain Nichols or Nicholas, to Mr Cross or Crosse and to Mr John Mercer. These were almost certainly at right angles to the Liffey and interacted in some way with Lazars Hill; and the need to retain them had to be answered, to the extent of arching the main new river quays over their entrances, as for instance can be seen today along the Schiavoni waterfront in Venice.

Behind the scenes, in protracted legal action, the Dockwra estate, represented principally by George Brooke, a grandson of Lord Dockwra, was proceeding against the city authorities to determine the primary ownership of the newly developed lands and the strands from which they had been reclaimed. In 1659 it was recorded that 'Lord Dowcra his heiresses do clayme the said strand to belong to them'. Aspects of this claim would pass through the courts well into the 18th century. In the outcome, a lease for ever of the whole north-side frontage of Lazars Hill from East Lombard Street to a line drawn along Corn Exchange Place and having a depth south–north of about 160 feet was awarded to the Dockwra estate. The areas between this holding and the river remained in the Mercer estate or in the ownership of the city.

During this time and during the rest of the 18th century the development of the Lazars Hill precinct continued. George's Quay, City Quay, Poolbeg Street and South Gloucester Street were laid out on an east–west axis, and George's Street and Shoe Lane, now combined in Tara Street, and also Luke Street, Moss Street and Prince's Street were laid out north to south. Rocque shows that by 1756 there was extensive building and planting of gardens along most of the frontages of these streets, although there would remain some plots along the north side of Lazars Hill not yet built on 80 years later when the first Ordnance Survey maps appeared in 1838.

The character of Lazars Hill as the high street of a long-established city precinct of the same name began to change early in the 19th century. The larger thoroughfare of Great Brunswick Street,

now Pearse Street, did not appear as a through route until 1838, when it emerged after a remarkably rapid development as a fully built street which had taken over as the main road through the city to Ringsend and the Sandymount shore. The ridge that had led to the name had been obliterated by filling in the low flanks. The very name of Lazars Hill was disappearing. Rocque used this name in 1756, and as late as 1815 Arthur Neville, writing as city surveyor, used it in a survey of the city liberties and franchises. However, Faden in 1797 was already making formal use of a new title of Townsend Street, a name of uncertain age and origin. This name became enshrined in the maps of the Ordnance Survey, and so brought to an end a road-name that had been in use in Dublin for probably 600 or more years.

[22, 37, 47, 106, 147, 149, 150; *CARD*, I, III–VI; BL, Pamphlets 1890, e.5; maps (Hatfield Plan *c.* 1592, Speed 1610, de Gomme 1673, Rocque 1756, Faden 1797, Taylor 1816, OS 1838)]

LAZARS HILL FORT
See FORT AT LAZARS HILL.

LAZARS HILL MANSION HOUSE
See LAZARS HILL.

LE HORE, RANDULF
See HORE, RANDULF LE.

LE PORTER, RADULF
In *c.* 1240 the citizens gave permission to Radulf le Porter to build with wood or stone a passage from St Audoen's Gate to the 'water of Avenlif . . . so that he can there make a suitable gate to be open at all proper hours and through which a cart loaded with hides and one sack of wool may . . . have passage to the water of Avenlif. The citizens also gave to le Porter and his heirs 'ten feet of their ground, in breadth, opposite the habitation of the Friars Preachers of the Holy Saviour, Dublin towards the west, and in length from the street so far as the thread of the water of Avenlif'.

This statement is difficult to interpret. The following is tentatively suggested. Le Porter was to make a firm track across land largely under-developed due north from St Audoen's Gate to the Liffey, a distance of some 140 m. There he was to make a gated slip with access to the river at all tides. Directly opposite on the north bank, east of St Saviour's Priory, he was to make a matching slip giving access from the relatively high river-bank down to 'the thread of the water' – that is to say, to the low-water channel in the river – again to be usable at all tides. It seems clear that use was not being made of the existing bridge upstream. A question might be asked: was Radulf le Porter a carrier by occupation?

[*CARD*, I]

Charles Lever (S. Pearce)

LEE'S LANE
See ASTON QUAY.

LEPROSY
See STEIN HOSPITAL.

LEVELS: WATER, TIDE AND GROUND
See WATER, TIDE AND GROUND LEVELS.

LEVER, CHARLES
Novelist and medical doctor, he was born in Dublin in 1806, and studied at Trinity College and Göttingen. He would have travelled on the cross-channel packets, using Kingstown and Howth, and probably the Pigeonhouse harbour, and in several of his books made reference to this crossing. For instance, in *Jack Hinton the Guardsman* (1843), the hero describes arousing himself

> from the depression of nearly thirty hours' sea-sickness, on hearing that at length we were in the bay of Dublin ... the sea ran high and swept the little craft from stem to stern; the spars bent like whips and our single topsail strained and stretched as though at every fresh plunge it would part company with us altogether.

The year was, as the novelist put it, 181–, so the harbour was probably at the Pigeonhouse.

Lever died in 1872 at Trieste, where he was British consul.

[54, 55]

LEVER, JAMES
James Lever is described in the *Dictionary of National Biography* as 'a builder with some pretensions to rank as an architect'. He came to Dublin from Manchester and worked on the construction of the New Custom House. He lived at 35 Amiens Street and it is here that his second son, Charles (see separate entry), was born – not, as has been suggested elsewhere, at Mulberry Lodge in Phillipsburgh Avenue. The house in Amiens Street was demolished in the building of the railway loopline from Amiens Street station to Westland Row station in 1888–91.

[31, 55]

LIBERTY HALL
Between 1820 and 1830 a complex named Northumberland Buildings was built on the corner of Eden Quay and Beresford Place. It contained shops, a hotel called the Northumberland Commercial and Family Hotel, and, later, Turkish baths. It is probable that Northumberland Market, mentioned in 1835, was in the complex.

passage on Wellington Quay and Essex Quay if reasonable gradients were to be used to approach the bridge. Accordingly, the Paving Board asked the Ballast Board to raise the parapets, and the result can be seen today in the series of nine steps in the coping east and west of the bridge.

The level of the quays today varies from 5.4 m to 7.5 m OD (Poolbeg) from Ringsend to Rory O'More Bridge. These levels were established not only to provide a freeboard above highest predicted tides, but to conform with bridge surface levels at intersections.

It is of interest to observe that some of the streets linking Essex Street East and Temple Bar with Wellington Quay rise rather than fall as they approach the quay. This derives from the need found to establish Wellington Quay at a higher level than Sir John Temple had considered necessary for Temple Bar when he made that street some 150 years earlier. The same feature can be observed elsewhere where quays have been built parallel to older streets, as, for instance, on the left bank of the Seine in Paris, where Rue Xavier Privas slopes upwards for 50 m from Rue de la Huchette to Quai St Michel.

East of O'Connell Bridge the walls of Eden Quay and Burgh Quay were built in the period 1812–16 as part of the Ballast Board's walls project; and, further downstream, the North Wall, George's Quay, City Quay and Rogerson's Quay were all substantially rebuilt in other projects during the 19th century, in particular between the years 1860 and 1890.

A general note on the levels of the early quays is given in the entry on Newman's Tower.

[87 (vols. 3, 10, 11), 90 (vol. 13: Purser Griffith), 99, 180, CARD, I, II, Dublin Corporation Archives, maps (Speed 1610, OS 1935/6)]

LIFFEY: QUAYS, GENERAL

The Liffey quays are related in many minds to Jack B. Yeats's painting 'The Liffey Swim'. He illustrates a race down the river that has taken place regularly for more than 70 years, over a course of about 2 km ending between O'Connell Bridge and Butt Bridge. It can attract 100 or more competitors, although few will emulate Mr Jack Kearney, who is reported

'The Liffey Swim' (J.B. Yeats, 1923)

as first competing in 1950 and who came in second in 1995. See also QUAYS IN DUBLIN: GENERAL.

[Private communication (S. Kearney)]

LIFFEY: THE RIVER AND ITS NAME

The Liffey rises in a circle of peat hags about 550 m above sea level and a short walk east of the mountain road from the Sally Gap to Glencree in County Wicklow. Passing under the little Liffey Head Bridge on that road some 3.2 km from Sally Gap, the stream flows west down through the Coronation Plantation to empty out as a substantial river into the Pollaphuca reservoir near Blessington. Joined in the reservoir by its first main

Anna Livia (sculptor: E. O'Doherty)

tributary, King's River, which rises at the Wicklow Gap, it flows west towards Ballymore Eustace and Kilcullen. It then turns first north and then northeast across Magh Life in County Kildare past Athgarvan, Newbridge, Clane, Straffan and Celbridge to Leixlip, where it is joined by its second major tributary, Rye Water, which rises near Kilcock.

Now flowing east, the river enters County Dublin and passes through Lucan and Chapelizod to the weir at Islandbridge, where it becomes tidal and the text of this book starts. Eleven kilometres further to the east it flows into Dublin Bay at its artificial mouth, man-made in the 18th and early 19th centuries between the Poolbeg and Bull lighthouses. While the total length of the Liffey's course to this place is 110 km, its distance as the crow flies from there to the source is only 23 km. Since the present mouth of the river is quite modern, and this text extends back to 900, the ancient mouth of the river is taken, arbitrarily, as a line crossing Dublin Bay from the Baily lighthouse to Dalkey Island.

The origin of the name of the river is uncertain. The *Annals of the Four Masters* record that the king of Ireland in 268 was Cairbre Liffeachair, and it is suggested that he was so named because he was fostered near the River Liffey. Later in the first millennium, that part of County Kildare lying within the loop of the river was named Airthear-Liffe and Naas was its principal town. In 712 Congal, king of Ireland, leaving the district after extracting tribute from its inhabitants, wrote, 'Bid me farewell, O Liffe! Long enough have I been in thy lap'; but he warned at the same time that he would if necessary return to 'rescorch' the plain of Liffe.

Some 40 variations for the name of the river have been recorded. They are divided into two groups, those beginning with the Irish word for river, such as Abhainn Liphthe (*Annals of the Four Masters*), Avenlif, Avenesliz, Avon Liffey and Anna Liffey, and those using only the river-name, such as Liphi (*Annals*), Liffe, Lyffye and Lybinum. The accepted name for the river at present is Liffey, although the form Anna Liffey has been frequently used in official documents in recent centuries. This form will have led to Joyce's use of Anna Livia Plurabelle in *Finnegans Wake*.

The description 'Ruirteach' or 'Ruirtech' was applied to the Liffey in early times. This signified 'raging' or 'furious' and bore testimony to the danger of flash-flooding, which in a matter of hours could transform the river from a quiet stream into a rushing torrent overflowing its banks. This occasional inundation in the Liffey was not brought under control until the hydroelectric dams were built at Pollaphuca, Golden Falls and Leixlip in the 1940s. [238]

LIFFEY BRIDGE

Sir Edwin Lutyens's original sketch for the proposed Lane gallery

Also known as the Cast Iron Bridge, Halfpenny Bridge, Iron Bridge, Metal Bridge and Wellington Bridge.

In March 1815 William Walsh, the lessee of the Liffey ferries in the city, presented a memorial to the Ballast Board seeking the replacement of the existing ferry from the Bagnio Slip to Liffey Street by a metal footbridge.

He had the support of Alderman John Claudius Beresford, and he submitted with his memorial a detailed proposal from the Colebrooke Dale (*sic*) Company of Shropshire for a metal arch. It is recorded that the bridge, to be made in cast iron with a single span of 140 feet and a rise of 11 feet, was designed by 'John Windsor, one of the works foremen' and was to be built at the Coalbrookdale Iron Works. The records of the company are, however, incomplete, and it is possible that Thomas Telford was consulted. The Ballast Board required Walsh to 'procure from Mr Johnson [*sic*] the Architect and Mr Semple the builder a certificate that the proposed Iron Bridge . . . would be in their opinion perfectly secure with a view to

The Halfpenny Bridge with advertisements, c. 1900

the safety of the public'. When the two certificates had been lodged, permission was given on 22 April 1815 for the bridge to be built.

During the autumn of that year the stone abutments were constructed, and in the spring of 1816 the site was ready for the placing of the metal arch. This consisted of three main ribs of cast iron, each made in six sections. These sections would probably have been cast at Coalbrookdale and floated down the River Severn to Bristol for transport by sailing-ship to Dublin. There is no account available of the erection procedure at the bridge site, but it seems likely that it took place during April and May 1816 and was based on the use of temporary timber supports. The *Dublin Chronicle* reported that on the night of Thursday, 28 March, a man going home from Aston Quay 'dropped into the Liffey at the breach in the Wall near the intended iron bridge' and was killed; and on 20 May *Carricks Morning Post* recorded that 'yesterday the passage over this beautiful piece of architectural ingenuity was thrown open to the public'. This could suggest that the whole of the metalwork in the arch ribs, and in the bracing members, deck and railings, was erected in a period of no more than seven weeks.

It is evident from the press reports that public opinion in the city varied where Alderman Beresford was concerned. *Saunders Newsletter*

was fulsome in praise, naming the bridge as Wellington Bridge and giving Beresford the credit as the 'sole planner of the work', which seems doubtful. On the other hand, the *Dublin Chronicle*, through the medium of an anonymous letter to the editor, challenged the 'unauthorized' naming of the bridge as Wellington Bridge. The *Chronicle* found little to praise either in the generosity of the 'humane alderman' in granting free passage across the bridge to the citizens for

Sir Hugh Lane (S. Harrison)

Liffey Bridge today

the first days, since the uncollected tolls were really no more than a first instalment of the £400,000 which the paper said he owed the city at that time. While it is not clear that Wellington's name was authorised, one must enjoy the fortuity of its choice. The *Freeman's Journal* rejoiced that 'a testimonial to the Hero of the British Army has at last been erected . . . we allude to the Arch of Cast Iron thrown over our river . . . which we understand with the express permission of the Illustrious Duke is to be called WELLINGTON BRIDGE'. The *Journal* noted that permission to build the bridge had been given two months before Waterloo, and that in fact building was already in progress at the time of the battle.

During April 1816 Beresford was given permission to erect 'receiving houses' at the ends of the bridge for the collection of tolls, but in October the Ballast Board, finding these toll-houses objectionable, ordered their removal. The toll of a halfpenny would, however, continue to be collected until *c.* 1916, and a photograph of around 1900 shows an arched toll-gate in position at the south end of the bridge.

In 1887 the *Dublin Evening Telegraph*, in an article deploring the continuing existence of the toll on the bridge, which it called the Metal Bridge, 'the last of our toll bridges', observed that the Walsh interest in the city ferries had been transferred to three new lessees, John Shanks, Alfred Killingley and Earnest (*sic*) William Harris. This transfer included the Metal Bridge, and the *Telegraph* noted with regret that the lessees 'have

meditated putting up hoardings along the sides of the bridge which would be covered with advertisments'. The Corporation had, however, 'very properly served them with notice of objection to any such innovation'. The article also observed that some repairs had been made to the bridge on foot of a report prepared by Spencer Harty, who became city engineer in that year.

Despite the official injunction on advertising, which may have been related as much to stability as to aesthetics, O'Connor shows that within 20 years or so, the bridge would, with devastating simplicity, be proclaiming Holloways Pills and Ointments on the arch, and Spratts Patent Chicken Meal and Dog Cakes on the abutments.

This abuse was to play its own part in a public controversy that sprang up at the time, and has not yet ended. In 1907 Hugh Lane had handed over a unique collection of French paintings to the Municipal Gallery of Dublin, 'provided the promised permanent building is erected [for them] on a suitable site within the next few years'. In 1912, no suitable site having been found, it was proposed – Lady Gregory believed by Lane himself – that 'the gallery should be built upon a bridge poised as it were between air and water'. In 1913 Lane wrote, 'The Corporation officials have agreed to pulling down the hideous metal bridge (covered with advertisements) and to build a gallery on a stonefaced bridge.' Sir Edwin Lutyens, who had already committed himself to designing a gallery for Lane 'in exchange for an Old Master', as Lane wrote, was enthusiastic about the bridge proposal and prepared a very splendid design. Yeats wrote, 'I have seen the Lutyens design – beautiful. Two buildings joined by a row of columns, there are to be statues on the top.' There was, however, opposition. The foundations were too costly and it would be impossible to ignore the 'effluvia ascending from the river'. More importantly, some in Dublin perhaps did not really want either the paintings or the architect. The opposition came to be orchestrated to a degree by the William Martin Murphy newspapers, and Lane's declining health led to the abandonment of the project. His death on the *Lusitania* in 1915 would effectively establish the position, as we know it today, of his generous bequest.

The metal arch is now 180 years old, and a significant structure both in the Irish heritage and in bridge engineering the world over. It remains in continuous 24-hour use. Indeed the development in the last 20 years of shopping precincts on both sides of the river has increased the numbers using it far above the daily 1,000 which was its tally for the first 10 days of its service in 1816.

The official name for this bridge may perplex. It carries no inscription. The commemoration of Wellington seems to have been short-lived, as officialdom in the form of the Ordnance Survey was to use the name Metal Bridge in 1838, presumably with Wellington's knowledge. The bridge is now officially known as Liffey Bridge. Dubliners, however, know it and have surely known it for the last 100 years or more as the Halfpenny Bridge, properly pronounced Haypenny; and that will not change. It is hoped that those who actually remember the coin will forgive the liberty taken with the spelling.

Details of the structure of this bridge are contained in *The Structural Engineer*, vol. 69, no. 3, February 1991.

[61, 85, 87, 92, various Dublin newspapers, map (OS 1838)]

LIFFEY CATCHMENT BASIN, MAP OF

In 1921 the Ordnance Survey Office, Dublin published a map, to a scale of 1:63,360, showing the catchment basin of the Liffey and its tributaries. Except for the extreme headwaters of

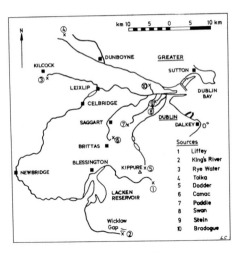

The River Liffey and its principal tributaries

the Tolka and the mouth of the Liffey below the Pigeonhouse precinct, it is comprehensive. Magh Life, the great plain in Kildare contained inside the loop of the Liffey, which was known as an area of rich land and fiercely disputed ownership in the earliest times, is shown very clearly. It is of interest to observe that this area, circumscribed by the Liffey and the Camac and extending from Kilcullen and Newbridge to Heuston railway station, is virtually an island, with the only dry link being a neck of land less than 100 m wide at the village of Brittas.

LIFFEY CHANNEL

In this book, the term 'channel' means the surface area occupied by the river and its tributaries and the bay, at low tide. The width of the channel in the river or in one of its tributaries at any section may vary with the amount of water passing it at any given time from the river or tributary catchment area upstream. For further comment, see Water, Tide and Ground Levels. See also LIFFEY TIDEWAY.

An exception must be made to this definition to admit Perrot's use of the term in 1585, mentioned in the entry on Newman's Tower.

LIFFEY FERRIES

See FERRIES ACROSS THE LIFFEY.

LIFFEY FREEZES

In 1338, 'so great a frost was this year from 2nd December to 10th February that the river Liffey was frozen over so hard as to bear dancing, running, playing football and making fires to broil herrings on'. Harvey recalls that the same happened for nine weeks in 1739–40; and this spell coincided with a period of nine weeks on the tidal Thames in London 'when coaches plied upon the Thames and festivities and diversions of all kinds were enjoyed upon the ice'. In another similar cold spell, Evelyn records in his diary for 24 January 1684:

> The frost still continuing more and more severe, the Thames before London was planted with bothes in formal streets as in a City . . . all commodities even to a printing presse where the people and ladys took a fansy to have their names printed on the Thames . . . Coaches now plied from Westminster to the Temple . . . as in the streetes . . . There was likewise bull-baiting, horse and coach races, pupet-plays and interludes, cookes and tipling and lewder places; so as it seemed . . . a carnoval on the water.

During the 19th century, Dixon records that ice on the Liffey in Dublin reached a thickness of 18 inches (450 mm) during the winter of 1838, and that in 1845 the Liffey froze as far downstream as King's Bridge.

[16, 28, 239, 245, *DHR* (Dixon)]

LIFFEY RUNS DRY

Harris has mentioned that in 1452 'the river Liffey at Dublin was intirely dry for the space of two minutes'. A virtually dry bed was always possible after a prolonged drought in the catchment area, but this would be only in that part of the west end of the city where the bed lay above the level reached by the low tide. Some draw-down of water level by swell action within the tidal movement could extend the area of dry river-bed for a very short period further into the city, and some such action may have led to the observation recorded 300 years later by Harris.

[16]

LIFFEY SHORELINE

See SHORELINE, THE 18TH-CENTURY; SHORELINE, THE MEDIEVAL; and SHORELINE, THE PRESENT.

LIFFEY-STRAND

A name given to the site of Kilmehanoc Ford. It probably denotes a small shingle or sandy strand at the ford.

LIFFEY STREET

The street running north from the Halfpenny Bridge consists today of three sections: Liffey Street Lower, from the quay to Abbey Street; Liffey Street Upper, from Abbey Street to Henry Street; Denmark Street Little, from Henry Street to Parnell Street (formerly Great Britain Street).

The same names were used in the OS map of 1838, except that Denmark Street Little was then Denmark Street.

Rocque (1756) and Brooking (1728) showed the same streets but named them respectively Liffey Street Lower, Middle and Upper. The streets did not exist in the late 17th century (see de Gomme 1673, Phillips 1685).

[Maps (as named)]

LIFFEY STREET WEST

A short street running north–south to connect Benburb Street (formerly Barrack Street) to Wolfe Tone Quay. Rocque (1756) shows it and names it Liffey Street. Brooking (1728) shows it but does not name it. On both these maps the street runs to the river-bank as there was no quay. The street did not exist in the late 17th century (see de Gomme 1673, Phillips 1685).

[Maps (as named)]

LIFFEY TIDEWAY

In this book, the term 'tideway' means the surface area occupied by the river and its tributaries and the bay, at high tide, whether between original natural banks or shorelines or between man-made walls or embankments. For further comment, see Water, Tide and Ground Levels.

LIFFEY TRIBUTARIES

Within the area covered by this book, there are said to be 32 tributary rivers and streams joining the Liffey and Dublin Bay, either directly or through other tributaries which do so.

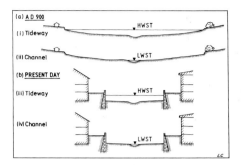

Notional cross-section of River Liffey from somewhere in Dublin at spring tide under prolonged dry weather conditions

Entries will be found under their own names for 13 of these tributaries. Moving west along the north shore, these are Santry River, Naniken Stream, Wad River, Tolka River, Bradogue River, Zoo Stream and Magazine Stream; and moving east along the south shore, Camac, Poddle, Stein, Swan and Dodder Rivers, and Glaslawer.

Other watercourses which have their own entries are Colmans Brook and Glib Water.

Consideration of the catchment areas for the named tributaries indicates that there must be or have been many other minor unnamed watercourses reaching the Liffey and the bay along both shores.

An extensive account of the Liffey tributaries is given by Sweeney.

[184]

LIFFEY VIADUCT

By the year 1860 Dublin had five railway termini, at Kingsbridge, Broadstone, Amiens Street, Westland Row and Harcourt Street. Each belonged to a different railway company and no two were connected except by long cross-country links. Seventeen years later, in 1877, the Great Southern and Western Railway, with its main terminus at Kingsbridge (now Heuston), was encouraged to establish a rail link with a new cross-channel facility being developed on the North Wall Quay between Guild Street and Wapping Street.

Accordingly, in that year a railway bridge, the Liffey Viaduct, was built across the river downstream from Sarah Bridge; and a half-mile-long tunnel, the longest railway tunnel in the city, was driven under Conyngham Road and the Phoenix Park to carry the railway from Kingsbridge past Cabra, Glasnevin and Drumcondra to North Wall Quay.

The bridge consists of a cambered metal lattice girder span over the river with three masonry arch approach spans at each end. The entry of the railway line under the Phoenix Park can be identified by the stone arch built into the park wall on Conyngham Road. The bridge can now be viewed close up from the residential development of Bridgewater Quay.

[214]

Liffey Viaduct (P. Hogan)

LIME STREET

(i) A street connecting Sir John Rogerson's Quay and Hanover Street East. It was shown first on Brooking's map of 1728 and continues to be shown on modern maps. A wall plaque at the south end of the street records, 'Edmund Ignatius Rice founder of the Order of the Christian Brothers opened his first school in Dublin on this site in the year MDCCCXII'.

(ii) A former street on the north shore of the Liffey. See EDEN GARDENS.

[Map (Brooking 1728)]

LINCOLN LANE

See ARRAN QUAY.

LITTLE GREEN

The de Gomme map of 1673 shows Little Green as an area bounded today by, roughly, Capel Street and Halston Street on the east and west, and Little Britain Street and North King Street on the south and north. It was a significant road junction throughout its history, with the main roads to Drogheda (Tradagh) and Howth (via Balliboght) meeting there, and the Finglas road leading to the north-west passing close by; and this importance continued into the coaching era, when many of the northbound coaches started from the north end of Capel Street, still part of Little Green.

The creeks and channels of the mouth of the River Bradogue extended up to Little Green from the Liffey. This tended to make the ground swampy, and probably for this reason the area remained largely unbuilt until the early 18th century. In 1727 it was decided to build a second church in Little Green for the new parish of St Michan's, and, to enable that to be done safely, the Bradogue where it passed through the intended site was deemed to require 'turning, covering and arching'. In 1736 the city's herb and root market was moved from Ormonde Quay to Little Green, and in 1773 the building of the new Newgate Prison was commenced on the southern part of the Green, to a design by Thomas Cooley. This prison, where Lord Edward Fitzgerald died in 1798, was demolished about 100 years ago, but

some evidence of its nature may be gauged today in the purlieus of the Green Street Courthouse as they now stand. In 1893 the Capuchin Franciscans established a church and friary on Halston Street.

Little Green was so known in the early 18th century. In the 16th century it had been called Abbey Green, and it appears under that name in 1673 in the de Gomme map.

[3, *CARD*, V, VII, VIII; *DHR* (Moore, Moylan); maps (de Gomme 1673, Rocque 1756, OS 1838)]

LITTLE HARBOUR OF ST MARY'S ABBEY

See ST MARY'S ABBEY.

LITTLE JOHN HIS SHOT

Gilbert records a 16th-century chronicle relating to the tradition of an astonishing feat of archery performed at Dublin in *c.* 1189 by Little John, a companion of the courteous outlaw Robert (Robin) Hood.

According to the account, 'There standeth in Osmantowne Greene an hillocke, named Little John his shot.' It goes on to say that when Robin Hood was betrayed,

Little John was faine to flee the realm by sailing into Ireland where he sojourned for a few daies at Dublin. The citizens being done to understand the wandering outcast to be an excellent archer, requested him hartilie to trie how far he could shoot at random; who yeelding to their behest stood on the Bridge of Dublin, and shot to that mole hill, leaving behind him a monument, rather by his posteritie to be wondered, than possiblie by anie man living to be counter-scored.

[18]

LITTON LANE

Also known as Littin's Lane. See BACHELORS WALK.

LOMBARD STREET EAST

The modern name for a street connecting City Quay and Pearse Street. It formerly consisted of two parts, Petersons Lane from City Quay to Townsend Street, and Lombard Street from Townsend Street to Pearse Street.

It was shown for the first time by Pool and Cash (1780), who did not name it. Wilson (1798) shows the whole street as Lombard Street. The northern part is named as Petersons Lane in OS 1838, and it retained this name until recently, when it was widened and the whole became Lombard Street East.

[Maps (Pool and Cash 1780, Wilson 1798, OS 1838, Dublin Port 1987)]

LONDON AND NORTH WESTERN HOTEL
See CROSS-CHANNEL PACKETS and NORTH WALL STATION.

LONDON BRIDGE
See BATH AVENUE.

LONG COACH
The long coach was the omnibus for the cross-channel packet. Maxwell describes it as a vehicle drawn by 4 horses, which could accommodate 32 people with their baggage, 16 inside and 16 outside. It could be very crowded and uncomfortable.

[30, 82]

LONG MEADOWS
Long Meadows is the name given to the strip of low-lying pasture between the north bank of the Liffey and the road from Dublin to Chapelizod. It may have included some part of that road, west of the Islandbridge weir. The area was subject to occasional inundation, and it was in this vicinity in 1535 that the bows of Skeffington's archers were damaged by immersion (see entry on Sir William Skeffington).

The name was used for a townland as far west as Chapelizod, but on the maps of Rocque (1756), Faden (1797) and Taylor (1816), it appears to have applied only to the section between modern Sarah Bridge and Sean Heuston Bridge. In 1838 the OS map shows that parts of this section had been built over, and the name was no longer being used east of Sarah Bridge. Following the removal of the danger of flash-flooding in the river in the decade 1940–50, much of this area has been intensively developed residentially and for industry and sport.

The extent of the recent Bridgewater Quay estate, built on the former flood plain below the site of Liffeybank House, demonstrates the new potential of this area.

[Maps (Rocque 1756, Faden 1797, Taylor 1816, OS 1838, current)]

LONG STONE, THE

The new Long Stone (sculptor: C. Cussen)

When the Norse sailed into Dublin, they erected, as was their custom, a pillar stone near their early landing-place in the Liffey at the mouth of the little tributary that came to be called the Stein (= stone). Similar stones have been recorded, for instance, in the Orkneys and the Isle of Man. The Dublin pillar was said to be uninscribed and to stand 3.6 m to 4.2 m high. Its purpose has been mentioned variously as an offering to the warrior-god Thor, as a symbol of taking possession, and, more prosaically, as a marker for sailors. It may have been all three.

It seems probable that the Long Stone stood just above the high-tide shoreline. The procession riding the city franchises in 1488 passed 'by the long stone of the Stayn', and in 1625 the road from the city to Lazars Hill was known as 'the lane leading to Long Stone'. In 1607 the pillar was being used as a mark in the work of land surveyors, and Petty in 1654 shows its location inside the shoreline.

Within ten years of Petty's map, Hawkins's Wall (1662–3) would place 150 m of dry ground between the Long Stone and the new high-tide shoreline. It would then become known in 1663 as 'the longe stone over against the Colledge'. It continued to be used as a land surveyor's mark until at least 1679, but had probably been pulled down and perhaps removed before 1700, having stood for 850 years. Its present location is unknown. It may be buried in the area and still intact.

It is thought that the site of the Long Stone was on the intersection of five modern city streets, College Street and Townsend Street (which together formed the original 'highway leadeinge to Lazie Hill'), Hawkins Street, D'Olier Street and Pearse Street. This site would later be used for the Crampton Memorial, and more recently, a granite pillar evoking the original Steyn, sculptured by Cliodna Cussen, was erected in 1986.

[6, *CARD*, I–V, map (Petty 1654)]

LONGSTICK LANE

See MERCHANTS QUAY.

LOOPLINE BRIDGE

As early as 1848 an engineer named Sankey proposed

> a bridge of one arch over the Liffey to cross opposite and pass through the Dock premises at an elevation of 50 feet above the level of high water and approached on either side by an inclined plane at an ascent of one in twenty. A communication to be established by this bridge between the Kingstown and Drogheda railways.

The Ballast Board did not at the time see any need for this work.

In the decade 1880–90 the desire to expedite British mail throughout Ireland, and to America, led to the construction in 1888–91 of a railway extension of the Dublin and Kingstown line from Westland Row (later Pearse Station) to link up with Amiens Street (later Connolly Station), and through these in 1892 to Broadstone and Kingsbridge (later Heuston Station). This required the bridge across the Liffey and the viaduct from the bridge to Connolly that we see today. The line was described in 1912 as being used by the City of Dublin Junction Railway.

The proposal to build this bridge had been under discussion for several years. In 1883 the Paving and Lighting Committee of Dublin Corporation had deplored the proposal, made then by the Dublin, Wicklow and Wexford Railway Company, and had urged that permission be refused. Later it was hoped that the bridge could be located to the east of the Custom House, but, with the realisation that there would be 'insurmountable difficulties to this being done', the plea became that the bridge 'should be made as convenient and the least objectionable as possible'.

In May 1884, 36 companies and individuals drawn from professional, business and academic groups lodged a protest with the lord mayor, saying:

> we request the Right Hon. the Lord Mayor to convene a public meeting of the citizens of Dublin at the Mansion House at an early day to consider the Dublin Railway Connecting Bill at present before parliament and to take steps to prevent the permanent disfigurement of the city by the Railway Bridge and Viaduct proposed to be erected across the river west of the Custom House.

The meeting was held on 6 June 1884, lists were opened for signatures, and on 18 June the *Dublin Evening Mail* reported that on the previous day workmen had been building a wooden model to show how the new bridge would obstruct the view of the Custom House.

Despite this widespread opposition, the bridge and viaduct were built. The bridge consists of three mild steel lattice girder spans with a total length of 118 m, supported on cast-iron cylinders, which rise out of the river. The bridge carries two tracks, with the clear width of the deck between the supporting girders being 8.53 m. The elevation of the bridge superstructure, liberally adorned with advertisements on the upstream face, is 3.66 m high, with the soffit of the deck about 6 m above quay level. It is not generally regarded as an elegant structure and it does interfere with the view of the Custom House.

In 1939 labour leader James Larkin commented that it was the Unionists and the Irish Parliamentary Party that 'were influenced to agree to the erection of the Loop Line which was the foulest thing that ever disgraced the city'.
[87 (vol. 19), 90 (vol. 38: Purser Griffith, vol. 65: Mallagh), *Dublin Evening Mail*, IEI competition data (1993), private communication (N. Torpey)]

LORD GALWAY'S WALK

Henri de Massue de Ruvigny, earl of Galway

Lord Galway's Walk was a pathway or avenue running east to west towards the Royal Hospital in Kilmainham across the meadowland on the south bank of the Liffey between Watling Street and Steevens's Lane. It has been seen also as simply that area of meadowland.

It appears on Rocque (1756) as Lord Gallway's Walk, starting at Watling Street and continuing the line of Dunghill Lane, now Island Street, some 75 m from the river-bank; and it is shown by Carrick in 1811 from Cooks Lane to 'Stevens Hospital'. This position remained the same on the OS map of 1838, but then it had become Galway Walk and was a short thoroughfare leading from Watling Street to the east side of the meadowland, but not extending to Steevens's Lane. As late as 1924 the Guinness estate maps continued to show it in the form given on OS 1838.

Lord Galway's Walk is not the Military Road from the end of Usher's Island Quay towards the Royal Hospital, a feature that appeared unnamed on Brooking (1728), and named on Carrick (1811) and OS (1838).

Henri de Massue de Ruvigny (1648–1720), a French Huguenot, was the elder son of Henri, first vicomte de Ruvigny, *député general* at the French court, who left France to live in England after the revocation of the Edict of Nantes, and died at Greenwich in 1689. Following the death of his younger brother, Pierre, with the duke of Schomberg at the battle of the Boyne in 1690, Henri, who had succeeded his father as *député general*, left France, and entered the Williamite army in Ireland to command troops that had been raised by his father. He became colonel of Huguenot cavalry in succession to the duke of Schomberg, commanded a corps at Aughrim, and took part in the negotiations for the treaty of Limerick. In 1692 he was made commander-in-chief of the forces in Ireland, and was created Viscount Galway and Baron Portarlington, with a grant of extensive estates. In 1697 he was appointed lord justice of Ireland, and later that year was made earl of Galway. He served in this role from 1697 to 1701, when he retired from government in Ireland, though in 1715–16 he would serve again as one of the lords justices. He died unmarried and his British titles became extinct.

In 1727 John Moncton-Arundel was created Viscount Galway. He was MP for Pontefract from 1734 onwards, and served as one of the commissioners of His Majesty's revenues in Ireland from 1734 to 1749. He died in 1751.

It has been suggested that it was Moncton-Arundel who gave the name to Lord Galway's Walk. Bearing in mind, however, that the Royal Hospital was the official residence of the commander-in-chief of the English forces in Ireland, and that the route from there to the Royal Barracks lay across Barrack Bridge, the balance of probability suggests that the Walk was named after Henri de Ruvigny.

[39, 55, 144, 298, maps (Brooking 1728, Rocque 1756, Carrick 1811, OS 1838), private communications (M. Germaine, P. Walsh)]

LOTS, JERVIS'S
See JERVIS'S LOTS.

LOTTS
See ORMONDE QUAY, UPPER.

LOTTS, NORTH
See NORTH LOTTS.

LOTTS, SOUTH
See SOUTH LOTTS.

LOUGH BUOY
The street now called Bow Street was named as Lough Buoy by Rocque in 1756. The name suggests a pond or lough, and the possibility of this existing in earlier days, particularly at the south end of the street, is strong, as the tideway of the Liffey could have lain close by. The nature of such a tidal lough is shown, for example, by Rocque's illustration of the Marsh in Sandymount on his map of 1760, and by Taylor in 1816.

Whether as a pond or as drained land, Lough Buoy was the subject of negotiation between the city and, separately, Sir Daniel Bellingham and Viscountess Massareene as early as 1660–70. These negotiations suggest that if there was a pond, it is possible that it lay roughly west of St Michan's Church. Young's Castle (see separate entry) lies near the north end of Lough Buoy.

Lough Buoy is also known as the Yellow Pool.

[CARD, IV, maps (Rocque 1756, Rocque 1760, Taylor 1816)]

LOUSY HILL
See LAZARS HILL.

LOVESTOKE'S LANE
Also known as Lowestock Lane. See MERCHANTS QUAY.

LOVETT'S GARDEN
During the 17th century Alderman Christopher Lovett was granted a lease on part of the land reclaimed by Jacob Newman in the Poddle estuary. This leasehold became known as Lovett's Garden. It was small, not more than 0.25 ha in extent, but, at the time, it was central in the developing city. In modern times, it extended from Crane Lane across much of Parliament Street and across Essex Gate and Essex Street. Close to its northern edge along the Liffey bank lay the new customs facilities initiated by James I, and also the ground that would become the south bank approach to Essex Bridge.

[CARD, V]

LOWTHER'S GARDEN
See MINT, PROPOSED.

LUCAS'S COFFEE HOUSE
See DAMES GATE PRECINCT.

LUCY LANE
Also known as Lucy's Lane, Lucas's Lane. See MASS LANE.

LUKE KELLY BRIDGE
This bridge was known as Ballybough Bridge from the beginning of the 14th century to 1985. It was then renamed Luke Kelly Bridge in memory of a musician in the group known as The Dubliners.

Harris records that 'in AD 1313, John Decer at this time a private citizen but formerly mayor of

Dublin built a bridge extending from the town of Balliboght to the causeway of the millpond at Clontarf which before was a very dangerous passage'. M'Cready suggests that the bridge was built in 1308 and was destroyed by flood in 1313. Ballybough village has always lain around the mouth of the Tolka, and it is generally accepted that Decer's bridge is the forerunner of the bridge we know today on the same site.

Decer's bridge had been rebuilt before 1488, when it is mentioned in the record of riding the city franchises: 'to Balliboght, and by the gate of Balliboght to the water of Tulkan by the bridge of Balliboght, and over that watir and so by that water southward'. The bridge of 1488 appears to be that described in 1858 as an 'ancient bridge of five rude unornamented arches'. There are records of its repair in 1676, when it was deemed to be 'insufficient as to the battlements, pavements and arches', and there is an uncertain reference to a need for funds for its repair in 1791.

It appears, singularly, on Phillips's map of 1685 as a six-arched structure, and on Greenvile Collins's draft map of 1686 as on 'the road to Baldoile'. Taylor and Skinner identify it in 1783, shortly before Annesley Bridge was built, as on the road from Dublin to Clontarf, Howth and 'Bull Doyle'. A drawing prepared in *c.* 1937, prior to a complete reconstruction, shows the five arches with spans varying in width up to a maximum of 5.5 m, supported on piers 3 m wide, and with a rise of approximately 1 m from the ends of the bridge to the centre. It appears probable that the pre-1937 bridge was substantially that rebuilt some 450 years earlier in 1488. If so, it becomes in terms of durability the most venerable bridge structure in Dublin.

The strategic position of Ballybough Bridge in the affairs of the city will be clear. Ball records that during the rebellion of Silken Thomas in 1534–5, an engagement took place 'between the insurgents and the forces of the Crown at Ballybough Bridge resulting in a great slaughter of Englishmen there and in Clontarf'. During the 18th century it was a place for the collection of 'tolls, customs, and petty customs', which were farmed out periodically to individuals. Thus, for the year of 1762, the letting was to one Snead at a rent of £56.

In 1797 Annesley Bridge was completed across the Tolka nearer to the bay, and the preferred route towards Howth began to be along the North Strand and directly across Annesley Bridge to Fairview, rather than by way of Summerhill, Ballybough Road and Phillipsburg Strand to Fairview.

In 1937 the ancient bridge at Ballybough was replaced by a reinforced concrete bridge of similar width between brick parapets, but with no significant rise from the ends to the centre. John J. Roughan was the designer. At this stage the channel spanned by the easternmost arch of the earlier bridge was filled in, with the land above it being reclaimed, and the new bridge consequently was reduced to one of four openings. In 1985 the bridge was widened on the upstream side, the older south brick parapet being retained, and a new brickwork and metal parapet was formed on the upstream side. Shortly after the completion of this work, the name of the bridge was changed to Luke Kelly Bridge.

O'Donovan has suggested that the early bridge known as Droichet Dubhgaill was located on the Tolka at the site of Ballybough Bridge. It appears more probable, however, that it was across the River Liffey close to the site of Áth Cliath.

[4, 13, 16, 39, 56, 120, *CARD*, I, V, XI, XIV, Dublin Corporation Archives, maps (Phillips 1685, Greenvile Collins 1686)]

LUKE STREET

This street runs north–south to connect Townsend Street (formerly Lazars Hill) to George's Quay. It appears first on Rocque's map of 1756 as St Luke's Street. Faden (1797) showed it as Luke Street, and it is still known by that name. Much of the street today is dominated by the railway viaduct and Tara Street railway station. The origin of the name is uncertain, but it may be associated with Luke Gardiner, who in 1741 acquired a long-term lease on lands behind George's Quay.

[Maps (as named)]

LUTYENS, SIR EDWIN

See ISLANDBRIDGE MEMORIAL PARK and LIFFEY BRIDGE.

M

MABBOT, GILBERT

Gilbert Mabbot had a brief eventful career in 17th-century Dublin, although he was never made a freeman of the city. He first appears in the Assembly records in 1669 when he is named by Nathaniel Fowkes, the newly appointed lessee of the city ferries, as one of a group of three influential citizens who have 'dayly stopt and interrupted' his boats. Mabbot was obviously engaged at that time in establishing his possession of lands and rights north of the Liffey opposite Hawkins's Ground, for in 1671 he was associated with Hawkins and others in a proposal to build a bridge across the Liffey near his lands.

The lease granted to Jonathan Amory in January 1675, which gave him permission to make new land along the north shore of the Liffey, named the 'water mill lately built by Mr Gilbert Mabbott' as the eastern limit of the grant. It mentioned also 'the corner of the wall beyond the said mill' as the eastern end of a highway to be made in conjunction with Amory's lease. This corner is shown plainly on de Gomme's map of 1673, and it is named on Bolton (1717) as the 'corner of Mabbot's wall'. The corner of Mabbot's Wall lay at or very near to the corner of modern Store Street and Amiens Street, close to the city morgue, and it has remained as an identifiable key point in the development of the North Strand district for over 300 years. Today Memorial Road joins Amiens Street at this same corner.

In 1684, and again in 1717, the limits of the new land to be divided into the North Lotts by the Corporation were seen as Mabbot's mill and the Furlong of Clontarf. The precise location of Mabbot's mill is unclear. In 1728 Brooking shows the junction of Mabbot Street and the Strand (Store Street had not yet been built) lying about 100 m west of the corner of Mabbot's Wall; and

Phillips in 1685, before Mabbot Street was laid out, showed an extensive tidal pool, which he described as a millpond, between that corner and the future Mabbot Street. It may be suggested that the mill lay behind Mabbot's Wall and near Mabbot Street.

It was a water-mill. The absence of any tributary flowing to the Liffey near this point and the nature of the terrain immediately to the north combine to make it unlikely that the water power came from a river. On the other hand, the presence of the large tidal millpond close by suggests strongly that the mill was a tidal mill. Two 'tide mills' at Portmarnock were included in the possessions of St Mary's Abbey following an inquisition taken in 1541, and Barton describes tide-mills existing in England at various times during a 700-year period (1233–1956). There is no reference to Mabbot's mill in Rocque's map of 1756, and, significantly, by that time Phillips's millpond of 1685 had been filled in to become gardens and pasture, although the corner of Mabbot's Wall was still very clearly shown.

Brooking, in 1728, is the first to show Mabbot Street. On his map it existed in its present location, extending from the Strand roadway northward to what Rocque in 1756 would call Great Martin's Lane (later Gloucester Street, now Sean Mac Dermott Street). The street had begun to be made before 1728. In 1722 John Moland leased to the city a dumping site, 108 m x 30 m in area, in Mabbot Street, for the use of the city scavengers. This continued in use for nearly 50 years but was taken back by Moland's son, Richard, in 1772, by which time one may presume it was completely filled and ready for development. In 1850 Mabbot Street contained 70 houses, of which 7 were tenements and 7 vacant. It consisted mainly of small shops and private houses, but included also the offices of Hugh Byrne, the city architect, and M.B. Mullins, who in 1859 would become president of the Institution of Civil Engineers of Ireland. The name of Mabbot Street remained in use until the early 20th century, but before 1935 it had been renamed as Corporation Street.

There is occasional reference to the name of Mabbot (Mabbott, Mabot, Mabbet) in parish registers in the period 1666–1786, but there is no reference to Gilbert Mabbot, and there appears no indication of a dynasty.

[22, 125, 146, *CARD*, IV, V, VII, XII, maps (de Gomme 1673, Phillips 1685, Bolton 1717, Brooking 1728, Rocque 1756, OS various)]

Mabbot Street
See Gilbert Mabbot.

Mabbot's Mill
See Gilbert Mabbot.

Mabbot's Wall
See Gilbert Mabbot.

Mac Gilla Mo Cholmoc, Domnall
Also known as Gillamacholmog, Gillemoholmoch, Gilmoholmock. See Battle of Hoggen Green.

Mac Murchada, Diarmait
In 1115 Donnchad Mac Murchada, king of Leinster, was killed by the Norse in Dublin and, according to Giraldus Cambrensis, buried shamefully, a dog being thrown into his grave. In *c.* 1126 his son, Diarmait Mac Murchada, bearing a hatred for the Dublin Norse, became king of Leinster. Diarmait was tall and well-built, a brave and warlike man among his people. He preferred to be feared by all than to be loved, and his voice was hoarse as a result of his constantly having been in the din of battle. He led a turbulent life, politically and socially. In 1146 he founded the convent of St Mary de Hogges, and in 1166, the year in which he founded the monastery of All Hallows, his castle at Ferns was destroyed by Tigernán Ua Ruairc, and he was banished from Ireland by the high king, Ruaidhri Ua Conchobair.

Diarmait now went to the court of Henry II in Aquitaine and sought his assistance in winning back his kingdom. This act of desperation helped to pave the way for the invasion of Ireland by the Anglo-Normans, and earned for Diarmait the dishonourable name of Diarmait na nGall (Dermot of the Foreigners), by which he is still known.

The few years remaining of his life would be tragic. In 1169 he joined Robert FitzStephen in the seizure of Wexford, and after the capture of Waterford in 1170 he gave, for a consideration, the hand of his daughter Aoife in marriage to Strongbow, Richard de Clare, earl of Pembroke. 'King Dermot then gave to the earl who was so renowned, Leinster he gave to him with his daughter whom he so much loved, provided only that he should have the lordship of Leinster during his life, and the earl granted to the King all his desire.'

Diarmait then led Strongbow to Dublin by a route through the mountains, because he had been warned 'by a scout whom he had sent that the Irish were in front about thirty thousand strong'. 'By the mountain did the King guide the English host that day. Without a battle and without a contest they arrived at the city.' On 21 September 1170, 'the day of Saint Matthew the Apostle, the city was taken that day beyond gainsaying', and the most recent occupation of Ireland began.

Following the seizure of Dublin 'the earl then abode while he pleased in the city and the King returned to Ferns in his own country'. He died there in 1171.

[22, 35, 36, 49, 147]

Mac Thorkil, Askulv
The Norse ruler at Dublin in 1170 when the Anglo-Normans captured the city.

From a family of Scandinavian earls who had come into power in Dublin in *c.* 1100, he had been in power or contending for it for many years before the conquest. Following the assault and capture of the city by Miles de Cogan and Raymond le Gros, 'The greater part of [the inhabitants], led by Askulv, went on board ship taking their most precious belongings and sailed off to the northern isles.'

He came back, however, around Pentecost in 1171, and put in to the banks of the Liffey with Norwegians and men from the Isles (Orkney and Man) in 60 boats, with the intention of taking the city. After a furious engagement on Hoggen Green, the Normans routed the attacking force (see Battle of Hoggen Green) and captured Askulv. He was brought before Miles de Cogan, who offered him his life for a ransom. But Askulv, the 'old hoary head', said, 'This time we have come in small numbers and this is only our first attempt. But if only I am spared this will soon be followed by other expeditions on a far larger scale, and having a very different outcome from this one.' Hearing this, on the order of de Cogan, 'on account of his outrageous conduct they speedily beheaded him in the presence of the sea folk'.

Variants on his name include Hasculf Mac Torkil and Asgall Mac Torcaill.

[35, 36, 49, 67]

MAC TORCAILL, ASGALL

See ASKULV MAC THORKIL.

MACARRELL'S WHARF

Macarrell's Wharf, described as Macarels Slip by Rocque, was a landing-place for vessels on the South Wall, probably near the end of the present Cambridge Road. It had been removed before the Ordnance Survey was carried out in 1837.

[DHR (Hammond), map (Rocque 1760)]

MACK, ROBERT

Robert Mack, 'a skilful man', was the stonemason, and perhaps, in the modern sense, the general contractor, for the first Essex Bridge.

[16]

MACKEN STREET BRIDGE (PROPOSED)

In 1939 the town planning consultants Abercrombie, Kelly and Robertson proposed the construction of a road bridge across the Liffey to join Cardiff's Lane to Guild Street. In 1993 this proposal was again being actively considered under the Dublin Transport Initiative.

See also Transporter Bridge at Guild Street.

[288]

MACKENZIE'S CHART

In 1751 Murdoch Mackenzie, senior, FRS, began a survey of the coasts of Ireland and the west side of

Great Britain. It was under the patronage of John, earl of Sandwich, then first lord of the Admiralty, and was for the guidance of mariners using the ports and harbours. In 1776 he published volume 1 of the Survey, 'containing the Maritim Survey of Ireland comprehended in XXVIII charts: also views of the land taken at sea. London. Engraved and printed for the Author and sold by the chart-sellers in Town and other seaports in Britain and Ireland. MDCCLXXVI.' The dates of publication of single charts, 'surveyed and navigated by M. Mackenzie, senr', and generally to a scale of 1:63,360, lay between May and November 1775. T. Bowen and G. Terry, both of London, were the engravers. The published volume of charts was accompanied by nautical descriptions and directions.

Mackenzie's survey appears to have been the first detailed survey ever to have been mapped for the coastal waters of Ireland as a whole. For a project of the mid-18th century, it must be seen as a work of considerable enterprise and achievement.

Chart No. 24 extends from Wicklow Head to Skerries, and contains Dublin Bay, showing the Liffey passing through Dublin. The presentation is unpolished. The south shoreline from Dunlary to Rings End is distorted, and the city is represented by a series of uniform rectangular blocks which convey the scale of the built-up area but offer no assistance with its detail. Useful information is given, however, on contemporary names for features on the shoreline from the Baily to Dalkey.

MACKLIN, J.

See NORTH LOTTS.

McMAHON, DR

See WATER, TIDE AND GROUND LEVELS.

MacMURROUGH, DERMOT

See DIARMAIT MAC MURCHADA.

MAEL SEACHNAILL II

See MALACHY, HIGH KING OF IRELAND.

MAGAZINE STREAM

The Magazine Stream rises at the north side of the Fifteen Acres in Phoenix Park, and flows east of the Magazine Fort to join the Liffey a little upstream of Sarah Bridge.

[Map (OS, current)]

MAGH MAISTEAN

See KILMEHANOC FORD.

MAIDEN ROCK

See LAMB ISLAND.

MAIDEN TOWER, PROPOSED

In 1582 Richard Condren, a water bailiff, was engaged to 'set upp .. a strong and sufficient beoie or perche uppon the barr', and to maintain it. Later in the same year, probably recognising the impermanence of a floating marker, the city invited two men, named Duff and Ball, to take over this work from Condren and, instead of a perche, to build 'a towre upon the Ringes end of such height and strength as shalbe of a perpetuall contynuance licke the towre at Drogheda'.

This change of policy may also have followed the granting of a charter by Elizabeth I giving monies to the city in aid of creating, at Poolbeg, a tower similar to that at Drogheda.

The Drogheda tower, which was built on oak piles on the beach at Mornington, still stands. It is about 19 m high and 3 m square overall. It contains inside just a flight of 55 steps to the top terrace, and the interior is lit only by occasional loopholes. It is known as the Maiden Tower because it was erected in the reign of Elizabeth I.

The work was not carried out at Poolbeg, and it would be nearly 200 years later, in 1767, that a permanent structure was built in the vicinity.

[80, *CARD*, II]

MAILS

See CROSS-CHANNEL PACKETS.

MALACHY, HIGH KING OF IRELAND

Malachy, otherwise Mael Seachnaill II Mac Domnaill, king of Mide, defeated the Norseman Olaf Cuarán (Olaf of the Sandals) at Tara in 980 and, in that year, became high king of Ireland. Olaf, who had ruled Dublin and Dyflinnarskiri since 945, retired to Iona as a pilgrim after his defeat, and died there within a year.

Malachy reigned as high king until 1002. During that time, he attacked and captured Dublin, in which there were Norse rulers, three times, in 981, 989 and 995. In 989 he imposed an annual tribute of an ounce of gold from every garth in the city. In 995 he took away from the city the sword of Carlus, associated with Charlemagne, and the Norse Ring of Thor, a precious armband worn by the ruler on ceremonial ritual occasions. This became, in the words of Thomas Moore, Malachy's 'collar of gold which he won from her proud invader'.

Malachy joined with Brian Bóruma to defeat the Norse and Maelmordha, king of Leinster, at Clontarf in 1014. Following the death of Brian in that battle, Malachy again became high king, ruling until his death in 1022.

Earlier, from 846 to 862, Mael Seachnaill I, great-great-grandfather of Malachy II, had been high king of Ireland.

[147, 150 (Curtis, Ryan)]

MALLET, J. AND R.

In 1801 Robert Mallet followed his father-in-law into his plumbing business in Ship Street, where apparently they operated a foundry. In 1804 Robert's nephew, John Mallet, took over this firm and moved it to premises at 7–9 Ryder's Row, off Capel Street. In 1820 John Mallet was described as an iron founder. In 1831 he had been joined by his son Robert, who later became a prominent civil engineer and internationally honoured scientist. The establishment became known as the Victoria Foundry, the owners from 1832 being J. and R. Mallet. Following this date, the firm expanded to provide structural iron and iron furniture for the new railway companies and the rapidly developing river and harbour works. Thus it provided the structural ironwork for the platform roofs in Kingsbridge railway station, as well as material for the Dublin and Kingstown railway, and cranes, bollards and mooring points for the harbours.

A remarkable use of cast iron is in the balusters for Inns Quay and for O'Donovan Rossa, Fr Mathew and Mellowes Bridges. These all date from 1815 to 1825, but they do not now offer any evidence of their makers' names.

In 1850 the Mallet company is recorded as John and Robert Mallet, plumbers, at 7–9 Ryder's Row, with J. Mallet, engineer, ironworker, at 98 Capel Street. The name Victoria Foundry is not mentioned. A fuller treatment, especially of Robert Mallet, is given by Cox.

[89, 146]

MALLIN STATION

See Dublin and Kingstown Railway.

MALTON, JAMES

The second son of Thomas Malton (1726–1801), architectural draftsman, James was born in c. 1764. He worked as an architectural draftsman for James Gandon from 1781 to 1784, when he was dismissed. Various accounts describe the animosity that the Malton family had towards Gandon.

James Malton is best known in Dublin for the series of illustrations he made in the 1790s under the title 'A Picturesque and Descriptive View of the City of Dublin'. The series appeared in six parts from 1792 to 1797, with the artist taking the opportunity to update his work as he made the engravings; and it was published in a single volume in 1799. He included six views that included the Liffey, and three maps. The views are as follows.

(i) Custom House
The quay walls are sloping stone walls faced with timber fenders about 1.5 m apart along the wall. These fenders support a heavy timber edging or sill at the top of the quay wall. There are no parapets above the quay level. The tide is close to full, and three large sailing-ships and some lesser crafts, including a wherry, are on the water. From this view, and many others, one can appreciate the problems of sailing such large vessels past the Bar and, even more, past the shallows between Ringsend and Lazars Hill, during the 18th century.

(ii) The Law Courts, looking up the Liffey
The Inns Quay has a stone wall, vertical for most of its length. There are some stone buttresses but no timber facing. By 1791 the use of this quay for shipping had ceased. There is no parapet. The elaborate cast-iron balustrade would come later. In the distance the Old Bridge in its 15th-century form, with four unequal arches, substantially closes off the river view. On the south bank a house on Wood Quay, perhaps at the site of Prickett's Tower, rises straight out of the river. The tide is low and small sailing-vessels are grounded along Merchants Quay. It seems that two great 'floats' of timber are being taken downstream under the control of a rowing-boat. This was the usual method of transporting timber, by unloading it in the estuary and forming it into a rough raft to be floated along the river. The water supply committee of the Corporation reported in 1756 that it had inspected a cargo of Norway fir imported by a Mr Gerrard and had 'agreed for one float which measured 22 tons'.

(iii) Marine School, looking up the Liffey
The governors and directors of the Hibernian Marine School or Nursery first opened a house at Ringsend in 1766 or 1767 for 20, and then 60, boys. In 1768 they took a plot at the lower end of Rogerson's Quay, and in 1773 opened there the Hibernian Marine School for 200 boys. The view shows the school and, immediately upstream on the same quay, 'The Marine Hotel, the house engaged with the Packets for the conveyance of the mail to and from London to Dublin'. The plate illustrates a low tide, with two sailing-ships grounded. Men are working on the exposed 'strand', and two of these appear to be manoeuvring a large timber raft while another raft lies on the strand behind them. Unlike the 'floats' in the Four Courts view, the Marine School rafts may well be of the form deliberately made for the transport of goods and merchandise and also called 'floats' in the 18th century. Semple

describes the part played by such a transport raft in the collapse of the Arran (now Mellowes) Bridge in 1763. While the view shows many sailing-vessels in the river, Malton comments that 'the Shipping in the Harbour and about the dock' is generally more crowded. A shipbuilding yard is shown in the left background.

(iv) View from Capel Street, looking over Essex Bridge

The engraving shows the Essex Bridge (now Grattan) in the form in which it had been rebuilt some 35 years earlier by Semple. The pronounced hump in the bridge, which was removed later in the Halpin and Stoney reconstructions, is shown, as also is the old Custom House, so soon to be taken out of service and to be used as a military barracks in 1798. In the left foreground appear the upper parts of a large sailing-ship that occupy a position which, while it must have pleased the artist, is navigationally both ungainly and quite unlikely in 1799.

(v) The Barracks

This view of the huge Royal Barracks, the building of which began in 1701, is seen from the escarpment on which James's Street runs today. From the viewpoint, meadows and pastures fall gently to the river, a rural scene with bushy hedges and trees, cattle grazing and hay being made. The river-banks are grassy, although the exercise yards of the barracks reach down towards the north bank. One can readily imagine John Garget busy repairing his fences in the 13th-century meadows in this area, or visualise Lord Galway enjoying his walk from Dunghill Lane towards the Royal Hospital. The area would quite soon vanish under the buildings and yards of St James's Gate brewery; and the barracks are now being converted for use by the National Museum.

(vi) Dublin from the Magazine, Phoenix Park

A particularly fine impression of the village of Kilmainham dominates this engraving, with a hint of the new Sarah Bridge, which Malton could not have shown in 1791. The city is very much in the distance. A busy road curves along through the Phoenix Park at high level towards the viewpoint, as the road within the park walls does today. The

sequence of houses along the Long Meadows marks the present Conyngham Road, shown by Taylor and Skinner as part of the road from Dublin to Sligo. The absence of the Kingsbridge (now Heuston) railway station complex, which would develop 50 years or so later, and the glossing over of the Artillery Barracks, which would be one of Emmet's targets in 1803, leave the field clear for appreciating the great expanse of the medieval meadow.

The three maps included in the 1799 book are: Faden's Plan of the City of Dublin, 1797; an embellished version of Speed's map of 1610; and 'A Correct Survey of the Bay of Dublin', 1795 (based on the Scalé and Richards map of 1765).

In addition to the Dublin series published in 1799, two other views of the Custom House by James Malton are mentioned by Elmes and Hewson. Malton died in 1803.

[11, 13, 54, 76, 77]

MAN-OF-WAR ROAD

An extensive deep-water anchorage in the bay shown, for instance, by Mackenzie in his chart of 1776, roughly midway between 'Dunlary' and the summit of Howth Head.

In 1655 Henry Cromwell, coming 'to feel his way before his appointment as Lord Lieutenant of Ireland', was rowed to Ringsend from a man-of-war that anchored off Dunleary, probably in the Man-of-war Road.

[56, map (Mackenzie 1776)]

MANSION HOUSE ON LAZARS HILL, PROPOSED

See Lazars Hill.

MAPS, PLANS, CHARTS: GENERAL

This text discusses individually maps and charts that include the Liffey at Dublin. The series begins with the Hatfield Plan of c. 1592, which is probably the first to show, to a useful scale, the relationship of a building in Dublin to the river; it ends substantially with the publication of the earliest Ordnance Survey maps of Dublin in 1838, although ten later specialised items are included. The series is not exhaustive. Many hundreds of lease maps and other small area maps covering several centuries survive. Some of these are included in a list of maps by the Dublin city surveyors published in 1983 by Dublin Corporation (Archives Section, City Libraries).

In the schedule which follows, the term 'city' means that the map finishes at or above Ringsend, the term 'harbour' includes the Liffey estuary down to the Bar of Dublin, and the 'bay' extends to a line joining the Baily lighthouse and the Muglins.

c. 1592	Hatfield Plan	Proposals for Trinity College
1610	Speed, J.	City
1618	Braun, G. and Hohenburgius, F.	City
1650	Merian	City
1654	Petty, W.	Halfe Barrony of Rathdowne (harbour and bay)
1673	de Gomme, B.	City
1673	de Gomme, B.	Harbour and bay
1674	Yarranton, A.	Proposals for new harbour
1685	Phillips, T.	City, harbour and bay
1685	Phillips, T.	Harbour and bay
1686	Collins, G.	Harbour and bay
1693	Collins, G.	Harbour and bay
1694	Revenue Board	Harbour and bay
1708	Pratt, H.	City
1714	Moll, H.	City
1717	Bolton, T. (Macklin, J.)	North Lotts (this map also known as Dublin Corporation map)
1725	Stokes, G.	Harbour and bay
1728	Bowen, E.	Harbour and bay
1728	Brooking, C.	City
1728/50	Stokes, G.	Site of the King's Inns
1730	Price, C.	Harbour and bay
1756	Rocque, J.	City (on four sheets)
1757	Rocque, J.	City (pocket plan)
1757	Rocque, J.	City, harbour, bay and environs (on four sheets)
1760	Rocque, J.	County Dublin (on five sheets)
1762	Semple, G.	Bay (eight charts)
1765	Scalé, B. and Richards, W.	Harbour and bay
1773	Rocque, J. with additions by Scalé, B.	City, harbour, bay and environs (on two sheets)
1776	Mackenzie, M.	Coastal waters of Ireland
1780	Pool, R. and Cash, J.	City
1797	Faden, W.	City
1798	Stockdale, J.	City
1798	Wilson, W.	City
1800	Cowan, J.	Harbour and bay
1800/3	Bligh, W.	Harbour and bay
1803	Wilson, W. (printed by Corbet, W.)	City
1811	Carrick, J. and J.	City
1811	Campbell, T.	City
1816	Taylor, J.	City, harbour, bay and environs (on two, or three, sheets)
1819	Giles, F.	North Bull
1821	Duncan, W.	City, harbour and bay
1823	Nimmo, A.	Harbour and bay
1824	Taylor, J.	Custom House stores and docks
1830	Nimmo, A.	Proposed railroad from Dublin to Kingstown
1831	Nimmo, A.	Coastal waters of Ireland, including Dublin Bay (on four sheets)
1833	SDUK	City
1838 and later	Ordnance Survey	City, harbour, bay and environs (on many sheets)
1838/42	Frazer, G.	The Liffey from Carlisle Bridge to the Bar
1875	Kerr, J.H.	Harbour and bay
1882	Sloane, J.	Walls of Dublin

1904	Strangways, L.	Walls of Dublin as in 1585
1915	Ordnance Survey	City and harbour (Geological Survey, drift edition)
1921	Ordnance Survey	Catchment basin of the River Liffey
1977	Walsh, P.J.	City (c. 840 to c. 1540)
1977	Royal Naval Hydrographic Chart (no. 1415)	Bay
1977	do. (no. 1447)	River
1978	Clarke, H.B.	City (medieval Dublin)
1987	Dublin Port	Port

[259, maps (as named)]

MARESCHAL, WILLIAM, EARL OF PEMBROKE

See STRONGBOW.

MARINE NURSERY

See HIBERNIAN MARINE SCHOOL.

MARINERS' CHURCH IN FORBES STREET

See FLOATING CHAPEL AT RINGSEND.

MARISCO, CHRISTIANA DE

See THORNCASTLE.

MARKETS, GENERAL

Markets close to the Liffey are mentioned in the text. They include Fish, Fleet, Herb and Root, New, New Hall (or New Gate), Northumberland, Old Crane, Ormonde, Roscommon and Wellesley. Each is listed under its own name.

MARNEY'S DOCK

Also Mourney's Dock. See NORTH WALL SLIP.

MARSH, THE

See SANDYMOUNT.

MARSHAL, WILLIAM, EARL OF PEMBROKE

See STRONGBOW.

MARSHAL ALLEY

See FLEECE ALLEY.

MARTELLO TOWERS

The Martello tower takes its name from Cape Mortella on the north-west coast of Corsica, where a circular stone defensive tower, though only lightly armed, resisted a land and sea attack by British forces in 1794. Large numbers of towers of this form were built soon afterwards along the coasts of Britain and Ireland, as part of the British defence system against threats of Napoleonic invasion.

Nine Martello towers were built around Dublin Bay in 1804. These were at Sutton on the north shore, and along the south shore at Sandymount, Williamstown, Seapoint, Dunleary, Glasthule, Sandycove, Bullock and Dalkey Island. The tower at Dunleary appears on Duncan's map of 1821, but was removed between 1834, when the Dublin and Kingstown railway was built, and 1838, when the line had been extended to the present Dún Laoghaire station. Ronan records that it stood on the site of the prehistoric *dún* of Dún Laoghaire; and he notes that it was located near the land end of the Old Pier and beneath the present roadway immediately to the south of the modern railway line. The tower at Glasthule was removed in the middle of the 19th century.

The other seven towers are still standing, and the Sandycove tower, which is the location for the opening of *Ulysses*, is now being used as the James Joyce Tower Museum.

Duncan shows that the tower at Sandymount was approached in 1821 by tracks along the seashore from Sandymount and the modern Merrion Gates. James describes this tower as it was in 1862, by which time Strand Road and Church

Road had been made. It was 50 feet (15 m) in external diameter. The external circular wall was 10 feet (3 m) thick, with the internal space being 30 feet (9 m) in diameter. It was entered on the land side at first-floor level by an external winding metal stairway 3 feet (0.9 m) wide; and machicolation in the parapet above made it possible for the garrison to drop missiles through vertical slots on to the heads of those attempting to force entrance.

The first floor was the living-quarters for the garrison of 12. The floor below, which was reached by a helical stairway 4 foot (1.2 m) in diameter and contained within the thickness of the wall, was used as the kitchen and for the master gunner's stores. It contained also the magazine, where 30 barrels of gunpowder could be held. Beneath this floor, which was brick-arched on thick stone walls, there was a water storage tank. The vaulted stone roof, protected by a parapet, was reached by the helical stairs. It supported guns, probably 18- or 24-pounders, which were mounted on a roller system that enabled them to be aimed in any direction over a wide arc. The roof adjacent to the machicolated segment contained a shot furnace that could make cannon-balls red-hot, to be used for setting fire to sails and timbers in wooden ships.

Modern excavation shows that the walls were founded on massive grillages of square-section pitch pine, arranged in three layers.

A small annexe to the tower on the bay side contained an external privy, an ashpit and a coal store, and there was also an internal privy built into the thickness of the circular wall.

The Martello towers were not identical, either in size or in garrison. Thus, the Sutton tower, which was quite remote and is still in open country, had a garrison of 16 men; and the tower at Sandycove, which was an outpost incorporated in a large battery, and which may have been primarily a watch-tower, is shown by James as only 42 feet (12.6 m) in external diameter.

In addition to the Martello towers, the south shore of Dublin Bay was protected by three strong coastal or shore batteries, mentioned in a separate entry (see Shore Batteries).

There is no evidence that any of the Martello towers was ever called into active service.
[134, 197, 220 (vol. 52, part 2, December 1932), *An Cosantóir*, May 1974 (Kerrigan), maps (Duncan 1821, OS 1838), private communication (D. O'Toole)]

MARTINS COURT
Harris (1766) records Martins Court as opening off Blind Quay.
[16]

MARTINS LANE
Harris (1766) records Martins Lane as opening off the Strand.
[16]

MASS LANE
In the second half of the 17th century, while the development of the King's Inns lands was in active progress along Inns Quay, a lane about 75 m long was made, running north from the quay outside the eastern boundary of the property. It is shown unnamed by Brooking in 1728, and is named as Mass Lane by Rocque in 1756. Both maps show it fully built up on both sides.

When the Four Courts were erected and the Richmond Bridge (O'Donovan Rossa) was built, Mass Lane was absorbed into the wider thoroughfare of Chancery Place. A chapel was built in Mass Lane, possibly during the reign of the Catholic monarch James II (1685–8), and was used first by Jesuits, and later in turn by Huguenots of the French Church and by a community of Protestant dissenters.

This lane was known also as Lucy, or Lucy's, or Lucas's Lane, and as May's Lane.
[201, 298, maps (Brooking 1728, Rocque 1756)]

MAYOR STREET
See NORTH LOTTS.

MAY'S LANE
See MASS LANE.

MEETING HOUSE YARD

See USHER'S QUAY.

MELLOWES BRIDGE

Mellowes Bridge

The first bridge on this site, Arran Bridge, was built in 1683, according to the records of the City Assembly. As such, it was one of the four bridges built across a 1-kilometre length of the Liffey within a period of 14 years from 1670 to 1683, in the unbridled rush to open up the north side of the river for development.

The responsibility for its erection lay with William Ellis, and it was named for Richard, earl of Arran, second son of the duke of Ormonde and his deputy from 1682 to 1684 as lord lieutenant of Ireland. It appears from a drawing made by Francis Place in 1698/9, 'Dublin from the Wooden Bridge' (NGI, 7515), to have been a four-span stone-arched bridge.

Arran Bridge, known as Arons Bridge in 1705, and later criticised by Pool and Cash as a 'mean building', collapsed in 1763, as the result of an unlikely accident which George Semple describes:

> A rapid land-flood broke the moorings of a raft of timber at the Barrack-slip and carried it down to Queen's [sic] Bridge, where it unluckily lodged quite across the middle arch. The piers of this bridge were built on the surface of the bed of the river, as most of the former bridges were. This raft of timber obstructing the current of the surface, in like manner increased the power of it at the bottom and within the space of a few hours totally demolished the bridge.

A new bridge was built in 1768 under the direction of Charles Vallancey and was named Queen's Bridge in honour of Queen Charlotte, wife of George III. Vallancey's bridge was a stone bridge of three arches with a total span of 42 m. It is, by far, the oldest surviving bridge across the Liffey in Dublin, although the parapets were replaced with cast-iron balustrades and stone copings in 1816–18; and it is regarded by many as the most elegant bridge in the city.

The name of the bridge was changed to Queen Maeve Bridge at a meeting of the Municipal Council on 2 January 1922, and in 1942 it was given the name of Mellowes Bridge. A plaque on the bridge in Irish and English uses the form Mellows, and reads as follows:

THE NAME OF THIS BRIDGE HAS BEEN
CHANGED TO
MELLOWS BRIDGE,
TO HONOUR THE MEMORY OF
LIEUT GENERAL LIAM MELLOWS
IRISH REPUBLICAN ARMY,
WHO GAVE HIS LIFE FOR THE REPUBLIC OF
IRELAND.
8th DECEMBER 1922
GO NDEINID DIA TRÓCAIRE AR ANAMNAIB AR
MARTAR UILE
ERECTED BY THE NATIONAL GRAVES
ASSOCIATION
1942

Mellowes Bridge has been known also as Bridewell Bridge, because of its proximity to the Smithfield Bridewell (1756), and as Ellis's Bridge, because of its association with Sir William and Sir John Ellis (1766).

[11, 87 (vols. 9, 10), 106, 121, 196, *CARD*, V, VI]

MEMORIAL ROAD

In 1927 the Old Dock beside the Custom House was filled in. In 1952 Beresford Place, which curved around the north side of the Custom House, was extended over the new ground to enclose the Custom House in a semicircular railed precinct.

This extension of Beresford Place, and a branch northwards to meet the junction of Store Street and Amiens Street, were named Memorial Road, to commemorate all sailors who sailed out of Dublin and died at sea.

[Private communications (B. Murphy, R. Tallon)]

MENDICITY INSTITUTION

See MOIRA HOUSE.

MERCER'S DOCK

See MERCER'S GROUND and WHITE'S LANE.

MERCER'S GROUND

In 1683 Phillip Croft was given the lease of 'a parcell of the Strand betwixt the north part of the buildings of the streete of Lazy Hill and the river conteineing in length from Mr Hawkins his wall in the west, eastward the number of two hundred, eightie four yards or thereabouts'.

As de Gomme showed in 1673, there were houses side by side along the north side of Lazars Hill (now Townsend Street), with fenced plots of land behind them. The north boundary of these plots would lie today near Rath Row. Between this boundary and the channel of the Liffey, there was a 'strand', represented today by the land along Poolbeg Street. This strand was exposed at low tide but covered at high tide, and this was the area that Croft intended to develop for a distance of 284 yards (256 m) eastward from modern Corn Exchange Place: that is, for a length from there to the east end of modern George's Quay.

Croft was to include in his work a 'street or dike' 40 feet wide roughly along Rath Row, and was also to form a riverside quay. The meaning of 'dike' in this context is obscure but it is evidently related to a perceived need for flood control in the area. This topic is mentioned also in the entry on Lazars Hill. Croft went ahead with his work, although the difficult political conditions of the time were a hindrance. By his own report, 'he laid out large sums of money in building of walls and filling to secure [the area] from water unto the time of the Popish Government', but then 'many boat loads of

stone [were] taken and carried away from the place in the late King James' time for the building malthouses at Wicklow when [Croft] was in England'.

In 1699 Croft died. His widow and her second husband lost interest in the project. In the opening years of the 18th century the area had come under the control of John Mercer, and in 1712 Croft's lease was transferred to him. The dimensions and indeed the conditions of the various leases are confusing, but it seems that Mercer now undertook to wall and take in a length of 100 perches or 700 yards of the Liffey strand. This is roughly equal to the whole length of the modern quays from Corn Exchange Place to the east end of City Quay at Creighton Street, where it would have abutted Rogerson's Quay, on which work started in 1713. Mercer was to provide, among other things, a riverside quay 40 feet wide in which there were to be arched openings leading to his own wharf (Mercer's Dock), at the west end of his holding, and to two existing wharves along Lazars Hill, Nichols's Quay and Crosse's Quay.

It soon became apparent, however, that Mercer was unlikely to complete the wall in his lease (see City Quay). The city accordingly paid him for the work he had done and took over the construction of the wall, beginning in 1715.

John Mercer died in 1718. His wharf or dock, which may in fact have been at White's Lane, modern Corn Exchange Place, passed into the hands of his widow, Grace Mercer; and in 1741 she and Luke Gardiner were awarded a lease for ever of the George's Quay property, which included the suggested site of Mercer's Dock.

[149, *CARD*, V–VII, IX, maps (de Gomme 1673, Brooking 1728, Rocque 1756)]

MERCHANTS ARCH

See MERCHANTS HALL.

MERCHANTS HALL

Records of the Guild Merchant of Dublin show that members were admitted to it as early as the 12th century. In the 15th century it became known as the Guild of the Holy Trinity.

municipal government, and the city was already over 900 years old when the establishment of the Wide Streets Commissioners in 1757 and the Ballast Board in 1786 first transferred part of that responsibility to other shoulders. Today, the port and maintenance of the Liffey east of Rory O'More Bridge, together with such other matters as public transport, policing and prisons, are controlled by bodies outside the City Council.

The term 'Corporation' as a title for the city government has been known since the 13th century and, for instance, was used by Charles II in 1665 when his charter committed the city ferries to the charge of the Corporation of Dublin. Today,

Dublin Corporation is the local authority for the city and consists of the elected representatives in Dublin City Council, and the civic officials headed by the city manager.

[6, 35, 149, 151 (Berry, Dudley Edwards), 187, 267, Dublin Corporation Archives]

MURROUGH, THE
See SANDYMOUNT.

MUSIC HALL, THE
See FISHAMBLE STREET.

N

NANIKEN STREAM

Naniken Stream rises in Killester and flows through St Anne's Park to discharge into Sutton Creek, west of the Bull Island causeway.

NAPPER TANDY, JAMES

See TANDY, JAMES NAPPER.

NARROW BRIDGE AT KILMAINHAM

See KILMAINHAM, NARROW BRIDGE AT.

NEW BRIDGE

The entry on William Vavasour mentions a new bridge across the tidal Dodder connecting Lansdowne Road and Herbert Road. This bridge was shown first, but not named, on the OS map of 1838, and was probably the wooden bridge mentioned in 1875 on Kerr's chart of Dublin Bay. The three-arched masonry structure now existing would then have been of later date. It is possible, however, that the appellation of 'wooden bridge' was given by Kerr in error, as the bridge now on this site resembles closely the stone structure of London Bridge built nearby in 1857 to replace a wooden bridge.

The name of New Bridge was first shown by the Ordnance Survey in its revision of 1935/6. This bridge has also been referred to as Herbert Bridge, probably reflecting the family name in the earldom of Pembroke.

[184, maps (OS 1838, Kerr 1875, OS 1935/6)]

NEW BRUNSWICK STREET

See PEARSE STREET.

NEW CRANE, THE

See CRANES AND CRANERS.

NEW CUSTOM HOUSE

See CUSTOM HOUSE, NEW.

NEW DOCKS, THE

This name appears to have been given both to the Grand Canal Docks (1796) and to the Custom House Docks (c. 1821–3).

[73, CARD, XIV]

NEW HALL MARKET

This market lay at the south end of Bridge Street in 1756, where part of Bridge Street Upper was later built. It is shown by Rocque in 1756, and its demolition is referred to in 1769. It is named by Brooking as New Gate Market in 1728.

[CARD, XII, maps (Brooking 1728, Rocque 1756)]

NEW HOLLAND

A name given in the early 19th century to part of the lands taken from the sea by Rogerson's Wall and the embankment of the Dodder, recognising it as low land seamed by water channels and close to sea level. The OS map of 1838 shows an isolated house named Newholland Lodge on Bath Avenue near the entrance to Vavasour Square.

[96, DHR (Dawson), map (OS 1838)]

NEW MARKET

See ORMONDE QUAY, UPPER.

NEW QUAY

In 1621 it was announced that a new wharf had been built at what would later become the Old Custom House Quay. In 1625 a complaint was laid before the City Assembly 'praying that a course might be taken for setting of ringes in the walls of newe Kea, which is much annoyed in foule weather by reason such as require that [those who use the] Kea fasten theire shippes, barques, and boats to the frame of the said Kea and also fix theire ankers on the pavement'.

[CARD, III]

NEWCOMEN BRIDGE

See NORTH STRAND.

NEWFOUNDLAND STREET

See ROYAL CANAL DOCKS.

NEWMAN, JACOB

Possibly the earliest speculative land developer along the Liffey in the history of the city. Many others in earlier centuries had taken in ground from the river around their own holdings, but Newman's work in the early 17th century was vastly more extensive. One must believe that 50 years before the post-Restoration surge of civil expansion, he recognised the obstacle caused by the Poddle estuary to the development of the city towards the mouth of the Liffey; and he would have been aware also of the potential of the north bank of the river, the development of which, by Jervis and others, he would in fact by his own work do so much to promote.

In 1602 Newman had come into possession of Isolde's Tower, also known as the Bakers' Tower, and later and to this day as Newman's Tower. This tower lay between Exchange Street Lower and the eastern end of Essex Quay (modern names are used throughout to identify locations). The tower was formally leased to him in 1604, at which time he was also granted land on the river strand adjacent to it.

In 1606 Newman initiated his grand plan of filling in the Poddle estuary and the river-bank lands on the south shore of the Liffey downstream. In that year, he was granted a lease of a 'voyde peace of ground' that may be identified roughly as a triangle with its apexes at the junction of Lower Fownes Street and Wellington Quay, the junction of Parliament Street and Dame Street, and a point on Essex Quay a little upstream of Grattan Bridge. This definition offers the scale of the project, but the actual boundaries of the leasehold are more complex.

The whole of this significant work, taking in about 2.5 ha of new ground from the tidal river and opening a potential route downstream along the river-bank, was completed in a little over ten years. In 1620 James I wrote to his deputy, Sir Oliver St John, ordering him 'to accept of a lease from Jacob Newman of a place in the port of Dublin

which is found to be convenient for erecting a crane and making a wharf and in lieu thereof to grant him for the term of ninety years the sum of £50 sterling per annum'. This negotiation would lead to the establishment of a quay and customs facilities in an area just downstream of the future site of Grattan Bridge, where a larger quay and Custom House would be constructed during the following 100 years.

Jacob Newman died shortly afterwards, and in 1637 the merchants of the city would be found negotiating with his widow, Rose Newman, for space for improved customs and goods-handling facilities near the riverside.

A comparison of Speed's map of 1610 with de Gomme's map of 1673 shows very clearly the importance of Newman's work.

[18, 160, *CARD*, II, III, *DHR* (KM), maps (Speed 1610, de Gomme 1673)]

NEWMAN'S TOWER

Reginald's Tower, Waterford

Newman's Tower was known previously as Isolde's Tower, and perhaps as the Bakers' Tower. An early reference to it appears in 1558 when the city granted that 'the master, wardens and corporacion of the bakers shall have Isold's towre for xli years, paing xxs Irish and doing all reparacions'. This wording suggests a greater age for the building, and it might be proposed that, like the other large riverside structures, it was built in the 13th or 14th century.

Stanihurst, in his description of Dublin in 1577, mentions 'a tower named Isouds tower. It took the name of la Beale Isoud, daughter to Anguish, King of Ireland. It seemeth to have beene a castle of pleasure for the kings to recreat themselves therein'. There is no evidence offered to support this.

In 1585 Sir John Perrot ordered a survey to be made of the walls of the city. In it, 'Issolde's towre' is described as a 'rownde towre towe storie hie, 18 foot square within the wall, and the wall 9 foote thicke and 40 foote hie from the channell, one timber lofte and a plate forme in the tope with three lowps in every rowme'. In external appearance and bulk, this tower could have closely resembled Reginald's Tower (AD 1003), still standing in good repair in Waterford.

The word 'channell' used by Perrot is of interest. He mentions it at Newman's Tower, and he describes Merchants Quay as having 'the Key 9 foote high from the chanell to the pavment'. Clearly he is referring to what in 1585 was a definite and reasonably constant level in that part of the tidal river along which quays had been made. It seems reasonable to say that the river-bed at any cross-section was lower in midstream than at the quay wall. The various dimensions then given by Perrot suggest strongly that the level known as the channel was the surface of the river-bed at the face of the quay wall. This surface would be exposed as mud or shingle at low tide, and covered by some feet of water at high tide. The level of the pavement of the quay would then be 9 feet or 2.7 m higher than the channel, and the ground floor of the riverside towers as recorded by Perrot would be at quay pavement level or perhaps 0.3 m below that level. Perrot's account also suggests that the depth of water at the quay face, presumably at some chosen high tide, varied from 1.8 m at Prickett's Tower to 1.2 m at Newman's Tower, with some shallower spots in between.

For a short time in 1601 Alderman John Elliott held the lease of the Bakers' Tower, but later that year it had passed into the hands of Jacob Newman, with the Assembly reserving the right of free access to it for the defence of the city. It would generally be known thenceforth as Newman's Tower. Newman was granted a lease for this tower in 1604 and quickly began to develop the riverbank in its vicinity.

The precise location of Newman's Tower has until recently been a matter of debate. It is now known that it lies close to the north side of Exchange Street Lower and about 50 m west of the centre-line of Grattan Bridge. This location is at variance with that shown on the Ramsey-Kendrick lease map of 1755, cited by Burke (bib. ref. 97). It should be remembered that Essex Quay did not exist in its present form in the 17th century, and Newman's Tower, in a salient position on the city wall, would have been very prominent in the river prospect. The reference earlier to its height 'from the channell' cannot be ignored.

Fifty years or so after the death of Jacob Newman, the tower was described in 1681 as being in a decayed condition and propped against collapse only by the support of adjacent buildings. This was surely an exaggeration, if only in view of the massiveness of the construction; and as late as 1786, when the property had passed into the possession of the Smyth family, the building was still being called 'that old ruined tower commonly called Isold's Tower'. It was referred to as being at the lower end of Kennedy's Lane, and a lease map of 1755 suggests that this was the unmarked dog-legged lane shown by Rocque in 1756 as joining Blind Quay and Essex Quay. Other evidence in 1779 suggests that by 1786 the tower may have been no more than a heap of rubble.

Part of the controversy surrounding the location of Newman's Tower arose from the statement by Semple that when building the Essex Bridge during 1754, in excavating for the south abutment, 'we raised part of the foundation of Newman's Tower which had been very judiciously laid on the solid rock'. There is no doubt that Semple, from his experience, would have recognised heavy stone masonry as distinct from natural rock, but one must now doubt that with the nearest part of the superstructure of the tower being roughly

45 m away from the bridge, the substructure would have extended so far. At the south end of Essex Bridge (Grattan) today, the rock surface is approximately 9 m below the street surface. It is now held that the masonry found by Semple formed part of Newman's early-17th-century river wall. Meanwhile, the uncovering of the base of Newman's Tower in 1992–3 at a foundation level of 2.8 m above OD (Poolbeg) is a significant discovery.

It is not certain that the occupation of Newman's Tower by the bakers in the 16th century gave it the name of Bakers' Tower, but it is likely to have been so called at that time. However, see Fitzsymon's Tower.

[2, 11, *CARD*, I, II, V, XIII, map (Rocque 1756), private communication (L. Simpson)]

NIALL GLUNDUBH, HIGH KING OF IRELAND

See CHRONOLOGY OF RULERS IN DUBLIN and KILMEHANOC FORD.

NICHOLAS'S BUILDINGS

See NICHOLS'S QUAY.

NICHOLAS'S QUAY

See NICHOLS'S QUAY.

NICHOLS'S QUAY

A quay or wharf at Lazars Hill dating almost certainly from the 17th century but not shown by Rocque as existing in 1756. This quay was also known as Nicholas's Quay.

On his map of 1673 de Gomme shows a group of structures named Captain Nicholas's Buildings on a lane south of Lazars Hill, roughly where Spring Garden Lane lies today. It is on this somewhat tenuous basis that a date has been suggested for the quay. The location of the cut containing Nichols's Quay appears to have lain at the east end of George's Quay near modern Moss Street.

[*CARD*, VI, maps (de Gomme 1673, Rocque 1756)]

NIGHTINGALE FORD

During the late 18th century the Ballast Office made two references to a shallow place called Nightingale Ford in the Liffey. Its location was not given, but it was to be the eastern limit of its work in dredging the channel of the river. In 1832 Alexander Nimmo, giving piloting directions for entering Dublin Harbour, recorded that 'a quarter of a mile below the Pigeon House there was a shoal called the Ford across the channel, the deepest water on the north side being three feet at low water'. He added, however, that 'a channel is now dredged entirely through this Shoal'.

It may be suggested that this was Nightingale Ford, with the shoal separating the Poolbeg from the Salmon Pool, and that it was located somewhat downstream of the two chimneys of the present Poolbeg generating station.

To use Nightingale Ford, if it was as described, one would have started from perhaps modern Oulton Road, west of Clontarf, and gone south-east to the ford. From there the route could have been south-west to Irishtown, making a total journey from shore to shore of about 5 km across the sands. The river would have been passable at the ford for only about an hour before and after low water, and not at all in time of storm or if the Liffey and Tolka were in spate.

[17, *CARD*, XI, XII, map (Greenvile Collins 1686)]

NIMMO, ALEXANDER

In 1811 Alexander Nimmo came to Ireland as an engineer for the Bogs Commissioners. He was then 28 years of age, having been born in Kirkcaldy in Fife in 1783. Most of his professional career from 1811 until his death in January 1832 at the early age of 49 would be in Ireland. His work as a public servant with the Bogs Commissioners, and later with the Commissioners of Irish Fisheries, the government's Irish Office in London, and the Admiralty, was voluminous and significant, and was honoured in an obituary published in Galway:

Honorary distinctions are but dust weighed in the balance when compared with the sterling talent and intrinsic merit of this excellent and lamented individual. Eulogium is unnecessary as the word

Alexander Nimmo (sculptor: J. Jones)

IRELAND alone will be both his most merited monument and suitable epitaph. No man so well understood the remedies required for its practical evils, and the effects not only of his foresight but his actual works will be felt long after the very remembrance of his name will have passed away.

Nimmo's private work as a consulting engineer was equally extensive. Examples from the period 1816–32 which may be seen today include the mail harbour at Dunmore East, County Waterford, Wellesley (now Sarsfield) Bridge across the Shannon at Limerick, and Pollaphuca Bridge in the upper reaches of the Liffey. His knowledge of the coastal waters of Ireland was encyclopaedic. His book, *New Piloting Directions for St Georges Channel and the Coast of Ireland*, published posthumously in 1832, demonstrates this, as does his hydrographic survey of Dublin Bay, made in 1823 for the Commissioners of Irish Fisheries.

The chart with which Nimmo illustrated his *New Piloting Directions* was published on four dissected sheets to a scale of approximately 1:375,000 and engraved by Josiah Neele, 352, Strand, London. 'Drawn chiefly from original surveys', it was dedicated to 'the Corporation for Improving the Port of Dublin . . . exhibiting the Sea

and Harbour lights under their management'. It included an insert on one sheet, showing Dublin Bay and Harbour to a scale of approximately 1:81,500, and marking on it soundings and a navigation line described as 'Custom House open of lighthouse', which led into the mouth of the river past the northern edge of Burford Bank and the southern edge of Rossbeg Bank.

Nimmo's home and office in Dublin were at 78 Marlborough Street. As one of the leading civil engineers practising in Ireland in 1820–30, it is not surprising that Nimmo was one of those invited to offer an opinion on the proposed ship canal from Kingstown to Ringsend, and that he was later appointed in 1831 to plan the line and construction of the Dublin and Kingstown railway. In 1830 he prepared a lithographed map entitled 'Plan of a proposed Rail Road from Dublin to Kingstown'. The line as built followed his proposals closely, except that he appears to have recommended the use of a tunnel under the lands of Lord Cloncurry and Sir Harcourt Lees near Blackrock, whereas in 1834 a deep cutting was used instead.

A bust of Alexander Nimmo, sculptured by John Jones, is in the collection of the Royal Dublin Society at Ballsbridge.

[17, *Galway Independent*, 28 January 1832, 'Alexander Nimmo, Engineer: Some Tentative Notes' (de Courcy, 1981, unpublished)]

NIMMO'S MAPS
See ALEXANDER NIMMO.

NIXON STREET
See ROYAL CANAL DOCKS.

NODDY
The noddy has been described as an 'improved machine', in comparison with the simpler Ringsend car. It was said to be a low small vehicle capable of holding two persons, and drawn by a single horse. Its description continues: 'it was covered in by a calash (or carriage hood) and open before, but the aperture was nearly closed by the back of the "Noddy boy" who was generally a large-

O'Donovan Rossa Bridge

by the Board of a design competition for the proposed new bridge. There were to be three awards, 100 guineas for the winner, and 60 and 40 guineas for those in second and third place. Entries were to be received in mid-October 1805; and a fortnight later, James Savage of Barbican, London was declared the winner, with W.H. Ashpitel of Homerton, London second, and John Semple third.

The Ballast Board was prepared to proceed at once with implementation of the winning design, but there was opposition. In 1806 the Dublin Grand Jury, which would be providing the funds, asked that new designs be sought for a stone bridge, and in 1807 Thomas Wilson was back in Dublin, offering his plan for a new bridge. In 1809 the Grand Jury accepted what must have been substantially Savage's design, but now a new obstacle arose with the controversy, discussed below, about where the bridge should be sited. Eventually in May 1812 the site for the bridge was agreed, and the Board was able in August of that year to invite tenders for its construction.

The new bridge was to be a stone bridge across the 'river Anna Liffey' at the foot of Winetavern Street. The design of James Savage would be followed in general, although some alterations to the profile, proposed by George Halpin, would be the subject of a small variation in the final cost of the bridge. In October 1812 George Knowles was appointed as contractor. In August 1813 the foundation-stone was laid by the duchess of Richmond, and on 17 March 1816 the bridge was opened to traffic.

The bridge has three arches, with a total span of 44 m. It is built in granite with an elaborate cast-iron and stone balustrade, the design of which is continued along Inns Quay and across the Fr Mathew Bridge. The keystones of the arches are embellished with heads cut in stone by John Smyth. On the east side are Plenty, Anna Liffey and Industry, and on the west, Commerce, Hibernia and Peace. There is no inscription on the bridge.

While construction was in progress, a temporary wooden bridge, built by Knowles, was made available, and tolls were taken on this bridge until the beginning of 1816.

It is recorded that in excavating for the foundations, some Tudor coins, a large millstone and the remains of two wooden boats were found below river-bed level. Each of the boats was 5 m long and in one was a human skeleton.

The suggested location for Richmond Bridge, as it then was, raised some controversy. There had been concern that it would be built on the former Ormonde Bridge site, but this was dismissed on both technical and planning grounds. There was, however, also a powerful lobby for its erection on the axis of the Four Courts, so as to increase the splendour of that building. This lobby proposed a street on the same axis from Merchants Quay to High Street, built on an embankment to give it a uniform gradient, and bridging over Cook Street. In the opinion of the lobby, Winetavern Street could not be used because 'the steepe at the west end of Christchurch is so great . . . that no carriage can safely go up or down'. It might also have noted how cluttered with buildings the quay was at the time, at the south end of the bridge as built. It was the opinion of this lobby that a new bridge in this vicinity had no value other than monumental, and that unless it were on the axis of the Four Courts, the citizens' money would be better spent by building a bridge at the west end of the Royal Barracks (where indeed King's Bridge would be erected not many years later).

The name of the bridge was changed by order of the Municipal Council on 2 January 1922. The new name commemorates the Fenian nationalist Jeremiah O'Donovan Rossa (1831–1915).

[3, 19, 29, 39, 54, 87 (vols. 5–9); *DHR* (Frazer); BL, MS 40196, f. 59]

O'HURLEY, DERMOT, ARCHBISHOP

Dermot O'Hurley, archbishop of Cashel, who was condemned to death by Elizabeth I in 1584, is said to have been hanged at the gallows near Parkgate Street.
[4]

OLAF CUARÁN

See MALACHY, HIGH KING OF IRELAND.

OLD BRIDGE, THE

See FR MATHEW BRIDGE.

OLD CRANE, THE

See CRANES AND CRANERS.

OLD CRANE MARKET

See CRANES AND CRANERS.

OLD CUSTOM HOUSE

See CUSTOM HOUSE, OLD.

OLD DOCK, THE

While the Custom House was being built, the Revenue Commissioners decided that an enclosed wet dock should be built beside it. They approached William Jessop, who would later become well known in Dublin for his design of the Grand Canal Docks, and in 1789 sought the finance for a project prepared by him. The scheme was, however, considered too costly. In 1792 they brought forward a revised scheme, which it is suggested may have been designed by James Gandon, incorporating a dock with stores to its east and north. Faden's map of 1797 suggests that the dock and the store to its east had been completed by then. In due course, after the building of George's Dock and the Inner or Revenue Dock downstream, this dock became known as the Old Dock.

The dimensions of the Old Dock were approximately 124 m north to south, and 60 m east to west. Its west quay was parallel to the east side of the Custom House and about 30 m from it. The south quay was in line with the front of the Custom House. Access to the river was through a lock about 12 m wide, and the continuity of the North Wall was preserved by a narrow swing-bridge.

During the following century the Old Dock fell into disuse, and in 1927 the entrance channel was closed and the dock filled in. Subsequently, Memorial Road was built over part of it to complete the semicircle of Beresford Place from Butt Bridge to the future Talbot Memorial Bridge. A plan drawn by John Taylor in 1824, entitled 'A General Plan of the Custom House Revenue Stores and Docks in Dublin', shows the precise location of the Old Dock. The dimensions given indicate that it underlies parts of Áras Mhic Dhiarmada, built in c. 1950, and parts of the recently built International Financial Services Centre.

The view of the Custom House looking up the Liffey has been a subject favoured by many artists, and several of these works, including S.F. Brocas (1828), include the entrance to the Old Dock, with some showing shipping moored in the dock.
[129, 182, maps (Faden 1797, Taylor 1824)]

OLD FERRY

See FERRIES ACROSS THE LIFFEY.

OLD LEATHER CRANE

See CRANES AND CRANERS.

OLD SHORE

See BANK OF IRELAND.

ORDNANCE DATUM

See WATER, TIDE AND GROUND LEVELS.

ORDNANCE DEPOT

See CLANCY BARRACKS.

ORDNANCE LANE

See CITY QUAY.

ORDNANCE SURVEY MAPS

The Ordnance Survey was established in London in 1791, primarily to make maps for military use in the anticipation of a possible French invasion. In 1824 parliament authorised the making of a survey of Ireland, with maps to be produced at a scale of 1:10,560, the so-called '6-inch' maps, and Lieutenant-Colonel Thomas Colby was appointed as director. In 1827 or 1828 the baseline for the principal triangulation, 41,641 feet (12.69218 km) in length, was set out on the east shore of Lough Foyle, County Derry. The publication of more than 1,900 sheets recording the survey was completed in 1846, making Ireland the first country in the world to complete a nationwide survey at such a scale. The survey teams were drawn from the Corps of Royal Engineers, although some scholars, such as John O'Donovan, were recruited to study special topics.

The 6-inch maps relating to this book are the following sheets of County Dublin:

XV   East end of Bull Island
XVIII   City of Dublin from Islandbridge to Sandymount
XIX   Dublin Bay, including the mouth of the Liffey
XXIII   Dublin Bay, including Blackrock, Dún Laoghaire and Dalkey.

Sheet XVIII was published in 1838 and the others at or about that time. The levels on these maps were based on a datum level, which was the 'low water mark of the spring tide on 8 April, 1837, at Poolbeg lighthouse'. This was adopted as the national datum in c. 1842. The datum level is described as being 21 feet below a mark on the base of Poolbeg lighthouse. In 1958 the national datum level was changed to be the 'mean sea level at Malin Head, Co. Donegal'. The present record, however, uses the Poolbeg datum throughout, as it has little occasion to quote post-1958 figures.

In 1849 a series of 33 maps, based on a local resurvey, was engraved to illustrate the city of Dublin at a scale of 1:1,056. These became known as the '5-foot' maps. Hand-coloured copies were available if required, and this series was generally said to constitute the finest town plan in Europe at the time.

In 1887 a resurvey of Ireland to a scale of 1:2,500 was authorised, and this work was substantially complete in 1913, the maps becoming known as the '25-inch' maps. The scale is such that each 6-inch map can be divided into sixteen 25-inch maps. The twenty-six 25-inch maps relating to this book are as follows:

Sheet XV   14, 15, 16
Sheet XVIII   6, 7, 8, 10, 11, 12
Sheet XIX   1, 2, 3, 4, 5, 6, 8, 9, 10, 13
Sheet XXIII   1, 5, 6, 7, 11, 12, 16.

During recent years a series of town plans at a scale of 1:1,000 has been produced for Dublin by the Ordnance Survey. These appear to meet the needs once served by the 5-foot maps.

The 6-inch and 25-inch maps are kept under review and now provide the best maps available of the city and bay. They are comprehensive and need no detailed discussion, although comparison of early editions and those issued 100 years later is always of value, especially in the port and in areas of new land intake.

[257, 258, maps (OS various; OS, Townland Index, County Dublin)]

ORMONDE, FIRST DUKE OF

See JAMES BUTLER, FIRST DUKE OF ORMONDE.

ORMONDE BRIDGE

Also known as Ormond Bridge, Ormond's Bridge and Coal Quay Bridge.

In April 1682 the Grand Jury decided it was necessary to build a timber bridge across the Liffey near Charles Street. The proposal had been made to it by Alderman Peter Wybrants, who lived on the north side of the river. The lord mayor of Dublin at the time was Sir Humphrey Jervis. The purpose of the new bridge was to provide even more direct access from the 'old city' to the new Ormonde Market than could be offered by the Essex Bridge, opened four years earlier.

Jervis offered to build the bridge, and completed it during the summer of 1682. It was a basic structure, probably trestled, and with no railings. During the autumn of 1682 Alderman West, who was sheriff that year, referred to the

The collapse of Ormonde Bridge, 2 December 1802 (R. Crofton)

urgency 'for the raileing of Ormond Bridge on both sides to prevent people falling off the Bridge into the river'. He offered to provide the railings at his own expense if permitted to provide 'small shops for selling apples etc. on each side of the bridge without narrowing the passage'. He was given permission to do this in December 1682.

During 1683 the control of the Ormonde Market was an issue being fought over in the city; and late that year or early in 1684, for reasons probably associated with that issue, the Corporation pulled down the timber bridge and began to build a new stone bridge, possibly immediately upstream of the timber structure. It was to be Semple's opinion 100 years later that the demolition of this stone bridge became necessary 'probably partly owing to the injudicious construction of it or more probably to the intolerable softness of the ground it was built upon'. It could also be, however, that differences of opinion between Jervis and the Corporation played some part.

The stone bridge was substantially completed in 1684. It had five spans, four being stone arches and the fifth a timber drawbridge. Again West applied for permission to have shops at or on the bridge, it is not clear which. This time he sought a long lease, and undertook by way of rent to 'draw up and lett downe the bridge' and 'to maintain the

[bridge] pavement and drawbridge in good order and repair'. He was given his lease, a condition being that he would not 'streighten the passage on the bridge'. It seems likely that the drawbridge was replaced by a stone arch almost at once. It would have served little purpose once the opening span at Essex Bridge downstream had been permanently closed in *c.* 1685.

In 1752, when Ormonde Bridge 'was in the utmost danger of sharing the same fate' as Essex Bridge – that is, of falling down – George Semple and his brother John were asked to examine it. They found that one pier had partially collapsed and had also lost part of its foundation. Subsequently, minor repairs were made, and the Corporation apparently decided it could remain in service. In 1776 George Semple, then an old man, observed that the pier he had examined had been 'built on the naked bed of the river', adding that it was 'somewhat surprising that it has stood so long'. Of the bridge as a whole he wrote, 'I do apprehend that within some very short time it must inevitably fall,' and he offered a design for a new bridge to be built on the same site, although he warned that the very poor quality of the river-bed just there would make the foundations very costly. Semple's offer was not accepted, and on 2 December 1802 the four southern arches of the bridge collapsed while the river was in spate, two of the piers being almost completely demolished. A contemporary etching by Crofton (BL, King's Topographical Collection, vol. 53, 20.e.2) shows the ruins.

Ormonde Bridge was never rebuilt. This was possibly because of the weakness of the river-bed, but more probably because civil and legal pressure was at the time already building up to have a new bridge instead on the axis of the Four Courts, as an enrichment of the recently completed buildings. Campbell (1811) shows a discontinuity in Wood Quay where the bridge had been.

This bridge is also mentioned in the entry on O'Donovan Rossa Bridge.

[3, 11, 16, 82, *CARD*, V, VI, X, XI, XIII, map (Campbell 1811)]

ORMONDE BRIDGE WATCH-HOUSE

The watchmen for the southern half of St Michan's parish had their watch-house in the 18th century on what was then Inns Quay, just upstream of the northern end of Ormonde Bridge. Rocque (1756) shows the location. There were 13 watchmen and an inspector attached to this watch-house. It appears that there was also a constable who remained at the watch-house and supervised the work of the others. The territory covered from Ormonde Bridge consisted substantially of the area bounded by Hammond Lane and Chancery Street to the north, the Ormonde, Inns and Arran Quays to the south, Arran Street East to the east and Pudding Lane to the west.

The watch lasted from ten o'clock at night until five the following morning during winter. Each watchman had his own 'stand' at some point around the periphery of the area, and it is reported that one of the men's duties was that 'if they find any person overtaken in drink, they are to see them safe to the next stand, and the other to the next, till the person be conveyed home'.

[*CARD*, XI, map (Rocque 1756)]

ORMONDE MARKET

See ORMONDE QUAY, UPPER.

ORMONDE QUAY

See ORMONDE QUAY, UPPER.

ORMONDE QUAY, LOWER

See ORMONDE QUAY, UPPER.

ORMONDE QUAY, UPPER

The names Ormond and Ormonde are both used in the maps and literature of Dublin, and there is scholarly support for both. In this book, in the interest of consistency, the form of Ormonde is used throughout.

Brooking in 1728 shows Ormonde Quay extending from Ormonde Bridge downstream to Liffey Street (Lower Liffey Street). Rocque in 1756 shows Upper Ormonde Quay extending from Ormonde Bridge to Essex (now Grattan) Bridge, and Lower Ormonde Quay from there to Lower Liffey Street. Upstream of Ormonde Bridge on these maps was Inns Quay or the Inns. Following the collapse of Ormonde Bridge in 1802, Upper Ormonde Quay was extended upstream to the new Richmond Bridge (now O'Donovan Rossa) when that bridge was completed in 1816.

Ormonde Market was located in the block bounded by Charles Street West, Chancery Street, Arran Street East and Upper Ormonde Quay. Ormonde Quay has also been known in 1766 as Jervis Quay, and Ormonde Market as New Market. The development of the Ormonde Quays and Ormonde Market are closely interlinked, and, for this reason, the three are discussed here in one entry.

Speed in 1610 shows this section of the north bank of the Liffey to consist of the fretted estuary of the Bradogue, or the Pill, extending downstream nearly to Capel Street, followed to the east by a wall probably associated with the former St Mary's Abbey and extending for about 100 m along the riverside, and then by open land.

Interest in the development of the 'Pill beyond the water' began in earnest early in the 17th century. In 1617 eight corporations representing the 17 craft guilds and the Guild of the Holy Trinity (the merchants) were granted by the city a lease of the land of the Pill in nine equal parts. In 1662 the lease for the Pill, and, as the records suggest, for the river-bank down to Mistress Piphoe's Park (near the present Abbey Theatre), passed to James Barry, Lord Santry. While it seems from de Gomme's map of 1673 that Barry had done some straightening of the river-bank by that date, the intensive development of the area did not begin until 1675. The legal complexities of ownership and lease entitlements in this part of the north bank are profound, and will not be analysed in this entry.

In January 1675 Jonathan Amory, a Dublin merchant, was granted a lease for 299 years of the north bank strand, extending downstream from a point between Arran Street and Capel Street on Upper Ormonde Quay to a point near the modern Áras Mhic Dhiarmada. The southern boundary of the leased ground, as in strand leases generally, was the low-water mark in the river (a somewhat indeterminate line). The northern boundary was roughly along the line of Little Strand Street, Great Strand Street and Lotts, which together form a modern east–west artery lying between Abbey Street and the quays. It is probable that the name of Strand Street, which was given by Brooking in 1728, indicates the position of the high-tide shoreline before the strand 'was taken in from the sea'.

Very shortly after Amory received his lease, Humphrey Jervis and his associates, probably in 1675, acquired the lands of the Pill and other lands north of the river, amounting in all to 20 acres. The Pill lands extended to the river-bank, and the other lands may have extended in a band immediately north of Amory's holding, from Arran Street East nearly to modern O'Connell Street; and they may have included, or been bounded by, the lane now called Lotts. Jervis, on acquiring these lands, had divided them into 28 lots, Jervis's Lots, which he offered for leasing at the time, not very successfully, for £10 each. Jervis appears also to have acquired at the same time an interest in some of Amory's holding along the riverside.

Prior to 1680 Jervis filled in the land at the Pill, possibly with some direct participation by the city;

The new Presbyterian church on Ormonde Quay, 1848 (architect: E.P. Gribbon), showing also Essex Bridge

he also built Essex Bridge (now Grattan) in 1676–8, with its north end on the junction of the Upper and Lower Ormonde Quays. He was lord mayor for two years from 1681 to 1683, and in 1682 built Ormonde Bridge opposite Charles Street at his own expense, but expecting to be recouped by the city. He was busily developing Ormonde Market at this time, and, in this process, generating bitter opposition in the city because of the proposed transfer of the main city markets to the north side of the river. One can understand the feelings of the great majority of the city population who lived south of the river in having to cross over and back to go to market. Jervis was accused of using the years of his mayoralty to 'forceably drive the markets out of the old city to his new grounds', and of building the bridges to further his own ends. Ormonde Market was opened in 1682, and quickly became the principal market for the city.

At this time also Jervis was developing Ormonde Quay. It had been his intention to build houses along the waterside with their backs to the river, but at the suggestion of the duke of Ormonde, then lord lieutenant, he agreed to keep the new quay open to the water, with houses only on the landward side. Craig, applauding this decision, which would be followed in all subsequent Liffey quays, observed that 'Otherwise Dublin might well have been like so many other towns through which the river slinks shamefacedly between tall buildings which give it no chance to be seen.' Jervis had offered some years earlier to name Ormonde Quay in honour of the duke of Ormonde in recognition of his support for the development project.

During the period from 1680 to 1690 Jervis sold one-sixth of his share to Sir John Davys, secretary of state, and a similar share to William Ellis, the strand leaseholder upstream of the King's Inns. Some years after this he would criticise Davys for having earlier fomented resistance to the new markets to make it possible for him to buy an interest for himself more cheaply. In 1684 it would be recognised by the city that 'the land on the north side of the river Annaliffee belongs to Sir John Davys'; and he in his turn compromised on the transfer of the markets by agreeing to share ownership of the city fish markets, north and south of the river, with John Quelch, the owner of a threatened fish market in Fishamble Street.

Phillips's map of 1685 suggests that Ormonde Quay, Upper and Lower, had been substantially formed by that date. It was, however, unprotected and was found to be dangerous in 1685 'by reason of the key not being fenced with a wall from the [Ormonde] bridge down to the slippe, [where] a poor man lately fell and drowned himselfe'. It was ordered that a parapet wall should be built along the waterside in that part of the quay, and that the apple-mongers who traded there should be required 'to place their baskets against that wall and leave the passage of the quay free for passengers'.

Nevertheless, the quay would continue to be used as a selling area. In 1692 permission was given for coal to be sold there, and in 1709 a city committee recommended that a yard 32 m long

and 5 m wide, to be surrounded by 2-metre-high walls and fitted with rails and tenterhooks, could reasonably be built on Upper Ormonde Quay for a 'hyde market'. The west end of the quay was recommended because 'the houses of most note where persons of quality do lodge do lie on the east end'.

The overflow from the Ormonde Market continued to operate on the quay during the 18th century. Fruit was still being sold there in 1764, while in 1736 dangerous structural conditions on the quay led to the removal of the herb and root market from there to Little Green. Tudor's engraving of 1753 (NLI, 377 TB), illustrating the Old Custom House, shows also the conditions and activities on Ormonde Quay Lower at the time.

In 1818, when Ormonde Market was already 136 years in use, it was reported that it contained 73 butchers' stalls, as well as stalls for poultry, bacon, butter, cheese, fruit, vegetables, and every sort of fresh or cured fish, 'nor perhaps was there any article of food according with the climate or season of the year or any sauce which luxury could require, which may not be had at this market'. In 1909 a contemporary writer noted that the market was then 'awaiting demolition at any moment'. The site is now Ormonde Square, a residential development in which the general outline of the original market can still be traced.

Shaw illustrates the whole of Lower Ormonde Quay and part of the Upper quay as they stood in 1850, and demonstrates the variety of uses to which houses on these quays were devoted. A feature on the Upper quay was the Presbyterian church, designed by E.P. Gribbon and illustrated in NLI, 628 TB, which stood near Capel Street. The Presbyterian congregation moved to this church from Usher's Quay in 1848 and remained there until 1938, when it combined with an existing congregation in the present Ormonde Quay and Scots Presbyterian church in Lower Abbey Street. The site on Ormonde Quay has been filled with a block of offices designed by Grafton Architects; the façade of the new building, which is named Grattan Bridge House, retains features of the earlier church structure.

Only four streets run north from the Ormonde Quays. Charles Street West and Arran Street East flank the former Ormonde Market behind the Upper quay, and the large artery of Capel Street meets the junction of the Lower and Upper quays. The fourth street, Swift's Row, is on the Lower quay, linking the quay to Abbey Street and continuing northward as Jervis Street. The name of Swift's Row possibly derives from Jonathan Swift (1667–1745). This name was shown in 1728 by Brooking, and there is no clear indication of how much earlier it had been in use. Jervis, in whose gift the name may have been, died in 1708 or 1709, and Swift's popularity in Dublin may not by then have reached the height of warranting a street named in his honour.

[2, 3, 6, 29, 77, 146; *CARD*, IV–VI; BL, Add. MS 28892, f. 113; maps (Speed 1610, de Gomme 1673, Phillips 1685, Brooking 1728, Rocque 1756)]

ORMONDE'S GROUND

See OXMANTOWN.

ORMOND'S GATE

See WINETAVERN STREET.

OSTMANS BRIDGE

See FR MATHEW BRIDGE.

OSTMANS GATE

See BRIDGE GATE.

OSTMANTON

See OXMANTOWN.

O'TOOLE, LAURENCE: SAINT, ARCHBISHOP

Laurence O'Toole was born in County Kildare in *c.* 1128, the son of Maurice O'Toole, ruler of Hy Murray. At ten years of age he was sent for two years as a hostage to Diarmait Mac Murchada, king of Leinster. In *c.* 1140 he was freed and started his formal schooling at the monastery of Glendalough, becoming its abbot in 1153. In 1162, at the age of

34, he was consecrated archbishop of Dublin in Christ Church Cathedral, in succession to Gregory or Grene, who had become the first archbishop of Dublin in 1152.

Norse influence was at the time very strong in Dublin. Even then, the city, which among its many commercial activities had a thriving international slave-trade, was seen as cosmopolitan, rather than wholly Irish. The *Four Masters* noted of Laurence's appointment that he was 'archbishop of the foreigners and of Leinster'.

When in 1170 Strongbow and Diarmait Mac Murchada, who was at this time Laurence's brother-in-law, appeared outside the walls of Dublin, Laurence, recognising their military strength, became the mediator between them and the Norse rulers of the city on terms for its surrender. His efforts, however, were forestalled by the savagery of Raymond Fitzgerald (le Gros) and Miles de Cogan, who took the city by violent force, even while the mediation was in progress.

A year later Laurence was again to act as mediator, this time between the small Anglo-Norman garrison besieged in Dublin, and Ruaidhri Ua Conchobair, high king of Ireland, along with his Irish and Norse allies, who surrounded it. As quoted in 'The Song of Dermot and the Earl', Strongbow said:

> We shall send the archbishop
> That I shall be willing to do to him fealty
> And will hold Leinster of him.

The account continues:

> An archbishop they sent
> Who was afterwards called Saint Laurence.

Giraldus Cambrensis recorded of this occasion, 'it was said that Laurence Archbishop of Dublin organised this siege out of patriotic motives'. This exclusive claim is said not to be corroborated by other evidence; and it is very much more probable that Laurence's actions, both in 1170 and in 1171, were, as a pastor, for protection and peace for the people of his archdiocese, the powerless victims of the fierce international political turmoil of the time in the city. His mediation in 1171 was also unsuccessful. Ruaidhri refused the overtures of the Dublin garrison, which resolved the matter in the customary Norman way by a rapid military action in which it attacked Ruaidhri unexpectedly, near Castleknock, and routed his army.

Laurence maintained the integrity of his archbishopric in an uneasy relationship with the new rulers of Dublin and with Henry II, who spent the winter of 1171–2 in Dublin; and he subsequently made many sea journeys out of Dublin to meet Henry in England, again acting more than once as mediator between Henry and Ruaidhri Ua Conchobair. In 1172 he joined in a Council of the Irish Church, convened by Henry at Cashel, and in 1176 he officiated in Christ Church at the funeral of Strongbow.

His primary concern for the people of Dublin and for the Church in Ireland generally was not pleasing to Henry II, and the participation of Laurence in the third Lateran Council at Rome in 1179, and his subsequent appointment as papal legate for Ireland, were noted by the king with disfavour. This opposition was to lead to the death of Laurence in exile. In 1180 he visited England to meet Henry, again as a mediator for Ruaidhri Ua Conchobair and having with him Ruaidhri's son, sent as a hostage to the king. Henry blocked Laurence's return to Ireland, and then left to visit

Normandy. Laurence followed him into France to seek reconciliation, reaching the town of Eu in Normandy in November 1180. He had been seriously ill, and in Eu his illness became fatal. He died there four days after his arrival, at 52 years of age.

The next appointment to the archbishopric of Dublin was an Anglo-Norman, John Comyn; and it was a subsequent archbishop, Henry of London, who advanced the cause of Laurence at Rome, which led to his canonisation in 1225, a charitable and prayerful man, and a lover of peace.

[35, 49, 120, 150 (Lawlor), 169]

OUR LADY, STATUE ON BULL WALL

See RÉALT NA MARA MEMORIAL.

OUR LADY OF DUBLIN

See ST MARY'S ABBEY.

OUZEL GALLEY

In 1695 a trading vessel, the barque *Ouzel*, later to be known as the *Ouzel Galley*, sailed out of Dublin, bound for Smyrna in Turkey. Her owners were Dublin merchants, Messrs Ferris, Twigg and

The Ouzel Galley

Cash, her captain was Eoghan Massey, and she carried a crew of 40. Three years later, no report having been received of her, she was deemed lost at sea, and an insurance claim by her owners was settled.

In 1700, within a few days of five years after her departure, the *Ouzel* sailed back into port in Dublin, still captained by Massey and carrying a valuable cargo of pirated goods. It appears that she had been captured by Algerine pirates, and had been used by them for some time as a pirate ship in the Mediterranean Sea while the members of her crew had been held in prison. An opportunity had then arisen for their escape. They regained control of the ship, finding on it a considerable quantity of pirated booty, and sailed back to Ireland.

The problem then arose in 1700 as to who owned the cargo, and the issue was referred to the courts for judgment. After five years of legal dispute, with consequent inroads into the value of the goods, the Dublin merchants withdrew the case from litigation and established their own arbitration process. This ended in a decision to devote the entire hoard to the establishment of a benevolent fund for impoverished merchants. Arising out of this happy outcome, the merchants then decided to form a society that would be prepared to act in arbitration of all disputes referred to them of matters relating to trade and commerce. They named it the Ouzel Galley Society, or simply the Ouzel Galley. Its membership was limited to 40, the complement of the vessel's crew, and its officers adopted seafaring titles, the chairman being known as the captain.

In a recorded period of 70 years from 1799, the Society dealt with 364 cases. In 1899, having fallen into desuetude, it wound itself up, distributing its funds – which amounted to £3,300 – equally between six Dublin hospitals.

A full account of the Ouzel and the Society is given by Little, and is the principal source of this entry. An 18th-century oil-painting of the vessel hangs in the boardroom of the Dublin Chamber of Commerce.

During the 19th century Wilson and Company of Dublin owned a barque of 262 tons named *Ouzel Galley*, which had been built in North America in 1845.

[51, 84]

OXMANTOWN

The modern name of Oxmantown represents an area north of the Liffey which, while it has been known for more than 900 years, has always been indefinite in extent. Earlier versions of the name, Houstmanebi, Ostmanby, Oustmanton, Ostmanton, The Ostmans' Town, reflect its origin as a Norse district. The establishment of St Michan's in Church Street as a parish church for the area in *c.* 1096 implies the existence of a significant population at that time. In this context the implications of the battle of Clontarf in 1014 cannot be overlooked. After 1170 there was large-scale migration of the Dublin Ostmen to this suburb, arising from the growing Anglo-Norman domination of the city, although, to quote Curtis, 'whether they were actually expelled or preferred to move away from the strangers who now flocked into Dublin we cannot tell'. That Oxmantown extended as far as the Liffey at that time is indicated by the fact that one of the buildings to be severely damaged in the fire that destroyed the suburb in 1304 was St Saviour's Priory on the river-bank.

Speed, in at least one edition, describes a large undefined area across the north of Dublin as 'Ostman or Ormuntowne'; and Clarke in his map of 1978 shows Oxmantown extending from Slighe Midluachra, which he identifies with the line of Lincoln Lane and Bow Street, on the west, to the River Bradogue on the east. It may be noted that another name used for St Mary's Abbey, which lay to the east of the Bradogue, was St Mary of Ostmanby (or Houstmanebi).

The name of Oxmantown does not appear, in any of its forms, as a place-name on any map other than Speed, although it continued to be used in documents. For instance, a parcel of land was declared in 1701 to be bounded by 'the brooke or rivolett called Braddoge next the Pill in Oxmandtowne'. The core of the area may perhaps be identified today in a very general manner by the location of Oxmantown Road and Lane near St Bricin's Military Hospital.

There was always associated with Oxmantown the large expanse of Oxmantown Green. Hanmer, quoting Richard Stanihurst, records that 'Anno 1095 there came certain Esterlings to the North side of Dublin adjoining to the Liffey and seated themselves there so that of them to this day the place is called Ostomontowne and corruptly Oxmonton', and then continues:

> The Faire-greene or Commune, now called Ostmontowne-greene, was all wood, and hee that diggeth at this day to any depth shall finde the ground full of great rootes. From thence Anno 1098 King William Rufus, by licence of Murchard, had that frame which made up the roofe of Westminster Hall, where no English Spider webbeth or breedeth to this day.

Oxmantown Green, or Common, defies precise location and is to be seen as an area of indefinite extent, varying from age to age, contained in the district of Oxmantown. The fairgreen proper, which may have occupied some common ground with the modern Smithfield, would have had some vague de facto boundaries, but the boundaries of the Green were not precise, although several references show that the river was its southern edge. In 1637, as one example, Charles I proposed to build a mint-house on Oxmantown Green, and one boundary of his site was to be the low-water mark in the Liffey near the Fr Mathew Bridge.

In the earliest times Oxmantown Green or Common might be seen as all the unassigned lands on the north shore of the Liffey from the Bradogue to Islandbridge and extending some indefinite distance northwards. The entry on Ellen Hore's Meadow shows that land near Islandbridge passed into the hands of the Parsons family in the 17th century, and a second title of baron of Oxmantown was conferred on the head of that family.

After the restoration of the monarchy, the city granted to the duke of Ormonde the lands shown by de Gomme (1673) as the 'Duke of Ormonde's Ground'. This enclosure, where the Royal Barracks would later be built, was presumably part of Oxmantown Common, and the area immediately

to its east was still marked as 'Common' by de Gomme. Further still to the east, de Gomme was able to record the decision taken by the city in 1664 when it resolved 'that the said (Oxmantown) Green be and is hereby divided into ninety six proportions (or lots) leaving a convenient highway and large market place'. The highway would become Queen Street, named after the consort of Charles II, and the market-place would be Smithfield.

The area shown by de Gomme as 'Common' was, however, not part of this apportionment. In 1756 Rocque still showed as Oxmantown Green an open area of about 4 ha with definite boundaries between the 1664 lots and the Royal Barracks. This area had as a focus the new Blue-coat School, which is now held by its successors, the Incorporated Law Society. No later map refers to Oxmantown Green.

In his map of 1673 de Gomme shows a formal fenced Bowling Green in Oxmantown. It is 135 m x 90 m in extent and is close to the Liffey, with its eastern edge on Queen Street. Francis Place describes it in his drawing of 1698/9 'Dublin from the Wooden Bridge' (NGI, 7515) as 'the famous bowling green'. Rocque shows a smaller area of irregular shape, which he names Bowling Green, in the same general location in 1756.

The game of bowls was described in England before 1200. It was viewed with official disapproval in early times, as a game 'alike dishonourable, useless, and unprofitable' in 1366, and as an 'illegal pursuit' in 1511–12. During the 16th century it became apparent that indoor bowling alleys rather than bowling greens were becoming the object of censure, and during that period the outdoor bowling green became an important feature in the gardens of great houses.

The public bowling green was already established in some form in Oxmantown in 1665, and was an object of pride to the city authorities, which in that year arranged for it to be shaded with elms and sycamores. It is recorded that in c. 1670 the duke of Ormonde asked Eleanor, widow of Oliver Fitzwilliam, earl of Tyrconnel, to allow the corporation to cut sods on her lands of Merrion 'for a bowling green which it was intended to make at Oxmantown'.

In Faden's map of 1797 a formal garden immediately to the west of the new Blue-coat School is identifiable with the Bowling Green, although he does not name it, and this garden area has continued to be shown on maps to the present day. [22, 56, 150 (Curtis), 196, 197, 198, 199, *CARD*, I, III, IV, VI, maps (Speed 1610, as in bib. ref. 76, de Gomme 1673, Rocque 1756, Faden 1797, OS 1935/6, Clarke 1978)]

OXMANTOWN GREEN

See OXMANTOWN.

OYSTERS AND OTHER SHELLFISH

Examination of household debris from pits made prior to the 13th century in Wood Quay and High Street shows that cockles and mussels were the shellfish most commonly eaten in Dublin at that time. Oyster and scallop shells were scarcer. It has been suggested that oysters were not then harvested as a particular species, but were gathered in when found during the picking of cockles and mussels. Natural oyster-beds occurred along the east coast near Dublin, certainly at a later date, from Skerries to Arklow and within the bay of Dublin.

In 1577 Richard Browne, a Dublin merchant and freeman, clearly knowing of one such bed, complained to the City Assembly that he was being obstructed in dredging oysters 'within the bar'. It was decided that any freeman should be permitted this right, although if he were found to be taking any other fish commercially he would be fined heavily at the exemplary rate of 40 shillings per fish. In 1595 it appears that dredging for oysters in Poolbeg was still unrestricted, and there is no evidence that this situation changed during the 17th century. It appears also that no leases were ever granted for harvesting oysters in the mainstream of the Liffey west of Ringsend.

In 1705 John Payne was given a lease for 21 years on the oyster-beds of Poolbeg. He was 'to keep well stockt with oysters the said bed' and to leave it well stocked on the expiration of his lease. This bed lay in the channel and sandbanks of the Liffey between the Pigeonhouse and Ringsend. When the Ballast Office was about to begin its work on the South Wall shortly afterwards, Payne complained, in 1715, that the bed had been destroyed by the new works at Rogerson's Wall above Ringsend, and sought an abatement of his lease and compensation. His complaint was accepted, and the Assembly decided that thenceforth, 'during the pleasure of the city' – that is, presumably, while the harbour works were in progress in the vicinity – 'all boats be given liberty to dredge for oysters in the said pool'.

The city, however, owned a very extensive oyster-bed between the Pool of Clontarf and the Clontarf shore, and in 1718 a lease for 61 years was given to Humphrey French, an ironmonger, for

full free and absolute power to lay down, bed, and take up oysters on that part of the strand belonging [to the city] commonly called Crabb Lough . . . bounded to the north east by the road below the shades of Clontarf, to the east by a channel running by the North Bull, to the South by Poolbeg, to the southwest by Clontarf Pool and to the west by the Beech or Furlong of Clontarf, containing in the whole 195 acres [Irish] or thereabouts.

In addition to a yearly rent for this lease, French was obliged to provide '10,000 of large oysters yearly to the Lord Mayor for the time being, and 2,000 to each of the sherriffs'. Citizens were to be free to fish for anything other than oysters, and in a privilege that stirs the imagination, French had to accept that 'the Lord Mayor . . . and citizens and their successors and there respective ladys shall have liberty one day in each year appointed by the Lord Mayor . . . to go upon the said strand of Crabb Lough and to eat as many oysters thereon as they shall think fitting'. One might recall, however, that at that time not more than perhaps 10 to 15 per cent of the population of Dublin were recognised as citizens.

In 1734 the Crablake oyster-beds had reverted to the city, and litigation was in progress between it and the Vernon family over ownership of the strand. Shortly afterwards, in 1748, the Poolbeg oyster-beds had been re-established, with the *Dublin Weekly Chronicle* advertising that 'Poolbeg Oyster Fishery being taken this year by Messrs

Bunit and Simpson of Ringsend [this title still exists as a shop name] they may be had fresh and in their purity at Mrs L'Swases at the Sign of the Good Woman in Ringsend'. In that year also, a Mr Pellissier leased inundated ground behind Rogerson's Wall to lay down oyster-beds, but no further reference appears to this venture.

In 1772 Rutty spoke of the great plenty and variety of shellfish which were 'the support of some thousands of families in supplying the city of Dublin'. He reported that the cockles and mussels were especially good along the North Bull near Clontarf, but observed that most of the crabs and lobsters reaching the Dublin market came from the Isle of Man. He divided the oyster-beds into two categories, those occurring naturally, which included Poolbeg and Dalkey Sound, and those which needed to be seeded at intervals, at Crablake and Sutton. He noted particularly the large brown-shelled oysters of Poolbeg, in which pearls might be found. The Crablake and Sutton beds are shown in graphic detail in the Rocque map of 1760 and the Rocque/Scalé map of 1773.

Oyster-farming in the bay and estuary continued into the 19th century. Despite Rutty's earlier assertion about Poolbeg, the Ballast Board found it necessary in 1820 to make rules to govern the Arklow fishermen who had for some years been laying down seed-oysters in the river between the Pigeonhouse and Ringsend; and in the same year, the Board gave the Dublin Fishery Company permission 'to lay down oysters' in that area. In 1819 Giles's map of the North Bull showed that the Crablake beds still existed.

In 1832 the city gave William Ingham a lease for an oyster-bed in the Liffey immediately north of the river wall of the Pigeonhouse harbour. The boundaries of this bed, which was 262 yards square, or 5.7 ha in area, were shown precisely on a map prepared for the lease by Arthur Neville, in the role of city surveyor, working from an address at 14 York Street. This lease was still being renewed annually to various lessees until 1844, despite legal challenges from the Ballast Board and the Herbert family.

The shellfish industry in the bay and estuary is now extinct. This may be attributed to the increased demands of the shipping traffic at Dublin Port, and to the gradual deterioration of the quality of the water in the river and the bay. It is likely that all of the earlier species of shellfish still exist, but they are no longer used as food.

[59, 87 (vols. 11, 18), 219, *CARD*, II, VI, VIII, XIX, *DHR* (Hammond), Dublin Corporation Archives, maps (Rocque 1760, Rocque/Scalé 1773, Giles 1819)]

P

PAGE, SIR THOMAS HYDE

Born in 1746, Thomas Hyde Page became an officer in the Royal Engineers, was wounded at Bunker's Hill in the American War of Independence in 1775, and was transferred to the Invalid Corps of the Royal Engineers in 1784. He acted as a consulting engineer for the Royal Canal Company, and proposed, prior to 1800, that docks be built in the North Lotts near the Custom House. He has been described as chief consulting engineer for the improvement of the port of Dublin, but it is not clear what works proposed by him were actually carried out. (See The Bar of Dublin; Howth, Proposed Canal; Sandycove, Proposed Breakwater at; Ship Canals Proposed at Dunleary and Sandycove.) In 1801 he published a volume of reports concerning the harbour. This publication was on the orders of the lord lieutenant, Marquis Cornwallis, who in the previous year had engaged Captain William Bligh in a hydrographic survey of the bay and harbour. Page died in 1821.

[29, 55, 70, 71]

PALACE OF HENRY II

See HENRY II.

PAPWORTH, GEORGE

The design selected by George IV for the King's Bridge, a gift from grateful subjects in Dublin, was made by George Papworth (1781–1855) during the 1820s. Papworth, one of a family well known in architecture in Britain, practised for many years as an architect in Dublin, and was the designer of the Church of Our Lady of Mount Carmel in Whitefriar Street for the Calced Carmelites in c. 1820. In 1840 he offered proposals, with a model, for the widening of Carlisle Bridge with 3.5-metre-wide footways on each side supported on iron arches; and in 1832 he prepared a design for new baths proposed to be built at Kingstown.

In 1846 he was elected as a member of the Institution of Civil Engineers of Ireland, one of a number of architects who joined the Institution in its early years.

[87 (vol. 17), 153, 186, 276 (Minutes, vol. 1), 287]

PARK GATE

See PHOENIX PARK.

PARKGATE STREET

In 1786 the Wide Streets Commissioners were given power 'to alter and widen the road westward from Barrack Street to Island Bridge'. This road had been shown by Brooking in 1728 but not named. The western part of the improved road became Conyngham Road. The eastern part from the Phoenix Park gate to Temple Street West, where Barrack Street began, appears to have been named first as Park Gate Street on a map prepared by Sherrard for the commissioners of the Royal Barracks in 1790 (WSC 15). Wilson also gives this name in 1803. It is now Parkgate Street.

At the time of construction of this street, neither King's Bridge nor the quay between it and Barrack Bridge had been made; and as late as 1825 Sherrard would show the north bank of the Liffey touching Parkgate Street, and the Steevens's Hospital ferry slip opening directly off the street.

The Ordnance Survey maps have, since their introduction, shown Parkgate Street running from Temple Street West to the park gate.

[BL, Add. MS 13911.b; Dublin Corporation Archives (WSC map 15, 1790); maps (Brooking 1728, Wilson 1803, OS 1838 and subsequent)]

PARLIAMENT HOUSE

See BANK OF IRELAND.

PARLIAMENT STREET

When Essex Bridge was opened to traffic in 1678, access to its southern end was limited for pedestrians to a footpath along the bank of the river to Wood Quay and a flight of steps leading down to Custom House Quay, and for vehicles to a maze of lanes connecting it with Essex Street and, through Essex Gate, with Dame Street. It seems evident from Phillips's map that in 1685 a street had been driven due south from the bridge to Essex Street, and this short wide street, unnamed, is shown by Brooking (1728) and by Rocque (1756). It is difficult to reconcile this evidence with Gilbert's statement that 'in 1757 the passage from the Bridge to Essex Street was narrow and irregular'; but it is accepted that some work to improve the street was done at that time.

In 1757 an act was passed for the making of a grand passage to the seat of government, and in 1762, under the superintendence of commissioners appointed 'for making wide and convenient passage from Essex Bridge to the Castle', the new street called Parliament Street was made. This was the first work of the body later known as the Commissioners for Making Wide and Convenient Streets. It was at first intended that the street should terminate at its southern end with a splendid square dominated by Dublin Castle and containing the equestrian statue of George I, then recently removed from its first site at Essex Bridge. This proposal was later dropped, and the Exchange, now the City Hall, was built where the square was to have been, with its foundation-stone being laid in 1769.

During the 18th century many dealers in woollen and silk goods had their premises in Parliament Street, and George Faulkner (1699–1775) published his *Dublin Journal* for many years at the corner of Essex Street and Parliament Street. In 1850, when the *Evening Mail* newspaper office had been established at the southern end of Parliament Street, the street had attracted some medical and legal practices, but it was still largely commercial.

[18, 28, 146, maps (Phillips 1685, Brooking 1728, Rocque 1756)]

PATENT SLIPS
See GRAVING.

PATRICK'S FORT
During the months of June and July in 1649 the marquis of Ormonde and the Royalist army besieged Dublin, which was held by the Parliamentarians, led by Colonel Michael Jones. It is recorded that, in an engagement during the siege, Ormonde captured 'Patricks Fort on the north bank of the Liffey'. It is not clear where this was located, although it may have been Phoenix House, overlooking Island Bridge, which was demolished in the early 18th century to permit the building of the Magazine Fort.

[19, 47, 56]

PAVING BOARD
The Commission for Paving, Lighting and Cleaning the Streets of Dublin, known for short as the Paving Board, was established by act of parliament (13 & 14 Geo. III, c. 22) in 1774. The title describes its function. The Board was abolished under the Dublin Improvement Act 1849 (12 & 13 Vic., c. 97), and its powers were transferred to Dublin Corporation.

The records of the Paving Board are contained principally in its 39 minute books and 35 letter books, which are held in the Corporation's archives.

[Dublin Corporation Archives]

PEARCE, EDWARD LOVETT
See BANK OF IRELAND.

PEARSE STATION
See DUBLIN AND KINGSTOWN RAILWAY.

PEARSE STREET
A map of Westlands Brickfields drawn by Thomas Mathews, city surveyor, in 1772 shows a short length of roadway called Handsard Street extending eastward along the line of modern Pearse Street from St Mark's Church. Rocque in 1756 and Faden in 1797 show this roadway starting at the same point but name it as Moss Lane. Faden shows it continuing eastward across the south strand to Ringsend Bridge.

It was not shown as extending westward beyond St Mark's Church until 1838, when the whole length from the Long Stone site to Ringsend Bridge was shown on the Ordnance Survey map under the single name of Great Brunswick Street (the longest street in the city at the time). The name New Brunswick Street had been in use in 1818.

Rocque's map and the OS map are of particular interest in showing the progress of the extension westward to the Long Stone site. Rocque shows that the new roadway was driven for much of its length through gardens and orchards, and the OS sheet shows that this roadway came into existence and became fully built up on both sides in the very short period between 1797 and 1838.

The name Great Brunswick Street was in honour of the reigning house of Hanover. The name of Pearse Street honours Patrick Pearse, signatory of the Proclamation of 1916, who was born there in 1879.

[29, 54; BL, Add. Charters 62763 B; maps (Rocque 1756, Faden 1797, OS 1838)]

PEMBROKE, EARLDOM OF

See STRONGBOW.

PEMBROKE QUAY

See SARSFIELD QUAY.

PERROT, SIR JOHN

Born in c. 1527, Perrot was commonly reputed to be the son of Henry VIII, whom he resembled in build and appearance. He was knighted by Edward VI in 1547, and was in Ireland as president of Munster from 1571 to 1573. In 1579 he commanded a squadron of ships off the west coast of Ireland on guard against Spanish vessels. He was appointed lord deputy in Ireland in 1584 and arrived into the harbour of Dalkey that year to take up his duties. In 1585 he caused a survey to be made in Dublin 'of the whole circuit of the citie walls from the towre called Bremegham's towre of the castell unto the easte gate called the Dameis gate of the said cittie'. This survey is the source for

much of the knowledge now existing of the walls, towers and gates of the early city.

Perrot was a man of great physical strength and had 'a violent and arbitrary disposition', which led him, at the age of 60, to blows with Sir Nicholas Bagenal on the floor of the Council Chamber. In 1588 he was accused of disloyalty to the queen (who was possibly his stepsister), and he surrendered his office in June of that year. Returning to London, he was charged with treason and was confined in the Tower of London in 1591. He was tried in April 1592, but in September, still held in the Tower, he died of natural causes.

[55, 56, *CARD*, II]

PERRY, CAPTAIN JOHN

Born in England in 1669. He joined the English navy, lost the use of his right arm in a naval engagement in 1690, and was promoted to the rank of captain in 1693. In that year he was court-martialled for alleged dereliction of duty and sentenced to ten years' imprisonment. Whether in prison or after early release, he published his *Recommendations for Seamen* in 1695. In 1698 he was brought to the notice of Czar Peter the Great and went with him to Russia to superintend the establishment of a royal fleet. He remained in Russia until 1712, reaching the position of comptroller of Russian marine works.

Returning to England, he became a consultant in marine works. He spent the period from September 1713 to April 1714 in Dublin, having been invited to the city by the Ballast Office committee, to which he had sent a proposal for removing the bar at the mouth of the Liffey. No immediate benefit appears to have sprung from his visit, and the committee, 'finding it expensive keeping the said Perry unemployed', acquiesced in his return to England. In 1721 Perry again visited Dublin and laid his proposals for the Bar and for a new 'bason' before a committee of the House of Commons, which, on 21 December, seems to have decided to accept them unreservedly, resolving

nemine contradicente, that an humble address be presented to his grace the lord lieutenant that he may be pleased to lay the said resolutions before his

outlines from time to time. Located close to the Salmon Pool and Poolbeg, it was an early staging-place for ships unloading to lighters in the estuary, and it was clearly a significant feature in the estuary when the Ballast Office initiated the South Wall project in 1715.

'The Piles' reached their westernmost point on the Green Patch in 1731, and it was appropriate that they should be met there by the Ballast Office Wall (1748–59), which both completed the channel protection and, with its roadway, linked Ringsend to the Green Patch. In 1766 the Ballast Office committee 'ordered two new wharfs to be built at the end of the new wall near the blockhouse, one at each side, for the more convenient landing any goods that may be necessary'.

The date of the blockhouse is not given in the reports of the Ballast Office, but this structure (see illustration on p. 301 for its location), in whatever form it took, appears to have been the first building erected in what will be called in this book the Pigeonhouse precinct. The blockhouse was used for the storage of tools and materials and as a repository for jetsam and flotsam claimed by the Corporation. It is said to have been built in 1760 and John Pigeon became its resident supervisor or caretaker in 1761. His name was quickly attached to the building for, in their map of 1765, Scalé and Richards name it as Pidgeon House. At that time, the Salmon Pool, or part of it known as the Pigeonhouse Hole, was used as a mooring-place for cross-channel boats, some of whose passengers were then landed by wherry on the Green Patch for journey onward by road. The Green Patch was also a place of excursion for Dubliners who wished to view the South Wall works at close hand. John Pigeon, aided by his wife and daughters, all of whom it seems were able to live in the blockhouse, established a resting-place with refreshments and a boat service for both sets of visitors, and he would continue to provide this amenity until his death in 1786.

Mackenzie's chart, drawn in 1775, shows three buildings on the Green Patch at that time. These are probably the blockhouse, the Revenue Barracks, about which little is recorded (one presumes it was basically a customs and excise post), and what appears to be a storehouse. It also suggests that a wall had been built to protect the south shore of the Green Patch against wave action. In a puzzling detail, Mackenzie also shows a harbour, opening to the Liffey channel, which had not then been built. Perhaps it was under discussion at the time.

A new period began for the Pigeonhouse precinct with the establishment of the Ballast Board in 1786. New 'blockhouse' accommodation was developed in 1787. It was now an eight-roomed lofted building, containing two rooms for the new supervisor, Francis Tunstall, two rooms for the contractors working in the precinct and on the South Wall, and two rooms for Patrick O'Brien and his wife, housekeepers, who were permitted to continue the Pigeonhouse tradition of refreshments for visitors. In 1791 a harbour to be called Pigeonhouse Harbour or Dock was planned. The existing South Wall formed its southern and eastern quays, and new walls were built in the channel of the Liffey to form the north and west sides of the basin. It came into service in 1793 and made it possible for passengers to disembark directly onto a quay. It must be said that it was never an efficient harbour, as it could dry out completely at low tide and was shown for instance on Frazer's survey of 1838/42 as dry and standing wholly on dry ground at low tide.

With the increase in cross-channel passenger traffic, it was considered that more elaborate accommodation should be provided for travellers. This led to the construction in c. 1793 of what was called the Pigeonhouse Hotel, an imposing cut-stone building in formal style, with Mrs Tunstall as manageress. It was ornately finished, according to contemporary records, with 2 chimney-pieces of mountain stone, 14 of black stone, 9 of Kilkenny marble, and with a large 'Tuscan frontispiece', cornices, moulded architraves and piers, and an arch over the front door. At this stage the same records were speaking of 'the Town of Pigeon House'.

In 1798 the rebellion of the United Irishmen led the government to ask the Ballast Board for the

Pigeonhouse Hotel

use of the Pigeonhouse precinct as a temporary military strong point. This began a military occupation of the precinct that would last until 1897. In 1800 Bligh noted on his map the existence of the Revenue Barracks and the 'Hotel Barracks', with a larger structure between them, along with a number of small buildings west of the hotel. He also showed that defensive gateways had been erected on the South Wall at both ends of the precinct, one guarding the approach from Ringsend, and the other preventing access along the South Wall from the east. The blockhouse of 1787 had apparently been demolished. According to a map prepared in 1813 by the army, and reading this in conjunction with a layout of the precinct prepared in 1861 (see illustration on p. 301), the buildings shown by Bligh included soldiers' quarters, stores, a magazine, and tanks for fresh water (piped water would not be made available by the city for another 30 years or more), and both gateways were protected with trenches cut in the paved surfaces and crossed by windlass-operated drawbridges.

During the early years of the 19th century the harbour continued to be used for the cross-channel packet-boats carrying mail and passengers. It was from this harbour that the *Prince of Wales* and the *Rochdale* sailed in November 1807 on the ill-fated voyage that was to end with shipwreck and many drownings on the South Bull between Blackrock and Sandymount some 36 hours later.

Between 1803, when the Pigeonhouse Fort was one of the barracks chosen for attack by Robert

Emmet, and 1813, the army built an armoury and a guardhouse commanding the road from Ringsend, and installed 24-pounder guns trained on the South Bull sands and the mouth of the river. In 1814 the government, citing the Defence Act and brushing aside Lord Fitzwilliam's claim that all the new land in the precinct and on the South Bull was his property, formalised its occupation of the precinct by buying it from the Ballast Board for approximately £100,000. Its purchase included the hotel and the harbour, together with a 180-metre length of the road towards Ringsend, a similar length of the South Wall east of the precinct, and a 120-metre-wide belt of sand on the South Bull strand south and east of the built precinct.

Although Haliday, who was a member of the Ballast Board in 1848, records that the hotel was still available until that year for dinner 'for good fellows', the hotel was in 1814 being used as officers' quarters, and a plan of the Pigeonhouse Fort, as it then became known, showed that by 1861 the Revenue Barracks, portrayed by Sadler as a substantial two-storey cut-stone building, had become the fort hospital. The everyday pursuits of the garrison had been catered for by the building of a handball alley, which can still be seen, a canteen which was the soldiers' eating and drinking area, and a prison. At that time the harbour, although out of use for the mails from 1813 onwards when Howth began to replace it, was still protected by a boom and presumably still used for military transport. The full complement of the fort in 1862 was 13 officers, 242 non-commissioned officers and men, and 12 horses. It is said, however, that the Pigeonhouse Fort troops were never called into active service except to menace with their guns those gathering for the monster Repeal of the Union meeting called by Daniel O'Connell across the river in Clontarf in October 1843. As a result the perceived need for the fort diminished during the century, until in 1897 it was vacated as a military post, and the precinct was sold to Dublin Corporation for £65,000, with the army retaining in perpetuity a right of way through it for its troops.

The Pigeonhouse precinct now entered its third

phase, this time as an area of service for the city of Dublin. Some years earlier, in 1878–81, the commissioners for the Rathmines and Pembroke townships had completed a comprehensive drainage project, in which the sewage of their area was pumped through a station at Londonbridge Road to discharge into the Liffey estuary through a penstock house still to be seen on the South Wall at the White Bank near Costello's, east of the Pigeonhouse Fort. The pipeline, 1.8 m in diameter, traversed the precinct, running beside the South Wall to the penstock house. This large main outfall sewer is of interest in that it remained in service for over 100 years, bypassing the Corporation works of 1896–1906 described below, and discharging sewage into the Liffey untreated except for the removal of sand and grit, which might otherwise have interfered with the channel of the river.

The purchase of the precinct in 1897 coincided with a long-delayed decision to develop a metropolitan sewerage system for a large area of the city. As part of this scheme, commenced in 1896 and opened with great splendour in 1906, sewage was treated in a battery of sludge beds which occupied about 90 per cent of the Pigeonhouse harbour. The effluent from this treatment was discharged to the river, and the settled solids were taken in a specially designed sludge boat for disposal at sea beyond the Baily lighthouse. A small area of the harbour at its east end was retained as a quay for berthing and loading the sludge boat.

Early in the 20th century the Corporation, which at the time controlled its own supply of electricity, found that its generating station at Fleet Street in the city was inadequate for the rapidly increasing demand for energy. In 1902 the foundation-stone for a new generating station in the Pigeonhouse precinct was laid by the lord mayor, Timothy Harrington, MP, and this began a history of electricity supply from the precinct that continues to this day. The first Pigeonhouse generating station, which met a demand of about 5,000 kilowatts, would remain in operation until 1971, being taken over by the Electricity Supply Board, established in 1927, and being developed in capacity over the decades up to about 95,000 kilowatts. In 1971 the coal-fired Pigeonhouse station was replaced by the Poolbeg station, using either oil or natural gas as fuel. It now has a capacity of 660 megawatts, which may be further increased.

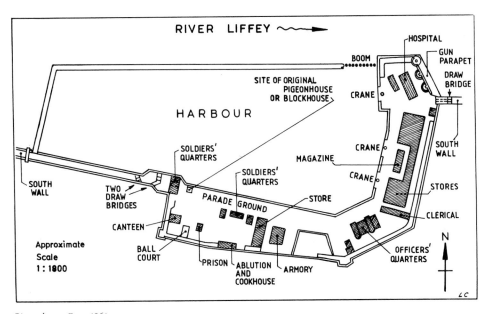

Pigeonhouse Fort, 1861

During the second half of the century the area south of the precinct was used for controlled refuse disposal, and a substantial hillock enlarging the Green Patch was formed on the edge of the South Bull, or, as it might now be called, Sandymount Strand. Inside this raised area, which now contains also Irishtown Conservation Park, the Corporation built a new sewage treatment plant, and brought it into service in 1985. This plant provides three-stage treatment for most of the sewage of Dublin south of the river, now including the former Rathmines and Pembroke townships. It discharges its residual effluent into the Liffey east of the electricity generating station, and dumps the consolidated sludge by boat north of a line extending due east from the Baily lighthouse. A jetty in the channel of the Liffey near the mouth of Pigeonhouse Harbour now allows the sludge boat to operate independently of the tide, and the sludge beds of the earlier plant are used today only to deal with storm overflows.

The Pigeonhouse precinct has continued to expand during the second half of the century. The Port and Docks Board has built three new quays along the Liffey west of the Poolbeg station. These are the South Quay, which is designed to handle container traffic, the South Bank Quay for roll-on/roll-off traffic, and the Coal Quay as the centre for coal importation. The Ringsend electricity generating station, with its coal conveyor gantry spanning over Pigeonhouse Road, lies at the western boundary of the precinct, and the oil storage tank farm attached to the Poolbeg generating station extends the original Green Patch eastwards to meet the remnant of the Shelly Banks strand that still separates it from the White Bank.

[6, 60, 87 (vols. 2, 3), 90, 129, 134, 154, 155, *CARD*, XI, *DHR* (Kelly, O'Donnell), *Engineers Journal*, vol. 41, no. 9 (de Courcy), maps (Revenue 1694, Bowen 1728, Scalé and Richards 1765, Mackenzie 1776, Bligh 1800/3, Frazer 1838/42, Dublin Port 1987)]

PIGEONHOUSE, REVENUE BARRACKS AT
See PIGEONHOUSE: A PRECINCT.

PIGEONHOUSE, TUNSTALL'S HOUSE AND OFFICE AT
See PIGEONHOUSE: A PRECINCT.

PIGEONHOUSE BARRACKS
See PIGEONHOUSE: A PRECINCT.

PIGEONHOUSE DOCK
See PIGEONHOUSE: A PRECINCT.

PIGEONHOUSE FORT
See PIGEONHOUSE: A PRECINCT.

PIGEONHOUSE GENERATING STATION
See PIGEONHOUSE: A PRECINCT.

PIGEONHOUSE HARBOUR
See PIGEONHOUSE: A PRECINCT.

PIGEONHOUSE HOLE
See POOLBEG.

PIGEONHOUSE HOTEL
See PIGEONHOUSE: A PRECINCT.

PIGEONHOUSE ROAD
See PIGEONHOUSE: A PRECINCT.

PIGEONHOUSE SEWAGE TREATMENT WORKS
See PIGEONHOUSE: A PRECINCT.

PILES, THE
See THE SOUTH WALL.

PILING ENGINE
See THE SOUTH WALL.

PILL, THE
The Pill, known in Dublin as 'the Pill beyond the water', was an area with imprecise boundaries,

consisting generally of the creeks, inlets and channels around the confluence of the River Bradogue with the Liffey, and the islets lying between them. It is likely to have been rank meadow and marsh, overflowed to some degree by high tide in the river, and was described in 1634 as 'wast and voide'. The improved land at St Mary's Abbey and at the Inns, formerly St Saviour's Priory, would have represented its east and west limits, and the entry for Little Green suggests something about its northern edge.

In 1614 the city authorities examined the titles of those who claimed rights to the Pill or parts of it. By 1618 they appear to have taken it under their control, for in that year they were dividing it into nine lots for leasing. By the year 1662 the leasehold for the area appears to have passed into the hands of Lord Santry, whose heirs are recorded as continuing to pay rent for it to the city 100 years later, in 1762.

In 1675 the Pill was still largely wasteland; and indeed one of the claims made by Sir Humphrey Jervis during his long legal battle with the city related to the cost of reclaiming the area by building a river wall along the Liffey and raising the general ground level. By his account, ten carts were constantly employed for four years carrying in earth for this reclamation.

By 1684 the Assembly Roll records that the 'lands called the Pill [are] now in the possession of the honorable sir John Davys, knight, his majesties principal secretary of state'; and, at this time, Jervis was apparently in some financial difficulties. It was in this land that the Ormonde Market was built.

The name of the Pill as a district remained in use late into the 18th century, and vestiges lasted even longer, with the thoroughfare now known as Chancery Street remaining as Pill Lane until 1890.
[16, *CARD*, III–VI, XI, *DHR* (Mac Giolla Phádraig)]

PILL, USHER'S

See USHER'S PILL.

PILL LANE

Pill Lane extended roughly parallel to the Liffey from Church Street to Arran Street East. It was a narrow but important artery on the route from the Old Bridge (Fr Mathew Bridge) to St Mary's Abbey, and as such probably existed from the 11th century, if not earlier.

It was known also as Pill Street. In 1890 its name was changed to Chancery Street.
[*DHR* (Mac Giolla Phádraig); BL, Add. MS 40196; maps (various)]

PILOTING IN DUBLIN HARBOUR

In England the work of pilots in early times was governed by rules that are mentioned in the Black Book of the Admiralty, and in the Oak Book of Southampton, which was compiled in 1300. When approaching a harbour which was not known to any of the mariners on a ship, the master was required to signal for a pilot or 'lodesman' who would then come aboard and be in charge until the vessel reached its berth. If, through ignorance or incompetence, the pilot caused the ship to be wrecked, he would, as a penalty, lose his right hand and left eye, or, if the majority of those on board so decided, might even be beheaded.

In 1514 Henry VIII founded, at Deptford, 'the Gild of the Holy Trinity', which consisted of the 40 Thames pilots under a master and warden. This later became Trinity House, which gradually came to manage also all the lighthouses around the coast of England and to control the examination of pilots. In Dublin the 16th century saw recognition of the need for the employment of competent pilots and for the control of the fees paid to them. In 1673 Captain James Sherland, who had been commander of the yacht *Mary*, engaged in the king's service in Ireland, petitioned Charles II, who wrote to the earl of Essex, his lord lieutenant, saying, 'there hath been many shipwrecks about the Bar and Port of the City of Dublin in few years last past for want of a skilful pilot duly authorised to attend the coming in and going out of ships there'. The king, possibly recalling the humiliation of the Dutch adventure into the Thames and Medway in 1667, referred also to the 'inconveniency and danger of foreigners taking upon themselves to sound and acquaint themselves with the depths, narrows, flats and shoals (in and about the Bar and

Port) whereby the ships lying in the said Port may be much exposed in time of war'. Charles's letter stated his 'will and pleasure in that you cause a grant of the said office of pilot . . . to be passed to the said James Sherland under our Great Seal . . . with such allowance of fees or duties as have been usually paid to persons hired and employed as pilots there'. Sherland was to 'prevent the concealment and embezzlement of any goods, customs, excise or duties', and was to work to instructions given by 'you, our lieutenant general'. Clearly Sherland was to be rather more than merely a pilot, and was to be answerable to the king, not to the city of Dublin.

In an early reference to a pilot service in Dublin, the names of seven pilots are listed in an address made by the city to George I in 1726. These were Brown, Bryan, Eustace, Lawler, Monks, Neale and Thompson.

In 1731 the Dublin merchants petitioned the House of Commons for the establishment of a Pilot Office. Later that year, parliament agreed the heads of a bill including provision 'for appointing sworn pilots in the harbour of Dublin', but pointed out that the establishment of such an office was the king's prerogative, and would require his consent. In 1739 the merchants asked the city to seek a charter from George II, and in 1747 the city prepared a petition to be sent to the lord lieutenant for the king's consideration. It was to seek 'skilful pilots', and to state 'that if a Pilot Office were under the same regulations as the Ballast Office it would answer the desired end'. It was emphasised that such an office should be under the authority of the city rather than be controlled by private interests.

In 1763 an act was passed vesting the authority for pilotage in the city, and the first Pilot Committee was appointed under this act in 1765. It consisted of the lord mayor, the 2 sheriffs, 5 aldermen, 10 common councillors, and 15 nominees of the Guild of Merchants, in all 33 members. This Committee, which also had responsibility for lighterage and havenage, had authority to appoint up to 50 pilots, and pilotage became compulsory for every ship arriving at Dublin or departing, except those carrying coal or grain.

New Pilot Committees were appointed periodically until 1786, when the Corporation for Preserving and Improving the Port of Dublin (the Ballast Board) replaced the Ballast Office. In 1774 the then Pilot Committee appointed a pilot master, with two early holders of this office being John Armstrong and Richard Greydon; and in 1776 it nominated 20 persons to be licensed as pilots.

In 1786 the Ballast Board was given the responsibility of appointing pilots, and since 1869 this work of pilotage has been carried forward by the Dublin Port and Docks Board.

Pilot boats and the pilotage service generally have been based at various stations in the river and bay. At the beginning of the 19th century Bullock Harbour was used, and a settlement of pilots' families built up there. In 1828 the pilotage office was at the new harbour then being built at Kingstown.

In 1846 the Tidal Harbours Commissioners noted that there were 9 river pilots, 36 sea pilots and 8 apprentices serving the port. They found that 'the distinction of river and sea pilots, the former earning double and not doing half the hard work of the latter, is unjust and prejudicial'. The distinction seems difficult to draw, but Robert Morton, a river pilot, said in evidence that 'he never went as far as the Kish'.

Since 1913 the general pilot station for the port has been at the Eastern Breakwater, close to the B. & I. freight terminal.

From quite early times there existed in the bay and estuary an unofficial group of adventurous and competitive boatmen who came to be known as hobblers. It was the hobbler's practice to put out to sea in a small boat to be taken on board an incoming vessel, accompany it to the harbour, perhaps even acting as a covert pilot, and moor it at its berth, for all which a fee was paid. As the control of pilots became stricter, the role of the hobblers was limited to mooring, although they continued to compete for trade, venturing out to sea in all weathers in search of work. This risky practice continued into the 20th century, and records speak of a crew of three hobblers who lost their lives when their boat was run down by a steamer in Dublin Bay in February 1926 (*The Irish Times*, 23 February 1926).

[129, 158, 197, 285; *CARD*, VII–IX, XI, XII; BL, Stowe MS 203, f. 66]

PIPE YARD

See BENBURB STREET.

PIPHOE (MISTRESS PIPHOE'S PARK)

The Phepoe or Piphoe family were long-established landowners in Dublin. A Richard de Pheypowe owned lands near Finglas in the 13th century. Through intermarriage with this family, the Beresfords came to own part of the lands of St Mary's Abbey where Tyrone House on Marlborough Street was built in *c.* 1740.

In 1662 Lord Santry, in negotiation with the city about the development of the Pill, agreed to provide a 21-foot-wide strip as highway 'all along the Liffie side . . . eastward to Mistress Piphoes park'.

From this limited evidence, it is tentatively suggested that Mistress Piphoe's Park had a frontage on the north bank of the Liffey, in the vicinity of Eden Quay.

[3, 106, 189, *CARD*, IV]

PIRACY

In 1632 the lords justices of Ireland wrote to the English Privy Council, 'There is at this moment a Biscayner pirate in the river. She chased some vessels which came in with last tide. This is an indignity and we are fitting out two barques to try and free the coasts of her.' They added, perhaps unexpectedly, 'It is a great mistake to have only English residents in command of the ships. If we were allowed to choose captains from residents here it would be very much better.'

Constant hostility between England and her maritime neighbours during the 17th and 18th centuries brought another style of pirate to the waters around Ireland. This was the privateer, a nominally loyalist pirate ship, privately owned, but commissioned by a state to plunder the shipping of enemies. In 1745 Dublin petitioned George II, saying:

The port and harbour of this city of Dublin are open and defenceless so that ships lying therein are exposed to and may be cut out by any privateer of moderate force. There is no ship of war stationed at Dublin or Waterford or northwards of this port nor any cruisers in St George's Channel. The navigation from this city to the southward or even to Liverpool or Chester is become hazardous and in a short time must be totally interrupted.

The Assembly noted at that time that 'within the last few days a French privateer near Tuskard has taken amongst others three ships bound from Dublin to Cork'.

Between 1778 and 1782 the army stationed two floating batteries or guard ships in Dublin Bay to discourage privateering on the doorstep. This drew an opinion from Lieutenant-Colonel Charles Vallancey that 'the fear of opposition has prevented many privateers from attempting to cut out ships at Poolbeg, but that a King's cutter stationed in the bay or harbour of Dublin would be of much greater use and not more expensive than the guard ships'.

Plunder within the port by land-based thieves was also seen as a form of piracy. In 1800 it was estimated that there were nearly 11,000 thieves and 500 receivers preying on the Thames traffic in London and that their yearly haul was about half a million pounds. This group divided itself into nine fraternities, each with its own special way of working. They were known as river pirates, night plunderers, light horsemen, heavy horsemen, game watermen, game lightermen, mud larks and scuffle-hunters, with the receivers being called copemen. One can be sure that equivalents existed in Dublin. In January 1790 George Stewart, who in London would have been a river pirate, cut a rope of the *Harry of Coulton* at Aston Quay to let it drift downstream. He was apprehended and 'a warrant under the Corporation seal was signed directed to the High Sheriffs of the City of Dublin requesting them to have George Stewart publicly whipped from Crampton Quay to the Marine School on Monday the 11th inst'. Perhaps he got off lightly for the times.

[68 (vol. 2), 87 (vol. 2), 160 (vol. 17), 216, *CARD*, IX]

PLAGUE, THE

A highly infectious disease transmitted by fleas from infected rats, which has occurred in epidemics of enormous size since the earliest times, and is still endemic in some parts of the world. It has three main forms, the best-known being bubonic, and until the development of 20th-century drugs it was generally fatal.

Six major epidemics of the Plague were recorded in Dublin from 1095–6 to 1603–5. Immeasurably the most serious of these was that known as the Black Death in the middle of the 14th century. It arrived in Europe from Asia in 1347, striking first in the Crimea, and it declined in 1351, having swept through the Continent, killing 25 million people, or about one-quarter of the entire population. It was first seen in Ireland at Dalkey, Howth and Drogheda early in August 1348. Before Christmas 14,000 had died of the disease in Dublin alone. It struck earliest at the ports and harbours, and the population of sailors and fishermen, in particular, suffered great losses, thus adding significant food shortages to the other afflictions of the city.

Not surprisingly, then, the outbreak of the Great Plague in London in 1664–5, an epidemic that would kill 70,000 of the city's population of 460,000, terrified Dublin. Steps were taken at once to control immigration by the building of 'pest houses' on Clontarf Island, in a foreshadowing of quarantine precautions. This must have helped, because in June 1665 it was possible to send a report to London saying that 'the plague as yet has proved fatal to no one in Ireland', and there was no later outbreak at that time.

[147, 160, 197, 239, CARD, IV, DHR (Boylan), Studies, vol. 24, March 1935 (A. Gwynn)]

PODDLE RIVER

The Poddle has been known as Sallagh, Soulagh, Podell, Puddell, Pottle, and, in 1506, as le Poddell. The river rises in Cookstown, near Tallaght, and flows into Dublin through Kimmage and Harold's Cross. In the city, it flows underground today through two main streams, one by way of New Row and one along the Coombe. These unite near Poddle Cross, the intersection of Patrick Street and the Coombe. The single or perhaps two-channel

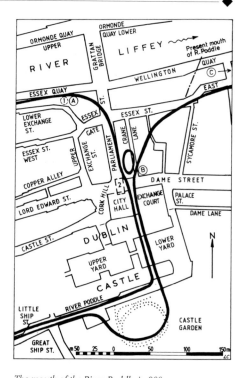

The mouth of the River Poddle in 900: an approximation
ABC: new land taken in by Newman, 1606–20
1: Newman's Tower   2: Dames Gate

stream then flows north between Patrick Street and Bride Street until it meets the great ridge of Christchurch. There it turns east and, passing south of St Werburgh's Church under Little Ship Street, and south and east of Dublin Castle, discharges into the Liffey through an arched opening at Wellington Quay.

This entry relates to that part of the Poddle which may have been influenced at some period in history by the tide in the Liffey. It does not consider the effect of storm flood conditions in the Poddle further upstream.

In any review of the lower Poddle, three eras in history should be recognised, namely:

(i) from the beginning (AD 900) to the building of a dam or dams (say 1240)

(ii) from the building of a dam to the reclamation of the land in the estuary (1240–1620)

(iii) from the reclamation of the estuary to the present time (1620–2000).

At the time of Perrot's survey in 1585, it was in the possession of a man named Prickett or Prichette. At that time it was a rectangular tower 9 m x 8.4 m out-to-out, with walls 10.2 m high and 1.02 m thick. It had a timber loft and a turret on its east side. There is no indication what it was used for. The dimension of 10.2 m is measured most probably from the level of the channel in the river, and the ground floor then would be at quay pavement level 2.7 m above the channel, or slightly lower at 2.4 m above the channel. This matter, and the particular meaning here of the term 'channel', is discussed generally in the entry on Newman's Tower.

Prickett's Tower was probably badly damaged in the gunpowder explosion of March 1597 (see Wood Quay), and it may not have been rebuilt, as there appears to be no further reference made to it. If it was rebuilt, it will have formed part of the cluster of houses shown by Rocque (1756) between Pudding Row and the river. It does not appear on OS 1838.

[150, CARD, I, II, map (Rocque 1756)]

PRINCE GEORGE OF DENMARK

See BALLAST OFFICE.

PRINCE OF WALES

During the afternoon of Wednesday, 18 November 1807, two vessels, the *Prince of Wales* and the *Rochdale*, sailed out of the Pigeonhouse harbour, as part of a flotilla of ships taking troops, accompanied by their families, away to foreign service. That night in the Irish Sea they ran into a violent storm of wind and snow. This persisted during the next day at such intensity that the captains decided to return to Dublin. They arrived in the bay as night had fallen and, being uncertain of their position, since snow was falling very heavily at the time, were carried past the small harbour at Dunleary and wrecked on the South Bull sands, the *Prince of Wales* under Blackrock and the *Rochdale* near the Martello tower at Seapoint. Three hundred and eighty people lost their lives, and this quite possibly in places where

they might have waded ashore had they known and were the waters quieter. For several days their bodies were washed up along the sands.

Some of the victims were buried in the graveyard at Booterstown, where a headstone was erected in their memory. The inscription reads:

Sacred to the memory of the Soldiers belonging to his Majesty's 18th Regiment of Foot and a bevy belonging to other Corps who Actuated by a desire of more Extensive Service Nobly Volunteered from the South Mayo and different Regements of Irish Militia into the line and who were unfortunately Shipwrecked on this coast in the Prince of Wales Packet and Perished on the night of the 19th of November 1807 this Tribute to their Memory has been placed on their tomb by order of General the Earl of Harrinton Commander of the Forces in Ireland.

Another stone stands to their memory in St Begnet's graveyard in Dalkey.

[87 (vol. 7), 241, *DHR* (O'Rourke)]

PRINCES STREET SOUTH

A street connecting City Quay and Townsend Street (Lazars Hill). It appears first on Brooking's map of 1728, where its name is exchanged in error with Moss Street, and it continues to be shown on modern maps.

[Maps (Brooking 1728, Rocque 1756, OS various)]

PRIVATEERING

See PIRACY.

PROUDFOOT'S CASTLE

Also known as Proudfitt's, Proutefort's, Profot, Prowdfoote's. See FYAN'S CASTLE.

PUBLIC LATRINES

It is recorded that there was a common 'pryve' or 'jacks' beside Izod's Tower before 1558. From that time the Liffey quays were always provided with public latrines. Thus there was a 'pryvie' to the east of Fyan's Castle in 1571, and a 'house of office' on Merchants Quay in 1626. In 1642 a new 'jakes' or 'common house of office' was built beside Fyan's Castle, and in 1691 John Denham was given a lease to make new land on the strand at Merchants Quay, provided that he built 'a good publick house of office into the river' and left 'a public passage with free ingrese, egrese, and regrese for all persons whatsoever'.

In 1737 permission was given to convert a former 'house of easement' or 'bog house' near the north-west corner of Ormonde Bridge into a shelter for the parish constables, and in 1757 it was noted that a new 'public house of ease' was required on Ormonde Quay because the existing 'necessary house' had been taken down during the rebuilding of Essex Bridge and there was no 'convenience of that sort' near the bridge.

[*CARD*, I–III, V, VIII, X]

PUDDING LANE

See ARRAN QUAY and WINETAVERN STREET.

PUDDING ROW

See WOOD QUAY.

PURSICTOR ALLEY

See ARCH LANE.

Q

QUARANTINE

The danger of transmitting serious diseases, such as the plague and cholera, through overseas travellers and their goods has been recognised from early medieval times. The building of the pesthouses on Clontarf Island as a reaction to the London plague epidemic of 1664–5 has been mentioned elsewhere. The first formal Quarantine Act in English law was, however, not promulgated until 1710. Its purpose was 'to oblige ships coming from places infested more effectively to perform their Quarentine'. At that time the suspected sources were 'on or near the Baltick Sea', from where of course Ireland was already importing timber. The act, which was reprinted by Andrew Crooke in Copper-alley in 1711, required that ships would 'be obliged to make their quarentine' in places directed, and that neither persons nor goods could leave a ship until this had been done. Anyone who broke the law would be compelled, and 'in case of resistance' would be compelled 'by Force and Violence to return on board [his] ship, there to remain during the time of Quarentine'.

It seems likely that, for Dublin, the place directed was in one of the pools in the estuary. In 1757 Rocque shows a 'quarantine sloop' in the Poolbeg, presumably on a fixed station; and in 1763 the crew of a quarantine wherry was thanked by the City Assembly for securing, 'at the manifest risk of their Lives', the floating light at the Bar, which had broken loose from its moorings.

The formal practice of quarantine in waters under English jurisdiction was gradually replaced by less stringent, or more locally directed, regulations during the 19th century. In 1788 a proposal was put forward to make a quarantine station on Dalkey Island, but nothing came of it.

[4, 6, 197, *CARD*, XI, map (Rocque 1757)]

QUAY WALLS AND FOOTPATHS

See LIFFEY: QUAY WALLS AND PAVINGS.

QUAYS IN DUBLIN: GENERAL

This book follows the *Concise Oxford Dictionary of Current English* in defining a quay as 'a solid stationary artificial landing-place lying alongside or projecting into water for loading and unloading ships'. To constitute a quay, the river-bank or sea coast must have been modified by man. Otherwise one is speaking of beaching or mooring at an existing bank or shore. There are exceptions to this definition but they are not known to exist at Dublin. This criterion makes it possible to suggest dates for the making of quays while accepting the fact that vessels may have loaded and unloaded at the various sites for many centuries previously. In Dublin as elsewhere, a quay tends to retain its title after it ceases to be used for loading and unloading ships, so it remains valid today to speak, for instance, of Usher's Quay or Merchants Quay, or indeed, in Brussels, of the Quai du Commerce, where there has been no water for 100 years.

The text lists, under their individual names, the quays along the Liffey and quays at other relevant places. The following names of quays are mentioned, but it will be seen in various entries that some are merely given as alternatives for others.

Quays on north side of Liffey

Albert	Alexandra	Alexandra East
Arran	Bachelors Walk	Back
Bridgewater	Custom House (New)	Dublin (North Wall)
East	Eden	Ellis
Inns	Iron	Jervis
King's Inns	North	North Quay Extension
North Strand	North Wall	North Wall Extension
North Wall Quay	Ormonde, Lower	Ormonde, Upper
Pembroke	St Mary's Abbey	Sand
Sarsfield	Wolfe Tone	

Quays on south side of Liffey

Aston	Blind	Bridge Street
Brooke's	Burgh	City
Coal (in city)	Coal (Ringsend)	Crampton
Crosse's	Custom House (Old)	Dublin
Essex	George's	Hawkins's
Merchants	New	Nicholas's
Nichols's	Rogerson's	South
South Bank	Usher's	Usher's Island
Victoria	Wellington	White's
Wood		

Quays at other relevant places

Britain	Charlotte	Fitzwilliam
Grand Canal	Great Britain	Hanover
Island	Tolka	

A separate entry on Liffey: Quay Walls and Pavings may also be consulted.

QUEEN MAEVE BRIDGE

See MELLOWES BRIDGE.

QUEEN STREET

See OXMANTOWN.

QUEEN'S BRIDGE

See MELLOWES BRIDGE.

R

RAHENY, MILL OF

Petty's map of the half-barony of Rathdown (1654) shows an unnamed windmill a little way back from the high-water coastline near the Sheds of Clontarf. Rocque (1760) shows three mills further east, in the vicinity of St Anne's Park, one 'Ratheny mill in ruins', and the other two 'Ratheny windmill' and 'windmill at Ratheny'. The significance of one of these mills is that, by the 18th century, the liberties of the city of Dublin, as ridden in the franchises, had their north-east corner at a little brook 130 perches north of 'the Mill of Raheny' (1773), or 130 perches north from 'the Mill of Raheny, now in ruins' (1815). The city had been gradually pushing its boundary eastwards over many hundreds of years, and the Petty windmill, not marked by Rocque, may possibly have been a boundary mark also.

The 'mill in ruins' was probably a water-mill, powered by the Santry River. The modern road beside the Santry River at this point is named Watermill Road.

[BL, 1890.e.5 (76) and (108); maps (Petty 1654, Rocque 1760)]

RAILWAY PROPOSED ACROSS CITY

See VIGNOLES, CHARLES BLACKER.

RAM LANE

Also Rame Lane. See MERCHANTS QUAY.

RAMYNELAN

See REINELAN.

RATHMINES, BATTLE OF

See BATTLE OF RATHMINES.

RAYMOND LE GROS

The son of William, or William of Carew, grandson of Gerald of Windsor, constable of Pembroke, and Nesta, daughter of Rhys ap Tewdr, prince of South Wales. Raymond came to Ireland in 1170 and, with Miles de Cogan, was in the company of young knights which took Dublin by storm in September that year.

He was a man 'of ample proportions', and a brave and resourceful warrior, one of the three leaders who broke Ruaidhri Ua Conchobair's siege of the city in 1171. Raymond married Basilia FitzGilbert, Strongbow's sister, in 1173 or 1174; they had no children. A castle was built for him near Wexford in 1181, and he died, probably between 1189 and 1200, by which date Basilia was the wife of Geoffrey FitzRobert. The year of his death and the place of his burial are not known.

What his family name was is not clear. He is described as Fitz William by Orpen, as FitzGerald by Giraldus, and as de (or of) Carew, the last being the name of his father's castle at Carew in Pembrokeshire. His brother, Odo de Carew, was the progenitor of the Carews of Cork.

[35, 37]

RÉALT NA MARA MEMORIAL

In 1972 a statue of Our Blessed Lady, Star of the Sea, was erected on the Bull Wall. It stands on a tall pylon formed with three slender prestressed concrete columns set in a base on the Wall. A foundation-stone at the foot of the pylon states that 'The memorial project was initiated by the dockers of the port of Dublin and mainly funded by them and other port workers'; and it acknowledges the designer and sculptor, Cecil King, the structural engineer, Bernard Le Cesne Byrne, and the contractor, William Lacy. Two further inscriptions on the stone read respectively, 'This foundation stone was blessed by His Eminence, Cardinal Gregory Agagianian, papal legate to the Dublin congress of the Patrician Year, prefect of the sacred congregation de propaganda fide, 16 June 1961'; and 'Réalt na Mara memorial. To the glory of God and in honour of the Blessed Virgin Mary this memorial was blessed and

*Réalt na Mara memorial on the
Bull Wall (sculptor: C. King)*

dedicated by Most Rev. Dr Dermot Ryan,
Archbishop of Dublin, on 24th September 1972'.

RED HOUSE, THE
See MUD ISLAND.

REFERENCE LEVELS
See WATER, TIDE AND GROUND LEVELS.

REFUSE DISPOSAL AND THE LIFFEY
In 1468 it was decreed that 'noo person ne
persones cast ne lay noo dunke at noo gatte ne in
none other place of the citte but oonly without
Hankman ys lane, in the holles and pittes ther, or
els in the holl beyan the Hogges butt'. Later, in
1571, the dump in Hoggen Green was to be
described as 'the greate holle by Allhallowes'. One
hundred years later, in 1557, additional city dumps
were named at 'Crokers Barris' and the 'Combe'.

A river has always been a convenient place to
throw away rubbish. In 1557 the city ordered
'whosomever [sic] henceforth do cast any donge
gravell or other fylth into the Keye of this cittie, he
shall forfaiet for every default two shillings', and in
1560 one Gylys Clyncher was given authority 'to
oversee the river that no donge ne ballast be cast
therin'. The mouth of the Poddle below the Castle

was also protected by its own order that 'no donge
shalbe laide by the Dams gate upon forfaieture of
iii s iiii d tociens quociens'. The 'custodes ipsi' had
their own inducement to see these laws observed.
In 1576 it was ordered that if the bailiffs did not
'enforce the law about filthred in the river they
would be fined ii s sterling and be committed to
Newgate for forty eight hours'.

During the succeeding 100 years the rivers
continued to be abused as handy dumping
grounds. In 1578 the Assembly ordered 'that the
oulde shippes and barkes which lieth at the Wod
Key shalbe presently carried awaie'. In 1612 it was
decreed that anyone who 'shall cast any filthred
into Colmans brooke or the ryver of the Lyffye'
would be fined, and the Assembly ordered the
'clensing of bouth the Keis, now at this present so
choackte uppe with filthred as noe barques boates
or gabbardes cann come neere the slipps'.

It appears that in the 18th century more
ordered steps were taken for the disposal of
refuse. A wharf was built at the east end of
Merchants Quay in 1740, quite probably for the
transport of material by boat to a dumping site
rented by the city at Mabbot Street. Scavengers
were appointed by contract, subject to penalty in a
decree of 1772 if 'they shall suffer any dirt or filth
to be thrown swept or emptied into the river Anna
Liffey'.

In that same year, the outspoken naturalist John
Rutty gave his opinion of his city. He found the air
to be 'greatly vitiated by the dirtiness of our streets
which is so great that one is frequently in danger of
being up to the knees in crossing them'; and he
adverted to 'the putrid animal effluvia exhaling
from charnel-houses and dunghills in the middle
of the city and in several of the avenues, and dead
animals, dogs and cats, and the excrements of
living ones, butchers' garbage and blood'.

The particular problem of domestic sewage
intensified as the population of the city grew. In
1818 it was recorded that 'the want of sewers was
much felt in Dublin . . . The waste water was
usually received in cesspools which were large
excavations made in front of each house and
covered in. It was supposed that the water would

filter through the soil. In Sackville Street and elsewhere these cesspools still continue.' Sackville Street was a wealthy area.

Districts near the river discharged untreated sewage directly into it, and in 1832 George Halpin would report, 'The Liffey in its present state may be considered as the main sewer of the city running from west to east into which all the other sewers empty and are discharged into the sea twice each day by the ebb tide.' His comment on this process, made more significant by his rank and background, was that it provided a 'salutary removal of filth'.

In 1847 an act was passed which included provisions for draining and cleansing the city (see City Surveyors and Engineers). The Liffey and bay would, however, for many years continue as the outlet for the raw untreated domestic sewage of Dublin. Conduits flowing north–south discharged through the quay walls, and the Rathmines and Pembroke drainage, completed in 1881, discharged untreated sewage to the river through the penstock house which may still be seen near Costello's on the South Wall. The centre city main drainage system, completed in 1906, laid intercepting sewers along the north and south quays, and piped the sewage through a pumping station at Ringsend to a simple treatment plant based on sludge beds, built in the former Pigeonhouse harbour.

In 1982–5 the several stages of an extensive sewage treatment works were completed in the Pigeonhouse precinct, with some of the main delivery pipes being laid in Sandymount Strand. The sludge from this works is transported by boat from a jetty built in the Liffey to enable loading at all stages of the tide, and dumped in the sea north of a line extending due east from the Baily lighthouse. The discharge of untreated sewage into the Liffey estuary has ended. The new treatment plant is also intended to process domestic sewage from the conurbations along the south shore of the bay.

The growth of the city and its industry during the 19th century and the associated building programmes led to a large increase in the quantities of other forms of domestic, industrial and civic refuse needing disposal. Towards the end of the century the concept emerged of using this material to form new land in the Liffey estuary and Dublin Bay. It is not clear when door-to-door refuse collection began in the city, but from 1907 onwards the city tramway network was being used by the Corporation. Incinerated material was taken by trains of vehicles drawn along the tramlines by electric locomotives from city depots to be used as filling in the making of Fairview Park. This practice continued until the late 1920s.

During the 20th century other new land has been formed (i) at the Clontarf linear park and the contiguous areas along Alfie Byrne Road towards the Tolka, (ii) in the great wedge of the South Bull strand between the South Wall and Strand Road at Sandymount, an area that now includes the new hill of Irishtown Conservation Park, together with extensive residential, industrial and recreational developments, and (iii) in creating large industrial areas within the port of Dublin.

[29, 59, 87 (vol. 14), 154, 155, 163, *CARD,* I–III, VIII, IX, XII, *Engineers Journal,* vol. 41 (de Courcy)]

REINELAN

The point of the island. Before the construction of the South Wall, the South Bull sandbank had at low tide a furthest north-east point somewhere between the Half Moon battery and the present Poolbeg lighthouse. This appears to be the point known for several hundred years as Reinelan or Rennivelan, the point from near which the spear was cast to determine the city boundary (see William Walsh and the Spear). Presumably from its proximity to the notorious sandbank known as the Dublin Bar, the point was also called Bar-foot. Other spellings of these names include Ramynelan, Rennivelain, Reymilan, Remelin, Rannelean, Rennyvelan, Ranielean, Bar Foote and Barr-foot.

[*CARD,* I]

RENNIE, JOHN, FRS

Born in Scotland in 1761, Rennie began his working life as a millwright but turned gradually

John Rennie (sculptor: P. Chantrey)

towards civil engineering. He built his first bridge in 1784 when he was 23, and he became involved in canal engineering some seven years later. His major marine work on docks and harbours began in *c.* 1800.

In that year, a determined effort was being made to improve the harbour and port of Dublin. The lord lieutenant, Marquis Cornwallis, had put Sir Thomas Hyde Page, a military officer, and Captain William Bligh, a naval officer, to work on a full study of the bay and the problems of the harbour; and in 1801 the Directors General of Inland Navigation (DGIN) were on the point of adopting, possibly in some modified form, Bligh's proposal for extending the North Wall out to the Spit Buoy: that is, roughly where the Bull lighthouse is today. However, following representations made during the summer of 1801 by the Corporation for Preserving and Improving the Port of Dublin, formerly the Ballast Office, to the DGIN, suggesting a new approach, namely the building of what, substantially, would later be the Bull Wall, the DGIN invited Rennie to visit Dublin and to examine the problems of the bay and harbour on their behalf.

Following one of his early visits, he was to write to the DGIN on 24 March 1802, 'The improvement of Dublin Harbour is perhaps one of the most difficult subjects which has ever come under the consideration of the civil engineer.' In his report, submitted in July 1802, and in other correspondence in that year, Rennie supported the 'Bull Wall' concept (which would not be realised for a further 20 years); and, recognising the value of maximising the scouring potential of an ebbing tide in the Liffey estuary, he proposed an embankment from the South Wall to Blackrock, to create a vast tidal reservoir on the South Bull, which would fill and empty with each flowing and ebbing tide through an opening in the South Wall near Ringsend. He also recommended the extension of the South Wall beyond the Poolbeg lighthouse to the Bar, and in a puzzling comment recommended also a corresponding parallel extension of the North Wall. This was possibly intended as an appendage to the conceptual Bull Wall, because there appears to be no evidence that Rennie supported Bligh's complete North Wall extension from the East Wall to the Spit Buoy. Clearly, the Bar was, as usual, causing concern.

On the south side of the bay, Rennie found himself having to comment on proposals just then being made to make a deep-sea harbour in Dalkey Sound, or behind a mile-long breakwater off Sandycove Point, and to drive a new ship canal right through from Sandycove or Dunleary to the new Grand Canal Docks above Ringsend. He favoured the idea of a ship canal, and in 1803 proposed a route following almost exactly the line of the Dublin and Kingstown railway, which was still some 30 years in the future. His personal support for a ship canal would be remembered when the project came up again for debate in 1833, 12 years after his death. If this idea seems whimsical today, one should recall that the first regular steamship service did not arrive in Dublin until 1821, and Rennie's canal proposal was based on the problems faced by sailing-ships.

In 1803 the committee appointed in Dublin for supplying the city with piped water, 'taking advantage of Mr Rennie's presence in the Kingdom', invited him to consider the adequacy of the city water supply, and, in particular, to consider whether, by installing appropriate machinery to pump water from the Liffey at Islandbridge, it could dispense with the Royal and Grand Canals as sources. Rennie's advice and co-operation were greatly appreciated by the committee, and in 1803, for 'his sound judgment in water works', his 'very conciliatory manner' and 'his great readiness and polite attention', he was made a freeman of the city.

In 1808 and 1809 Rennie submitted proposals for harbours at, respectively, Howth and Dunleary. The harbour at Howth, which was not very successful, was built between 1809 and 1819. The work on the East Pier at Dunleary began in 1817, and by 1821 was completed substantially as we know it today. In 1821, also, Rennie was engaged in the construction of the Custom House Docks, and had embarked on a study of the drainage and navigation of the River Shannon. More immediately, he was completing the final details of his proposals for a new London Bridge in London. He died on 4 October in that year.

He was survived by six children, among them two civil engineers, George (1791–1866) and John (1794–1874), who was knighted in 1831 upon the completion of London Bridge.

[55, 56, 57, 68 (vol. 2), 70, *CARD*, XV–XVII]

RENNIVELAN

See REINELAN.

REVENUE BARRACKS AT PIGEONHOUSE

See PIGEONHOUSE: A PRECINCT.

REVENUE DOCK, THE

See CUSTOM HOUSE DOCKS.

REVENUE MAP OF DUBLIN BAY

Egerton Manuscript 790 is entitled 'The accounts of His Majesty's Revenue in Ireland for five years vizt. from the landing of Duke Schonberg in August 1689 to Christmas 1693'. The manuscript includes a careful and exquisitely coloured map of 'Dublin Citty and Bay', made in 1694, which appears to be based on those of Greenvile Collins

and Phillips. It contains several interesting named features in the Liffey downstream of Lazars Hill. Thus, it may be the only map that actually names the North and South Channels of the Liffey as such, between there and Ringsend.

[BL, Egerton MS 790, ff. 59–61 and 70]

RICHMOND BRIDGE

See O'DONOVAN ROSSA BRIDGE.

RICHMOND GUARD TOWER

During the late 17th century and throughout the 18th, there was a meeting of four vehicle routes at the west end of the south quays as it then existed. Usher's Island Quay met Watling Street at the south end of Bloody Bridge. From this junction an avenue led west across the river meadows, probably close to Lord Galway's Walk, to Steevens's Lane. The general arrangement is shown by Brooking (1728), Rocque (1756) and Faden (1797). The avenue, which would later be known as the Military Road, was part of the route from the Royal Barracks to the Royal Hospital, where the commander-in-chief of the army had his quarters. Victoria Quay, extending west from the junction, would not be made until *c.* 1845.

In 1811 or 1812, when there would have been little need to protect the avenue across the meadows, a strong gateway, named the Richmond Guard Tower, was built at the junction, to the design of Francis Johnston. The lord lieutenant at that time was Charles Lennox, fourth duke of Richmond. The tower, some 10 m broad in front elevation and 12 m high, contained an arched gate 3.8 m wide, which appears to have been protected by or perhaps merely ornamented with a portcullis. A turret rose from ground level at one corner to a height of approximately 3 m above the main tower. This tower continued the line of the buildings on the west side of Watling Street down to the bank of the Liffey and so formed a strong visual termination to the south quays.

The gate may have been kept closed at first, but in 1818 the avenue lay open for public use. The tower was seen as an attraction for visitors and it

Richmond Guard Tower, showing also Barrack Bridge and part of the Military Road (M. Connor)

became a favourite subject for artists. The National Library holds illustrations by G. Petrie (634 TA), M. Connor (410 TA) and an unknown artist (553 TA), and W.H. Bartlett also included it among his drawings.

In 1846 the Great Southern and Western Railway Company sought the removal of the whole tower, on the grounds that it was obstructing the traffic route to its new terminus at Kingsbridge (now Heuston). It offered to defray the cost of taking it down and rebuilding it at the western entrance to the Royal Hospital. It is reported that this was done in 1847, and the rebuilt gateway may now be seen in its new position.

It seems that until the 19th century the route to the Royal Hospital from the Royal Barracks followed the avenue to Steevens's Lane, and then used that lane and Bow Lane to cross the Camac at Bow Bridge above the reach of high tide, and so to the Hospital. In 1838 the OS map shows that, while the avenue from the tower to Steevens's Lane remained as before, the route from Steevens's Lane now passed north of Dr Steevens's Hospital and turned through a right angle to approach the Royal Hospital from the north. This whole route then became known as the Military Road. Today the former avenue across the river meadows is within the yards of the Guinness Brewery, and the western portion follows part of St John's Road past Heuston

railway station and turns south along the road that is now called Military Road.

[7, 19, 29, 77, *DHR* (Jacob), maps (Brooking 1728, Rocque 1756, Faden 1797, Campbell 1811, OS 1838 and current)]

RIDELISFORD, WALTER DE

An Anglo-Norman knight who is named as the slayer of John the Wode at the battle of Hoggen Green. He was granted extensive lands east of Dublin, including Thorncastle, a district stretching along the coast from Ringsend through Merrion to Blackrock.

[35, 56]

RINGSEND

'Galleys of the Lochlanns ran here to beach, in quest of prey, their bloodbeaked prows riding low on a molten pewter surf' (Joyce, *Ulysses*). Watching them from 100 m away would have been one of the earliest communities on Dublin Bay, the people of the Point, An Rinn. Freeman comments that 'from the beginnings, the first evidence of settlement [at Dublin] suggests occupation of two patches of dry ground of which the more important was the spur on which the castle was built near the main ford of the river; the other was the low gravel ridge at Ringsend'.

the passes and defiles of the mountains to the Holy City. The Templars were active in Ireland in the 12th and 13th centuries until their statutory suppression by Edward II, and they were at times strongly hostile to the Order of the Knights Hospitallers of St John of Jerusalem. However, even in the 13th century there could be uncertainty about their separate identities, as a document of 1220 refers to the younger body as 'the Templars or Hospitallers'.

The choice by Strongbow of the eastern nose of the plateau as a site for the new priory may have been influenced by his recognition of the strategic importance of the site in the defence of Dublin. Six hundred years later, in 1798, Lieutenant-General Vallancey, military surveyor-general of the English army in Ireland, would choose the same location, the Royal Hospital at Kilmainham, as the best site available for conversion into a fortress or temporary citadel for transacting government business 'in case of a sudden insurrection in Dublin'; and it was occupied again by 2,500 British troops during the Easter rising in 1916.

The priory and hospital remained under the control of the Knights of St John of Jerusalem until 1540, when a statute of Henry VIII declared the order 'utterly dissolved and void' in his jurisdiction, and vested its property in the monarchy. By that time, it had moved its headquarters, first to Margat in the Holy Land, and then successively to Cyprus, Rhodes and finally, in 1530, Malta, where members of the order would become generally known as 'Knights of Malta'.

In 1541 the prior of Kilmainham, John Rawson, later Viscount Clontarf, surrendered the priory and all its possessions to Henry. The buildings were spacious and pleasantly located, and they would be used as a country residence by successive lords lieutenant and lord deputies until c. 1617, when the splendid new Phoenix House, built by Sir Edward Fisher on the site of the future Magazine Fort, was adopted as the official viceregal residence.

During the decade 1670–80 Charles II consented to the erection of a retirement home for old soldiers of the Irish forces, to be modelled on the Hôtel des Invalides in Paris. In 1679 the site of Kilmainham Priory, by then unused and in decay, was chosen as its location. At the time, this land formed part of the Phoenix Park or Deer Park. The architect for the new Royal Hospital was William Robinson, engineer and surveyor-general of the fortifications and buildings in Ireland. The foundation-stone was laid by the lord lieutenant, the duke of Ormonde, in April 1680. In 1684 the building was being lived in, but the work was not completed until 1701, when the tower was built. The Hospital continued to be used as such until 1927, during most of which time it also provided the residence for the commander of the army in Ireland, who was usually its governor. After 1927 the Hospital was used for some time by the Garda Síochána.

A building on the hill to the south above Islandbridge has been a well-known feature of the tidal Liffey throughout the entire time covered by this book, and its recognition by the illustrators of the river, from Francis Place in 1698/9 to the present day, is evidence of its visual importance. [3, 22, 56, 66, 147, 174, 181, 216, 218; *DHR* (O'Dea); *An Cosantóir*, August 1973; BL, 4813, Pococke MSS, ff. 45–6]

ROYAL HOSPITAL GATEWAY
See RICHMOND GUARD TOWER.

ROYAL PHOENIX IRON WORKS
The Royal Phoenix Iron Works, or Phoenix Iron Works, known also in 1831 as Robinson's Iron Works, at which the metalwork for Sean Heuston Bridge was cast, were on the north bank of the Liffey immediately adjacent to the bridge. The strongly walled site was in use during the First World War as a factory for making bombs, and these were then carried down the river in barges that were loaded at a jetty beside the factory. The site continues today to be used for industrial purposes. [Dublin Corporation Archives (WSC map 33/2), Irish Army Archives (private communication)]

RUIRTECH
See LIFFEY: THE RIVER AND ITS NAME.

RULERS IN DUBLIN
See CHRONOLOGY OF RULERS IN DUBLIN.

S

St Augustine Street

See USHER'S QUAY.

St Augustine's Friary

Also known as the Monastery of the Holy Trinity, it was founded in 1270–75 for the Order of Hermits of St Augustine, and would become a general college for all the friars of that order in Ireland. It was located on about 4 acres (1.6 ha) of land extending from Dame Street to the Liffey and bounded broadly by modern Temple Lane South and Fownes Street. Speed shows this site in 1610, although by that time the monastery buildings and yards, which had covered about 0.6 acres, had largely been demolished.

In 1540, during the suppression of the monasteries, St Augustine's was handed over to the king. In 1541 the lands and buildings, with other property, were granted to Walter Tyrrel, a merchant. They passed quickly through several hands, and by 1627 were owned by William Crowe, who had already erected buildings there that he called 'Crowe's Nest'. At about this time, the link between the site and the river was being broken by the south bank river works of Newman and his successors.

It was from the 'Crowe's Nest' that William Petty directed the Down Survey in 1654–6; and it was there in 1684 that the Dublin Philosophical Society, founded in that year 'agreeable to the design of the Royal Society of London', held many of its early meetings.

A music hall was built on part of the site in 1730, and in 1757 this was superseded by Crow Street Theatre. In 1836 the Company of the Apothecaries Hall of Dublin bought part of the theatre in Cecilia Street (as Crow Street had become known in c. 1837) for laboratories, and in 1852 it sold this building to the Catholic University of Ireland, which established its medical school there.

Recent excavations have revealed parts of the medieval friary.

[18, 22, 231, *DHR* (Mac Giolla Phádraig), maps (Speed 1610, OS 1838)]

St Begnet's Island

Also known as St Bennant's or St Benedict's Island. See DALKEY ISLAND.

St Clement's Chapel

Alen records that there was a chapel of St Clement near the Stein Hospital in medieval time.

[189]

St James's Bridge

(i) See RORY O'MORE BRIDGE.

(ii) Walsh on his map names a bridge across the Stein near the Thomas Moore statue in College Street as St James's Bridge.

[Map (Walsh 1977)]

St James's Hospital

See HENRY OF LONDON, ARCHBISHOP.

St John of Jerusalem, Order of

See ROYAL HOSPITAL, KILMAINHAM.

St John's Street

See FISHAMBLE STREET.

St John's Well at Islandbridge

See ISLANDBRIDGE, ST JOHN'S WELL AT.

St Laurence O'Toole

See LAURENCE O'TOOLE: SAINT, ARCHBISHOP.

St Maighneann, Priory of

See ROYAL HOSPITAL, KILMAINHAM.

St Margaret of Cortona, Hospital of

See HOSPITAL FOR INCURABLES.

ST MARY DE HOGGES, CONVENT OF

In *c.* 1146 Diarmait Mac Murchada founded a convent for nuns of the Arroasian Order of St Augustine in the hamlet of Hogges beside Dublin. The site was near modern Suffolk Street, close to the Stein and perhaps 100 m from the high-tide shoreline of the Liffey. It was a rule of the convent that only women over 30 years of age could be accepted as nuns, and it is said that Mor (named also as Alice), who was wife of Mac Murchada and sister of St Laurence O'Toole, died there as a member of the community.

It is recorded that after the Anglo-Norman invasion, John regarded this convent very highly for having given sanctuary to some English who had been attacked by the Irish, and he had it rebuilt and richly endowed.

The convent was suppressed by Henry VIII in 1540. The buildings were soon demolished, leaving only the walls standing, with other materials being removed to Dublin Castle for its repair. In 1550 a former mayor of the city, Richard Fyan, with strong support from the chancellor and Irish parliament, sought a lease for the site and the remains of the buildings. He proposed to set up six looms and to employ spinners and weavers to make linen and woollen cloth. He attacked the Dublin merchants for exporting unprocessed yarn, and urged that they should 'studye and practise thuse of those commodyties amongst themselves; and for the suerty of this poore lande see the people sett to labour and worke as they doo in other countries, whoose common weales by mayntenance of artificers doo floorishe and prosper'.

It is not clear whether this initiative succeeded, for in 1552 the site was granted to a James Sedgrave and the name of Fyan does not appear again.

Speed does not show this convent on his map of 1610.

[18, 22, 160, 231; BL, 4813, Pococke MSS]

ST MARY DEL DAM, CHURCH OF

See DAMES GATE PRECINCT.

ST MARY OF OSTMANBY (HOUSTMANEBI)

See ST MARY'S ABBEY.

ST MARY ON THE BRIDGE

In 1348 Edward III gave letters patent to a John de Grauntsete to found and construct a chapel at the north end of the stone bridge of Dublin in honour of the Virgin Mary. It was to be endowed with a stipend for the attendance of two chaplains, who were to say mass there each day. In *c.* 1478 the Fraternity of the Blessed Virgin Mary, which formed the Guild of English Merchants Trading in Ireland, was established in the chapel, then called Chapel del Marie du Grace on the Brygge End. After the dissolution of the monasteries, it passed into the hands of Ralph Grimesditch, who built a stairway beside it (illegally), presumably for access to the river, and he was still in possession in 1592.

It has been suggested that this building was beside the north end of the bridge rather than on it. Kenny proposes that it may have been one of the cluster of houses on the river-bank east of the Old Bridge (Fr Mathew), and that it may have been known also as the 'Chappel to the cloysters', the cloysters being the quadrangle in the King's Inns complex. The cluster of houses on the river-bank was demolished early in the 19th century.

[18, 201, *CARD,* II, *Proc. RIA* (vol. 90C: de Courcy)]

ST MARY'S ABBEY

The Chapter House of St Mary's Abbey

There is a tradition noted in the Pococke manuscripts that the Danish rulers of Dublin founded a Benedictine abbey in 948 at the site of

St Mary's Abbey, in thanksgiving for a miraculous cure from blindness. The monastery known in history, however, as St Mary's Abbey was a Savigniac foundation of 1139 which became a Cistercian house in *c.* 1147. The site of the abbey buildings was close to the high-water shoreline of the Liffey and east of the marshy mouth of the River Bradogue, in an area now bounded by Arran Street East (formerly Boot Lane), Little Mary Street, Capel Street and Mary's Abbey.

In *c.* 1156 St Mary's Abbey became affiliated to Buildwas Abbey in Shropshire. Following the Anglo-Norman conquest of Dublin in 1170, the abbey received many grants of land and other privileges, and by the year 1213 it held a substantial part of the environs of Dublin north of the Liffey. This estate was bounded by Church Street, Grangegorman and the road to Drumcondra on the west and north, and the Tolka and the Liffey on the east and south.

The authority of the order was great. In 1224 it handed over its ownership of a church which it had built near the present Four Courts to the Dominican Order, which later developed it into St Saviour's Priory, the other great monastic institution of the north bank of the river. Already in the 13th century the abbey had its own quay and harbour on the north bank and controlled a deep-sea port at Bullock near Dalkey. The monks had their own ships to use for trade with England and France, and the abbey, despite a disastrous fire in 1304, became the recognised guest-house for noblemen and officials visiting Dublin from England. The abbey also built up schools for education at several levels, and offered its halls for meetings of the Council of State.

The abbot and community were very jealous of the freedom of their abbey and its immediate precincts from the jurisdiction of the city of Dublin. Friction arose at the riding of the franchises by the city authorities. A determined confrontation occurred in 1488 between the abbot, who forbade the official procession to pass between the abbey and the river, an act that would take the abbey precinct into the city liberties, and the mayor, who claimed historical precedent for his right to do so. It appears that the mayor had his

Our Lady of Dublin, now at Carmelite church, Whitefriar Street, Dublin

way. The difficulty could not arise when Sir John Terrell (Tyrell) rode the franchises as mayor in 1603. The Dissolution Act had been passed in 1536, the abbey was falling into ruins, its prerogatives had vanished, and the procession moved unopposed 'without the sowth syde of the stone wall of Saint Marye Abbaye betwixt it and the river'.

When the particular order was made for the dissolution of St Mary's Abbey, the lord deputy pleaded for its survival because of its use by important visitors from England, and in general because of the benefits it brought to others than its own community. The plea was in vain. In 1543 the abbey was granted to James, 15th earl of Desmond, 'for the keeping of his horses and train at the time of his repairing to parliament or council'. James had himself been a rebel, but had submitted to Henry VIII in 1536 and been pardoned; in 1542 he had been made lord high treasurer of Ireland, an office he held until 1558.

It is obvious that the buildings and enclosure of St Mary's still existed in some form when Speed made his map in 1610, as did the traditional Cistercian cross on the roadway outside the entrance to the abbey. The strong wall surrounding the polygonal precinct of the abbey building, as shown by Speed, presents a puzzle: why one large segment at its north side is missing. Either that segment had been removed before 1610 for building stone, or it had never been built. This second possibility, which the detail of Speed's map could suggest, might arise if one reason for the enclosing wall had been to keep out high tide or floodwater and if the levels of the ground outside the wall made it clear that inundation could not come from the north.

The fabric of the abbey and its enclosure has now vanished almost completely. In 1676 Humphrey Jervis used it as a source for stone to build the first Essex Bridge. Later, the new north bank building and development programmes erased the traces of its layout, and new businesses, including in 1782 or 1783 the first Bank of Ireland premises, were established on the site.

The only element of the abbey remaining today is the Chapter House in Meeting House Lane. This small vaulted chamber, associated in history with Silken Thomas Fitzgerald's challenge to Henry VIII in 1534, offers also significant evidence of a link between the Liffey and the city. The floor level in the chamber lies at approximately 4.6 m above OD (Poolbeg), and is today about 2 m lower than the surface of the adjoining street. This floor level is to be seen in the context of the highest annual tide level in any given year in medieval times, which it is suggested is substantially the same as that applying today, namely 4.7 m above OD (Poolbeg). This topic is discussed under the heading Water, Tide and Ground Levels.

The other relic remaining of St Mary's Abbey is the oak statue of Our Lady of Dublin, known also as the Black Madonna, that stands in the church of the Calced Carmelites at Whitefriar Street. This statue of Our Blessed Lady and the infant Jesus is said to have been hidden in an inn yard after the dissolution of the abbey. It was subsequently set up in a small Catholic chapel known as Mary's Lane, served by the Society of Jesus, where it was seen in 1749. It was later discarded, to be found and bought from a second-hand shop by the Carmelites and set up at Whitefriar Street in 1827.

St Mary's Abbey had been known by many names:

- St Mary of Houstmanebi (1192)
- St Mary's Abbey of Ostmanby (1324)
- House of the Blessed Virgin Mary near Dublin (c. 1385)
- St Marye Abbaye (1603)
- Mary's Abbey (modern name for street in vicinity).

[22, 34, 56, 147, 181; CARD, I; *DHR* (Mac Giolla Phádraig); BL, 4813, Pococke MSS; map (Speed 1610); private communication (B. Doran)]

ST MARY'S ABBEY QUAY
See ST MARY'S ABBEY.

ST MARY'S GATE
See DAMES GATE PRECINCT.

ST MATTHEW'S CHURCH, IRISHTOWN
Late in the 17th century the Protestant community of Ringsend, which had just then been augmented by a new revenue and customs presence in the village, complained that access to its parish church at Donnybrook was uncertain and difficult because of uncontrollable flooding in the Dodder, and asked for a new church nearby. An act to enable this to be built was passed in 1703, a site was chosen near the seashore in Irishtown, and the building of the 'Royal Chapel of Saint Matthew at Ringsend' was begun in 1704. Progress was slow. In 1706 the city, which was contributing to the cost, agreed to a payment of £50, to be made 'when the said church is rooft and not sooner'.

The city authorities recognised the prominent position of the new church on the shoreline of Dublin Bay, and agreed in 1711 to pay for a tall

St Matthew's Church, Irishtown

tower to be built there, 'the same being intended to be a landmark for safety of the shipping'. Work on the tower, which still stands, was in progress in 1713, and it is shown complete on Bolton's map of 1717. A significant feature of the tower structure was the inclusion of a stiffening ring beam of oak, described as 'four beams of oak to lay in the middle of the steeple walls at the height as now it is, and to be duvtailed to each other at the quoins, in order to prevent cracks'.

The monarch was the patron of St Matthew's, and it was George I who appointed a new minister on the death of the first incumbent, Revd John Borrough, in 1726. Two members of the Brocas family, Theophilus and John, would hold the curacy in succession from 1750 to 1795.

The importance of the tower as a landmark continued. Scalé and Richards in 1765 and Bligh in 1800/3 follow Bolton in showing a thumbnail sketch of the church and tower on their maps. Nimmo shows it on his map of 1823, and in his piloting directions of 1832 indicates its use in practice: 'to sail in by the South Channel,' he wrote, 'bring Irishtown Church to the right of Saint Patrick's steeple'.

In 1810 the church was still being described as the 'Royal Chapel of Saint Matthew, Ringsend'. It is now known as St Matthew's Church, Irishtown.

In 1878–9 the church was restored and enlarged, under the direction of the architect J.S. Fuller.

[1, 4, 17, 65, *CARD*, VI, XVI, maps (Bolton 1717, Scalé and Richards 1765, Bligh 1800/3, Nimmo 1823)]

ST MICHAEL'S HILL

See WINETAVERN STREET.

ST MICHAN'S CHURCH

See OXMANTOWN.

ST OLAVE'S CHURCH

This church stood on the west side of Fishamble Street approximately 70 m south of Fyan's Castle. It was named in *c.* 1050 for St Olaf (*c.* 993–1030), king of Norway from 1015 to 1030, when he was killed in battle. The church was described as having been converted to profane use, although there was still reference to it in 1702, when St John's parish granted a lease for 'an ancient house called the Priest's Chamber of St Olave's alias St Toolog's, situate in Fishamble-Street'. No trace of the church exists today, although human remains were found there about 50 years ago.

The section of Fishamble Street from St Olave's Church to Wood Quay was formerly known as St Tullock's Lane. This name leads to the existence of two theories regarding the foundation of the church. In the first, the church was founded by Duilech or Doolagh in about the 8th century, and rededicated to St Olaf in the 11th century, the street name altering with time from Doolagh to Tullock. In the second, the church was founded in the 11th century, and the street name changed from Olaf to Tullock, by way of the form Tooley, a form of Olaf found in London.

[18, 99 (H.B. Clarke), *DHR* (J.K. Clarke)]

ST PATRICK'S CHURCH, RINGSEND

In the early 19th century there was a Catholic chapel at Irishtown which served also the community at Ringsend.

In 1859 a Catholic church was built at the junction of Thorncastle Street and Bridge Street in Ringsend. In 1911–12 this church, which was in danger of collapse, was replaced by the present Church of St Patrick, designed by W.H. Byrne, which stands on the same site with a garden overlooking the Dodder behind it.

[186, 225 (vol. 53, 1911), 302]

St Paul's Church, Arran Quay

See Arran Quay.

St Saviour's Priory

The history of St Saviour's Priory began with a foundation by William Mareschal in c. 1202 and a grant of land in 1218 by Audren Brun and Richard de Bedeford. The grant was to the Cistercians of St Mary's Abbey, who built a small church, and handed it over to the Dominicans, the Order of Friars Preachers, in 1224. The site of the church was on the east side of the north end of the Old Bridge (now Fr Mathew) and was 120 feet (36 m) long by 114 feet (34.2 m) broad. It appears to have stood back from the river-bank, and the curve of the river at this point suggests the possibility that there was there a dry bluff that made the location suitable. Speed (1610) shows a roadway between the priory site and the river, and this could well have been the situation also in the 13th century.

In 1238 a larger church was built. It seems that the monastic buildings were also built at this time, as in c. 1250 the city had carried a 5-inch-diameter (125 mm) pipe across the bridge to provide water to St Saviour's, a condition being that the size of the pipe within the house should be such 'that its opening may be stopped by the insertion of a man's little finger'.

A fire that swept through Oxmantown in 1304 burned down much of the priory, but it was quite rapidly rebuilt. In 1317 a significant part of the church fabric was destroyed to improve the city's defences against Edward Bruce, but Edward II subsequently required the citizens to restore the buildings, observing that 'although laws were squatted in warre, yet notwithstanding they ought to be revived in peace'.

With the suppression of the monasteries by Henry VIII, Patrick Hay, the last prior of St Saviour's, surrendered the priory to the Crown in 1539. In 1541 it was decreed that the church in the priory should be demolished, and Speed's map of 1610, which shows an empty space on the south side of the quadrangle, is taken as showing that this was done.

The buildings were assigned to be the King's Inns in 1542 and the area was then occupied in a general manner by the lawyers, with the property in increasingly dilapidated condition, until c. 1785, when the buildings were demolished to make room for the Four Courts, which occupy the site today. The title to the site in the 16th century was based on a series of short leases, with the earl of Ormonde as the owner for a period following 1578. It has been recorded by Collins that as recently as 1913 some significant traces of the original buildings still existed below ground level. An archaeological excavation and study made in 1984 by McMahon (Proc. RIA, vol. 88C) examines some details of the medieval buildings.

Other constructions associated with St Saviour's include the Dominican School at Usher's Quay, the Bridge, in certain aspects, and the King's Inns.

[12, 22, 28, 29, 34, 201, CARD, I, II, DHR (O'Sullivan), map (Speed 1610)]

St Stephen's Hall

See Bridge Street.

St Tullock's Lane

See Blind Quay, Fishamble Street and St Olave's Church.

St Vincent's Seminary at Usher's Quay

See Usher's Quay and Castleknock College.

St Woolstan's

In 1577 Stanihurst referred to the Old Bridge (now Fr Mathew) 'that reacheth over the Liffie' as being 'hard by Saint Woolstan's'. In 1529–34 Alen recorded that 'at Saint Ulstan's are canons regular of Saint Augustine'. It might be suggested that Ulstan and Woolstan are two forms of the same name.

These scanty references appear to have been to a religious house. The Augustinian Hospital of St John the Baptist, a foundation confirmed in 1188, lay between the Liffey and Thomas Street. It could scarcely be described as 'hard by' the river, although it was not so far removed from Usher's Pill, which existed at that time. There seems a possibility that St Woolstan's was associated with the hospital.

[189, 231, *CARD*, II]

STS MICHAEL AND JOHN CHURCH

A church in honour of St Michael the Archangel is said to have been built by Donatus (Dunan), the first bishop of Dublin, in *c.* 1038. It was rebuilt several times, and was finally replaced on the same site after 1870 by the Synod Hall at Christ Church. The tower of one of the earlier constructions was retained, and may still be seen as part of the Medieval Trust Museum and Exhibition Centre that succeeded the Synod Hall.

A church in honour of St John the Evangelist is said to have been built with an endowment from Domnall Mac Gilla Mo Cholmoc, probably in the late 12th century. It was located at the junction of St John's Lane East and Fishamble Street. Rebuilt several times, it was finally taken down in 1885.

Speed shows the two churches on his map of 1610.

In the late 18th century the combined Catholic parish of Sts Michael and John had its church in Rosemary Lane. This fell into decay, and in 1810 the building of a new church, Sts Michael and John, was started on a site bounded by the Blind Quay (now Lower Exchange Street) and Smock Alley. The work was very advanced in 1813, and in that year the Wide Streets Commissioners described it as 'the new Roman Catholic Chapel Smock Alley' in discussing the possible opening of access to it direct from Essex Quay. This was found to be outside the powers of the Commissioners, but some vista was provided, as Wright recorded that 'this very elegant building is seen . . . from the

opposite side of the river'. A bell was hung in the church tower in *c.* 1818, and Craig observes that this was 'the first Catholic bell to sound in Dublin since the Reformation'.

Sts Michael and John was in 1993 a church in the Catholic parish of Merchants Quay. It was not in use. Its development as a museum is now being actively considered.

[3, 18, 34, 41, 208, *DHR* (Mac Giolla Phádraig), map (Speed 1610)]

SALLCOCK'S WOOD

Also known as Salcock's Wood. It was situated probably towards the east end of Blackhorse Avenue in an area still shown as well wooded in 1837. Dillon Cosgrave suggests more precisely that it lay on the intersection today of Quarry Road and Cabra Road.

[31, map (OS 1838)]

SALMON POOL AT ISLANDBRIDGE

A pool in the River Liffey just below the Islandbridge weir.

SALMON POOL IN THE ESTUARY

See POOLBEG.

SALT-WORKS AT CLONTARF AND RINGSEND

There are no natural salt deposits near Dublin. It appears clear, however, from the Revenue map of 1694, which shows evaporation beds on the shoreline near the landward end of the Bull Wall and describes them as 'salt works', that the process of recovering salt from sea water was then in use at Clontarf. It was probably linked to the vigorous fishing industry then based at the Clontarf Sheds.

At this same time Greenvile Collins (1686) showed a similar salt-works between modern Merrion Gates and Booterstown, and an Assembly reference to a salt-works at Ringsend in 1763 suggests the possibility that the fishing industry there was also recovering salt from sea water.

[176; *CARD*, XI; BL, Egerton MS 790, ff. 59–61; map (Greenvile Collins 1686)]

SAND ISLAND
See BULL ISLAND.

SAND QUAY
See SARSFIELD QUAY.

SANDWITH STREET
Modern Sandwith Street runs north-west to south-east through a district in which the streets otherwise are substantially east–west and north–south. The reason for this is that it was until the 18th century the thoroughfare along the high-tide shoreline of the Liffey, and is shown as such on the 17th-century maps. Faden in 1797 called this street The Folly, and a late-18th-century map, undated, names it as The Folly Road. See the entries for the Fort at Lazars Hill and Lazars Hill.
[Dublin Corporation Archives (C1/SI/59 n.d.), maps (de Gomme 1673, Greenvile Collins 1686, Faden 1797)]

SANDYCOVE, PROPOSED BREAKWATER AT
In 1800, in an attempt to provide an asylum for ships caught in stormy weather near Dublin, Thomas Hyde Page proposed the construction of a mile-long breakwater in the bay off Sandycove Point at a cost of over a million pounds. The Directors General of Inland Navigation saw the value of this breakwater in providing shelter for ships in transit seeking temporary refuge in the bay. As an adjunct to Dublin trade, however, they dismissed it, saying that 'no trading ship that could pass the Bar would run behind Sandycove Pier unless perhaps for the purpose of smuggling'.
[70, 75]

SANDYCOVE, PROPOSED SHIP CANALS AT
See SHIP CANALS PROPOSED AT DUNLEARY AND SANDYCOVE.

SANDYGO
In making his proposal for a breakwater off Sandycove Point in 1800, Thomas Hyde Page gave the name of the district as Sandygo. See SANDYCOVE, PROPOSED BREAKWATER AT.

SANDYMOUNT
For about the first 1,000 years covered by this text, the shoreline at high-water level from where Merrion Gates is today to the Conniving House was probably marked by a broad bank of sand, shingle and clay. Behind this bank lay rough marshy scrub land partly below high-tide level and containing at least one large pond or lough, where Park Avenue now is. This lough was linked to the Cock or Cockle Lake by a narrow gut that passed just west of the site of the Martello tower at Sandymount, and is described as 'The Marsh' on Taylor's map of 1816. The dry part of this little wilderness was a rabbit warren, or coneyburrow or conyer. Thus it is recorded that in 1564 'Mr Thomas Fitzwilliams of Bagatrath' was awarded in fee farm 'the two conyers and the moraghe' that comprised the area. A moraghe is a marshy place separated from the sea by a bank, as, for example, the area that is today called the Murrough in Wicklow formerly was.

Early in the 18th century the clay in this area was found to be suitable for making bricks, and an industry grew up, presumably to join other brickfields in serving the Georgian building programme just beginning at that time in and around Merrion Square in the city. The workforce grew, under the direction of the owners, the Fitzwilliams, lords of Merrion, and gradually formed a new community in an area then called Scallet or Scallot or Scald Hill. The name of the new village became Brick Town or Brickfield Town, and it appears under this second name in Rocque's map of 1760.

At that time, the Strand Road did not yet exist, and Brickfield Town lay as an isolated village surrounded by country, reputedly dangerous by night. A road led south towards Simmonscourt, and tracks followed the present route of the Sandymount and Tritonville Roads westward towards Irishtown. The road to Dunleary passed not far away but one may note that Taylor and Skinner in 1783 did not find it necessary to mention the village under any of its names in their map of that road.

Early in the 19th century, certainly by 1830–35, and perhaps 30 years earlier, the situation had changed. The village had altered in name and nature. It was now Sandymount (Emmet had used this name in his account of 1803), and its built area had been extended out to the shoreline along Seafort Avenue. It had become a seaside resort for Dublin people, urging its superiority over neighbouring Irishtown, as Joyce records, by charging a bathing fee on its shore of twopence, whereas one could bathe at Irishtown for a penny. (See also Bathing and Bathers.) The formal road-link to Irishtown and Ringsend had been completed, following the line of the earlier track. The Beach Road had not, however, been made in 1837 and Bath Street through Irishtown led at its east end straight to the shore, where it stopped near Cranfield's Baths. Farther east along the coast, the Martello tower stood in isolation on the ancient bank, not to be reached by a formal road until the Strand Road was constructed, probably during the 1820s and early 1830s.

With the building of the Strand Road and its linking to Irishtown by the Beach Road in the 20th century, Sandymount ceased to play a role in this account of the Liffey and its estuary.

[13, 65, *CARD*, II, *DHR* (Hussey), maps (Rocque 1760, Taylor 1816, OS various)]

SANDYMOUNT BATHS
See MERRION PIER AND BATHS.

SANDYMOUNT STRAND
The name generally given to the large portion of the South Bull that is bordered by Strand Road.

SANDYMOUNT TOWER
See MARTELLO TOWERS.

SANTRY RIVER
The Santry River rises north of Finglas and flows into Sutton Creek immediately to the east of Watermill Road and the Bull Island causeway.

SARAH BRIDGE
See ISLAND BRIDGE.

SARSFIELD BRIDGE
See SEAN HEUSTON BRIDGE.

SARSFIELD QUAY
The short length of the north bank of the river from Rory O'More Bridge upstream to Liffey Street West has had three different names, having first appeared on de Gomme's map of 1673 as a riverside track, fenced but with no buildings.

In Brooking (1728), buildings, probably erected following the then recent completion of the Royal Barracks nearby, face on to an unwalled river-bank, and this situation is shown also by Rocque in 1756. It is possible that during this period the river-bank was known as Sand Quay.

In 1766 Harris records the name of the quay as Pembroke Quay, and this name was shown by Pool and Cash in 1780. The name of Pembroke Quay was still in use in 1882, but M'Cready reports that in 1886 the quay was called Sarsfield Quay, the name that it retains.

[16, 31, 39, 133, maps (de Gomme 1673, Brooking 1728, Rocque 1756, Pool and Cash 1780)]

SAVAGE, JAMES
James Savage, designer of the O'Donovan Rossa and Fr Mathew Bridges, was born in London in 1779. In 1800, at the age of 21, he was awarded second premium for his scheme to improve the city of Aberdeen. In 1823 he came second to John Rennie and his sons for the commission to design the new London Bridge, being deprived of success only by the casting vote of the chairman of the House of Commons committee. He studied at the Royal Academy schools, and exhibited at the Academy from 1799 to 1832.

In 1808 and 1809 he delivered, in two sessions, his essay on bridge-building to the London Architectural Society. In this, he discussed the aesthetics and analysis of masonry bridge structures, noting the difference between circular, true elliptical and segmental arches. In his comments on design, he distinguished between properties of matter, which included friction, cohesion, and *vis inertiae* (which he described as 'the disposition that matter has to remain at rest'), and resources of art, in which he listed such items as cement, joggles and cramps.

Savage was a member of the Institute of British Architects for a short time until a disagreement caused him to retire, and he became a member of the Institution of Civil Engineers. He built up a practice in the design of churches and public buildings, and in arbitration. He is said to have built, at St Luke's Church in Chelsea in 1820–24, the first stone vault of the Gothic Revival.

He was awarded the commission for the Richmond Bridge (now O'Donovan Rossa) in 1808, and this was built (1812–16) after some discussion in Dublin with George Halpin about the precise profile of the arches. The Whitworth Bridge (now Fr Mathew) was afterwards built to substantially the same design (1816–18).

James Savage died in 1852, and is buried at St Luke's Church.

[87, 138, 139, 140]

SAVIGNIAC FOUNDATIONS

The Congregation of Savigny was part of the Order of Fontevraud founded in the Benedictine tradition in 1100. The congregation was united in 1148 to the Cistercian Order, which had been founded in 1098.

[197]

SCALD HILL

Also known as Scallet or Scallot Hill. See SANDYMOUNT.

SCALDBROTHER

See GALLOWS NEAR PARKGATE STREET.

SCALÉ'S AND RICHARDS'S CHART

In 1765 Bernard Scalé and William Richards, land surveyors and hydrographers, compiled *The Coasting Pilot from the Harbour of Balbriggn in the County of Dublin to Tarrow Hill in the County of Wexford*. An introduction recommending the work was written by Nathaniel Card, a member of the Pilot Committee. It was accompanied by a chart made to a scale of approximately 1:48,700, and dedicated to the commissioners and governors (named) of His Majesty's Revenue of Ireland and to the Society of Merchants of Dublin. The chart shows the shoreline of Dublin Bay in detail and shows depths of water at low-water spring tide in the river, bay and Irish Sea.

The text relating to Dublin reads:

> The Harbour of Dublin is difficult for a Stranger to make, because of the Bar lying across the Entrance. The East Channel is the best. Bring the Pigeon-House on Irishtown Church, and you go through the best of the Channel, keeping the East Buoy on the Larboard Hand. To go through the West Channel, you must bring the Light-house at the Piles on Raheny Wind-Mill, keeping the South Buoy on the Starboard Hand. There is a Buoy fixed on a Spit of the North-Bull, almost abreast of the Light-House on the Piles, which you must keep on the Starboard Hand coming in. You are in the best Anchorage, when you bring the big Sugar-Loaf to the Westward of Carrigalligin. N.B. As the Light-House on the Piles is not finished, the Light-Ship continues to display her Ensign from Half Flood to Half Ebb in the Day; and her Lanthorns Light from Half Flood to Half Ebb in the Night.

The third edition of this work, which was printed by T. Jefferys in London in 1768, shows the completed Poolbeg lighthouse.

[161]

SCALÉ'S MAPS

See ROCQUE'S MAPS and SCALÉ'S AND RICHARDS'S CHART.

SCALLOT HILL

Also known as Scallet Hill, Scald Hill. See SANDYMOUNT.

SCANLAN, JAMES

See DUBLIN'S WATER SUPPLY AND THE LIFFEY.

SCARLET LANE

See BLIND QUAY.

SCHERZER BRIDGES

See BRIDGES ON CUSTOM HOUSE QUAY, BRIDGES ON NORTH WALL QUAY and EAST LINK TOLL BRIDGE.

SCHOOL AT USHER'S QUAY

See DOMINICAN SCHOOL AT USHER'S QUAY.

SDUK MAP

In 1833 Baldwin and Cradock of London published a map entitled 'Dublin, Published under the Superintendance of the Society for the Diffusion of Useful Knowledge'. This map, made to a scale of approximately 1:14,900, showed the River Liffey from Island Bridge to Ringsend. It was probably the first map to show the steam packet stations at the North Wall Quay following the introduction of steamships to the cross-channel routes during the period from 1815 to 1825 (see Cross-channel Packets). The map also shows the Artichoke Road from the Maquay Bridge over the Grand Canal to the Bath Avenue junction. At the west of the city it shows Conyngham Road petering out near Island Bridge and labels the modern winding road inside the Phoenix Park as 'the road to Chapelizod'. It is in error in showing Richmond Bridge (now O'Donovan Rossa) on the site of the earlier Ormonde Bridge.

An interesting feature of this sheet is a series of precisely drawn thumbnail elevations made by W.B. Clarke, architect, that show a comparison of what he considered the 13 principal buildings of Dublin. He includes in the series the Custom House, the Four Courts and the Bank of Ireland. [84]

SEA LANE

See DAME STREET.

SEAL OF DUBLIN

The citizens of Dublin were assured of civic independence by John in a charter of 1215. This was underwritten in 1229 by Henry III, whose charter apparently led to the provision of a common seal for the city, which was used in that

Dublin city seal, 13th century (reverse side)

year for a grant of land made at the first meeting of the city council. The bronze moulds for the two faces of this seal are still held by the Corporation in a heptagonal box, or hanaper, although the present hanaper may not date before the 17th century.

The obverse of the seal shows a three-towered castle. On the reverse,

on waves of the sea in which fish can be seen, is a galley in full sail. From the masthead flies a pennant with an indistinguishable device; an anchor hangs at the bow. At the bow and stern are embattled platforms (the fore-castle and stern-castle), with in each a figure blowing a horn. In the galley are four persons: a man, bust only showing, wearing a crown, and facing him a woman; next to them a man offering a cup; at the stern a sailor hauling the bunt of the sail.

An inscription around the circular rim reads '+SIGILLUM: COMMUNE: CIUIUM: DUBLINIE'. It seems reasonable to suggest that the crowned figure is a king. *Lèse-majesté* was then a more perilous act than now. But whether it represents John, who did visit Dublin in the summer of 1210, or Henry III, who never came to Ireland, is not known.

W.G. Strickland ('The Ancient Official Seals of the City of Dublin', *JRSAI*, vol. 53, 1923; or see bib. ref. 151), who is quoted above, records that the vessel shown on this seal is a warship, and he associates this with the Great Galley of Dublin.

Strickland deals also with other seals of Dublin, including the seal of the staple. In 1326 Edward II appointed Dublin to be a staple town, that is to say, one of the towns at which royal customs were to be collected and from which, consequently, staple goods such as wool and hides and some metals could be exported legally. Officers of the staple continued to be appointed by the merchants and later by the Corporation until the early 19th century, but these posts became nominal from the late 17th century onwards. [151]

SEAN HEUSTON BRIDGE

George IV, c. 1814 (T. Lawrence)

Following the building of the Royal Barracks (now Collins) in the first decade of the 18th century, the need was frequently raised for a direct route from it to the Royal Hospital, to replace the ferry granted to the trustees of Dr Steevens's Hospital. As early as 1720 a tentative proposal existed for a bridge. A visit to Dublin by George IV in 1821 led to an opportunity to use funds of £14,000, publicly subscribed to commemorate the royal occasion, to build a bridge, this being the expressed wish of the king.

Several designs were prepared by Dublin architects, and it is recorded that these were 'submitted to His Majesty's choice who was pleased to select that from which the present bridge has been erected'. The bridge is a single-arched seven-ribbed cast-iron structure designed by George Papworth. Details of the project were recorded in an inscription on a copper plate inserted in the foundation-stone. It is not clear where that stone was laid, but the inscription reads as follows:

ON THE 12TH DAY OF DECEMBER, 1827,
HIS EXCELLENCY THE MOST NOBLE
RICHARD MARQUESS WELLESLEY,
KNIGHT OF THE GARTER,
LORD-LIEUTENANT GENERAL,
AND
GENERAL GOVERNOR OF IRELAND,
LAID THE FIRST
STONE OF THIS BRIDGE,
ERECTED BY SUBSCRIPTION, AS A NATIONAL
TESTIMONIAL,
IN COMMEMORATION OF THE MOST
GRACIOUS VISIT OF
HIS MAJESTY KING GEORGE THE FOURTH
TO IRELAND ON THE 12TH DAY OF AUGUST,
1821.
GEORGE PAPWORTH ESQ
ARCHITECT
MR RICHARD ROBINSON
OF THE ROYAL PHOENIX IRON WORKS
CONTRACTOR
SIR ABRAHAM BRADLEY KING, BART.
CHAIRMAN OF THE MANAGING COMMITTEE.
THE HONBLE AND REVD JOHN POMEROY,
SECRETARY.

The width of the bridge between parapets was 9.3 m and the distance between the river walls was 53.4 m. As George Petrie shows, however, in his fine drawing of the east face of the bridge (NLI, 552 TA), substantial abutments projected into the river from both banks, thus reducing the arch span between springings to not more than approximately 35 m.

King's Bridge, looking downstream, c. 1829 (G. Petrie)

The bridge, which was possibly the earliest arched road bridge made in Ireland with cast iron, was opened to traffic in 1828. The completed bridge was generally admired at the time of its erection, although more recently it has been categorised as 'an agreeably vulgar affair'. The date of the royal visit, 1821, remains on the balustrades, but the crowns which adorned both parapets at midspan have been removed.

Dublin Municipal Council at its meeting on 2 January 1922 adopted a report prepared by a committee in 1921 and changed the names of several of the Liffey bridges. King's Bridge became Sarsfield Bridge at that time, but there is little evidence that the new name ever came into common use. In 1941, 25 years after the Easter rising, the bridge was renamed Sean Heuston Bridge and it now carries the following inscription:

Sé ainm an droiċid seo anois ná
Droiċead Seán Heuston
i gcuiṁne
an Ċapt Seán Heuston
(Fianna Éireann)
a ṫug a anam ar son poblaċt na hÉireann
8ú Bealtaine, 1916
Ar ḋeasláiṁ Dé go raiḃ a anam
Cumann na nUaiġeann Náisiúnta a ṫóg 1955

The bridge, now a little shabby in appearance, is still in service, although the introduction of Frank Sherwin Bridge has left it with a greatly reduced volume of traffic.

[3, 121, 211, 215; *CARD*, VII; BL, Add. MS 13914 D]

SEAN MOORE PARK

An extensive park has been formed on land taken in from the sea along Beach Road from the Green of Irishtown to Sandymount Strand. A memorial stone records that 'this park is named after Sean Moore (1917–1986) who was Lord Mayor of Dublin in 1963/64, and was a TD and City Councillor for many years, in recognition of his devoted services to the City of Dublin'. The park contains two other new sculptured stone monuments, a 'finger stone' and a stone with incised symbols, both uninscribed.

SEMPLE, GEORGE AND JOHN

There are Semples recorded as associated with building on and around the Liffey in Dublin during the 17th, 18th and 19th centuries. There was at least one named George and were at least three named John, but it is not always clear how they were related.

George Semple, designer and builder of the new Essex Bridge in the years 1752–5, recorded that 'my father (who was a workman about the year 1675) often told me [about techniques in masonry]'.

George was born in c. 1700 and may have been the man who at Christmas 1735 became a freeman of Dublin as a bricklayer and member of the Guild of Carpenters, Millers, Masons and Heliers. He practised as architect, engineer and builder. In 1751 he designed a temporary repair for Essex Bridge. In 1752 he prepared, with 'the assistance of my brother John', an estimate of cost for the complete rebuilding of that bridge for the sum of £20,500 0s 3d, and he carried out this work in the years 1753–5. In 1762 he offered the Ballast Office proposals for the development of the harbour of Dublin. These were illustrated on eight charts now held by the Dublin Port and Docks Board.

In 1776, then living at Queen Street, he published his treatise, in which he advised the 'young and unexperienced readers' to whom the book was 'principally addressed and peculiarly adapted' that they should study the works of the masters. 'The young Student', he wrote, 'should always be on his Guard when he is about designing any Thing, that a too lively or over-heated Imagination does not lead him into Chimeras, which sober Judgement would not approve'. George Semple died in c. 1782. He was at that time receiving a pension of £100 a year from parliament. It has been recorded that his immediate descendants were also architects.

John, the brother of George, and in this entry named as John 1, is known explicitly for the assistance he gave George in 1752. He may have been (i) the John who at Christmas 1749 became a freeman of the city as a bricklayer, (ii) the craftsman described as 'Semple the bricklayer' who worked on the Blue-coat School from 1773 to 1779, and (iii) the 'bricklayer and rough mason' named as one of 'the chief artificers' at the new Custom House in 1781. He may also have been (iv) the John who in 1795–6 was building (probably as a contractor) quay walls at Custom House Docks and Carlisle Bridge, presumably as a nominee of Gandon. He would, of course, have been quite old at that time.

There are two other men named John Semple who are relevant to this entry. They are known here as John 2 and John 3, but it is not suggested that they were necessarily direct descendants of John 1, or, indeed, of George.

John Semple 2 was made a freeman of the city in 1792 as a bricklayer. He could at this time have been in his early twenties. He was the son of a freeman bricklayer, possibly George or John. He may also have been (i) the John Semple who received, in 1805, the third premium of 40 guineas for his design for a bridge to replace Ormonde Bridge, (ii) the engineer who in 1815 joined Francis Johnston in vouching for the adequacy of the proposed cast-iron structure for the Halfpenny Bridge, and (iii) the John Semple who was presented in 1821 with 200 guineas for his work on the new 'King's Room' or Round Room in the Mansion House. This John held the civic rank of sheriff's peer from 1799 until the Dublin City Assembly was replaced by Dublin City Council in 1841.

John Semple 3 was born in c. 1801. He was admitted a freeman of the city in 1830 as a member of the Guild of Merchants, and was sheriff of Dublin in the civic year 1831–2. He was engineer for the civic committee for water supply for much of the period from 1832 to 1841, when the Assembly was replaced by the Council. He was probably the John Semple who was elected as a member of the Institution of Civil Engineers of Ireland in 1836, and who offered a proposal for the widening of Carlisle Bridge (now O'Connell) in 1838. He died in c. 1873.

John Semple, the noted church architect, was almost certainly either John 2 or John 3. On balance it seems more likely that he was John 2. John 3 would have been only 20 years of age when the Round Room was built at the Mansion House, and 29 when St Mary's Chapel of Ease (the Black Church) was built to a Semple design in 1830. At that time, Semple, the church architect, was architect to the Board of First Fruits for the Province of Dublin of the Church of Ireland, and seven years earlier, in 1823, had been appointed architect to Dublin Corporation. These appointments and works would seem more appropriate to a man born in about 1770 than to one born in 1801. One must also accept, however, that both John 2 and John 3 were recognised architects.

The further study of this family (with many more names listed in various records) would be rewarding.

[3, 11, 55, 87 (vols. 4, 5, 9, 17), 90 (vol. 13), 153, 186, 276 (*Minutes*, vol. 1), *Proc. RIA* (vol. 93C, no. 3, pp. 81–105: G. Daly), Dublin Corporation Archives]

SEMPLE'S CHARTS OF DUBLIN BAY

In 1762 George Semple presented to the Ballast Office a set of eight charts of Dublin Bay. In these, he 'collected and carefully laid down some of the most authentick surveys of this harbour for some hundred years past', and added his own ambitious proposals for developing the mouth of the river, and his plan for a harbour at Dún Laoghaire.

This material is presented and analysed in a paper by Gerald Daly published in 1993 in *Proc. RIA* (vol. 93C, no. 3).

SHALLOWAY'S BATHS

The enclosed bathing establishment known as Shalloway's Baths stood at the junction of Mayor Street and East Wall Road, on ground that would later become part of the Great Southern and Western Railway goods station. It appears first on Wilson's map of 1798 and then on several later maps, although it is not named on any of them.

It is probable that the baths were erected only shortly before 1798, as it is recorded that during the building of the new Custom House (1781–91) the only sea baths existing north of the Liffey were those known as the Annesley Bridge Baths, said to have been frequented by the earl of Charlemont, at the corner of East Wall Road and North Strand Road (see WSC map 257), where a fire station now stands.

Shalloway's Baths appear as a navigational seamark on Duncan's map of 1821. The buildings were demolished in c. 1875, when the goods station was built.

[31, 94, Dublin Corporation Archives (WSC map 257), maps (Wilson 1798, Bligh 1800/3, Taylor 1816, Duncan 1821, OS 1838)]

SHEAHAN MEMORIAL

A monument in the form of a cross on a plinth stands on Burgh Quay in the mouth of Hawkins Street. The inscription reads:

This memorial was erected in memory of Patrick Sheahan a constable in the Dublin Metropolitan Police force who lost his life on the sixth day of May 1905 in a noble and self-sacrificing effort to rescue John Fleming who had in the discharge of his duties descended the main sewer close by this spot and was overcome by sewer gas. It was also intended to commemorate the bravery of a number of other citizens who also descended the sewer to assist in rescuing the before-mentioned thereby risking their lives to save those of their fellow men.

The inscription is given also in Irish.

The monument was erected by the Mansion House Committee 1906. The designer was P. O'Neill, architect.

SHEEP STREET
See PODDLE RIVER.

SHELLFISH
See OYSTERS AND OTHER SHELLFISH.

SHELLY BANKS
See PIGEONHOUSE: A PRECINCT.

SHERIFF STREET
See NORTH LOTTS.

SHERRARD, THOMAS AND OTHERS

The Wide Streets Commission was established in 1757 and the Commissioners functioned from 1758 to c. 1851, two years after their formal abolition in 1849. In 1782 Thomas Sherrard was appointed as surveyor to the Commissioners, and in 1789 he was appointed to act also as their secretary and clerk. He kept the minutes of their meetings, and supervised the execution of their instructions, dealing with landowners, architects and builders, and with other statutory bodies.

In 1803 William Sherrard joined Thomas as clerk and surveyor. In 1814 William was replaced by

David Henry Sherrard, and he and Thomas were joint secretaries in 1816. David Henry appears to have served the Commissioners as secretary and surveyor until their abolition in 1849 and in their subsequent winding-down period, and was in practice in Dorset Street as a land agent in 1850.

Members of the Sherrard family prepared many maps in their official capacity. They also carried on a private practice as surveyors. Thus in 1796 Thomas Sherrard received a fee from the Ballast Board for surveys he made in the Lotts, and in 1816 Messrs Sherrard, Brassington and Greene were engaged by the Ballast Board to survey the North Bull region, and were paid for that work.

In 1825 Thomas Sherrard and Company prepared a plan for the realignment of the Liffey between the future King's Bridge and Barrack Bridge (see Victoria Quay). In 1840 a firm of Brassington and Gale was engaged by the Commissioners (see WSC map 1991-1).

It is not always clear whether certain items of Thomas Sherrard's work were prepared in his official capacity or in his private practice. Perhaps this is not an important distinction. His most dramatic map was that entitled 'A Survey of Part of the River Anna Liffey Dublin Showing the Proposed Improvements by Opening and Widening from Park Gate Street to Carlisle Bridge'. This large sheet, which is in the archives of Dublin Corporation, has a text measuring 2.4 m x 0.45 m drawn to a scale of 1:960. It is undated, but internal evidence suggests that it was probably prepared in 1801 or 1802. It carries the signature of Thomas Sherrard, but is not explicitly addressed to the Commissioners. Dealing in particular with the realignment of the quay walls on both sides of the river, it coincides in time with the early stages of the major project of the Ballast Board to remake the walls, in a programme that would continue until 1820. This map is discussed further in Liffey: Quay Walls and Pavings.

Other maps prepared by Thomas Sherrard which are not addressed directly to the Commissioners include:
(i) WSC map 15, 1790, 'A Survey of Ground Contiguous to the Barrack Dublin by Order of the

Right Honourable and Honourable the Commissioners of His Majesty's Barracks'.
(ii) British Library, Add. MS 40232, ff. 323–5, 1813, a map illustrating 'Observations' made by Sherrard 'on the eligibility and advantage of the site of the old Custom-house for the Post Office'.

[87 (vols. 4, 9), 146, 208 (vols. 18, 26); BL, Add. MS 13911.b, Add. MS 40253, f. 88; Dublin Corporation Archives]

SHILLINGEFORDE'S GARDEN
In 1582 this piece of land, probably near St Mary's Abbey, was granted for ever by Elizabeth I to Thomas, earl of Ormonde.

[22]

SHIP BUILDINGS
In the 17th century a street running east from the earlier St Mary's Abbey led ultimately to the open strand near modern Liberty Hall. Phillips shows this street in 1685, without naming it. The eastern end of the street between Marlborough Street and the strand was known in 1747 as the 'ship building', and was named by Rocque in 1756 as Ship Buildings. By 1797 a new street, Lower Abbey Street, had been constructed to the north of Ship Buildings, to link Middle Abbey Street to the newly developed Beresford Place. In modern terms, the new Lower Abbey Street lies to the north of the Abbey Theatre, while Ship Buildings, now called Abbey Street Old, lies to its south and is no longer a main thoroughfare.

The proximity of the Iron Quay or Iron Yard, combined with the title of the street, suggests that ships were built at this place. It has been recorded, however, that in the 18th century there were five shipbuilding yards in Dublin, two at George's Quay, two at Rogerson's Quay and one in Ringsend. No mention has been made of the building of ships on the north side of the Liffey at that time. The street name may have had some other connotation, but the existence of Marney's Dock close by makes this unlikely. See Dublin Shipbuilders.

[202, CARD, IX, maps (Phillips 1685, Rocque 1756, Faden 1797)]

SHIP CANALS PROPOSED AT DUNLEARY AND SANDYCOVE

In 1800, despite Bligh's assertion that the Bar at the river-mouth had largely disappeared, this obstacle to navigation still existed in the thinking of the harbour authorities, as well as, to a high degree, in fact. In addition, the dangers of the bay and the Bull sands in stormy weather were very much in their minds; and indeed the disaster of the *Prince of Wales* and the *Rochdale*, which occurred only a few years later, would show their anxieties well founded.

Getting past the Bar at low tide and having safe access to Dublin in storm were seen by some as two problems that could be solved by a single answer. An account of Hyde Page's proposal for a breakwater at Sandycove appears elsewhere in this text. Inside the shelter of that breakwater, he planned a ship canal to start from Sandycove and to run 'through the country' to the newly opened Grand Canal Docks at Ringsend. Mr (William?) Vavasour, developing this idea in 1800, won the approval of Hyde Page for a route for that canal to pass by Monkstown church and the Stillorgan Obelisk, to cross the line of Mount Merrion Avenue and to pass over the Dodder on an aqueduct near Milltown, and so down to Ringsend. The quantity of locking could have been stupendous, but it was believed that there was enough water available to service such a system. William Jessop's proposal of the same year would have kept the canal closer to sea level, and he would have brought the necessary feed water to it from 'near the sources of the river Liffey'. Perhaps it is not surprising that neither of these proposals attracted support. The note on John Rennie elsewhere in this record shows his effort to find a workable solution in 1802–3, although again the proposal was not adopted.

The agitation for a major harbour at Dunleary which would provide an asylum in storm, and its actual building in the period 1817–21, pushed the ship canal concept into the background for many years. It was, however, to be brought forward again, and even more vigorously pursued. During the 1820s some members of the Grand Canal Company, probably concerned with the indifferent success of its docks at Ringsend, invited John Killaly to design a canal to link the new harbour at what was by now Kingstown to the Grand Canal Docks. Killaly's cost plan for his project was considered too high, and at that stage a suggestion was made in the company for a steam railway, intended, one might presume, in the first instance as a carrier for goods traffic. Alexander Nimmo was invited to prepare a scheme, the project won support, and an act to enable its execution was promulgated in 1831. The resulting Dublin and Kingstown railway, designed in the event largely by Vignoles, would be opened in 1834 and would go on to provide a successful passenger service and to form part of the Dublin Area Rapid Transit (DART) system 150 years later.

The possibility that this railway would be constructed made the already complicated conflict of opinions regarding a ship canal even more involved in the years 1832 and 1833. The Dublin and Kingstown Railway Company resisted a canal because it was now hoping to provide the link for goods traffic; and the Corporation for Improving and Preserving the Port of Dublin resisted it because it was all the time pursuing the development of the acceptable direct-access port in the Liffey, which, as we now know, it would later achieve. On the other side, the traders and merchants of the city wanted safe access at once for shipping to the Liffey quays, and did not believe that either the Bar or the low-water conditions in the Liffey channel above Ringsend could ever be made satisfactory; and some faction in the Grand Canal Company which had earlier sought Killaly's advice still wanted a water-borne traffic link between its canal vessels and seagoing shipping.

Many eminent engineers were called in. Separate schemes were prepared by Killaly, Nimmo and William Cubitt. All of these proposed quite direct routes from Kingstown Harbour across the South Bull to Ringsend, and all relied mainly if not totally on tidal water to keep their channels filled. The Cubitt proposal, which was favoured, was for a broad canal having its floor at the same level as that of the Kingstown harbour and having only one formed embankment, along its seaward side, to maintain still water in its channel even with

available to him. It appeared as the frontispiece for Cosgrave's and Strangways's *Dictionary of Dublin* in 1908.

This work, which should be seen, is based primarily on the survey ordered by Perrot in 1585. The detail along the Liffey at Merchants Quay and Wood Quay must be questioned, and the arrangement and some details of the walls and towers at the mouth of the Poddle in the north-east corner of the ancient city, together with the inclusion of a double wall at this corner, are now known to be incorrect.

At least one later version of Strangways's map exists, but it merely aggravates the errors. Healy's paper on the town walls of Dublin describes present knowledge and may be consulted with advantage. Also, following recent excavations (1992–3) the precise location of Isolde's (Newman's) Tower is known, and may be viewed.

[1, 150 (Healy)]

STRONE

Strand: in particular the South Bull sandbank, between Reinelan and Blackrock.

[*CARD*, I]

STRONE, NEWTOWN OF THE

A name for Blackrock used in the 16th century and probably earlier.

[*CARD*, I]

STRONGBOW

Richard de Clare FitzGilbert, lord of Strigoil, second earl of Pembroke, born *c.* 1130, having obtained leave from Henry II 'to trust himself to Fate and Fortune in foreign lands', sent Raymond le Gros into Ireland in May 1170, and followed him with a large army in August or September. He captured Waterford, married Aoife, daughter of Diarmait Mac Murchada, and, with Diarmait, marched on Dublin. The town was taken on 21 September 1170.

In 1173 Strongbow, who had earned the displeasure of Henry II for what were considered his insubordinate actions in Ireland, had again gained the king's favour and was appointed by him as governor or custos of Ireland. He died in 1176 'of an ulcer he got on his foot'. Unfriendly records suggest, however, that his death resulted from a 'wasting sickness in punishment for all the churches he had plundered and ravaged'. His tomb is in Christ Church.

Strongbow was described by Giraldus Cambrensis as tall in build with reddish hair and freckles, grey eyes, a feminine face, a weak voice and a short neck. In temperament he found him generous and easygoing, but he was resolute and 'stood firm as an immovable standard' in battle.

Strongbow's title of earl of Pembroke came to him from his father, and passed to his widow, Isabel, who became countess of Pembroke. Following her subsequent marriage to William Marshal (Mareschal), he was created earl of Pembroke at the time of the coronation of John in 1199. Five sons of William succeeded serially to the title, but as none of them had an heir, the earldom reverted to the Crown in 1245.

In *c.* 1300 Aymer de Valence, through his relationship to one of William Marshal's daughters, became earl of Pembroke, and was succeeded by his nephew, Laurence de Hastinges, in 1339. The title remained with the de Hastinges family until 1389, when the holder, John, died without issue, and again the earldom reverted to the Crown.

From 1414 to 1495 the title became a prize for favourites close to the monarchy, though sometimes ill-starred. The earldom was held by Humphrey of Lancaster (1414–c. 1446), William de la Pole (c. 1446–50, when he was beheaded at sea) and Jasper Tudor (1452–95). During the time of Jasper Tudor, William Herbert, 'an ardent Yorkist', captured Pembroke Castle in 1461 and was granted the lordship of Pembroke (this meant there were then two earls). In 1469 he was beheaded and the title passed to his son, William Herbert, who held it until 1475, when he resigned on receiving further honours. In 1479 the child Edward Plantagenet, prince of Wales and heir apparent to Edward IV, was created earl of Pembroke. He was killed in 1483, shortly after his accession to the throne as Edward V. On Jasper's death in 1495 all his honours, including Pembroke, became extinct. The anomaly of two contemporaneous earldoms may have arisen from the fact that Jasper Tudor was attainted twice during the period 1452–95, and may have been stripped of his titles while out of favour.

The Pembroke title then moved for a short time even closer to the monarch. In 1532 Henry VIII created his second wife, Anne Boleyn, the marchioness of Pembroke. In 1536 she was beheaded. She died without male issue, and 'her peerage if not already forfeited became extinct'.

In 1551 William Herbert, grandson of the earlier William who had been beheaded in 1469, was created earl of Pembroke. He was a brother-in-law of Henry VIII through the marriage of his wife's sister, Catherine Parr, to the king. The title has remained in the Herbert family since then.

[35, 147, 232]

STRONGE, CATHERINE

One of the very few women named as holding a contract from the Corporation, Catherine Stronge was the city refuse collector in 1632. She was accused in that year of emptying 'filthred and dounge' into the Liffey to such an extent that loaded gabbards could reach the quay, probably Wood Quay, only at spring tides. The alderman and constable of Damastreete were ordered to prevent further abuse.

[CARD, III]

SUMMER ISLANDS, THE

See THE SOMMER ILANDS.

SUNDIAL ON THE BRIDGE, THE

In 1666 the City Assembly agreed that a 'knowing artist' should be engaged to erect a good sundial on the Bridge of Dublin 'for the benefit and honour of this antient citty'. It is not clear whether this work was ever done.

[CARD, IV]

SUTTON

A study of kitchen middens on a raised beach about 1 km east of Sutton Cross indicates that early neolithic man lived there in c. 3000 BC. At that time Howth was an island, and it and Dalkey Island, inhabited in the same period, are possibly the two earliest places of human habitation in the area covered by this book. By the beginning of historical time, Howth was connected to the mainland by a narrow isthmus in the vicinity of Sutton Cross.

In 1686 Greenvile Collins showed Sutton as a named hamlet centred on modern Strand Road and St Fintan's Road. In 1765 Scalé and Richards showed it as a single large house in the same area, and in 1800/3 Bligh showed it, again as a single house, but nearer to Red Rock. It is now a district centred on Sutton Cross that stands on an isthmus, roughly 450 m wide, which is a raised beach with an average ground level 6.5 m above OD (Poolbeg). The level of the beach of 5,000 BP has been shown to be from 6.0 to 7.6 m above OD (Poolbeg).

Before the advent of steam and the control of the bar at the mouth of the Liffey, Sutton figured often in the schemes of those who were working for safer access for shipping to the port of Dublin. Other entries mentioning Sutton may be consulted, and reference may be made also to Howth, Proposed Canal; Perry's Canal and his Other Harbour Proposals; Thomas Rogers: Proposal for Canal.

The establishment of a Martello tower close by, and the use of Corr Castle as a navigation mark, may also be noted.

[220 (vols. 86 and 102: Mitchell), maps (Greenvile Collins 1686, Scalé and Richards 1765, Bligh 1800/3, OS 1948, Dublin Administrative Edition)]

SUTTON BAR

The Scalé and Richards navigation map of 1765 shows Sutton Bar or Barr off the west shore of Howth Head at the bay end of Sutton Creek. It would have had significance in the 18th century in the context of developing Sutton Creek as an access canal to the port of Dublin. Its position today would be off the east end of Bull Island.

[Map (Scalé and Richards 1765)]

SUTTON CREEK

See THE NORTH BULL and PERRY'S CANAL AND HIS OTHER HARBOUR PROPOSALS.

SUTTON ISTHMUS: PROPOSED CANAL

See THOMAS ROGERS: PROPOSAL FOR CANAL.

SWAN ALLEY

See MERCHANTS QUAY.

SWAN RIVER

Also known as Swan Water, it is, as Sweeney describes, a complex network of streams which has as its catchment large sections of Terenure, Rathgar, Rathmines, Ranelagh and Ballsbridge.

In earlier times, one of its main streams rose in a quarry near Lower Kimmage Road, to use modern names, crossed Rathgar, flowed northward east of and parallel to Rathmines Road (Swan Place) and turned east to pass under Mount Pleasant to the east end of Leeson Park. From there it flowed past Bloomfield Avenue (Swanbrook) and along Clyde Road to pass down the west end of Lansdowne Road, once known as Watery Lane. It then turned and followed Shelbourne Road to discharge into the delta of the Dodder.

The Swan was also the main drain for the area in early times, and during the centuries much of it was arched over and covered. In the 19th century the Swan Sewer, as it was then called, was diverted to flow from Shelbourne Road through the future Lansdowne Road football grounds to join the Dodder upstream of London Bridge, and in 1867 this section was culverted.

As part of the Rathmines and Pembroke Townships Main Drainage Scheme (1878–81), the Swan Sewer was reconstituted and carried forward in new works from Clyde Road to a new treatment plant at Pigeonhouse, and the culverted outlet to the Dodder became a storm-water sewer.

In its earlier history, the Swan was shown by Phillips in 1685 with a branched outlet that added to the complexity of the Dodder delta. It was mentioned also in 1778. In that year, the Ballast Office was proposing that the Dodder be diverted to flow from New Bridge directly to the South Bull strand (Sandymount) south of St Matthew's Church in Irishtown. The committee proposed 'making a cut from Mr Robinson's wheel and joining to it [the Dodder] the water from Ranelagh'. This reference is to the Swan, and Robinson's Wheel was probably the mill-wheel for the distillery or other water-mill that stood at that time on land close to the present Marian College.
[90 (vol. 13: Crook), 184, *CARD*, XIII, maps (Phillips 1685, Taylor 1816)]

SWIFT'S ROW

See ORMONDE QUAY, UPPER.

SWIVEL BRIDGE

See BUTT BRIDGE.

SYCAMORE ALLEY

Now Sycamore Street. See POOLEY'S WOOD YARD.

SYNAGOGUES

See CRANE LANE.

T

TAAFE'S VILLAGE
See POPLAR ROW.

TALBOT, VENERABLE MATT
See TALBOT MEMORIAL BRIDGE.

TALBOT MEMORIAL BRIDGE
The increasing traffic demands in the decade from 1960 to 1970 made it necessary to convert Butt Bridge into a one-way northbound crossing, and to build a new one-way bridge for southbound traffic downstream of the Custom House to link Memorial Road to Moss Street. The construction of the new bridge, which would eventually be named Talbot Memorial Bridge, was started in 1976 and the bridge was opened for traffic on 13 February 1978. Its peak traffic capacity is rated as 2,400 vehicles per hour.

This bridge was the first Liffey bridge in Dublin to use prestressed concrete as a structural medium. It has three spans, with an aggregated length of 80 m, and a width of 22 m between the parapets. The centre span is 34 m long. The maximum depth of water under the bridge (HWOST) is 8.9 m. The designers were DeLeuw, Chadwick and Ó hEocha, who consulted Mott, Hay and Anderson, of London, and, for visual aspects of the design, Tyndall Hogan Hurley, of Dublin. The builders were Ascon Limited.

The name of the bridge makes a twofold commemoration. Firstly it honours Venerable Matt Talbot (1856–1925), a Dublin man of heroic sanctity, who worked first in the Dublin Port and Docks Board, then for some years as a casual labourer, and for the last 25 years of his life in the timber yard of Messrs T. and C. Martin on the North Wall. It is named also as a memorial to all sailors who sailed out of Dublin and died at sea.

A plaque on the bridge carries the following inscription in Irish and in English:

Talbot Memorial Bridge

THIS BRIDGE WAS OPENED OFFICIALLY BY
THE RIGHT HONOURABLE THE LORD MAYOR,
COUNCILLOR MICHAEL COLLINS;
14 FEBRUARY 1978
[90 (vol. 102: Stephens and Dowling)]

TANDY, JAMES NAPPER

James Napper Tandy

Born in 1740, son of a tradesman, James Napper Tandy went into trade as an ironmonger and land agent. He was elected to the City Assembly as a member of the Merchants' Guild and served for 18 years. He was active in advocating municipal and parliamentary reform, and came to be a popular favourite in Dublin through, for instance, his support of the rights of the Assembly against the Revenue Commissioners in the first months of the Custom House project. He joined the duke of Leinster's corps of the Volunteers in 1778, but, being expelled from it, formed in 1780 a new corps, named the Independent Dublin Volunteers.

He helped Wolfe Tone and Thomas Russell in the foundation of the Society of United Irishmen in 1791, but fled to America shortly afterwards to escape arrest. Returning to Europe in 1798, he sailed for Donegal later that year in command of a French vessel attached to Bompard's expedition. He took no part in the fighting in Ireland, but was later captured in Hamburg and sentenced to

imprisonment. In 1802 he was released on the intervention of Napoleon, and retired to Bordeaux, where he died in 1803. His portrait appears in volume XIV of Gilbert's edition of the *Calendar of the Ancient Records of Dublin*, and in a painting in the National Gallery (NGI, 429).

History has not treated him gently. Perhaps it would be fair to say that he tried, but that his capabilities did not match the drama of the stage on which he found himself an eager player.

[54, 185, 190, *CARD,* XIV]

TARA STREET

This street extends today from George's Quay to Pearse Street (formerly Great Brunswick Street). It was shown first by Brooking in 1728 as George's Street, running from George's Quay to Townsend Street (named by him as Lazers Hill). Rocque (1756) and Faden (1797) show the same detail. In 1838 the Ordnance Survey showed the northern part of the street from the quay to Poolbeg Street as George's Street, and the rest, to Townsend Street, as Shoe Lane. In 1850 the two streets were run-down and consisted between them of 40 houses let in tenements. In 1907/8 the district had been redeveloped, possibly following the construction of the Swivel Bridge, and the whole street, now extending from the quay to Pearse Street, was named as Tara Street.

[146, maps (Brooking 1728, Rocque 1756, Faden 1797, OS 1838, 1907/8)]

TATE'S GARDEN

A holding in the vicinity of Foster Place in 1663. It was used as a landmark for an extensive lease of land to the earl of Anglesey in the ground reclaimed by William Hawkins.

TAYLOR'S MAPS

John Taylor (*fl.* 1790–1830) is best known as an engraver, but he made two maps that are relevant to this book.

In 1760 Rocque made a map of County Dublin. Over 50 years later, this was still the only map showing Dublin with its hinterland to a useful scale. In October 1816 'Taylors Map of the

Environs of Dublin extending 10 to 14 Miles from the Castle by Actual Survey on a scale of 2 Inches to One Mile' was published, and dedicated to Earl Whitworth, the viceroy, and Earls O'Neill and Rosse, the postmaster-general. The scale, of Irish miles, represents a ratio of 1:40,320. The map was first published on two sheets of unequal size.

The main interest of this quite graphic map in the present context is the presentation of the bay and its shoreline. Andrews, in a detailed analysis, points out Taylor's use of the hydrographic data established earlier by Bligh, and remarks on the confusion that arose when Taylor 'combined Bligh's soundings with his own very differently shaped coastline'. One should, however, note such details as Dunleary Harbour with only the east pier built, the small island 400 m long that had by then developed on the North Bull, and the use of the name of London Bridge for the crossing of the Dodder at Bath Avenue; and one accepts that Taylor must have found that the same four wrecks seen on the Bull sands by Bligh were still in existence when he showed them in the same positions in 1816.

This map with amendments reached a fifth edition in 1828, and a facsimile of the 1816 edition was produced by Phoenix Maps in 1989.

The second map was made by Taylor in 1824. It was 'A General Plan of the Custom House Revenue Stores and Docks in Dublin, for public letting by Winstanley and Sons, London'. It was made to a scale of approximately 1:1,750, and printed in London. It illustrates, with figured dimensions, the Custom House, the Old Dock, George's Dock and the Inner Dock. It shows in detail the entries to the docks from the Liffey, and the arrangement of streets leading on to Beresford Place. It names the former Ship Buildings, now Abbey Street Old, as Stable Lane.

[255, map (Bligh 1800/3)]

TELFORD, THOMAS

The name of Thomas Telford (1757–1834), among the leading engineers of his period, has been associated with important works in Ireland. While he did not himself design any specific structures in this country, he was on several occasions invited to give opinions as an adviser on works in progress or projected. Thus, in 1822 he visited the Bull Wall, designed by Halpin and Giles and then under construction, and gave his opinion on the work being done. In 1823 he visited the Custom House Docks and noted that the work, designed by Rennie, 'was proceeding in a very satisfactory manner'. On this occasion, he was also able to confirm that cast-iron work required for the project had been prepared at Shrewsbury, where he had seen it a few days previously, and was ready for dispatch.

[118; PRO, cust. 21, Engineers' Reports, 1823–4, vol. 19]

TEMPLE BAR

In 1656 Sir John Temple was granted, at the north side of his family home and garden at Dame Street, a lease on about 0.4 ha of ground, extending along the south shore of the Liffey from the line of Temple Lane to Fownes Street, to use modern names. This was a 'wast peece of ground', part of which would have been liable to tidal submersion twice daily. The plot straddled the line of the street now known as Temple Bar.

In 1662–3 William Hawkins built his wall, which extended along the river from Burgh Quay to the line of Temple Lane. To quote de Gomme's words of 1673, this wall led to a large new area being 'ground taken in from the sea'. As a result, the whole area from Temple Lane to Hawkins Street, and, very roughly, from the line of Cecilia Street to the Liffey, became land usable for building and free of tidal interference. This new land, located, as it was, end to end with Newman's work on the Poddle estuary (1606–20), established virtually the whole length of the south shore of the Liffey from Hawkins Street to Fr Mathew Bridge as ready for development.

Taking advantage of Hawkins's Wall, Temple quickly established the street called Temple Bar, and already in 1673 de Gomme showed its modern length, naming it as Temple Bar. At that date, it was simply a lane through fields, and going nowhere. By 1728, however, Brooking could show it as fully built up on both sides, and linked end to end with the new streets Essex Street East to the west and Fleet Street to the east. The whole length of the street called Temple Bar at present is from Temple Lane South to Anglesea Street; but the name of Temple Bar is now being given to a social precinct containing the street and covering some 2 ha in area, a precinct at present undergoing intensive development.

In the 17th and 18th centuries Temple Lane, then called Dirty Lane, had its south end at Dame Street, and extended northwards along the east boundary of Pooley's Wood Yard to the bank of the Liffey, where it was the terminal for a ferry. The short northern section from Temple Bar to the river was closed, probably when Wellington Quay was formed early in the 19th century. Dirty Lane had formerly been known as Hog's Lane or Hog Lane, the name used for it by Stanihurst in 1577.

[*CARD*, II, IV, maps (Speed 1610, de Gomme 1673, Brooking 1728, Rocque 1756, OS various)]

TEMPLE LANE
See TEMPLE BAR.

TENGMOUTH STREET
See DAME STREET.

TEYNMOUTH STREET
See DAME STREET.

THOMPSON'S DOCK
See NORTH WALL SLIP.

THOMPSON'S YARD
In 1728 Marney's Dock on the north bank of the Liffey was being described as Mr Thompson's Dock. An Assembly reference to Mr Thompson's Yard in 1724 could indicate the same area, but the phrasing also suggests that Thompson's Yard may have been on the south bank, roughly across the river from Thompson's Dock.

[*CARD*, VII]

THOM'S DIRECTORY
See DIRECTORIES OF DUBLIN.

THORNCASTLE
Also Thorncastil. In 1306 it was held that the lands of Thorncastle belonged to Christiana de Marisco, having come to her through her ancestors, who held them as a grant of King John. These lands extended 'from the rivulet called Glaslawer running to the sea near the boundaries of the land of Carrickbrenan towards the East to the rivulet called Clarade running to the sea near the boundaries of the land of the city of Dublin towards the West'.

Christiana's great-grandfather was Walter de Ridelisford, who is said to have slain John the Wode at the battle of Hoggen Green. Glaslawer is probably the stream that still flows under Temple Road to discharge east of Idrone Terrace in Blackrock. Carrickbrenan was probably in the present area of Monkstown, where there is today Carrickbrennan Road. The rivulet called Clarade is the Dodder, which in fact discharges into the Liffey at the west end of what was Clarade. Thorncastle is recalled in Thorncastle Street in Ringsend, which was part of the Thorncastle lands.

The same record describes the River Dodder as running to Karna, which may be Rathfarnham, or, as described on an early map, Rathfarna. Alternatively, the name Karna, or, as given elsewhere, Carnan, may have been used for the mouth of the Dodder – that is, as a name for Ringsend. Note, however, that the name appears also in the south-west of the city.

Christiana de Marisco inherited the lands of Thorncastle as an infant in 1244 from her grandfather, also Walter de Ridelisford, through her mother, a daughter of Walter. Christiana's father, Robert de Marisco, had died earlier. She never married. She was a close friend of Eleanor, widowed queen of Henry III, and probably followed her into a religious community.

Christiana, having a large estate in England also, assigned her Irish lands to the Crown. During the 14th century these lands of Thorncastle were held from the Crown by, successively, William le Deveneis (1300), Walter de Islip, Robert de Nottingham (1320), Thomas Bagod of Baggotrath, John de Bathe, and Sir John Cruise (1366). In c. 1400 the properties passed to the Fitzwilliam family, where they were held for about 400 years.

After the death of the seventh Viscount Fitzwilliam in 1816, the estate passed to his cousin George Herbert, then earl of Pembroke, and has remained in that family.

[35, 56, 181]

THREEPENNY CUSTOMS
See ADMIRALTY PREROGATIVES.

TIDAL HARBOURS COMMISSION
In 1845 Victoria established the Tidal Harbours Commission with ten members to 'enquire into the state and condition of the tidal and other harbours, shores, and navigable rivers of our United Kingdom of Great Britain and Ireland'.

In their Second Report, issued on 20 March 1846, the Commissioners included all the chief harbours in Ireland. They found that in Dublin much had been done, but considered that, with better planning, more benefit could have been gained for the money spent. They criticised the Ballast Board for its composition and process of election.

Their final report read:

Within the last thirty years many improvements have taken place; the depth of water over the bar and up to the city quays has been increased several feet, by dredging and by the bold measure of running out the great north wall; the traffic and consequent revenue of the port have more than doubled; and the latter has risen to 34,000 l. a-year. Yet the evidence shows that the foundation of the quays is generally so imperfect that they will not in their present state admit of the river being further deepened; that the south quay, the resort of three-fourths of the shipping of the port is encumbered at its foot by heaps of mud; that the entrance into the Grand Canal Docks is all but blocked up by sand-banks; that there is a grave want of graving docks; that there is but one public crane; that the port charges are very high; and that the ballast of which, by act of parliament, the Ballast Office has a monopoly, and for which it charges about double the market price, is in many cases bad.

This report was based on the reports of the Examining Commissioners, which in turn were based on the texts of listed letters and reports that had been issued between the years 1800 and 1846 and on the evidence taken during a one-day hearing on 10 October 1845. The texts and evidence were reproduced in full, and the report was illustrated by Frazer's map of 1838/42.

[285]

TIDAL MILLS
See MABBOT'S MILL.

TIDE LEVELS
See WATER, TIDE AND GROUND LEVELS.

TIDE SURVEYORS AND TIDEWAITERS
A note in 'The accounts of His Majesty's Revenue in Ireland for five years vizt. from the landing of Duke Schonberg in August 1689 to Christmas 1693' (BL, Egerton MS 790, ff. 59–61) describes the customs control procedure at that time for vessels sailing in to Dublin: 'On arrival of every ship she is boarded by the Tide surveyor who upon examining and inspecting of all things leaves on board one or more tidewaiters'. Then, 'after the ship is unloaden the tide surveyor goes aboard, rummages the ship and takes off the tidewaiters, and if afterwards any goods are found on board and concealed from the tide surveyor on rummaging and clearing the ship as aforesaid, such goods are seized and the master is liable to forfeitures'.

TIGHE STREET
See BENBURB STREET.

TIMBER TRADE AND TRAFFIC ON THE LIFFEY
See DUBLIN'S WATER SUPPLY AND THE LIFFEY and SHIPS AND BOATS ON THE LIFFEY.

TIRELESFORD (TYRELLFORD)
In 1324 Edward II names Tirelesford as a stage in the riding of the city franchises. From various descriptions, this was a ford in the River Camac north of Bow Bridge. It is mentioned again by Richard II in 1395, under the name Tyrellford.

[189, *CARD*, I]

V

VALLANCEY, GENERAL CHARLES

Charles Vallancey (attributed to H.D. Hamilton)

Military engineer and antiquary, lived 1725–1812. Vallancey appears to have spent much of his life in Ireland. He became 'engineer in ordinary in Ireland' in 1762, was lieutenant-colonel and 'director of engineering' in 1777, was promoted lieutenant-general in 1798 and general in 1803. He designed the greatly admired Queen's Bridge (Mellowes), which was built in 1768, and he supervised the construction of one of the earlier piers at Dunleary, which was approaching completion in 1767.

In 1777 Vallancey prepared a report for transmission to the lord lieutenant in which he considered the problems of protecting the bay and estuary from attacks by pirates, and providing asylum in the bay for vessels that were stormbound or awaiting suitable tide to enter the port. For protection, he suggested cannon positions at Baily, Candlestick, Poolbeg lighthouse, Pigeonhouse, Dunleary, Dalkey Island and Sorrento. For asylum, he suggested using convict labour, by those under

sentence of transportation, to build a wall from Dalkey Island to the mainland, converting Dalkey Sound into two back-to-back harbours. For the general protection of Dublin, he resurrected de Gomme's idea for a fortress at Ringsend, noting, as had others, that the area could be transformed into an island. His report was accompanied by a map of the bay and estuary drawn to a scale of 1:63,360.

A comprehensive memoir of Vallancey is given by Nevin.

[55, 56, 82, 106, 220 (vol. 46, 1916: Westropp; vol. 123, 1993: Nevin); NLI, MS 13058]

VAVASOUR, WILLIAM

In 1792 Counsellor William Vavasour, who had earlier developed part of the area in Williamstown where Blackrock College now is, proposed a scheme to the Ballast Board for embanking the River Dodder below Ballsbridge. This was opposed by the Grand Canal Company and its consulting engineer, William Jessop, who feared that the proposal would damage the entrance to the Grand Canal Docks. The Ballast Board supported Vavasour, who had become a lessee in the area in 1795, and the work was completed in 1798.

Rocque (1760) shows the lower Dodder as a many-channelled marshy area from Ballsbridge to Ringsend, and Faden suggests that this was still the situation in 1797. The OS map of 1838, however, shows the influence of Vavasour's embankment. A single channel has been formed and passes under a new bridge at the north-east end of Haigs Lane, now part of Lansdowne Road. This channel turns through 90 degrees below the bridge and flows in a straight line to Ringsend Bridge. The OS map shows also the new road, Bath Avenue, crossing the Dodder at London Bridge; and shows that the ground on which later the Lansdowne Road and Londonbridge Road sports grounds would be laid out, and the residential squares named after Vavasour and Havelock, as well as the development north of Bath Avenue, would be built, had been taken in from the former marshy meadowland of the estuary.

[56, 87 (vol. 4), maps (Rocque 1760, Faden 1797, OS 1838)]

VEHICLES AND VEHICLE TYPES

While it is clear that pack-animals were the principal load-carriers in the earliest times, the Oseberg tapestry shows that in the ninth century the Norse were already using large four-wheeled horse-drawn carts for their goods. One may assume that they brought this practice to Dublin and that it continued on from there through the medieval city wherever there were surfaces that wheeled carts or wagons could use.

In 1624 it was stated in the City Assembly that 'the multiplicitie of carmen . . . throng to the Wood Kea and Merchant Kea in such numbers togeather as coaches carriadges and other necessaries can hardlie have passadge without danger of hurte', and the Assembly decreed that all carmen were to be licensed and taxed, and all cars and carts were to bear a badge showing the arms of the city.

Yarranton observed in 1674 that the transport of boat passengers by road between Ringsend and the city was costing at least £500 each year, and in 1703 it is recorded that the regulation of hackney coaches was introduced in Dublin, with 150 licences being issued in that year.

Reference to the separate entries in this book on the jingle, long coach, noddy and Ringsend car will show that 1,000 years had brought few major improvements to vehicle design, and it is difficult now to appreciate the instant and amazing impact of the Dublin and Kingstown railway in 1834, when vehicles suddenly began to run under control at speeds of over 40 miles an hour along the shoreline of the bay.

[116, 168, *CARD*, III, V]

VERNONS OF CLONTARF

Shortly after the foundation of the priory at Kilmainham in *c.* 1174, a religious commandery was established at Clontarf on lands given by Hugh de Lacy to Adam de Phephoe. From the beginning this commandery was associated with the Knights Templars. Early in the 14th century the Templars were suppressed, and the manor of Clontarf was bestowed on Richard de Burgo by Edward II, who, however, retained the Templars' building, naming it 'our royal House of Clontarf' and placing it under the control of the Knights of St John of Jerusalem at Kilmainham.

In 1600, about 40 years after the dissolution of the Kilmainham priory, the lands and house of Clontarf were granted to Sir Geoffrey Fenton, and in *c.* 1640 they passed into the hands of Matthew King. They remained for only a short time in the King family, as during the commonwealth period the property was seized and granted under Cromwell's authority to John Vernon. In 1660 Colonel Edward Vernon, who had been a loyal follower of both Charles I and Charles II, and who owned estates also in England, was given far-reaching legal rights to the manor of Clontarf, 'together with all anchorages, fisheries, creeks, sands and seashores, wrecks of the sea etc.'.

Throughout the 18th century the city and the Vernon family were in legal dispute about the ownership and rights of Clontarf, with particular emphasis on the foreshore and fisheries. In 1716 the Vernons were selling stone, as of right, from the Clontarf foreshore to John Rogerson for his wall, and in 1729 they were claiming wreckage cast up on the shore at Clontarf, and were claiming also the ownership of the fisheries at Crab Lough and at part of the Poolbeg. In 1730 John Vernon was seeking amicable discussion with the city authorities to resolve their differences, but in 1731 he denied the right of the Corporation to take in his manor of Clontarf as part of the city liberties when riding the franchises, arguing that his lands were those anciently granted to the Knights Templars and so excluded from the city lands by the charter of John.

In 1734 the Vernons took their case for the ownership of Crab Lough to the House of Lords in London and were successful. The legal confrontation continued, however, into the 19th century, with, in one case, George Vernon being awarded one shilling in 1814 in acknowledgment of his 'right of fishery' on the strand near part of the North Lotts. In 1820, correspondence in the records of the Ballast Board suggests that the Corporation was then acquiring the Vernon rights at the North Bull, and in 1823 it was recorded that the North Bull fishery had been let by the city to William Campbell for an annual rent of £35.

The present building on the site of the medieval commandery carries the inscription, 'Clontarf Castle was founded by the Knights Templars in the 12th century and rebuilt by J.C.V. Vernon Esq. AD 1837'. [4, 87 (vols. 10–12), *CARD*, VII, VIII]

VICEROY, OFFICE OF
See JUSTICIAR, OFFICE OF.

VICTORIA
The cross-channel steamship *Victoria* (or *Queen Victoria*), bound from Liverpool to Dublin with 100 passengers and cargo, struck Howth Head near the Baily lighthouse in a snowstorm during the night of 14/15 February 1853. Fifty-five persons, including the ship's captain, were drowned. The survivors were rescued by the lifeboats of the steamship *Roscommon*.
[65, *DHR* (Dixon)]

VICTORIA AND ALBERT BRIDGE
See RORY O'MORE BRIDGE.

VICTORIA BRIDGE
See RORY O'MORE BRIDGE.

VICTORIA FOUNDRY

Queen Victoria (G. Hayter)

See J. AND R. MALLET.

VICTORIA QUAY
At the beginning of the 19th century, the south quays ended at Barrack Bridge (now Rory O'More) at the west end of Usher's Island. From there, the

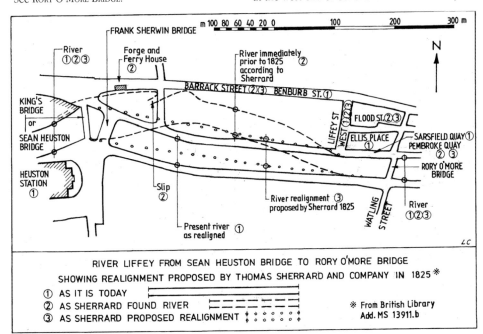

Realignment of the Liffey between Sean Heuston Bridge and Rory O'More Bridge

avenue known as the Military Road led towards the Royal Hospital across open fields bounded on the north by the river-bank. The entrance to this avenue from 1811 or 1812 onwards was through the Richmond Guard Tower, which closed the line of the quays. In 1828 the King's Bridge was opened where the Steevens's Hospital ferry had formerly plied.

At that period the channel of the Liffey followed its ancient course north of east past the ferry and then through a gentle S-bend to reach Barrack Bridge, there flowing due east as it does today. Rocque (1756) and OS (1838) show this course.

In 1825 Thomas Sherrard and Company, Dublin surveyors, prepared proposals for the realignment of the river to flow in a substantially straight course from the ferry crossing to Barrack Bridge. This was part of a scheme for providing new quays, and a new access route to Phoenix Park and the west along the north bank of the river. This work had not been carried out when the area was surveyed in 1837 for the first Ordnance Survey maps, although the King's Bridge had been built and opened on the line of the ferry in 1828.

In 1846 Kingsbridge railway terminus was opened to traffic, and in 1847 the Richmond Guard Tower was removed as it was considered to be an obstacle to the increasing traffic along the quays. By 1847 the OS map shows that the course of the river had now been changed, and wide unnamed quays had been made along its two banks.

The new course did not follow Sherrard's straight line. Instead it ran east-south-east from King's Bridge for about 180 m, bending then to flow nearly due east to Barrack Bridge. The magnitude of the realignment may be gauged from the fact that, for a substantial length, the new north bank of the river lay south of the old south bank. This course, which necessitated a quite abrupt change of direction for the river at King's Bridge, is discussed further in the entry on Wolfe Tone Quay.

In 1861 Queen Victoria, during her third Irish visit, drove along the new quay in an open barouche *en route* from Kingsbridge Station to Westland Row Station, but it is probable that her name was not given to it until some years later. In

1873 Arthur Guinness Sons and Company began to extend its brewery complex northward from James's Street to Victoria Quay. In that year, it started to use steam barges on the river to carry its export stout and porter downstream for loading on to deep-sea vessels near the Custom House. It began at the time the construction of timber wharves at Victoria Quay and would continue to expand that riverside system until 1913. The quay continued to serve as its river terminus until 1961. By then, it had been the only working quay west of O'Connell Bridge for more than 150 years, and the only quay in that area ever to accommodate steam vessels on any regular basis.

Victoria Quay was shortened slightly in 1982 by the opening of Frank Sherwin Bridge to the east of King's Bridge.

[19; maps (Rocque 1756, OS 1838, 1847); BL, Add. MS 13911.b; private communication (P. Walsh)]

VICUS PISCARIORUM

See FISHAMBLE STREET.

VIERPYL, SIMON

Sculptor, born *c.* 1725, who worked on the Casino in Marino in 1757. He was also a member of the City Assembly, who supervised the strengthening of the abutments and platform for the Poolbeg lighthouse from 1775, when its designer, John Smith, died, until 1780, when he retired from the Corporation. He died in 1810.

[95, *CARD*, XII, XIII]

VIGNOLES, CHARLES BLACKER

A civil engineer born in Enniscorthy, County Wexford in 1793 and brought up in the West Indies. Following engineering experience in North America, he set up in practice in England, and in Dublin at 3 Westland Row. He completed the designs for the Dublin and Kingstown railway and supervised its construction in 1833–4, and he designed and supervised the construction of the atmospheric railway from Kingstown to Dalkey, which opened for service in March 1844 and operated for ten years. His later works were in

The LAT datum is 0.20 m above the Ordnance Datum (Poolbeg). Thus in referring to the Poolbeg datum, which appears on many Ordnance maps currently in use, the high and low tide levels mentioned above become 4.70 m (15.67 feet) above OD (Poolbeg) and 0.35 m (1.2 feet) above OD (Poolbeg).

These figures may be used, as an example, to demonstrate that the level of City Quay, namely 18.00 feet or 5.40 m above OD (Poolbeg), is 2.33 feet or 0.70 m above the highest predicted tide level in 1991. This freeboard of 2.33 feet or 0.70 m is based on calm water and may be reduced in wind or storm.

Records held by Dublin Port and Docks Board since 1923 show that storm-driven water has been known to reach levels in the river (North Wall light) up to 0.6 m (2 feet) above highest predicted tide levels. Such a level could reduce the City Quay freeboard to 0.1 m or 4 inches.

It is of interest to note here that the crest of the Liffey weir at Islandbridge is 5.85 m or 19.51 feet above OD (Poolbeg), or 1.15 m or 3.84 feet above the level predicted to be reached by the highest tide of 1991.

As the soundings in the bay shown by the Admiralty chart are related to the LAT datum, it follows, for instance, that where the chart records that the channel through the Bar is 'dredged to 7.8 m', this means that the level of the bed of the channel is 7.80 m below LAT datum, or 7.60 m below OD (Poolbeg); and it indicates that the depths of water in the channel at the times of the highest and lowest predicted tides for 1991 were, respectively, 12.30 m (41.00 feet) and 7.95 m (26.50 feet).

Another reference level used occasionally in the port is the old Dublin Port Datum, which is 0.23 m above LAT datum or 0.43 m above Ordnance Datum (Poolbeg). This ODP datum is not used in the present work.

In 1958 the Ordnance Survey adopted a new national reference datum based on Malin Head in County Donegal. This OD (Malin), which is 2.71 m above OD (Poolbeg), will appear on new editions of maps. Since, however, the use of the Poolbeg datum extends back in time through several editions to the first Ordnance Survey maps published in 1838, and as many of these maps at present in circulation do not show the Malin reference, this book in general uses the Poolbeg datum.

There is a difference of 0.06 m between the tide levels, both high and low, occurring at the North Wall and the Bar, but this is not considered significant in the present context. A similar difference of 2 inches (0.05 m) between the Poolbeg lighthouse and the Custom House was recorded by a Dr McMahon before 1804.

Perrot, in his survey of the walls of Dublin in 1585, refers to the channel of the river in the vicinity of Merchants Quay and Wood Quay, and his record is important in the context of the levels of the early quays. This matter is treated generally in the entry on Newman's Tower.

After careful review, it is held throughout this book that, in the short space of geological time covered, there has been no significant change in the absolute level of high water at ordinary spring tides at Dublin, or in the tidal ranges. Thus, for example, if such a high tide today could reach the earthen bank that was built under the Christ Church escarpment at Wood Quay in c. 900, it would reach substantially the same level in relation to the top of the bank as it did then. See also Trial Boreholes.

It should be noted that the levels in this entry do not take into account higher water levels reached in occasional inundation that has arisen from storm flooding in the Liffey catchment.

[CARD, II; Dublin Port Tide Tables, 1991; Dublin Port and Docks Board Archive; BL, Hardwicke Papers, vol. 583, Add. MS 35931; map (RN Hydrographic Chart, no. 1415 of 1977, new ed. 1979)]

WATER ROW

The narrow street leading from Ormonde Quay to the circle in the centre of Ormonde Market. It is mentioned in the Assembly records in 1736 and is recorded in 1818 as close to the mouth of the Bradogue. It is identified by Shaw in 1850, when it contained 14 houses let in tenements.

[29, 146, CARD, VIII, map (OS 1838)]

WATER SUPPLY FOR DUBLIN FROM THE LIFFEY

See DUBLIN'S WATER SUPPLY AND THE LIFFEY.

WATERSHEDS IN DUBLIN

In the early history of Dublin the watersheds between the Liffey and its principal tributaries were notable features in the perceived topography of the town. The steep-sided prow between the Liffey and the Camac had military implications. The ridge of High Street between the catchments of the Liffey and the Poddle was a focus for the first settlements and also influenced the water supply system of the early city from the beginning.

The long ridge gradually developing from west to east between the Liffey and the Tolka, down the nose of which the Royal Canal would at the end of the 18th century be so precipitately carried, appeared to many people of the early times as their northern horizon and was a region rarely visited by them. When Rocque published his survey of the county of Dublin in 1760, the dominance of this ridge had become obscured by extensive building and road development. When, however, less than 100 years previously the de Gomme maps of 1673 were drafted, the ridge was shown quite graphically. One sheet described it as 'the top of the hills', while the other called it the 'heighte or top of the hills', and showed beyond it 'a great valley' that was in fact the course of the Tolka.

[Maps (de Gomme, city, 1673, de Gomme, harbour and bay, 1673, Rocque 1760)]

WATLING STREET

This street possibly began as a country path from the west side of St James's Gate on James's Street down the hill to a mill on the river-bank. In 1670 Bloody Bridge (now Rory O'More) was built close to the mill, and in 1673 de Gomme used the name Twatling Street for the path from James's Street, a name which Brooking repeated in 1728.

In 1758 the city decided to lay a 5- to 6-inch-bore (125 to 150 mm) elm water main in what the records then called Watling Street. Pool and Cash used this name in their map of 1780, and it has continued in that form since then.

[CARD, X, maps (de Gomme 1673, Brooking 1728, Pool and Cash 1780)]

WEEKES'S WHARF

In the late 18th century a wooden jetty was constructed by a philanthropist, Mr Weekes, immediately to the west of Clontarf Point (or Head). Its location and purpose were noted by Bligh on his map, 'Weeks wharf: for ships to water at free of cost: done at the expense of Mr Weeks'. The water-pipes were slung under the jetty, and at its sea end there was a platform with seating where strollers could sit to enjoy the sea breezes. A view of Weekes's Wharf appears on La Porte's engraving (1796) 'Dublin Bay from Clontarf' (BL, King's Topographical Collection, vol. 53, 21.c; see illustration on p. 81). The jetty fell into disrepair early in the 19th century.

[29, map (Bligh 1800/3)]

WEIR AT ISLANDBRIDGE

See ISLANDBRIDGE WEIR.

WEIR WALL

See TOLKA RIVER.

WELLESLEY MARKET

In 1826 George Holme (Home) built the Wellesley Market on Usher's Quay. It was to be a centre for the sale of Irish textiles, and, in that context, contained 80 ware rooms and a large central display and sales gallery. The building also housed Home's Hotel, 'containing 200 bedrooms originally designed for the accommodation of legal gentlemen . . . and denominated in consequence "Law Chambers"'. In 1832 the hotel was advertised in the *Treble Almanack* as 'the most extensive hotel in Europe'.

In 1843 the White Quakers became the occupiers of part or all of the premises. They were a small community formed from within the Religious Society of Friends and under the leadership of Joshua Jacob (1801–77). They taught the common ownership of property and got their name from their simplicity of dress, which they wore unbleached and undyed. While in Usher's

Home's Hotel and Queen's Bridge, c. 1829 (W.H. Bartlett)

Quay, they were occupied principally in weaving and in charitable works in the city. The community also held the former Lord Kilwarden's estate at Newlands near Clondalkin, to which it appears to have withdrawn before 1850. In that year James Ganly is named as the occupier of the premises at Usher's Quay, and his successors would carry on an auctioneering business there until 1977, when the building was demolished.

An illustration by Bartlett in 1831 shows that the building was an imposing composition that dominated Usher's Quay with its massive open portico based on seven two-storey fluted columns. [113, 146, *DHR* (Jacob), *Journal, Co. Kildare Archaeological Society*, vol. 16, no. 4, 1983–4 (Boylan)]

WELLINGTON BRIDGE

See LIFFEY BRIDGE.

WELLINGTON QUAY

Wellington Quay extends along the south bank of the Liffey from Crampton Quay at Asdill's Row to Grattan Bridge.

In 1621 a quay was built just downstream of Grattan Bridge to serve new customs facilities for the port, and in 1651 this was known as Custom House Quay. In 1705 the quay was widened by taking in from the river a strip of new land about 2 m wide. In 1756 Rocque showed the length of the quay as 105 m, with its west end about 27 m downstream of Grattan Bridge. The level of this quay may have been at approximately 5.4 m OD (Poolbeg), which would be 2.7 m below the present street level at the south end of Grattan Bridge. This quay, Old Custom House Quay, remained in existence until it was buried in the new construction of Wellington Quay.

In 1641 Richard Bamber was granted a lease by proxy for a length of 1,000 feet (300 m) of the south bank of the river west of Chichester House. This area would have been, in some part, river strand, and it would have extended as far west as Old Custom House Quay. Bamber undertook to build a quay along the river-bank, and this was to include the provision of a 'convenient way from one end of the ground to the other of seaven yardes broade next the wall aforsaid'. This lease came to nothing, and the entries on Aston Quay and Crampton Quay describe how those quays were eventually built.

During the 18th century the waterfront between Crampton Quay and Old Custom House Quay was a series of private holdings, with little pattern. Two public ways each led to a ferry terminal at the river-bank. One was the Bagnio Slip, now modern

Lower Fownes Street. The other was Temple Lane Slip, on the line of modern Temple Lane, an extension of that street which was blocked off when Wellington Quay was made. Two other gated access lanes were shown by Rocque in 1756, one on the line of Eustace Street (which would later become a public extension of Eustace Street to Wellington Quay) and the other near the present confluence of the River Poddle and the Liffey. A slope upwards towards the river in Fownes Street Lower and Eustace Street from, respectively, Temple Bar and Essex Street may be seen clearly today. This arose from the necessity of establishing the quay at a higher level than the parallel street to meet high-tide conditions in the Liffey.

As early as 1757 a city committee recommended that a quay be built from Aston Quay to Old Custom House Quay. This recommendation led immediately to the building of Crampton Quay, but it was not until the early 19th century that a decision was taken to build the rest. The delay may have arisen because, as Rocque shows, considerable new land would still have been required between the two slips to establish a direct line for a new quay. In 1812, however, the Wide Streets Commissioners began to discuss the opening of a quay, and purchased properties on the Bagnio Slip. In 1813 a map was prepared for the 'intended improvement of the new quay', and in November that year the Ballast Board asked that 'a row of stakes should be driven in the river from the west end of Crampton Quay to Essex Bridge to mark the line of the intended new wall' and to facilitate 'the erection of any new buildings'. The construction programme advanced with exemplary speed. In March 1815 the Ballast Office warned that the south abutment for the Halfpenny Bridge would need 'to be connected with the wall for which purpose it will be necessary to build [it] at the same time the new wall is erecting . . . to bear up against the pressure of the arch'; and later that year it was announced that 'the opening of the quay to Essex Bridge is about to take place immediately'.

In 1813 Arthur Wellesley, Viscount Wellington, a descendant of the Dublin family of Usher and former chief secretary for Ireland, was engaged in the Peninsular War against France. On 24 March of that year the Wide Streets Commissioners decided formally that the new quay was to be named Wellington Quay.

The development of the quay continued for several years. In 1822 the paving of the carriageway was being completed, and in 1823 old buildings that projected onto the quay were being demolished. In 1836 a petition to have the quay widened by up to 5 m was refused because of lack of funds. In 1850 Wellington Quay was predominantly a street of shopkeepers. The occupancies of the 43 houses listed on it included 35 merchants and traders and 1 public house. Thirteen solicitors had their offices there, and there were 5 private houses.

Later, in c. 1886, Dollard's would develop its printing-house on the quay near Grattan Bridge. Its site was beside the present Clarence Hotel, which opened for business in 1939 on a site where an earlier hotel had stood.

[87 (vols. 8, 15), 146, 208 (vol. 25), *CARD*, III, XVI, XVIII, map (Rocque 1756)]

WEST ROAD
See THE EAST WALL.

WESTLANDS BRICKFIELDS
See BRICKFIELDS AT WESTLAND ROW.

WESTMINSTER HALL
See CHRONOLOGY OF RULERS IN DUBLIN.

WESTMORELAND HOSPITAL
Also known as the Lock Hospital. See HOSPITAL FOR INCURABLES.

WESTMORELAND STREET
Until William Hawkins built his wall in 1662–3, the area which now includes Westmoreland Street and D'Olier Street was liable to be overflowed twice every day by the tide rising in the Liffey. From that date onward this area developed into a warren of little buildings served by narrow lanes and passages, the most important of these being Fleet

Alley and Fleet Lane. One significant thoroughfare, Fleet Street, passed through it on the route from the Old Custom House to Lazars Hill. The ground in this area was irregular, containing 'sudden and great declivities' that would tax James Gandon's architectural skills when he came to build the extension to the Parliament House in 1785.

In June 1799 George III gave his assent to an act of parliament (ch. 53) which stated that 'it would tend much to the public convenience that new and convenient passages should be opened from Carlisle-bridge to the south side of the city as far as College Green and Townsend Street' through

College Street and thence to College Green'. The street was to be 150 feet (45 m) wide. At that meeting, the Commissioners resolved formally that the street from the bridge to the college would be called Westmoreland Street. John Fane, tenth earl of Westmoreland, was then lord lieutenant, having been sworn into office in January 1790.

Preliminary development works for the new street may have begun at that time. In 1785 the construction of the east portico of the House of Lords had been started, to Gandon's design. It consisted of 'six Corinthian columns surmounted

Westmoreland Street and D'Olier Street, 1820 (S.F. Brocas)

lands owned by Trinity College. The purpose of the act was to enable these lands to be purchased, and it recorded that it had been publicly known in 1790 that the construction of Carlisle Bridge was intended and that a new street or streets would be opened 'from thence to College Green and Townshend Street'.

These works came within the programme of the Wide Streets Commissioners, and were already under discussion by them in the decade 1780–90, following the decision of parliament early in that period to open new communication between the north and south sides of the city. In 1790 their surveyor, Thomas Sherrard, laid before them plans for a street 'to be carried in one straight line in to

by a pediment originally approached by two steps', although a sketch drawn in 1790 (NLI, 598 TA; see illustration on p. 21) shows the podium approached by four steps from street level. The street level was, however, subsequently raised, as can be seen today, and as illustrated by Petrie in his drawing of Trinity College in 1821 (NLI, 722 TA), which shows the street surface at the level of the column bases, the steps being buried under the raised carriageway.

During the decade between 1790 and 1800 the Commissioners frequently discussed Westmoreland Street. In 1795 Carlisle Bridge was opened to traffic, and in 1797 Faden could show the positions of both Westmoreland Street and D'Olier Street, which was at that time still unnamed. At a meeting in May 1799 the Commissioners were still finding it appropriate to consider 'the best and speediest method of opening the communication from the Houses of Parliament to Carlisle Bridge', appointing a committee of five to deal with this matter, which related only to Westmoreland Street. At the same meeting they resolved that

> the buildings to be erected in said street shall stand upon a colonade of twelve feet wide and fifteen feet high both in the clear so as to form an extended piazza for the length of the street on either side. The superstructure to be supported on stone pillars of the Doric order, the said piazza to be vaulted underneath and flagged and to occupy the space of the footway so that the carriageway at the entrance on the Quay shall be sixty feet wide.

Unfortunately this ambitious resolution came to nothing, and a later proposal omitting the colonnade was adopted in 1800.

In 1796 Jeremiah D'Olier was elected as a Wide Streets Commissioner on the proposal of Luke Gardiner, Viscount Mountjoy. D'Olier, of Huguenot stock, had been a sheriff of Dublin, and in 1799 was governor of the Bank of Ireland. In that year, the bank sought to buy the land between modern College Green and the bridge as a site for a new headquarters. This offer, which would be withdrawn in 1802 when the bank purchased the abandoned Houses of Parliament, was warmly welcomed by the Commissioners. At their meeting of 1 August 1799 they resolved that 'the avenue on the east side of said ground let for the Bank leading from Carlisle Bridge to Townsend Street aforesaid be named D'Olier Street'.

It is clear that following the passage of the act of 1799, the carriageways on both Westmoreland Street and D'Olier Street were rapidly completed. Influenced to some degree by the Act of Union (1800), the sale of the building lots along the two streets was much slower. Some plots on Westmoreland Street were not sold until 1804, and sites were still available on D'Olier Street in 1811.

[77, 147 (vol. 9), 192, 208 (vols. 9, 14, 15), 209, map (Faden 1797)]

WHARF ROAD

See THE EAST WALL.

WHIDBEY (WHIDBY), JOSEPH

Joseph Whidbey was a sailing-master in the Royal Navy. He sailed around the world with George Vancouver in a voyage ending in 1795, and later became master attendant at Woolwich Dockyard. He assisted John Rennie in his preparatory studies for works at Plymouth Harbour early in the 19th century.

Whidbey became a visiting adviser at Dublin Port, probably on Rennie's recommendation. Addressed there as Captain Whidby, he recommended in 1822–3 the construction of a new wall and channel for the Tolka to carry it due south from Clontarf Island to meet the Liffey opposite Ringsend. This proposal was overtaken by the extensive new port developments later in the century.

[68 (vol. 2), 87 (vol. 11)]

WHITE BANK, THE

The construction of the South Wall inevitably led to a shifting of the sands of the South Bull in its vicinity. A prominent feature that developed during the 18th century was the White Bank, probably so called because of a profusion of shells, but perhaps also because its sands, generally or permanently dry, contrasted with the darker often-wetted colour of the rest.

Mackenzie mentions the White Bank on his chart published in 1776, Bligh shows it as 'dry' on the map of his survey of 1800, and Corneille shows it very clearly on his map of 1804. It appears there as a narrow ridge or spit about 700 m long stretching south-west from the South Wall, which it joins some 800 m east of the Pigeonhouse Fort, with a 90-metre-wide junction. It is implied on the Corneille map that this bank remains dry at high tide, and an area, some 30 m by 60 m, is shown as covered with grass.

Although it was suggested then that this spit might lead to the expectation 'that in the process of time the works at the Pigeon House will appear standing on a mound of dry sand', we also know that, while this has effectively happened, but with man's intervention, the process begun at the White Bank did not develop.

Early in its lifetime, the White Bank became one more bone of contention between the city and the Fitzwilliam estate. Obviously expecting the continuing development of new land, a committee of the City Assembly reported in 1807 that it had 'directed a dwelling house to be erected on the White Bank of the South Bull, part of your honours' estate, at a cost of £14-17-10', the purpose being not to ease the housing shortage but 'to ascertain and establish a right to the ground now formed there'. Lord Fitzwilliam forthwith began legal proceedings for an ejectment order against the city. The outcome is unclear. The 'wooden building' shown on the bank by OS 1838 may be the structure referred to.

In 1881 the commissioners for the Rathmines and Pembroke townships completed a sewerage system for their district, and established an outfall into the Liffey downstream of the Pigeonhouse complex. The position of the now disused outfall was close to the existing disused penstock house on the South Wall, and this station building is sited on the east edge of the White Bank. The derelict walled area lying immediately west of the penstock station constitutes part of the White Bank, but the southern part of Corneille's 700-metre-long bank, which lay outside the walled area, has been eroded. The purpose for which the walled area, sometimes known as Costello's or Crosbie's, and the several buildings contained in it, all now in ruins, was developed is uncertain. (See also Kerr's Chart of Dublin Bay, Lifeboat Service and Pigeonhouse: A Precinct.)

For comment on Corneille's map, see the entry on Captain Daniel Corneille.

[75, 90 (vol. 13: Crook), *CARD*, XVI, maps (Mackenzie 1776, Bligh 1800/3, OS 1838)]

WHITE QUAKERS, THE
See WELLESLEY MARKET.

WHITE'S LANE
Rocque's map of 1756 shows George's Quay extending west of George's Street (now Tara Street) as far as White's Lane (now Corn Exchange Place). It is possible that Mercer's Dock lay in a part of George's Quay that had probably been part of Hawkins's Ground, at White's Lane.

M'Cready includes White's Quay in George's Quay, and it seems reasonable to link White's Quay to White's Lane and possibly also to Mercer's Dock. The map given in Morgan of a 1741 lease to Grace Mercer and Luke Gardiner includes land on both sides of White's Lane, and is of interest in considering the location of Mercer's Dock.

[39, 149, map (Rocque 1756)]

WHITE'S QUAY
See WHITE'S LANE.

WHITWORTH BRIDGE
See FR MATHEW BRIDGE.

WHITWORTH PIER AND BASIN
When the army closed the Pigeonhouse harbour to civilian traffic, the Ballast Board decided, in September 1814, to build new facilities 300 m upstream of the harbour and projecting about 120 m into the river. They were to be called the Whitworth Pier and Basin in honour of the lord lieutenant. In December of that year it was reported that the work was in progress, but that the army authorities were enquiring about any buildings that might be created as a result at the new harbour. As there seems to be no later reference to this project in written records, and as it does not appear on any map, it may well be that the fears of the army led to its abandonment.

This site is now occupied by the Coal Quay.

[87 (vol. 9)]

WIDE STREETS COMMISSIONERS
The Commission for Making Wide and Convenient Ways Streets and Passages in the City of Dublin was established as a body, independent of the city, by an act of parliament in 1757 (31 Geo. II, ch. 19). The first 21 Commissioners, all powerful and

influential men, held their first minuted meeting on 1 May 1758. The Commission was abolished in the Dublin Improvement Act of 1849 (12 & 13 Vic., ch. 97), and it wound itself down and disbanded, following its last meeting on 2 January 1851.

The number of Commissioners rose gradually to 25, but while they continued to be recruited from those with influence in the city, it is some measure of the decline of their power after the Union that in 1791 13 of the 23 Commissioners were members of the Irish parliament, whereas in 1818 only 7 out of 25 were members of the parliament of the United Kingdom. The Commissioners were for several decades empowered and funded to lay out new streets and to develop those existing, to initiate works, and to buy land and property for these purposes. Their role was reduced, however, in 1826, to controlling the work of others, without access to their own development funds.

During its time of office the Commission realised many projects of great civil merit along both banks of the Liffey from the Custom House to Parkgate Street. These are mentioned elsewhere in this book.

The records of the Commission are held in the archives of Dublin Corporation. They consist principally of the 50 volumes of minutes of its meetings, an extensive collection of maps and drawings, and various legal and financial records.
[149, 182, 209, Dublin Corporation Archives]

WIDOW MAGRATH'S TAVERN

The public house on Rogerson's Quay where, in April 1798, Town Major Sirr arrested a group of 11 men accused of plotting for the rebellion.
[DHR (Hammond)]

WILDE'S LANE

Harris, in 1766, mentions this lane as connecting to Rogerson's Quay. It is not shown on any map.
[16]

WILLIAM AND WILLIAM OF AIER

It is recorded that in November 1696, 'The William pacquet-boat with two mails and about 80 passengers (among whom was Brigadier Fitzpatrick, Mr O'Neal, and many other persons of distinction) was cast away in a violent storm in Dublin bay, near Sutton, only the master and a boy saved.'

Earlier, in January 1609, 'the good shippe called the William of Aier in Scotland, of the burthen of fyfty tunns riding at ancre at Powle Begge near Dublin by great tempest was overthrown, and the marryners and others the shippemen therin weare loste'.
[16, CARD, I]

WILLIAMS ROW

See BACHELORS WALK.

WILLIAMSTOWN BEACH

Taylor (1816) shows a shingle bank projecting across the South Bull west of Blackrock. Immediately to the west of this bank near modern Blackrock Park, the South Bull strand was known as Williamstown Beach in the 19th century.
[Map (Taylor 1816)]

WILSON'S MAPS

During the late 18th and early 19th centuries Peter Wilson published Wilson's Dublin Directory annually. The directory for 1803, issued a year after his death, was printed by W. Corbet at 57 Great Britain Street, and contained as a folded sheet a 'new plan of the city of Dublin', drawn to a scale of approximately 1:11,500. It is of interest as showing the Liffey at the beginning of the 19th century.

The inadequacy of Carlisle Bridge as a link between the wide thoroughfare north and south of the river is clear. The street system in the new land on the south strand behind Rogerson's Quay is largely named although obviously little used. The triangle between Westmoreland Street, D'Olier Street and College Street (then called Bank Street) on the ground taken in from the sea by Hawkins in 1662-3 is still described as 'the scite of the Bank of Ireland'. Pearse Street (Great Brunswick Street) does not exist between Westland Row and D'Olier Street, and an enigmatic symbol, 'Str.', is shown where the Long Stone is thought to have stood. Burgh Quay is still unconnected to George's Quay, and Eden Quay (Bachelors Walk) does not extend to the Custom House.

A map to the same scale, but more richly embellished and dissected on a linen base for folding, was issued with the directory of 1798.

WINDMILL LANE

A dog-legged street connecting Creighton Street to Sir John Rogerson's Quay, which OS (1838) was the first to show in this form and to name. Elements of this lane appear unnamed on earlier maps from Brooking (1728) onwards.

[Maps (Brooking 1728, OS 1838, other early maps)]

WINDMILLS

It has been suggested that European windmills originated in the eastern Mediterranean and were brought to western Europe by the Knights Hospitallers. Possibly the earliest picture of a windmill in Dublin is that shown on the map illustrating a lease of part of the strand at Lazars Hill given to Phillip Croft in 1683. This shows 'Mr Hawkins windmill' on the river-bank at the north-east corner of the ground taken in by Hawkins from the sea 20 years earlier. See illustration on p. 219.

In general, cartographers paid little attention to windmills as such. The only windmill to be shown formally on any map is on the North Wall, some 100 m east of the mouth of the Royal Canal. This appears for the first time on Taylor's map of 1816, although it had in fact burned down late in 1810. Possibly it was reconstructed but it is not shown on OS (1838), and the site later became railway sidings and stores. An account of this conflagration is quoted by Dixon in *Technology Ireland* (vol. 7, no. 2, 1975).

Other windmills near the Liffey that appear in pictures are:

(i) three shown by Brooking in the prospect of the city included in his map of 1728. They appear near the north bank of the Liffey. Did they ever exist?

(ii) one in Windmill Lane, which is shown very clearly with its sails, on an engraving made *c.* 1834

'A View of the Late Fire on the North Wall', 1810 (Brocas, junior)

The Irish House, formerly on the corner of Wood Quay (F. Mitchell)

looking north-east from the vicinity of Westland Row railway station (now Pearse). This mill, now gone, appears also to be that shown by T.S. Roberts in his view looking east along the Liffey from the Four Courts (*c.* 1820, bib. ref. 28).

(iii) one at the junction of Thomas Street and Watling Street, which was working when the Roe family bought that property in 1757. This mill is shown with its sails on several editions of the late-18th-century picture of Dublin from Phoenix Park. The very large tower of this mill, carefully maintained by the Guinness Brewery, may still be seen. (See *Technology Ireland*: 'Industrial Archaeology', no. 3.)

A windmill at Raheny is mentioned as a seamark by Scalé and Richards in their chart of 1765.

[28, 239, *Technology Ireland* (Corran, Dixon), Dublin Corporation Archives, maps (Brooking 1728, Scalé and Richards 1765, Taylor 1816, OS 1838)]

WINETAVERN GATE

See WINETAVERN STREET.

WINETAVERN STREET

One of the very early streets of Dublin, it ran from south of the King's Gate down to the Liffey at Wood Quay. Coupled with Christchurch Lane, or, as it later became known, Christchurch Place or St Michael's Hill, which ran from south of the King's Gate up to High Street, this thoroughfare linked the High Street precinct with Wood Quay from the 11th century, if not earlier.

The King's Gate, dedicated to Richard I, and probably a 12th-century structure, lay in the city wall about 20 m south of Cook Street. It would be known as Winetavern Gate in the 16th century and would appear, surprisingly, as Ormonds Gate on Speed's map of 1610. It is not shown 63 years later by de Gomme and it does not appear on later maps. It existed for a mere 450–500 years!

In the earliest records, Winetavern Street is named as the street of the tavern keepers, vicus tabernariorum vini. The name remains to the present time, although Shaw's record of 1850 shows that there was then no tavern in either

Winetavern Street or its southern extension to High Street, which he named as Michael's Hill.

In pre-Norman time, the people of Dublin had a public court and meeting-hall in Winetavern Street. This, becoming known as a Guildhall, continued in use through the years of the conquest, and did not fall into decay until the 14th century.

From early medieval times until the late 17th century Winetavern Street was busy in the water-borne trade of the city. The Crane, which was also a centre for the collection of customs, stood at its junction with Merchants Quay, and the street was clearly part of the quay precinct. In 1578 the City Assembly, being displeased with the amount of rubbish accumulating in the river, ordered that 'Mr Maior shall cause a man out of every howse in the Wyntavarne street and Wodd Key to travail to make clean the former filthred', and in 1611 it ordered that 'from hensforth noe milstones shalbe laid or sett upon the Key or Wynetaverne street to the nuzans of the neighbors'. This puzzling proliferation of millstones dumped on the city quays or thrown into the river is referred to several times in the city records.

The construction of Essex (now Grattan) Bridge in 1676–8 diminished the volume of shipping reaching the older quays, and the commercial pattern changed. During the early 18th century, buildings began to appear in increasing numbers along the water's edge at Wood Quay and Merchants Quay, and in Brooking (1728) and, in more detail, in Rocque (1756) Winetavern Street was shown blocked off from direct access to the quayside by a range of houses at Pudding Row. These would remain until the 19th century, when it was noted in 1818 that the Wide Streets Commissioners had 'removed the obstructions which deformed our quays at the bottom of Winetavern Street'.

In 1800 there were, and had been for perhaps 800 years, three serious defects in the Winetavern Street/St Michael's Hill artery as a passage for vehicles. It was too steep, it was too narrow, and there was an abrupt Z-bend where it crossed St John's Lane. Rocque (1756) shows two of these defects clearly. The width of the street between houses near the bend is only 5 to 6 m, and the displacement at St John's Lane is about 16 m.

When the proposal to locate the new Richmond Bridge (now O'Donovan Rossa) on the axis of Winetavern Street was made early in the 19th century, a protest was lodged, probably in 1814, by a group of influential citizens. Part of their criticism was that 'the steepe at the west end of Christchurch is so great and the passage so narrow that no carriage can safely go up or down'. This assessment was justified. The street was too narrow, and the gradient, which had been increasing gradually since folk first began to live on the High Street ridge, had reached perhaps 1 in 13 in the southern section in the 19th century. The protest was denied, however, and the bridge was built as planned.

At the same time, the Wide Streets Commissioners did move quickly to improve the street and its alignment. Before 1818 they had removed the Pudding Row houses, and in that year, they announced their intention to demolish the whole western side of Winetavern Street in order to widen it. The OS map of 1838 shows that not only had this work been done, but new houses had been built along the whole length of the new frontage.

In the middle of the 20th century many of the buildings along Winetavern Street and St Michael's Hill were falling into decay. The city, wishing to build new offices for the civil administration, obtained, in 1964, powers for the compulsory purchase of the additional lands it needed for this purpose, including the east side of Winetavern Street. The pattern of the new Winetavern Street is now emerging.

[1, 8, 18, 29, 99 (Haworth, Walsh), 146; *CARD*, II, III; BL, Add. MS 40196; maps (Speed 1610, de Gomme 1673, Brooking 1728, Rocque 1756, OS 1838, 1935/6)]

WOLFE TONE QUAY

The Royal Barracks (now Collins) was built during the first decade of the 18th century on what de Gomme in 1673 described as the 'Duke of Ormonds Ground' north of the Liffey. Early in the 18th century a street named Barrack Street was made along the south front of the barracks. It is shown by Brooking in 1728. Between this street and the river there was, as he showed, an open field along the river-bank with some houses built along Barrack Street facing the barracks. In 1766 a short quay named Pembroke Quay (now Sarsfield Quay) ran from Rory O'More Bridge to the east side of this field. Malton's view of the Royal Barracks, drawn in 1796, offers an impression of the area.

Some time in the period 1822–4 an undated memorial with approximately 100 signatories was sent to the lord lieutenant, Richard, Marquis Wellesley, inviting him 'to support the improvement of his native city'. It pointed out that Barrack Street had become 'a very insufficient passage overcrowded and dirty on the five market days in each week'. It regretted having to say that because of the contiguity of a numerous garrison, 'this street is infested with women of the most abandoned character and Public Houses of the lowest description' and could not properly be used by persons of decent moral habits who wanted to enjoy Phoenix Park. It appealed with righteousness to a military man about 'the continued prevalence of contagious disease in that ill-ventilated and demoralised district and its injurious effects on the health and discipline of the Garrison'.

The memorial pointed out that a plan and estimate prepared in 1814 for extending Pembroke Quay westwards along the river-bank had been abandoned on the grounds of expense, and it concluded by offering to build a bridge to commemorate the visit of George IV in 1821 'so soon as the quay shall be extended to the Phoenix Iron Works'.

The bridge, King's Bridge, was opened in 1828, but it was not until the 1840s that the river was realigned and quays were made along the north and south banks. A fuller description of the realignment of the river is given in the entry on Victoria Quay. In 1847 these quays were still unnamed. It is likely that during the 1860s the quay on the north bank was named as Albert Quay, after the prince consort, and it would retain this name until c. 1940, when it was changed to Wolfe Tone Quay.

The realignment of the Liffey in the 1840s offers a perplexity. It would seem more efficient to have taken the channel in a straight line from King's Bridge to Barrack Bridge, but instead it was diverted to flow first southwards and then east, as described in the entry on Victoria Quay. One may suggest that the reasons for this included a wish to minimise incursion on the area of mass burials known as the Croppies Acre.

[BL, Add. MS 13914.D; maps (de Gomme 1673, Brooking 1728, OS 1838, 1847, 5-foot scale, 1936/7, 1943)]

WOOD, SANCTON

See HEUSTON RAILWAY STATION.

WOOD QUAY

Thirteenth-century wooden revetments (archaeologist: P.F. Wallace)

Wood Quay is the oldest quay in Dublin. In 841 the Viking longphort was established in a bay of the tidal Liffey that might be called Christchurch Bay between modern Fishamble Street and Winetavern Street. Archaeological excavation shows that an earthen bank was constructed under the Christ Church escarpment in c. 900, and that, for 400 years afterwards, a series of earthen banks, timber revetments and stone walls steadily pushed the high-tide waterfront northwards for a distance of about 80 m, ending in c. 1300 with a stone wall roughly along the south side of modern Wood Quay. The area progressively taken in from the water was used for dwellings, with new structures superimposed on the remains of earlier ones, and

Dublin Civic Offices (architects: phase 1, Samuel Stephenson; phase 2, Scott, Tallon, Walker)

there was probably always some clear open space near the quayside. A full treatment of this development from *c*. 917 onward is given by Wallace in bib. ref. 305.

The Wood Quay we now know came to be demarcated by two houses, Prickett's Tower, opposite the end of Winetavern Street, and Fyan's Castle, at the foot of Fishamble Street. Since these were both known at the beginning of the 14th century and since they are shown by Speed in 1610 as standing on the quayside, the location of Wood Quay is established within reasonable, although not necessarily precise, limits. It appears that the quay level at those times may have been about 2.5 m above the surface of the strand at the foot of the quay wall.

In 1327 Wood Quay was described as part of 'the kaye of the water of Avenlyf', and, with Merchants Quay, it would remain the focus of water-borne trade for the city for a further 350 years.

Speed, in 1610, shows that the quay had developed into a wide street with houses on both sides, those to the north rising straight off the river wall. If his illustration is correct, the access to the water can have been only by slips that passed through the houses, or watergates, unlike Merchants Quay, where there were some gaps between houses.

The late 16th and early 17th centuries were periods of bustle and development. Cargoes cluttered the quays, 'tymber, plankes, slates and millstones, paving stones and other great materialles'. In the river it was necessary to order that 'oulde shipps and barkes which lieth at the Wod Key shalbe presently carried awaie'.

In March 1597 one cargo caused the greatest disaster ever to arise from accident in the history of the city. Twenty-five tons of gunpowder had been sent to Dublin, and the final seven tons, packed in 150 firkins, were lying on Wood Quay awaiting delivery to Dublin Castle. A chance spark, struck from a horse's hoof or by children at play, caused the seven tons of powder to explode. Some 200 people were killed, 20 houses were knocked down, and it was said that not one house within the walls of the city escaped damage. A full account of this disaster and the subsequent inquiries is given by Gilbert in his history of Dublin.

It appears that at the beginning of the 17th century Wood Quay was considered to extend east of Fyan's Castle, as far at least as Isolde's Tower, some 100 m distant. In 1605 Jacob Newman, possibly the earliest recorded land developer as such in the city, was given a lease adjoining his holding 'upon the Wood Key near Isolde's tower'. Speed shows that part of the quay as quite wide, although he may in fact be regarding the Blind

Quay as a riverside part of Wood Quay. The issue of improving Wood Quay and of providing adequate access for wheeled traffic from it towards the east was live during the early 17th century. In 1607 Richard Prudfoote, whose name would become associated with Fyan's Castle, was given a lease for the new land he had taken in 7 yards out into the tideway of the river over a length of 16 yards in the vicinity of the castle; and a general widening of the quay by a like amount followed in 1628.

In 1684–5, following the construction of Essex Bridge and Ormonde Bridge, a further extension of Wood Quay to a new quay wall line 9 m north of Fyan's Castle was completed under the supervision of Sir Humphrey Jervis and William Moland, using stone from houses demolished near Newgate. This widening extended for the whole length of both Wood Quay and the riverside east of it, from the new Essex Bridge to the new Ormonde Bridge, or possibly to the line of Winetavern Street. The eastern portion from Fyan's Castle to Essex Bridge would be formalised as Essex Quay during the early decades of the 18th century.

There would be no further building on the river side of Wood Quay except west of Ormonde Bridge, where a group of houses, shown first by Brooking in 1728 and illustrated by Malton in 1799, restricted the access between Wood Quay and Merchants Quay to the narrow street called Pudding Row. These houses, and with them Pudding Row, had disappeared by 1816, and are not shown by Taylor in his map.

Other developments on Wood Quay during the 17th century included (i) the limiting of the sale of coal to that quay and to Merchants Quay, a ruling that, perhaps earlier, gave Wood Quay its alternative name of Coal Quay, (ii) a proposal to build an Exchange on the quay, which originated in c. 1627 and had been partially accomplished in 1644, only to be abandoned in c. 1657, and (iii) a restriction on the 'aplemen' in 1620, that, because they were obstructing the shipping, they could tie up only at Wood Quay and were not to remain 'above thirty daies in selling theire said aples'.

The 800 years of Wood Quay in the focus of Dublin's deep-sea traffic ended with the permanent closure of the opening span in Essex Bridge in c. 1687. Rocque underlines this in 1756 when he shows Wood Quay swarming with a gaggle of gabbards and other lighters, with the large sailing-vessels restricted to the water below Essex Bridge.

Wood Quay did, however, continue as a busy and socially active landing-place. The parochial constabulary of St John had its watch-house on the quay, with a complement of 1 constable and 12 men. In 1732 its members had to complain of nightly quarrels and riots caused by people abroad at unseasonable hours; they were then given a plot of ground 8 feet square beside the watch-house 'in order to fix a cage of wood there to confine such idle strollers and night walkers till they may be brought to justice in the morning'.

During the 19th century, and particularly with the building of the new quay walls, Wood Quay, while still an imposing open space and thoroughfare 100 m long and 30 m broad, faded out as an area for water-borne trade. It had been a place for merchants to live in and work in, and it is reported that, in 1782, 2 of the then remaining 11 wooden houses in the city were on Wood Quay. In 1850, when there were 22 houses listed on the quay, the maritime trade had gone, and 7 of the 17 occupied houses were associated with boot- and shoemaking. Osborne's painting of the Four Courts (NGI, no. 1916) in c. 1901 gives a somewhat morose impression of Wood Quay at the beginning of this century.

An internationally significant archaeological excavation programme was carried out on several parts of the ancient Wood Quay in the years 1973–81. An account of this and of events surrounding it is given by Bradley, and the occasion may possibly be apostrophised by the first verse of Paddy Healy's ballad, 'Ye Olde Wode Quay', published by the O'Brien Press, and to be sung to the air of 'The Sash':

It was old but it was beautiful
And its structure was of wood.
It was stratified by the Liffeyside
Where the Viking fortress stood.
These men of old were brave and bold
And they shared our forefathers' blood
But we will fight for the Wood Quay site
And the banks of Viking mud.

During the period from 1977 to 1994, new civic offices were built for Dublin on the Wood Quay site from the earthen banks to the modern quay. The construction was in two phases, the first being two tall blocks in the southern part of the site, designed by Samuel Stephenson, and the second, linear buildings along the modern quay to the design of Messrs Scott, Tallon, Walker.

[18, 34, 99, 146, 305, *CARD*, I–III, V, VI, VIII, maps (Speed 1610, Brooking 1728, Rocque 1756, Taylor 1816); Paddy Healy's permission to include his ballad is gratefully acknowledged]

WOODEN BRIDGE
See RORY O'MORE BRIDGE.

WOODEN BRIDGE PROPOSED AT MOUTH OF DODDER
See DODDER, WOODEN BRIDGE PROPOSED AT MOUTH OF.

WOODSTOCK LANE
See MERCHANTS QUAY.

WORLD'S END LANE
The present Foley Street was formerly Montgomery Street, a name which it was given in *c.* 1770. Prior to that it had been World's End Lane, and was so called by Rocque in 1756. Brooking shows the roadway but does not name it. Bolton (1717) does not show it. The east end of the lane, where it joined the Strand, which at the time was the seashore, was known as World's End. This is the present junction of Buckingham Street and Amiens Street.

[16, 31, *DHR* (Hammond), maps (Brooking 1728, Rocque 1756)]

WORTHINGTON, SIR WILLIAM
See ISLANDBRIDGE WEIR.

WORTHINGTON'S STONE
See ISLANDBRIDGE WEIR.

WRECKS
Between the exposure of the bay, the Bar and the other sandbanks, the difficulty of the channel right

Wrecks that have been mentioned in this book include:

Unnamed 'ould hulke'	Pole of Clontarfe	Prior to 1593
William of Aier	Powle Begge	1609
(see separate entry)		
Unnamed collier	Forecourt of Sir Patrick Dun's Hospital	1690
William packet-boat	Sutton	1696
(see separate entry)		
Aldborough man-of-war	Polebegg	1725
(see separate entry)		
Friendship	North Bull	1728
Burford man-of-war	Burford Bank	1770
Dolly cargo boat	Standfast Dick	1773
Hope	North Bull	1789
Prince of Wales troop-ship	Blackrock	1807
Rochdale troop-ship	Seapoint	1807
(see separate entries for two above)		
Victoria cross-channel ferry	Howth Head	1853
(see separate entry)		
Antelope schooner	North Bull	1950
Kilkenny container cargo ship	East of Poolbeg lighthouse	1991
(see separate entry)		

up to the quays in the city, the absence for 1,000 years of any harbour of refuge in the bay, and the risks taken by seafarers and their land-based masters, the Liffey and Dublin Bay have been the scene of many wrecks, particularly of sailing-vessels.

Fynes Moryson describes sailing into Dublin in September 1600 and passing by a ship 'cast away in passing from one shoar to another wherein a Bishop and his whole Family were drowned'. Later, Boate, writing in c. 1641, with a fatalism not so understandable today, described a storm 'in the beginning of November, An. 1637, when in one night ten or twelve barks had that misfortune [to be carried away from their anchors, and driven into the sea] befaln them, of the most part whereof never no news hath been heard since'.

Later in that century, Yarranton has recorded that while he was in Dublin in the month of November 1674, 'there happened a great storm which very much shattered the ships lying in the harbour and blew one to sea where ship and men perished; and blew another upon the rocks near the point of Hoth where she was staved and broke to pieces; her lading and part of the men perished'.

Bligh marks five wrecks on the map of his survey of 1800, four along the edges of the North and South Bulls and one in the bay; and in his report, in which he speaks of 'many wrecks', he is critical of the inadequacies of the gear carried by many ships for dealing with storm conditions.

The number of unrecorded wrecks of seagoing vessels over 1,200 years must have run into many hundreds, and indeed Ball has written that 'as many as twenty [ships] are said to have been annually lost or seriously injured while lying [in the open bay of Dublin]'.

The profits accruing from salvage engaged many minds. Already in the 12th and 13th centuries the privilege of 'seizing wrecks' from the sea had been granted to those who owned coastal lands. Thus in 1174 Henry II granted the abbot of Buildwas in Shropshire the rights of St Mary's Abbey in Dublin, including lands at Clunliff (Clonliffe) and Rathena (Ratheny) 'and all shipwrecks that might happen on their lands'. In 1684 the rights along the South Bull were being argued between the Admiralty and the city. Henry Forrest found it necessary to ask the city to defend him at law, which the Assembly agreed to do, because 'he having taken from some persons near Ringsend a cable found upon the strand of Merion . . . belonging to a vessel cast away in December last . . . and having given it to the Lord Mayor . . . is now being threatened by the judge of the admiralty'.

A little later, in 1728, as part of long-lasting dissension between the city and the Vernon family of Clontarf, one finds the Assembly

> setting forth that Captain Vernon assumes the right of the honourable city by taking upon him to seize such things that are cast on shore at Clontarf by shipwreck, pretending a right thereto as lord of the manor, which is the undoubted right of the city of Dublin . . . whereupon it was ordered that such method be taken for ascertaining the city's rights in law and equity as Mr Recorder shall advise.

Wherever the right to salvage lay, it is clear that a rich haul could await whomever reached a wrecked ship first, whether landlord or mob. It is not therefore surprising that the Corporation awarded the freedom of the city to Mr Richard Nevil in 1776, 'for procuring an Act to prevent the plundering of shipwrecks'.

In a file of protests to Edward Hamerton, Tabellion Publick, regarding vessels wrecked, stranded or otherwise damaged between 1797 and 1800 in the harbour of Dublin, the names of 58 vessels are listed. In his book on shipwrecks, Bourke mentions about 70 named vessels and 10 unnamed that were wrecked at various times in Dublin Bay; and further information is given by de Courcy Ireland in bib. ref. 304.

[15, 16, 17, 22, 42, 56, 58, 179, 262, 286, 304, *CARD*, I, II, V, VII, XII, *DHR* (Dixon, Hammond, Tutty), *The Irish Times*, 23 November 1991, map (Bligh 1800/3)]

X Y Z

Xystus Proposed by Vignoles

See Vignoles, Charles Blacker.

Yarranton, Andrew

Born in 1616 in England. He became a captain in the Parliamentary army, but retired prior to 1652 and devoted himself to studying engineering aspects of English waterways and their importance in commerce. He fell foul of the Restoration authorities and spent some time in prison. Cleared of all charges against him, he visited Saxony in 1667 to investigate aspects of the iron industry on behalf of English interests. Now styling himself as a consulting engineer, he came to Ireland in November 1674 to survey iron works, and timber sources for shipbuilding, in the south-east of the country. During his visit to Dublin, where he experienced a severe storm in the bay, he was requested by the lord mayor to propose a scheme for improving the harbour. His proposal is treated in a separate entry.

Yarranton died in c. 1684. A book written by him and published posthumously in 1698 under an 18-line title, which commences *England's Improvement by Sea and Land*, includes a description of his scheme for Dublin Harbour. He was being described in the mid-19th century as 'the founder of English political economy' and as 'the first man in England who saw and said that peace was better than war, that trade was better than plunder, that honest industry was better than martial greatness, and that the best occupation of a government was to secure prosperity at home and to let other nations alone'.

[42, 55, 57, *CARD*, V]

Yarranton's Proposal for Harbour

During a visit to Dublin in 1674, Andrew Yarranton made a proposal for a new harbour for Dublin. It

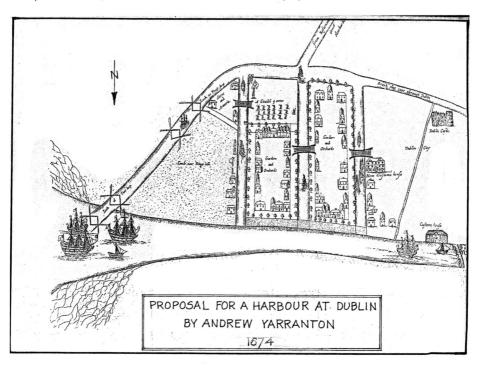

PROPOSAL FOR A HARBOUR AT DUBLIN
BY ANDREW YARRANTON
1674

Andrew Yarranton's proposal for a harbour at Dublin, 1674

was to be formed in the intertidal lowlands between Ringsend and Lazars Hill. He proposed three new channels, parallel to one another, linked at their south ends, at right angles to the Liffey but cut off from it. The easternmost of the three would be the present Dodder up to perhaps Newbridge. Access to the harbour for shipping would be by way of a fourth channel, picking up the south link between the three and cutting across the South Bull from near Newbridge to enter the Liffey near the Salmon Pool. This entry would be controlled by two locks, with the water in the harbour being at all times 4 m deep. The supply of replacement water for the locking system would be obtained from the Dodder, augmented by the Poddle, which would be diverted at Dublin Castle to flow across George's Lane and 'through a waste piece of land of Sir William Pettie and so down to Lasey Hill'. A citadel covering 4 acres and a new Custom House would be provided, and the berthing would be so safe that 'a boy and a dog' could take care of a ship. It is not clear, however, what Yarranton had in mind for Trinity College, as one of his channels might well have been sited in College Park. There is no record that Yarranton's proposal ever received formal consideration.

Yarranton's map is reproduced in volume V of the *Calendar of the Ancient Records of Dublin*. In addition to the proposed harbour, it appears to show Essex Bridge, the building of which in fact did not begin until 1676.

[42, *CARD*, V]

YELLOW POOL, THE

See LOUGH BUOY.

YOUNG'S CASTLE

The watch-house shown by Rocque (1756) at the junction of Oxmantown, now North King Street, and Church Street is known as the Young's Castle Watch-house. From there, in 1730, the constabulary of the northern half of St Michan's parish made its rounds.

See also Ormonde Bridge Watch-house.

[*CARD*, XI]

ZOLA, CHURCH OF THE DAUGHTER OF

The following are references in 20th-century literature to the Church of the Daughter of Zola:

(i) Diarmait Mac Murchada in his charter of *c.* 1166 'granted land called Ballidubgail with its men and appurtenances to his spiritual father and confessor Edan, Bishop of Louth, for the use of the canons of the church of the daughter of Zola and their successors' (bib. ref. 244);

(ii) 'the Church of the Daughter of Zola (the predecessors of All Hallows at the present College Green' (*DHR*: Ronan, 'St Stephen's Hospital, Dublin').

This title does not appear in standard reference works, but a possible explanation of it is offered by Brunskill in *JRSAI*, vol. 34 (1904), p. 272.

The sixth-century monastery of Louth (Lughmadh), burned down in 1148, was refounded in the same year by Edan O'Kelly, bishop of Oriel, and Donough O'Carroll, king of Oriel, under the new name of St Mary's Priory OSA. Edan placed his see there and was buried there in 1182.

Brunskill states:

> The solution of this difficulty [i.e. the name Zola] is to be found in Sweetman's 'Calendar of Documents relating to Ireland' where, under the year 1268, we find an exemplification of the Charter of Dermot M'Murrough, most probably copied from the original document, the copy of which in the 'All Hallows' Register' was made more than 100 years later. In it we read that the grant to Edan, bishop of Louth, was made 'to the use of the Canons of the only Daughter of that Church [ecclesiae filiae solae]'.

It is suggested that the copyist may have written Zola by mistake.

Brunskill adds that the fact that the monks of All Hallows and Louth were Augustinian canons supports the statement that the former was the daughter-house of the latter.

[220 (1904: Brunskill), 244, *DHR* (Ronan)]

ZOO STREAM

The Zoo Stream rises in the north of Phoenix Park and flows through the ponds and lakes in Áras an Uachtaráin and the Zoological Gardens. It joins the Liffey a little upstream of Sean Heuston Bridge.

[Maps (OS)]

74   Report . . . at a Meeting of Gentlemen
     Merchants and Traders . . . on 11 August
     1833 . . . to Promote . . . the Construction of
     a Ship Canal from Kingstown Harbour to
     Dublin, Dublin, printed by E. Ponsonby, 1
     Grafton Street, 1833

75   'Representation for the Improvement of
     Dublin Harbour Submitted to His Excellency
     the Lord Lieutenant . . . by the Directors
     General of Inland Navigation in Ireland, 19
     December 1804', BL, Hardwicke Papers, vol.
     583, Add. MS 35931

76   James Malton, A Picturesque and
     Descriptive View of the City of Dublin,
     reproduced from the edition of 1799 with an
     introduction by the Knight of Glin, Dublin,
     Dolmen Press in association with the Irish
     Georgian Society, 1978

77   Rosalind M. Elmes, Catalogue of Irish
     Topographical Prints and Original
     Drawings, new edition revised and enlarged
     by M. Hewson, Dublin, Malton Press (for NLI
     Society), 1975

78   T.W. Freeman, Ireland: A General and
     Regional Geography, London, Methuen and
     Co., 1950

79   Ted Ruddock, Arch Bridges and their
     Builders 1735–1835, Cambridge University
     Press, 1979

80   John D'Alton, The History of Drogheda with
     its Environs and an Introductory Memoir of
     the Dublin and Drogheda Railway, Dublin,
     published by the author, 1844

81   Catherine de Courcy and Ann Maher, Fifty
     Views of Ireland, Dublin, NGI, 1985

82   John Carr, The Stranger in Ireland or a
     Tour in the Southern and Western Parts of
     that Country in the Year 1805, London,
     Richard Phillips, 6 Bridge Street, Blackfriars,
     1806

83   John Ferrar, A View of Ancient and Modern
     Dublin with its Latest Improvements to
     which is added a Tour to Bellevue in the
     County of Wicklow, 2nd edn, Dublin,

printed by the editors of Graisberry and
     Campbell, 1807

84   Ernest B. Anderson, Sailing Ships of Ireland,
     reprint, Dublin, Morris and Co., Cavendish
     Row, 1951

85   Lady Gregory, Hugh Lane's Life and
     Achievement with Some Account of the
     Dublin Galleries, London, John Murray,
     1921

86   The Architecture of Sir Edwin Lutyens
     (2 vols.), London, Country Life Ltd, 1950

87   Port Journal of the Corporation for
     Preserving and Improving the Port of Dublin
     (later Port and Docks Board), manuscript
     journals, vol. 1, 1786 onwards, National
     Archives, Dublin

88   George A. Little, Dublin before the Vikings,
     Dublin, M.H. Gill and Son, 1957

89   R.C. Cox (ed.), Robert Mallet 1810–1881,
     Transactions of Centenary Seminar, Dublin,
     IEI and the Royal Irish Academy, 1982

90   Transactions of the Institution of Civil
     Engineers of Ireland (later the Institution of
     Engineers of Ireland), vol. 1, 1845, ongoing,
     Dublin, ICEI (IEI)

91   R.J.B. Walker, Old Westminster Bridge: The
     Bridge of Fools, Newton Abbot, David and
     Charles, 1979

92   Laurence O'Connor, Lost Ireland, Dublin,
     Rainbow Publications, 1984

93   Kevin B. Nowlan (ed.), Travel and
     Transport in Ireland, Dublin, Gill &
     Macmillan, 1973

94   James Gandon/Thomas J. Mulvany, The Life
     of James Gandon Esq., Material Assembled
     by his Son, James Gandon, prepared for
     publication by Thomas J. Mulvany, Dublin,
     Hodges and Smith, 1846

95   Walter George Strickland, A Dictionary of
     Irish Artists (2 vols.), Dublin and London,
     Maunsel and Co., 1913

96   Ann M. Stewart (compiler), Royal Hibernian
     Academy of Arts, vol. 1: A to G, Index of

Exhibitors and their Work 1826–1979, Dublin, Manton Publishing, 1986

97 Nuala Burke, 'Dublin's North-eastern City Wall: Early Reclamation and Development at the Poddle–Liffey Confluence', *Proc. RIA*, vol. 74C, Dublin, Royal Irish Academy, 1974

98 Herbert A. Kenny, *Literary Dublin: A History*, New York, Taplinger Publishing Company; Dublin, Gill & Macmillan, 1974

99 John Bradley (ed.), *Viking Dublin Exposed: The Wood Quay Saga*, Dublin, O'Brien Press, 1984

100 Adrian Le Harivel (compiler), *National Gallery of Ireland: Illustrated Summary Catalogue of Drawings Watercolours and Miniatures*, Dublin, NGI, 1983

101 Flora H. Mitchell, *Vanishing Dublin*, Dublin, Allen Figgis, 1966

102 W.H. Bartlett (text by J. Stirling Coyne, N.P. Willis, etc.), *The Scenery and Antiquities of Ireland*, London, James S. Virtue (also known as George Virtue: bib. ref 77), 1842 (date from bib. ref. 77)

103 Anne Crookshank and the Knight of Glin, *The Painters of Ireland* c. *1660–1920*, London, Barrie and Jenkins, 1978

104 Kenneth McConkey, *A Free Spirit: Irish Art 1860–1960*, London, Antique Collectors' Club in association with Pyms Gallery, 1990

105 Patricia Butler, *Three Hundred Years of Irish Watercolours and Drawings*, London, Weidenfeld and Nicolson, 1990

106 Robert Pool and John Cash, *Views of the Most Remarkable Public Buildings Monuments and Other Edifices in the City of Dublin delineated by Robert Pool and John Cash*, Dublin, printed for J. Williams, 21 Skinner Row, 1780

107 Anon. (introduction by Homan Potterton), *National Gallery of Ireland Illustrated Summary Catalogue of Paintings*, Dublin, Gill & Macmillan, 1981

108 *Dublin Port and Docks Board Custom House Docks Report on Redevelopment 1980 (Study directed by Ronald Tallon, Scott Tallon Walker, Architects)*, Dublin Port and Docks Board, 1980

109 Anon.: Irish Transport and General Workers' Union, *Fifty Years of Liberty Hall 1909–1959*, Dublin, ITGWU, 1959

110 Maurice Gorham, *Dublin from Old Photographs*, London, B.T. Batsford, 1972

111 George Morrison, *An Irish Camera*, London, Pan Books, 1979

112 Tom Kennedy (ed.), *Victorian Dublin*, Dublin, Albertine Kennedy Publishing, 1980

113 Frederick O'Dwyer, *Lost Dublin*, Dublin, Gill & Macmillan, 1981

114 Gordon Jackson, *The History and Archaeology of Ports*, Tadworth, World's Work, 1983

115 Brian Kennedy (ed.), *Concise Catalogue of the Drawings, Paintings and Sculptures in the Ulster Museum*, Belfast, UM, 1986

116 John Edward Walsh, *Rakes and Ruffians: The Underworld of Georgian Dublin*, Dublin, Four Courts Press, 1979 (first published 1847 under the title *Ireland Sixty Years Ago*)

117 Georges-Denis Zimmermann, *Songs of Irish Rebellion*, Dublin, Allen Figgis, 1967

118 I.J. Mann, *River Bars*, London, Crosby Lockwood and Co., 1881

119 G.A. Hayes McCoy, *Irish Battles*, London, Longmans, 1969

120 John O'Donovan (ed.), *Annals of the Kingdom of Ireland by the Four Masters from the Earliest Period to the Year 1616*, Dublin, Hodges and Smith, 1851

121 *Minutes of the Municipal Council of the City of Dublin* and *Reports and Printed Documents of the Corporation of Dublin*, printers: various, dates: various

122 E.H.H. Archibald, *Dictionary of Sea Painters*, 2nd edn, London, Antique Collectors' Club, 1989

123 John Harris, *The Artist and the Country House*, rev. ed., London, Sotheby's Publications, 1985

124 Col. M.H. Grant, *The Old English Landscape Painters* (8 vols. 1926–61), Leigh-on-Sea, F. Lewis

125 Nicholas Barton, *The Lost Rivers of London*, New Barnet, Historical Publications Ltd, 1982 (first published 1962 by Phoenix House and Leicester University Press)

126 David G. Wilson, *The Thames: Record of a Working Waterway*, London, B.T. Batsford, 1987

127 Ruth and Jonathan Mindell, *Bridges over the Thames*, Poole, Blandford Press, 1985

128 Ulick O'Connor, *Oliver St John Gogarty*, London, Granada, 1981 (first published 1964 by Jonathan Cape, London)

129 Henry A. Gilligan, *A History of the Port of Dublin*, Dublin, Gill & Macmillan, 1988

130 Oliver St John Gogarty, *The Collected Poems*, London, Constable, 1951

131 Oliver St John Gogarty, *It Isn't this Time of Year at All*, London, Macgibbon and Kee, 1954

132 Peter Townend (ed.), *Burke's Genealogical and Heraldic History of the Landed Gentry*, 18th edn 1965–72, London, Burke's Peerage Ltd

133 Anne Crookshank and the Knight of Glin, *The Watercolours of Ireland: c. 1600–1914*, London, Barrie and Jenkins, 1994

134 'Plans of the Barracks etc. in the County of Dublin, being part of the Dublin or Northern District Zincographed in the Topographical Department of the War Office Col: Sir Henry James. R.E. F.R.S. etc.', BL map collection, 1862

135 Peter Kemp (ed.), *The Oxford Companion to Ships and the Sea*, London, Oxford University Press, 1976

136 *Le Chasse-Marée, Revue Bimestrielle*, director: Bernard Cadoret, Douarnenez, France

137 A. Jal, *Glossaire Nautique, Répertoire Polyglotte de Termes de Marin Anciens*, Paris, Chez Firmin Didot Frères, 1848

138 *Essays of the London Architectural Society*, London, LAS, part 1: 1808; part 2: 1810

139 *Macmillan's Encyclopaedia of Architects*, London, Free Press, Collier Macmillan Publishers, 1982

140 Dora Ware, *A Short Dictionary of British Architects*, London, George Allen and Unwin, 1967

141 A.H.W. Robinson, *Marine Cartography in Britain: A History of the Sea Chart to 1855*, Leicester University Press, 1962

142 Governours of the Workhouse, *By-laws Rules and Orders for the Better Regulating of Hackney-coaches, Chairs, Brewers Drays Carts and Carrs*, Dublin, printed by Sylvanus Pepyat, Skinner-Row, 1729

143 Alfred Barnard, *The Whiskey Distilleries of the United Kingdom*, centenary edn, Edinburgh, Mainstream Publishing Company; Moffet, Lochar Publishing, 1987

144 John Lodge (rev. Mervyn Archdall), *The Peerage of Ireland* (7 vols.), Dublin, James Moore, 1789

145 Joseph Haydn (continued by Horace Cekerby), *The Book of Dignities*, London, W.H. Allen and Co., 1894

146 Henry Shaw, *New City Pictorial Directory 1850*, 1850

147 T.W. Moody, F.X. Martin and F.J. Byrne (eds.), *A New History of Ireland*: vol. 8, *A Chronology of Irish History to 1976*; vol. 9, *Maps, Genealogies, Lists, etc.*; Oxford, Clarendon Press, 1982

148 Sir Bernard Burke, *A Genealogical History of the Dormant Abeyant Forfeited and Extinct Peerages of the British Empire*, London, Harrison and Sons, 1883

149 Francis Morgan (arranger), *Mapped Rental of the Estates of the Right Honorable the Lord Mayor Aldermen and Burgesses of Dublin*, 1867

150 H.B. Clarke (ed.), *Medieval Dublin: The Making of a Metropolis*, Dublin, Irish Academic Press, 1990

151 H.B. Clarke (ed.), *Medieval Dublin: The Living City*, Dublin, Irish Academic Press, 1990

152 Cheyne Brady, *The History of the Hospital for Incurables*, Dublin, Browne and Nolan, 1875

153 H.M. Colvin, *A Biographical Dictionary of English Architects 1660–1840*, London, John Murray, 1954

154 Anon., *Dublin Main Drainage Scheme; Souvenir Handbook*, Dublin, Sealy, Bryers and Walker, 1906

155 Anon. (foreword by Frank Feely, Dublin city and county manager), *The Greater Dublin Drainage Scheme*, Dublin Corporation/ Dublin County Council, 1986

156 Wm. M. Hennessy (ed.), *Annals of Loch Ce, A Chronicle of Irish Affairs from* AD *1014 to* AD *1590*, vol. 1, London, Longman and Co. (etc.), 1871

157 John Purser Griffith, 'The Improvement of the Bar of Dublin Harbour by Artificial Scour', *Proceedings of the Institution of Civil Engineers*, vol. 58, London, 1878–9

158 L.F. Salzman, *English Trade in the Middle Ages*, Oxford, Clarendon Press, 1931

159 James Ware, *The Whole Works of Sir James Ware Concerning Ireland* (3 vols.), vol. 1, *Containing the History of the Bishops of that Kingdom etc.*, Dublin, E. Jones, Clarendon Street, 1739

160 H.C. Hamilton (ed.) (other editors for later volumes), *Calendar of State Papers Relating to Ireland*, London, Longman Green, Longman and Roberts, 1860 and later

161 Anon., *The Coasting Pilot from the Harbour of Balbriggn in the County of Dublin to Tarrow Hill in the County of Wexford*, 3rd edn, with additions, Dublin (printed in London), 1768

162 Captain Greenvile Collins, *Great Britain's Coasting Pilot, The First Part*, London, printed by Freeman Collins, 1693

163 Anon., *Dublin Bay: Water Quality*, Dublin, Environmental Research Unit, 1989

164 Arthur Dobbs, *An Essay on the Trade and Improvement of Ireland*, Dublin, A. Rhames for J. Smith and W. Bruce, Blind Quay, part 1: 1729; part 2: 1731

165 Peter Pearson, *Urban Heritage Series 2: Dun Laoghaire Kingstown*, Dublin, O'Brien Press, 1981

166 The Marquis of Lansdowne (ed.), *The Double Bottom or Twin-hulled Ship of Sir William Petty*, Oxford, Roxburghe Club, 1931

167 T.W. Moody and F.X. Martin (eds.), *The Course of Irish History*, Cork, Mercier Press, 1967

168 Gwyn Jones, *A History of the Vikings*, Oxford University Press, 1968

169 Desmond Forristal, *The Man in the Middle: St Laurence O'Toole*, Dublin, Veritas, 1988

170 Louis Hyman, *The Jews of Ireland*, Shannon, Irish University Press, 1972

171 Charles Hadfield and A.W. Skempton, *William Jessop, Engineer*, Newton Abbot, David and Charles, 1979

172 Alan McGowan, *The Ship Tiller and Whipstaff*, London, HM Stationery Office, 1981

173 E.E. O'Donnell, *The Annals of Dublin – Fair City*, Dublin, Wolfhound Press, 1987

174 James Henthorn Todd (trans.), *The War of the Gaedhil with the Gaill (or The Invasions of Ireland by the Danes and other Norsemen)*, London, Longmans, Green, Reader, and Dyer, 1867

175 J.T. Gilbert, *History of the Viceroys of Ireland*, Dublin and London, James Duffy, 1865

176 Robert Kane, *The Industrial Resources of Ireland*, 2nd edn, Dublin, Hodges and Smith, 1845

177 J. Mitchel, *The Last Conquest of Ireland (Perhaps)*, author's edn, London, Burns, Oates, and Washbourne, n.d.

178 John de Courcy Ireland, *Ireland's Sea Fisheries: A History*, Dublin, Glendale Press, 1981

179 'Numbers of Vessels which have been Wrecked Stranded or Otherwise Damaged in the Bay Port or Harbour of Dublin from 8th February 1797 to 23rd August 1800', attested copies of protests taken and extended before Edward Hamerton and others, National Archives, Dublin

180 Ronald C. Cox, *Bindon Blood Stoney: Biography of a Port Engineer*, Dublin, IEI, 1990

181 H.S. Sweetman (ed.) (other editors for later volumes), *Calendar of Documents Relating to Ireland*, London, Longman and Co., 1875–86

182 Edward McParland, *James Gandon Vitruvius Hibernicus*, London, A. Zwemmer, 1985

183 James Joyce, *Finnegans Wake*, London, Faber & Faber, 1939

184 Clair L. Sweeney, *The Rivers of Dublin*, Dublin Corporation, 1991

185 John Mitchel, *History of Ireland*, Glasgow and London, Cameron and Ferguson and Co., n.d.

186 Douglas Bennett, *Encyclopaedia of Dublin*, Dublin, Gill & Macmillan, 1991

187 J.T. Gilbert (ed.), *Historic and Municipal Documents of Ireland AD 1172–1320 from the Archives of the City of Dublin etc.*, London, Longmans Green and Co., 1870

188 Rev. William Ball Wright, *The Ussher Memoirs or Genealogical Memoirs of the Ussher Families in Ireland*, Dublin, Sealy, Bryers and Walker, 1889

189 Charles McNeill (ed.), *Calendar of Archbishop Alen's Register c. 1172–1534*, Dublin, Royal Society of Antiquaries of Ireland, 1950

190 R.F. Foster, *Modern Ireland 1600–1972*, London, Penguin Books, 1989

191 Vivien Igoe, *James Joyce's Dublin Houses*, London, Mandarin Paperbacks, 1990

192 John T. Gilbert, *An Account of the Parliament House, Dublin*, Dublin, Hodges Figgis and Co., 1896

193 Cecil Woodham-Smith, *The Great Hunger: Ireland 1845–9*, London, Hamish Hamilton, 1962

194 Helen Landreth, *The Pursuit of Robert Emmet*, Dublin, Browne and Nolan: Richview Press, 1949

195 F.H.A. Aalen and Kevin Whelan (eds.), *Dublin City and County: From Prehistory to Present; Studies in Honour of J.H. Andrews*, Dublin, Geography Publications, 1992

196 Anon., *The Irish Compendium: Or Rudiments of Honour*, 5th edn, London, printed for J. Knapton, etc., 1756

197 *Encyclopaedia Britannica*, 10th edn, Edinburgh, Adam and Charles Black, 1903

198 N. Donnelly, *History of Dublin Parishes* (parts 1–17), Dublin, Catholic Truth Society, 1907 and later

199 *Ancient Irish Histories: Spencer, Campion, Hanmer, Marleburrough Chronicles of Ireland Meredith Hanmer (1571)*, Dublin, Society of Stationers, 1633, reprinted at the Hibernia Press, 1809

200 Anon., *Dublin Diocesan Guidebook 1993*, produced for the archdiocese of Dublin by Brendan Byrne and Associates, Carlow, 1992

201 Colum Kenny, *King's Inns and the Kingdom of Ireland, The Irish 'Inn of Court' 1541–1800*, Dublin, Irish Academic Press in association with the Irish Legal History Society, 1992

202 John de Courcy Ireland, *Ireland and the Irish in Maritime History*, Dún Laoghaire, County Dublin, Glendale Press, 1986

203 Ulick O'Connor, *A Terrible Beauty is Born: The Irish Troubles 1912–1922*, London, Hamish Hamilton, 1975

204   Bulmer Hobson, *Ireland Yesterday and Tomorrow*, Tralee, Anvil Books, 1968

205   T.C. Luby, *The Life and Times of Daniel O'Connell*, Cameron Ferguson and Co., n.d.

206   Niall McCullough, *Dublin; An Urban History*, Dublin, Anne Street Press, 1989

207   Colm Lennon, *The Lords of Dublin in the Age of Reformation*, Dublin, Irish Academic Press, 1989

208   Minutes of the Commissioners for Making Wide and Convenient Streets in the City of Dublin, 50 manuscript volumes, 1758–1851 (WSC leases included also under this reference number)

209   Niall McCullough (ed.), *A Vision of the City: Dublin and the Wide Streets Commissioners*, exhibition catalogue, Dublin Corporation, 1991

210   A. Peter, *Dublin Fragments, Social and Historic*, Dublin, Hodges Figgis and Co., 1925

211   The Liffey Bridges Survey Team, *The Liffey Bridges*, Dublin, Liberties Association, n.d. (introduction dated 1987)

212   V.T.H and D.R. Delany, *The Canals of the South of Ireland*, Newton Abbot, David and Charles, 1966

213   Miscellaneous authors and anon., 'Single Sheets Relating to Ireland', BL, 1890.e.5

214   Oliver Doyle and Stephen Hirsch, *Railways in Ireland*, Dublin, Signal Press, 1983

215   G.N. Wright (drawings by G. Petrie, W.H. Bartlett, Baynes), *Ireland Illustrated from Original Drawings*, London, H. Fisher, Son, and Jackson, 1829

216   J.J. Crooks, *History of the Royal Irish Artillery*, Dublin, Browne and Nolan, 1914

217   Dorothy Macardle, *The Irish Republic*, London, Victor Gollancz, 1937

218   Richard Woof, *A Sketch of the Knights Templars and the Knights Hospitallers of Saint John of Jerusalem*, London, Robert Hardwicke, 1865

219   G.F. Mitchell, *Archaeology and Environment in Early Dublin*, Medieval Dublin Excavations 1962–81, series C, vol. 1, Dublin, Royal Irish Academy, 1987

220   *Journal of the Royal Society of Antiquaries of Ireland*, vol. 1, 1849, printed by John O'Daly, Dublin; ongoing, later volumes by various printers

221   Liam Price, *An Eighteenth Century Antiquary (The Sketches, Notes and Diaries of Austin Cooper, 1759–1830)*, Dublin, John Falconer, 1942

222   Pettigrew and Oulton, *The Dublin Almanac and General Register of Ireland* (see entry on Directories of Dublin)

223   Watson, *Gentleman's and Citizen's Almanack* (see entry on Directories of Dublin)

224   Thom, *Thom's Irish Almanac and Official Directory*, first published in Dublin, 1844 (see entry on Directories of Dublin)

225   *Irish Builder* (later *Irish Builder and Engineer*), Dublin: vol. 1, 1859; ceased publication 1983

226   Patrick Flanagan, *Transport in Ireland 1880–1910*, Dublin, Transport Research Associates, 1969

227   Calton Younger, *Ireland's Civil War*, Fontana/Collins edn, London, Fontana Books, 1970

228   Roger H. Harper, *Victorian Architectural Competitions*, London, Mansell Publishing, 1983

229   Jeanne Sheehy, *Kingsbridge Station*, Gatherum Series No. 1, Ballycotton, County Cork, Gifford and Craven, 1973

230   Gareth Dunleavy, *Douglas Hyde*, Lewisburg, USA, Bucknell University Press, 1974

231   Thomas C. Butler, *John's Lane*, Dublin, St John's Priory, 1983

232   G.E.C. [George Edward Cokayne] (ed.), *The Complete Peerage of England Scotland Ireland, Great Britain and the United Kingdom* (13 vols.), rev. and ed. by the

Hon. Vicary Gibbs, London, Saint Catherine Press, 1910–40 (later revised and enlarged by Doubleday, White and Howard de Walden)

233 Kenneth MacGowan, *Our Lady of Dublin*, Dublin, Carmelite Publications, 1970

234 John Mitchel, *Jail Journal*, Dublin, M.H. Gill and Son, reprinted from *The Citizen*, New York, 1854

235 Aonghus Moloney et al., *Survey of the Raised Bogs of County Longford*, Dublin, Irish Archaeological Wetland Unit, 1993

236 John O'Donovan (ed.), *The Book of Rights (Leabhar na gCeart)*, Dublin, Celtic Society, 1847

237 G.K. Chesterton, *Christendom in Dublin*, Dublin, Sheed and Ward, 1932

238 S. Conlin and J. de Courcy, *Anna Liffey*, Dublin, O'Brien Press, 1988

239 Benjamin Vincent (ed. of 20th edn), *Haydn's Dictionary of Dates*, London, Ward Lock, Bowden and Co., 1892

240 Dr William Petty, *The History of the Survey of Ireland Commonly Called the Down Survey*, Dublin, published for the Irish Archaeological Society, 1851

241 Emer Malone (ed.), *Dalkey Saint Begnet's Church and Graveyard*, Dalkey, Dunlaoghaire Borough Heritage Society, n.d.

242 William Makepeace Thackeray, *The Irish Sketch Book*, London, Henry Frowde, Oxford University Press, 1863 (first published 1842)

243 E. Healy, C. Moriarty and G. O'Flaherty, *The Book of the Liffey from the Source to the Sea*, Dublin, Wolfhound Press, 1988

244 A. Gwynn and R.N. Hadcock, *Medieval Religious Houses in Ireland*, London, Longman Group, 1970

245 E.S. de Beer (ed.), *The Diary of John Evelyn* [1620–1706], London, Oxford University Press, 1959

246 William Beresford, *Correspondence of the Right Honorable John Beresford*, London, Woodfall and Kinder, 1854

247 E.M. Stephens (ed.), *Dublin Civic Week 1929: Official Handbook*, Dublin, Civic Week Council, 1929

248 R.A. Skelton, *Decorative Printed Maps of the 15th to 18th Centuries*, London, Spring Books, 1965 (first published 1952)

249 Maurice Craig, *The City of Dublin 1728: Charles Brooking*, Dublin, Irish Architectural Archive and Friends of the Library, Trinity College, Dublin, 1983

250 J.H. Andrews (introduction), *Two Maps of 18th Century Dublin and its Surroundings*, Lympne Castle, Harry Margary, 1977

251 Thomas Davis, *Literary and Historical Essays*, James Duffy and Co., n.d., based on edition of 1883 (first published 1845)

252 Right Honorable John, Earl of Clare, *Report from the Committee of Secrecy of the House of Lords of Ireland*, London, John Stockdale, 1798

253 Anon., *Historical Documents: Historic Dublin Maps*, Dublin, NLI, n.d.

254 P. Wyse Jackson, *The Building Stones of Dublin*, Dublin, Town House and Country House, 1993

255 J.H. Andrews, *John Taylor's Map of the Environs of Dublin*, Dublin, Phoenix Maps, 1989

256 Anon., *Ordnance Survey*, catalogue of a 1983 exhibition, Dublin, Ordnance Survey of Ireland, n.d.

257 John Andrews, *Ireland in Maps: Introduction to an Exhibition: 1961*, Dublin, Dolmen Press, 1961

258 Staff of OS of Ireland and OS of Northern Ireland, *Ordnance Survey in Ireland*, printed in Dublin, 1991

259 Mary Clark, *The Book of Maps of the Dublin City Surveyors 1695–1827*, Dublin Corporation, Public Libraries Department, 1983

260 Alfred Dudszus and Ernest Henriot, *Dictionary of Ship Types* (translation from German), London, Conway Maritime Press, 1986

261 Hilaire Belloc, *The Book of the Bayeux Tapestry*, London, Chatto and Windus, 1914

262 Fynes Moryson, *An Itinerary Containing his Ten Years Travell through Twelve Dominions*, London, printed by John Beale, 1617

263 Sean McGrail, *Medieval Boat and Ship Timbers from Dublin*, Dublin, Royal Irish Academy, 1993

264 Sean McGrail, *Ancient Boats*, Aylesbury, Shire Publications, 1953

265 Laurin Zilliacus, *From Pillar to Post*, London, Wm. Heinemann, 1956

266 Mary Purcell, *The Story of the Vincentians*, Dublin, All Hallows College, 1973

267 Mary Clark and Raymond Refaussé (eds.), *Directory of Historic Dublin Guilds,* Dublin Public Libraries, 1993

268 Bill Long, *Bright Light, White Water*, Dublin, New Island Books, 1993

269 *Archaeology Ireland*, vol. 1, 1987, ongoing, Archaeology Ireland Ltd, Bray, County Wicklow

270 T.K. Cromwell, *Cromwell's Excursions through Ireland* (3 vols.), London, Longman, 1820

271 Pat Liddy, *Dublin Stolen from Time*, Dublin, Oisin Art Gallery and Chadworth, 1990

272 Pat Liddy, *Dublin Be Proud*, Dublin, Chadworth, 1987

273 Brian Lalor, *Dublin*, London, Routledge & Kegan Paul, 1981

274 Brian Lalor, *Dublin Bay*, Dublin, O'Brien Press, 1989

275 Anon., *Annual Directory and Year Book*, Dublin, Institute of Public Administration, 1967 onwards

276 ICEI, *Minutes* and *Reports*, Dublin, 1835 onwards

277 Chiang Yee, *The Traveller in Dublin*, London, Methuen and Co., 1953

278 Jonah Barrington, *Recollections of Jonah Barrington*, Dublin, Talbot Press, n.d.

279 F.G. Hall, *The Bank of Ireland*, Dublin, Hodges Figgis & Co., 1949

280 Edward McParland, *The Custom House Dublin*, Dublin, Office of Public Works, 1991

281 Bernard Share, *The Flight of the Iolar*, Dublin, Gill & Macmillan, 1986

282 Ruth Delany, *A Celebration of 250 Years of Ireland's Inland Waterways*, Belfast, Appletree Press, 1986

283 Charles Hamilton Teeling, *History of the Irish Rebellion of 1798*, Glasgow, Cameron and Ferguson, 1876 (first published 1828)

284 John Lindsay, *The Shining Life and Death of Lord Edward Fitzgerald*, London, Rich and Cowan, n.d.

285 Tidal Harbours Commission, Second Report, Parliamentary Papers, vol. 18, part 1: *Tidal Harbours (Part 1)*, London, 1846

286 Edward J. Bourke, *Shipwrecks of the Irish Coast, 1105 to 1993*, Dublin, 1994

287 Rena Lohan, *Guide to the Archives of the Office of Public Works*, Dublin, Stationery Office, 1994

288 Patrick Abercrombie, Sydney Kelly and Manning Robertson, *County Borough of Dublin and Neighbourhood: Town Planning Report: Sketch Development Plan*, Dublin Corporation, 1941

289 Gustav Milne, *The Port of Roman London*, London, B.T. Batsford, 1985

290 Colm Lennon, *Richard Stanihurst the Dubliner*, Dublin, Irish Academic Press, 1981

291 xxxxx xxxx Esq., *The Liffy: A Fable in Imitation of the Metamorphoses of Ovid etc.*, printed for Tho. Warner at the Black-Boy in Pater-noster-Row, 1726, BL 1001. h. 28. (1.)

Edward II, King, 44–5, **139–40**, 180, 353, 408
Edward III, King, 1, 22–3, 109, 126
Edward V, King, 387
Edward VII, King, 5
Edwards, Edward, 2
Egan, Darby, 373
electricity generation, **140**
Electricity Supply Board, 163, 301
Elizabeth I, Queen, 2, 6, 98, 171, 329
  charter, 243
Ellen Hore's Meadow, **140–41**, 289
Elliott, Alderman John, 264
Ellis, John, 210
Ellis, Thomas, 373
Ellis, William, 10, 141, 208, 210, 249, 285, 336, 365
Ellis Bridge, 249
Ellis family, 11
Ellis Place, **141**
Ellis Quay, **141–2**, 225, 366
Ellis Street, 22, **142–3**
Ellsworth, William, 2
Elwood, Samuel, 406
Emancipation Bridge, 337
Emmet, Robert, xxxvii, 46, 76, 93, 97, 108, 117, **143–4**, 155, 300, 350
engineers, city, **75–6**
Ennis, Michael, 128
Ennocneganhoc, **144**
Esmonde, Dr John, **146**
Esplanade, 97
Essex, earl of, 146, 303
Essex Bridge, 64, 101, 107, 128, 209, 226–7, 242, 281, 284, 292–3, 326–7, 330, 345, 423, 426. *see also* Grattan Bridge
  collapse, 163
  faction-fighting, 149
  Malton view, 245
  rebuilt, 155, 264–5, 316, 354–5
  statue, 145
Essex Gate, 40, 60, 64, **146**, 238, 308
Essex Quay, 26, 40, 64, **146–7**, 161, 225, 226, 308, 348, 405, 426
Essex Street, 17, 19, 64, 107, 149, 238, 293, 308, 312, 392
  Ballast Office, 89
  construction, 40, 92, 146
Eucharistic Congress (1932), **147–8**, 278
Eugenius, 275
Eustace, pilot, 304
Eustace, Sir Maurice, 206
Eustace Street, 308, 416
Evening Mail, 293
Exchange Court, 307
Exchange Street, 40–41
Exchequer Street, 193

faction-fighting, **149**
Faddle Alley, 431
Faden, W., 39
  map, **149**
Fagan family, 54
Fagan's orchard, **149**
Fairview, xxxvi, 395
Fairview Park, 270, 321
Fairview Strand, 8, **149**, 297, 367
Fariss, William, 204, 206–7
Fr Mathew Bridge, xxx, xxxv, 14, **149–51**, 185, 244, 350. *see also* Old Bridge
Faulkner, George, 293
Feinaglian Institution, 3
Fenton, Sir Geoffrey, 408
Fenwick, James, 76
ferries, **152–5**
Ferryboat Lane, 401
Fingal, 133
Fish Slip, **158–9**
Fish Street, 66, 269
Fishamble Street, 157, 158, **159**, 162, 285, 346, 348, 425
Fisher, Colonel, 384
Fisher, Sir Edward, 297, 341
fishing, fisheries, **155–8**
FitzAldelin, William, 213
Fitzgerald, Lord Edward, 41, **159–60**, 234, 257
Fitzgerald, Gerald, earl of Kildare, 213
Fitzgerald, Silken Thomas, xxxi, 4, 6, 12, 131, **160**, 215, 239, 345, 368, 369
Fitzgibbon, John, 143, 217
Fitznicholas, Robert, 381
FitzRobert, Geoffrey, 319
FitzStephen, Robert, 83, 241
Fitzsymon's Tower, **160–61**
Fitzwilliam, Eleanor, 289–90
Fitzwilliam, Lord, 161, 300, 419
Fitzwilliam, Colonel Oliver, 330
Fitzwilliam family, 254, 325, 393
Fitzwilliam Quay, **161**
Fitzwilliam Square, 145
Fitzwilliams, Thomas, 65, 157, 349
Five Lamps, **161–2**
Fleece Alley, **162**
Fleet Alley, 13, 162, 416–17
Fleet Lane, 162, 417
Fleet Market, **162**
Fleet Street, 140, **162**, 195, 301, 392, 417
Fleming, Dr Thomas, OFM, 198
floating batteries, **162–3**
floating chapel, Ringsend, **163**
Flood Street, 141
floods, 35, **163–4**
Florence Place, 308
Floyd, Lt.-Gen., 336
Foley Street, 427